GREG MOODIE
VERSUS THE UNION

ONE MAN'S STRUGGLE WITH A 300-YEAR-OLD MONSTER

The Complete Indyref Cartoons

May contain tubas.
www.gregmoodie.com

For David Moodie

Published by Greg Moodie
Copyright © Greg Moodie 2014

A catalogue record for this book is available from the National Library of Scotland and the British Library.

ISBN 978-0-9930133-0-0

Design and layout by Greg Moodie.
Printed in Scotland by Bell & Bain Ltd.

If the author had a publisher and had not been forced to do everything his bleeding self, these are the other books you could be enjoying right now:

The Unbearable Stupidity Of Being

Six Degrees Of Stupidity

And who knows, with this one out of the way, the author may yet complete the third novel in his 'Stupid' trilogy:

Stupid Animals

www.gregmoodie.com

"Funny, irreverent and designed to ensure that none of us get to take ourselves too seriously."
Nicola Sturgeon MSP, Deputy First Minister

"A great contribution to the debate and to Scotland. Brilliant stuff."
Elaine C. Smith, actress and comedienne

"Greg's illustrations and characters show that a different kind of radical politics and Scotland is not only possible, but exists in the here and now."
Gerry Hassan, author, Caledonian Dreaming: The Quest for a Different Scotland

"The referendum campaign has produced a Caledonian forest of talent in which Greg Moodie stands tall."
Joan McAlpine MSP

"Greg Moodie should be put in charge of a vast new satirical-industrial complex, buried deep in the reactor core of the SBC."
Pat Kane, author, The Play Ethic

"Like every artist I've ever known, the boy needs therapy."
Liz Lochhead, poet and playwright

"At least it's funny and takes ten years off me."
Jim Murphy MP

"Better to make your point with a smile rather than a scowl."
Lord Foulkes, Labour peer

"My favourite cartoonist is Gary Larson."
Duncan Hothersall, Labour Party activist

"The best lay we ever had."
A Thousand Flowers

"Greg Moodie has the talent to be the next Rolf Harris!"
BBC Scotlandshire

"Ye dancin? Greg Moodie wiz. He's a grumpy bastard but jeezo, he's got some moves!"
Lady Alba, icon

"Greg Moodie once kissed me on the mouth."
Ross Aitchison, National Collective

"You got *Farquharson* to write the foreword?"
Rev. Stuart Campbell, Wings Over Scotland

"He's not right bright and he stole all my best jokes, but he really knows how to trace."
Rose Garnett, author, Carnalis (available soon from Permuted Press.)

As well as Blair McDougall, Johann Lamont, Alistair Carmichael, Ruth Davidson and Alistair Darling (who obviously did not say "Totes amazeballs"), I also requested quotes from Tony Blair (I offered cash), Daniel O'Donnell (said I was a big fan of his work), Mel Gibson (said I wasn't familiar with his work but heard he made a film about Scotland), Sarah Palin (said her views on Scottish independence were fascinating), David Hasselhoff (said it was the least he could do after having thrown up in my wardrobe), Darius Campbell (said I wasn't sure if he was still alive), Donald Trump, David Starkey and Katie Hopkins. None were forthcoming.

ACKNOWLEDGEMENTS

I didn't set out to be a cartoonist, but somewhere along the way I appear to have been mistaken for one. I blame Kenny Farquharson for this, amongst other things, as it was he who identified the vast yawning void in the independence debate where fun and colour were meant to be, and suggested someone try to fill it. I'd say he was the Godfather of this collection but he's twisted enough to consider that a good thing.

Shortly I'll be going back to making things difficult for my design clients and finishing my stupid third novel, but in the meantime here's 'Greg Moodie Versus The Union'. Make of it what you will because the last two years are a bit of a blur to me. One minute I thought it would be funny if Johann Lamont and Margaret Curran were sipping Cosmopolitans on a beach, the next I was getting indignant tweets if I hadn't come up with a new strip by Sunday lunchtime.

The front cover is a parody of Delacroix's Liberty Crossing The Barricades and I have Gerry Hassan to thank for that - first for commissioning an early version of it for his own book Caledonian Dreaming, and then for having the good sense to reject it.

Thanks to National Collective, A Thousand Flowers, Wings Over Scotland, Bella Caledonia, Newsnet Scotland, BBC Scotlandshire and Peter Curran. We don't all see eye to eye but that's because we're a hugely diverse group – and that's the way I like it.

Thanks to Chris Hurst for unceasing technical brilliance and for being Chris Hurst.

Thanks to anyone whose picture I may have lifted or whose joke I stole. It wouldn't be worth your while to sue.

Thanks especially to Rose Garnett, who is much funnier, darker and more perverse than I'll ever be. It's as well she can't draw.

Of course in reality, it's not Greg Moodie Versus The Union, it's a massive independence movement challenging the dreary, unimaginative, self-serving and morally reprehensible British establishment. At the time of writing, the outcome of the referendum is unknown, but yes or no, independence is not going away. Thank you to everyone who is playing a part.

I hope you enjoy these cartoons as much as I did when I first realised there would come a time when we wouldn't have to suffer many of the people in them any longer.

Greg Moodie
August 1st 2014

1 One of Johann Lamont's 'wee things'.
2 Cone. Moves in mysterious ways.
3 Muriel Gray's parrot. Vocal critic of Scottish journalism.
4 Alasdair Gray. Artist and writer.
5 Nicola Sturgeon MSP.
6 Greg Moodie. Accidental cartoonist.
7 LaFlamme. Raven-haired but otherwise scarlet.
8 Twin-lever corkscrew. Has saved lives.
9 Patrick Harvie MSP.
10 Liz Lochhead. Poet and Makar.
11 Troll. Best avoided.
12 Fred Goodwin. Banker. Casts no shadow.
13 Tuba. See also (23) Blair McDougall.
14 Emergency cute fluffy bunny.
15 Alistair Darling MP. Joy-free zone.
16 Lupe (1996-2013).
17 Football. National sport. Reason unknown.
18 "Very odd chancellor" George 'Giddy' Osborne MP.
19 A representative of the Scottish media.
20 Mel Gibson. Unionists' favourite movie star.
21 David Cameron MP. UK Prime Minister. Debate-shy.
22 Alistair Carmichael MP. Cardboard cutout Scottish Secretary.
23 Blair McDougall. See also (13) Tuba.
24 Nick Clegg MP. Possibly pointless.
25 Lord Robertson of Port Ellen. Seer of seers.
26 Beer. Has been a friend to me.
27 Brigadoon. Please go away.
28 Lord Foulkes of Cumnock. In a box.
29 Ruth Davidson MSP. Was once chased by a dalek.
30 Deely boppers. And Johann Lamont MSP.
31 Gordon Brown MP. Gogszilla to his friends.
32 That woman.
33 Ed Miliband MP. Has dubious adviser by name of Corky.

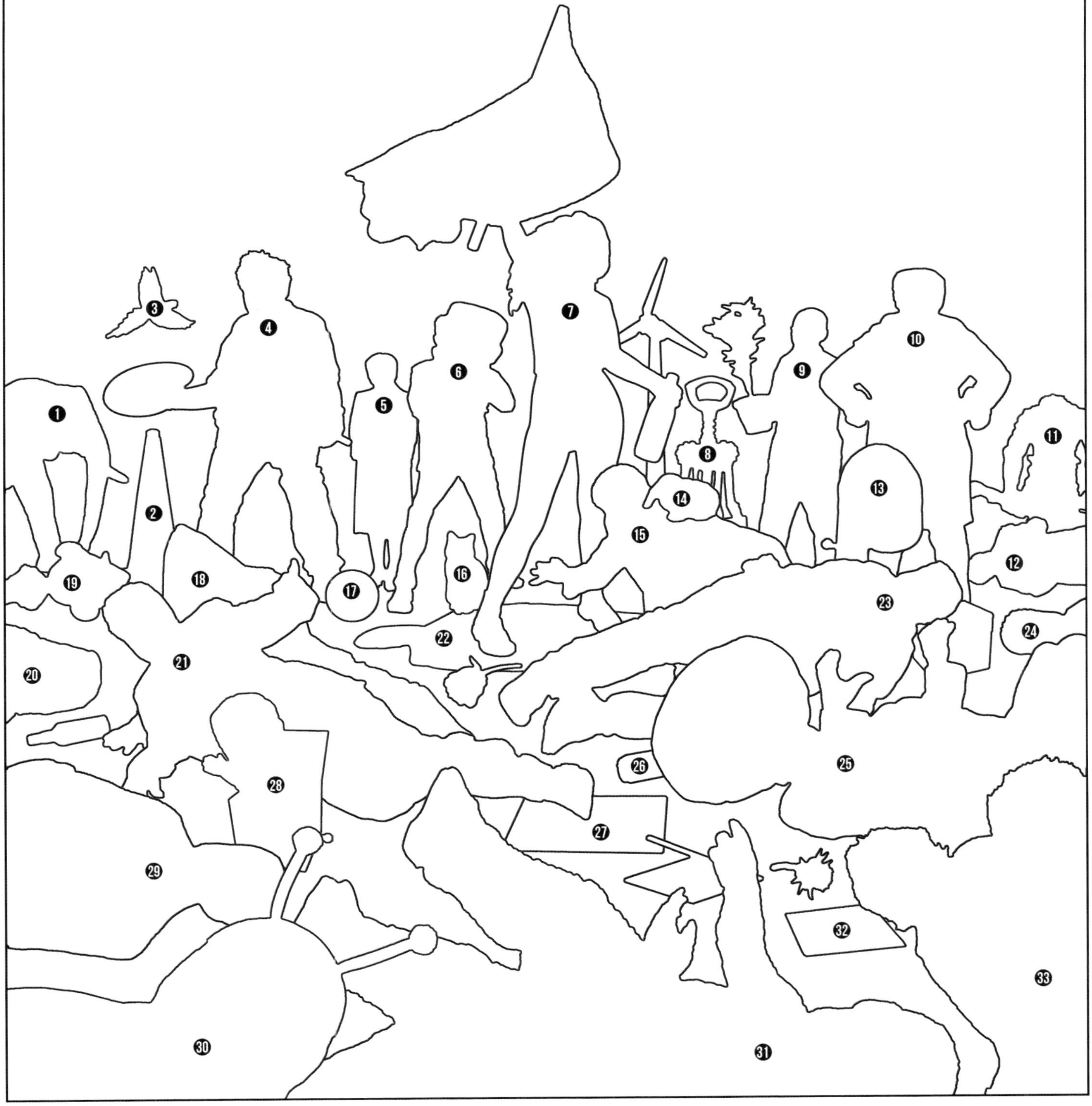

1
2
3
4
5
6
7
8
9
10
11
12
13
14
15
16
17
18
19
20
21
22
23
24
25
26
27
28
29
30
31
32
33

FOREWORD

Greg Moodie blames me for him becoming a political cartoonist. I happily accept my culpability. It happened like this.

Early in the referendum campaign a group of enthusiastic young Scots started an organisation called National Collective. With a blithe indifference to the distinction between a noun and an adjective, they presented themselves as "artists and creatives for independence".

"Creatives". Ugh.

They were smart, energetic and idealistic. Their work had a bit of style. I liked them a lot, and defended them on Twitter when they got pelters from sundry supporters of the UK.

But I had a criticism of how they were operating. Their output was heavy on political analysis but light on political art. In the indyref there was already lots of the former and almost none of the latter. So I suggested they take on the responsibility of remedying that imbalance.

Greg Moodie immediately took this suggestion to heart. A little older than most of the National Collective's young scallywags, he was perhaps not as fully imbued with their sunny positivity. The prospect of spending the long campaign "making wish trees" and being relentlessly upbeat was daunting.

Instead he embraced the cruel, cynical and unforgiving ruthlessness that is the prerequisite of the good political cartoonist. A much happier outcome.

Scotland has a superb track record in comic art. We gifted the world the Beano, the Dandy, the Broons and Oor Wullie, all created in Moodie's home town of Dundee.

Scots have been pioneers in the international comic book world dominated by Marvel and DC. The genre's globally-recognised geniuses include a number of Scots, such as Alan Grant, Frank Quitely, Grant Morrison and Mark Millar.

But a curiosity of the comic book world is that its stars are either writers or artists. Somebody does the words and somebody else draws the pictures. Rarely are both done by the same person. Moodie does both, and with a devastating flair that has made him one of the cultural discoveries of this fascinating period in Scotland's national life.

Moodie's great gift is the surreal detail that nevertheless makes perfect sense. Blair McDougall's tuba. Alistair Carmichael as a cut-out. Johann Lamont with a traffic cone on her head. Alistair Darling as Sam Eagle. George Foulkes as a wind-up jack-in-the-box. Anas Sarwar as a toy robot.

Each of them feels exactly right. This is the kind of characterisation a politician can be stuck with for life. Who now can think of John Major without visualising him wearing his Y-fronts over his trousers, courtesy of Steve Bell?

Do not underestimate the shrewd political analysis required to identify the right absurdity. Nor the graphic skill required to articulate it so simply on the page. Moodie makes both look easy.

My only regret is that Moodie's skills have only been deployed on one side of the binary referendum debate. How would he have characterised Alex Salmond, Blair Jenkins, Elaine C Smith, Nicola Sturgeon, Kenny MacAskill?

Perhaps after 18 September 2014, in whatever state we find this small, wonderful, infuriating country of ours, we'll find out. I look forward to that prospect immensely.

Kenny Farquharson
Deputy Editor, The Scotsman & Scotland on Sunday
July 31st 2014

⊚⊚

CONTENTS

JOHANN AND MARGARET'S HOLIDAY IN MAJORCA

OCTOBER 25TH 2012

I could imagine Johann Lamont and Margaret Curran sipping Cosmopolitans and chillaxing at some beach resort. But you know it wouldn't take long for the conversation to move towards one subject in particular.

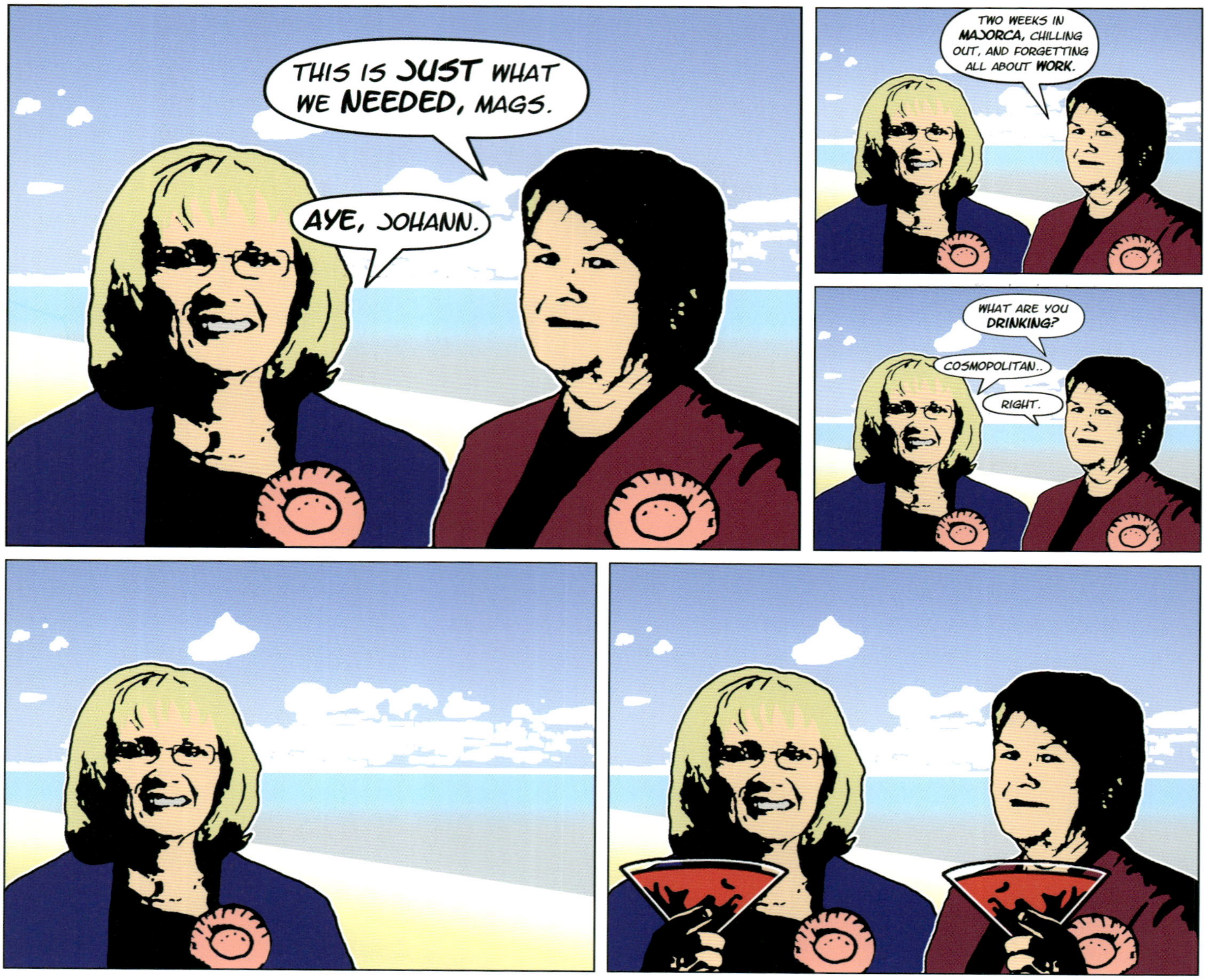

THIS IS JUST WHAT WE NEEDED, MAGS.
AYE, JOHANN.
TWO WEEKS IN MAJORCA, CHILLING OUT, AND FORGETTING ALL ABOUT WORK.
WHAT ARE YOU DRINKING?
COSMOPOLITAN..
RIGHT.

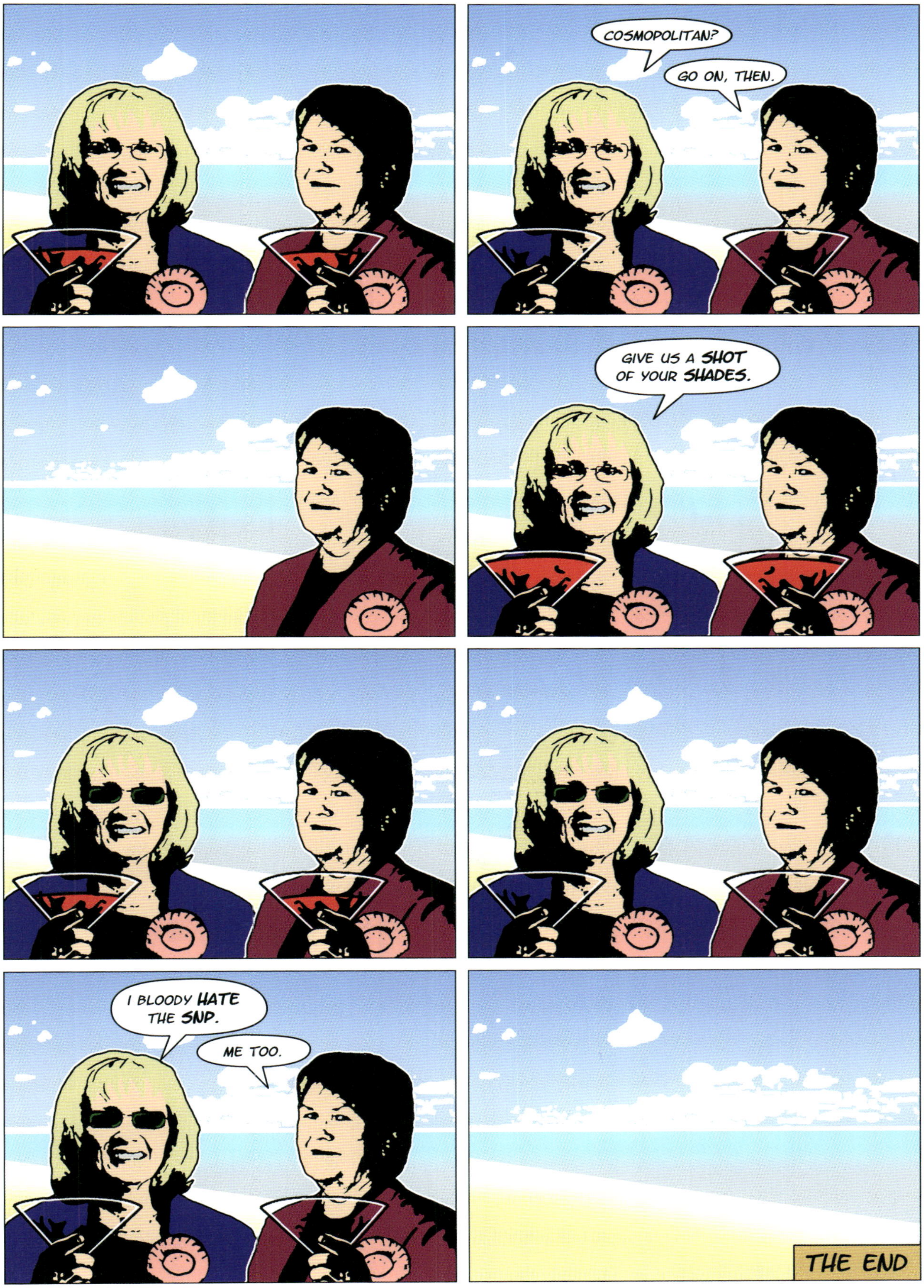
COSMOPOLITAN?
GO ON, THEN.
GIVE US A SHOT OF YOUR SHADES.
I BLOODY HATE THE SNP.
ME TOO.
THE END

WESTMINSTER WORLD

DECEMBER 1ST 2012

When BAE Systems discussed closing either Portsmouth or one of the two shipyards on the Clyde, Jim Murphy, MP for East Renfrewshire, made it clear where his priorities lay: "Why keep open two yards that could potentially be in a foreign country by 2016?"

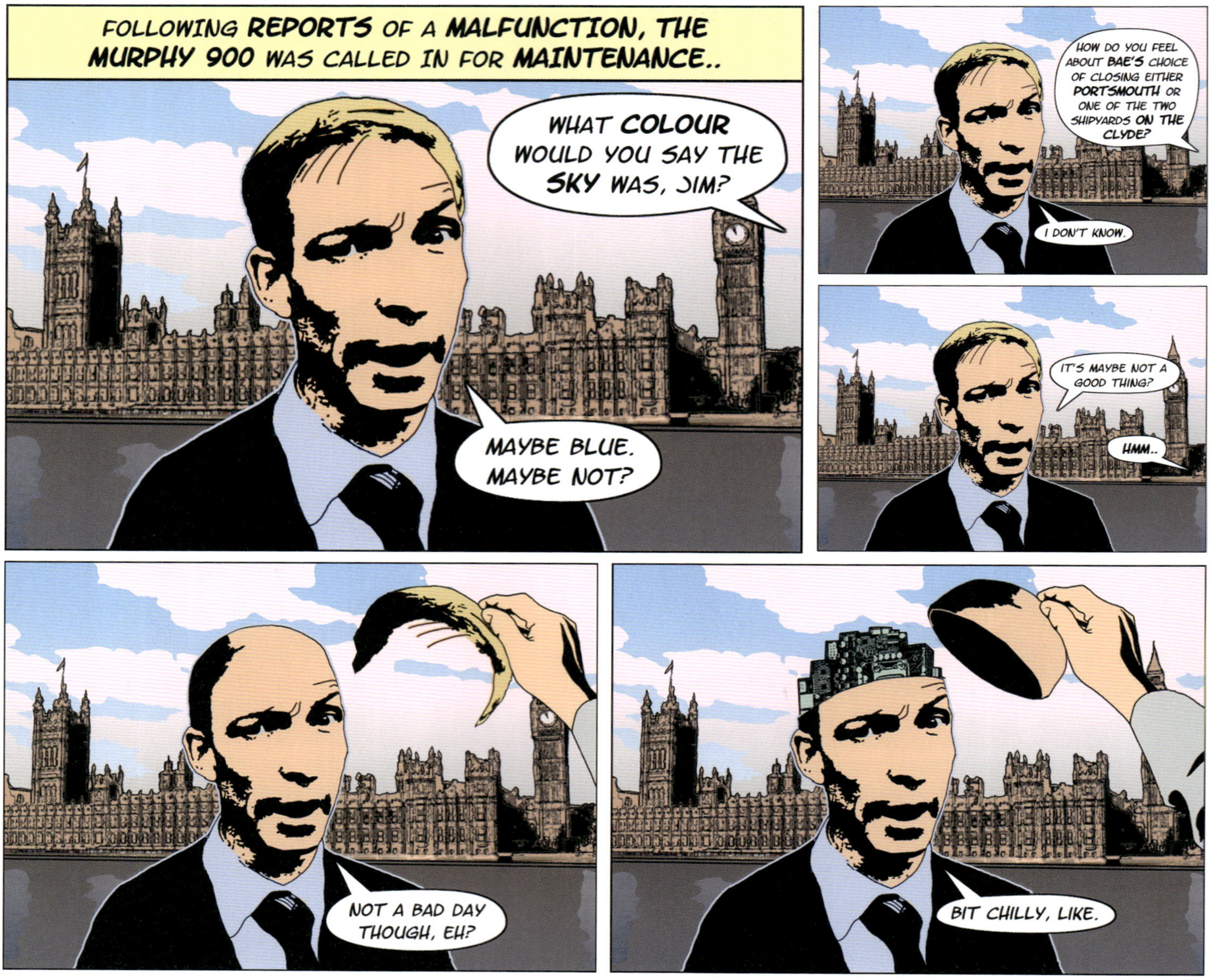

FOLLOWING REPORTS OF A MALFUNCTION, THE MURPHY 900 WAS CALLED IN FOR MAINTENANCE..
WHAT COLOUR WOULD YOU SAY THE SKY WAS, JIM?
MAYBE BLUE. MAYBE NOT?
HOW DO YOU FEEL ABOUT BAE'S CHOICE OF CLOSING EITHER PORTSMOUTH OR ONE OF THE TWO SHIPYARDS ON THE CLYDE?
I DON'T KNOW.
IT'S MAYBE NOT A GOOD THING?
HMM..
NOT A BAD DAY THOUGH, EH?
BIT CHILLY, LIKE.

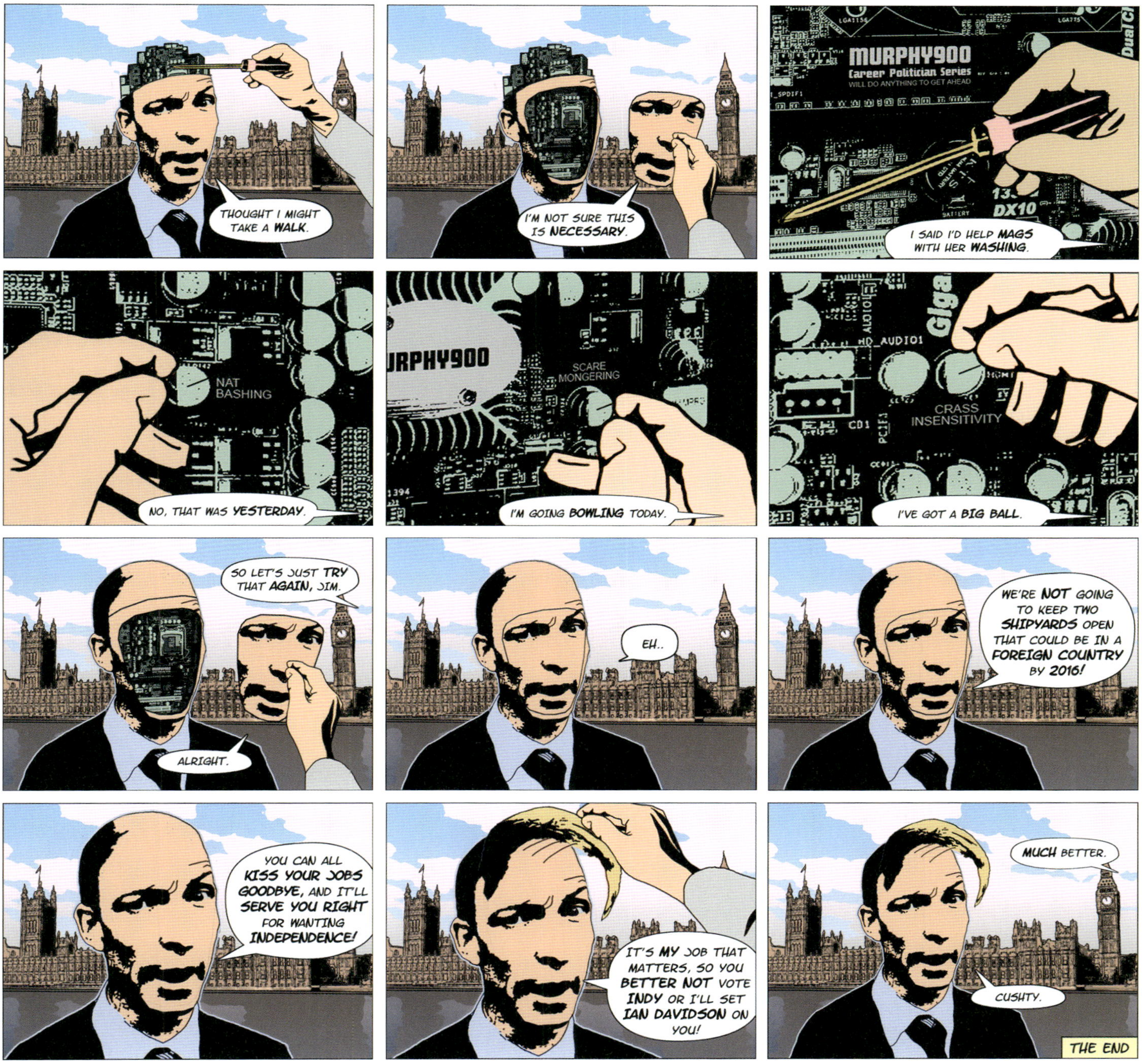
THOUGHT I MIGHT TAKE A WALK.
I'M NOT SURE THIS IS NECESSARY.
MURPHY900
Career Politician Series
WILL DO ANYTHING TO GET AHEAD
I SAID I'D HELP MAGS WITH HER WASHING.
NAT BASHING
NO, THAT WAS YESTERDAY.
SCARE MONGERING
I'M GOING BOWLING TODAY.
CRASS INSENSITIVITY
I'VE GOT A BIG BALL.
SO LET'S JUST TRY THAT AGAIN, JIM.
ALRIGHT.
EH..
WE'RE NOT GOING TO KEEP TWO SHIPYARDS OPEN THAT COULD BE IN A FOREIGN COUNTRY BY 2016!
YOU CAN ALL KISS YOUR JOBS GOODBYE, AND IT'LL SERVE YOU RIGHT FOR WANTING INDEPENDENCE!
IT'S MY JOB THAT MATTERS, SO YOU BETTER NOT VOTE INDY OR I'LL SET IAN DAVIDSON ON YOU!
MUCH BETTER.
CUSHTY.
THE END

THE THOROUGHLY REPUTABLE CAMPAIGN DONOR

APRIL 21ST 2013

"To learn who rules over you, simply find out who you are not allowed to criticise." - Voltaire. When National Collective broke the story about the 'not at all dodgy' background of Better Together's main donor, Ian Taylor, head of oil company Vitol, Taylor threatened them with legal action.

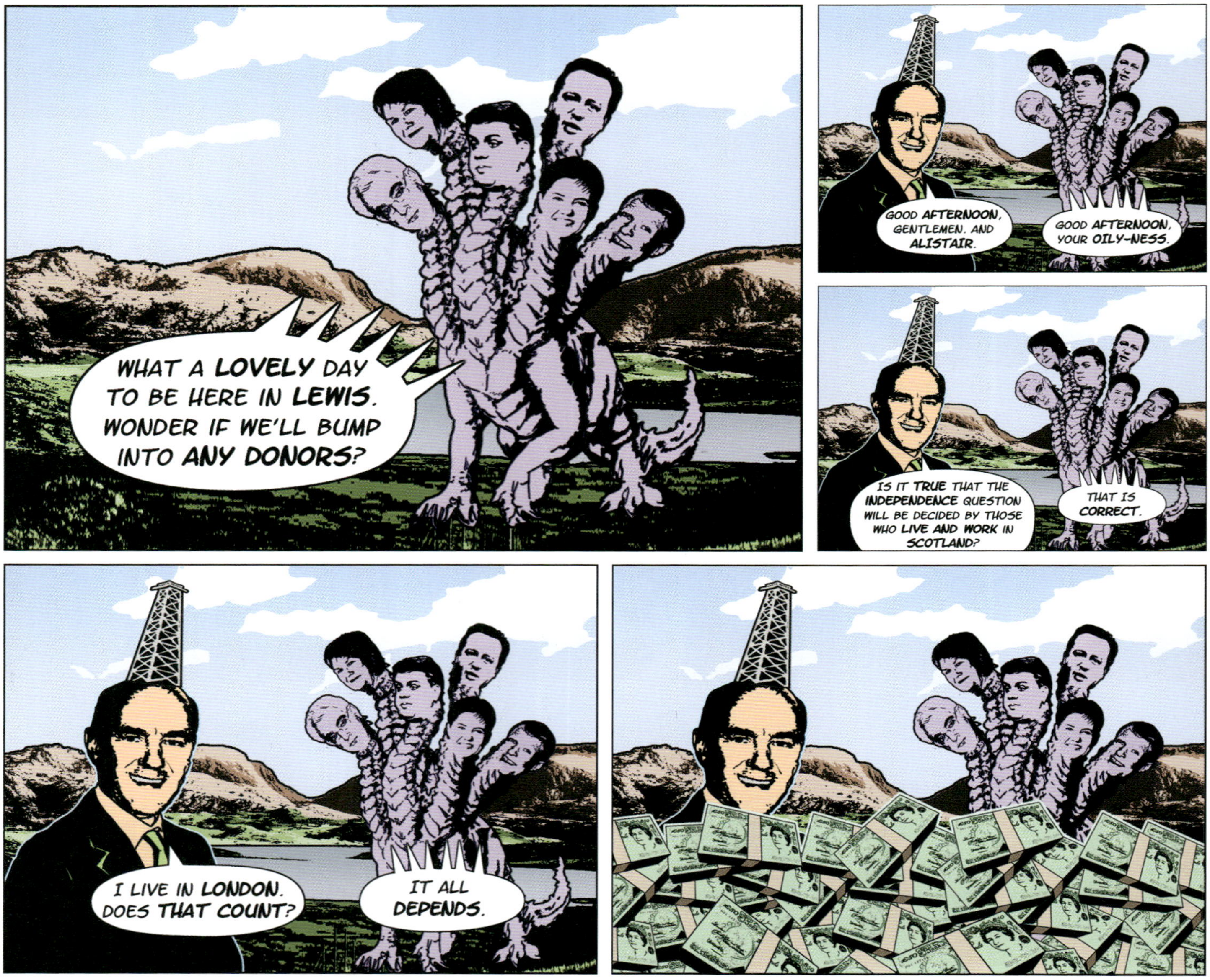

WHAT A LOVELY DAY TO BE HERE IN LEWIS. WONDER IF WE'LL BUMP INTO ANY DONORS?
GOOD AFTERNOON, GENTLEMEN. AND ALISTAIR.
GOOD AFTERNOON, YOUR OILY-NESS.
IS IT TRUE THAT THE INDEPENDENCE QUESTION WILL BE DECIDED BY THOSE WHO LIVE AND WORK IN SCOTLAND?
THAT IS CORRECT.
I LIVE IN LONDON. DOES THAT COUNT?
IT ALL DEPENDS.

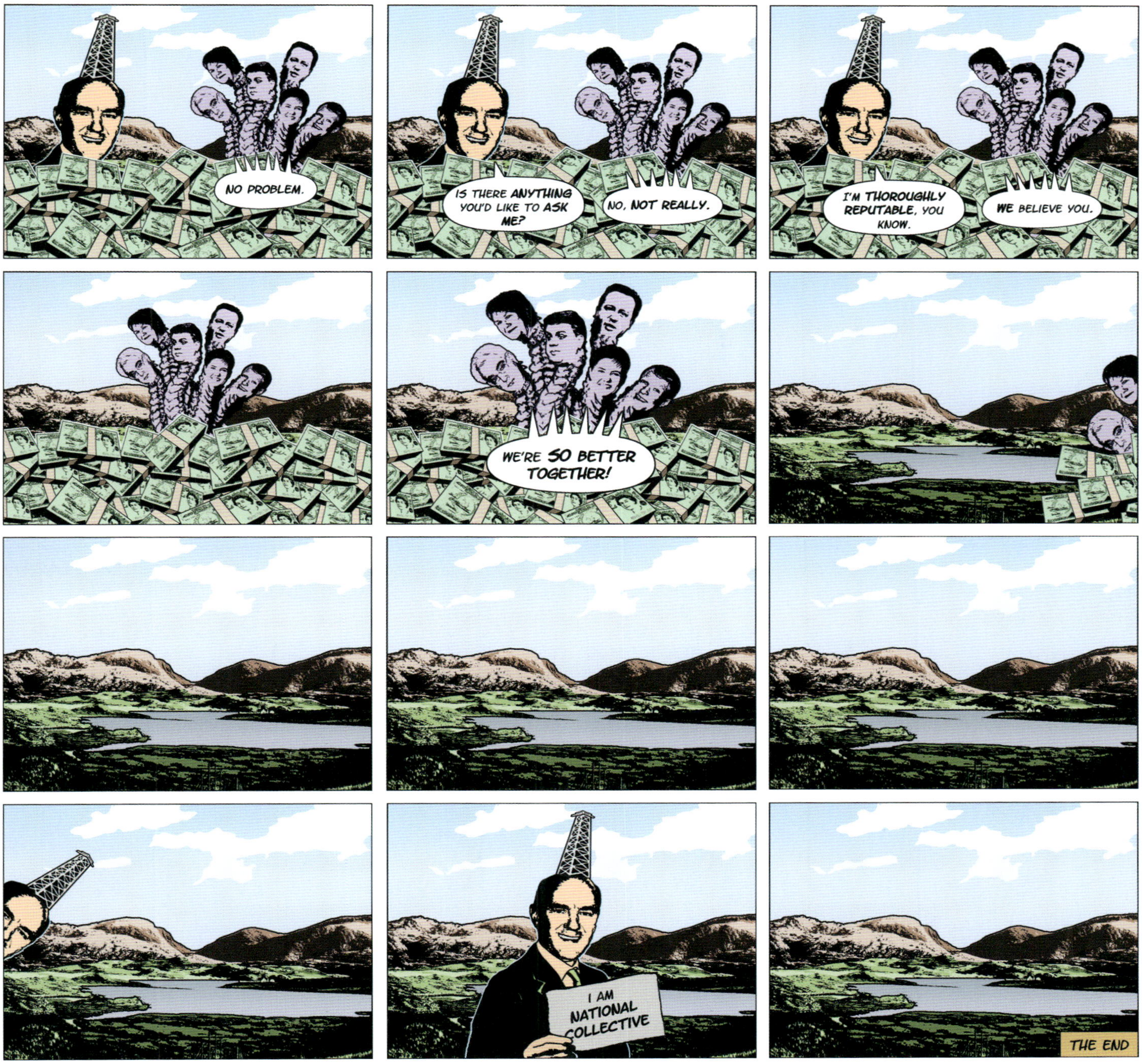
NO PROBLEM.
IS THERE ANYTHING YOU'D LIKE TO ASK ME?
NO, NOT REALLY.
I'M THOROUGHLY REPUTABLE, YOU KNOW.
WE BELIEVE YOU.
WE'RE SO BETTER TOGETHER!
I AM NATIONAL COLLECTIVE
THE END

CHARM SCHOOL WITH IAN SMART

MAY 11TH 2013

Prominent lawyer, Labour activist and 'No' campaigner Ian Smart is known for making ill-tempered pronouncements. But nobody outside of the indyref bubble has any idea who he is, so after this little adventure I washed my hands of him. Took some scrubbing.

THERE'S NOTHING IN THE WORLD LIKE ETIQUETTE, IN KINGLY CHAMBERS OR IMPERIAL HALLS.
THE TRUE MEASURE OF A GENTLEMAN IS NOT BASED ON WHAT THEY HAVE, BUT RATHER ON WHO THEY ARE.
BEING A MALE IS A MATTER OF BIRTH, BEING A MAN IS A MATTER OF AGE, BEING A GENTLEMAN IS A MATTER OF CHOICE.
BETTER 100 YEARS OF THE TORIES THAN THE TURN ON THE POLES AND THE PAKIS THAT WOULD FOLLOW INDEPENDENCE FAILING TO DELIVER.*
*ACTUAL QUOTE.

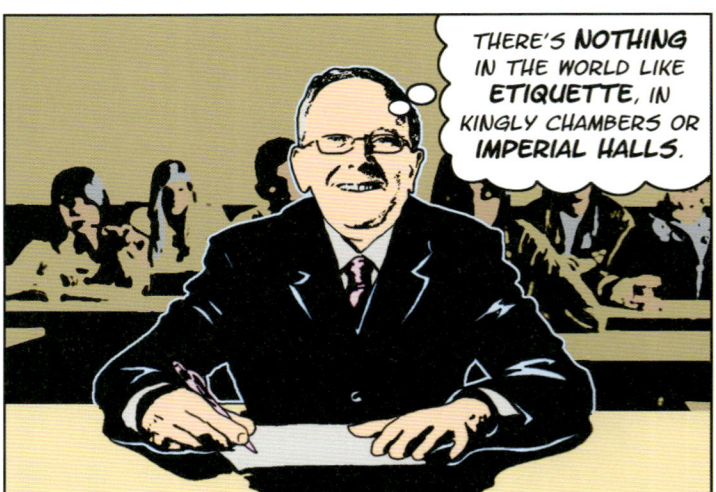

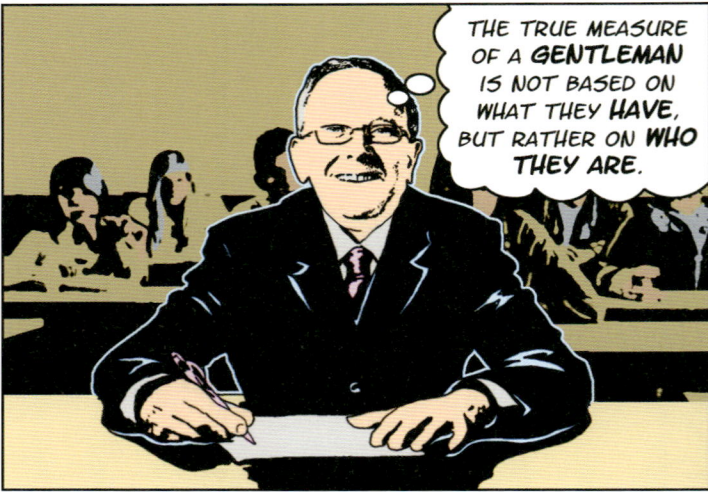

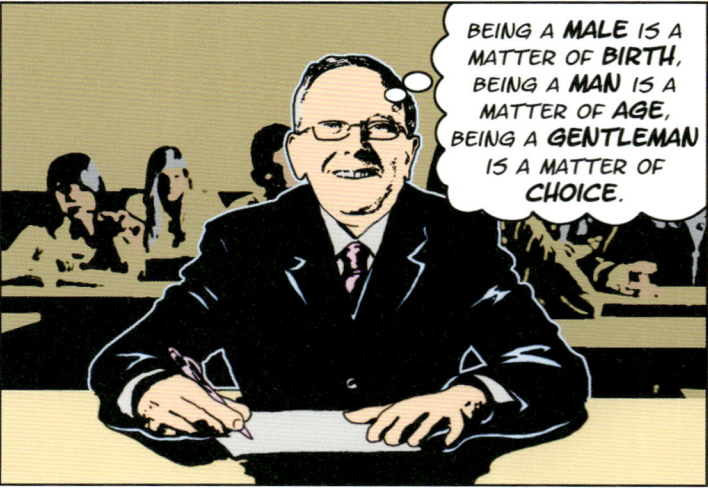

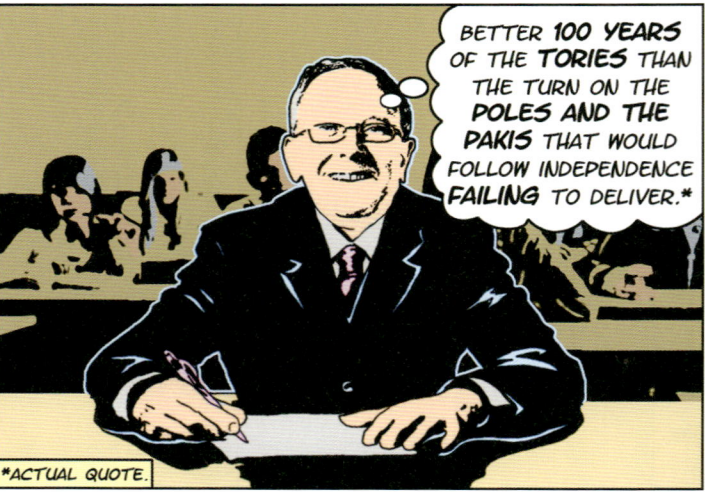

BUGGER.
I SHOULD HAVE PUT "POLES AND PAKIS" IN QUOTATION MARKS.*
D
*ACTUAL QUOTE.
THE END.

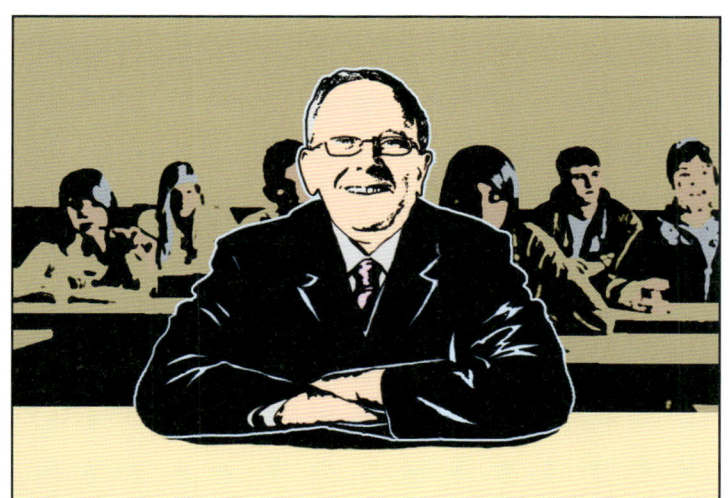

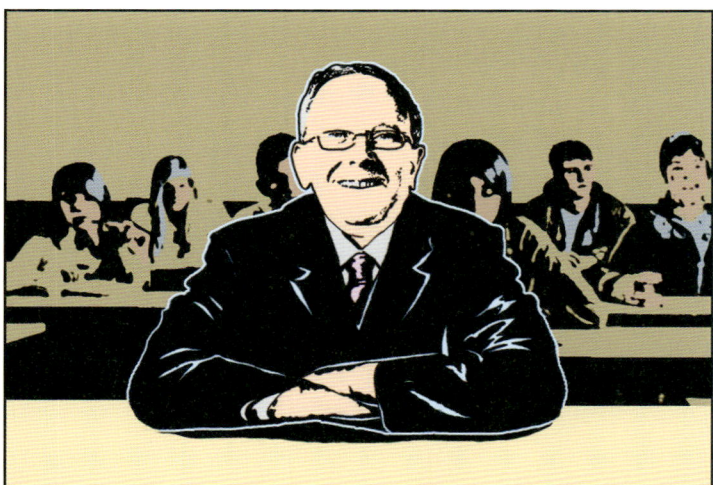

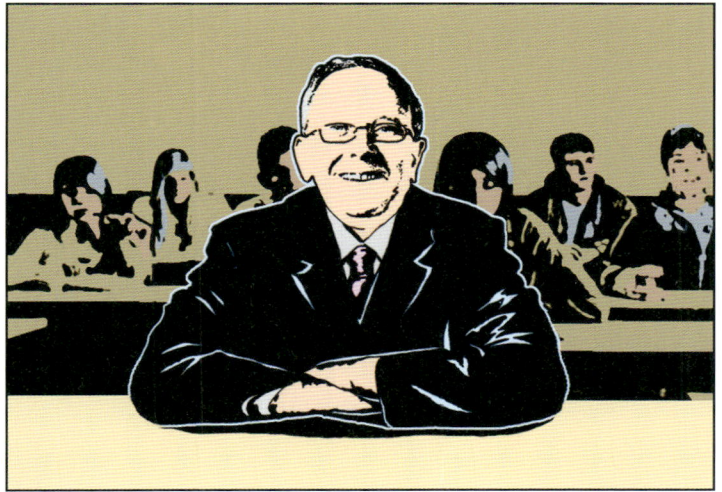

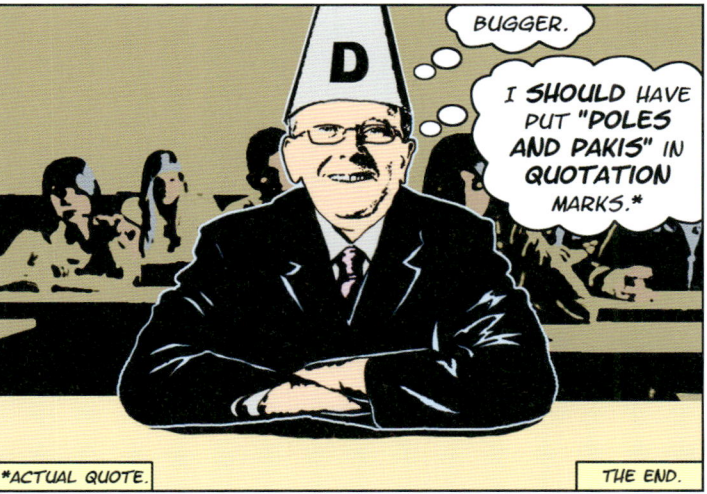

NIGEL FARAGE WOOS SCOTLAND

MAY 19TH 2013

Nigel Farage paid a visit to Edinburgh's Canons' Gait Bar and was surprised to find that the locals did not fall at his feet. With a large group of protesters outside, he eventually had to be locked in the bar for his own safety until a police escort arrived.

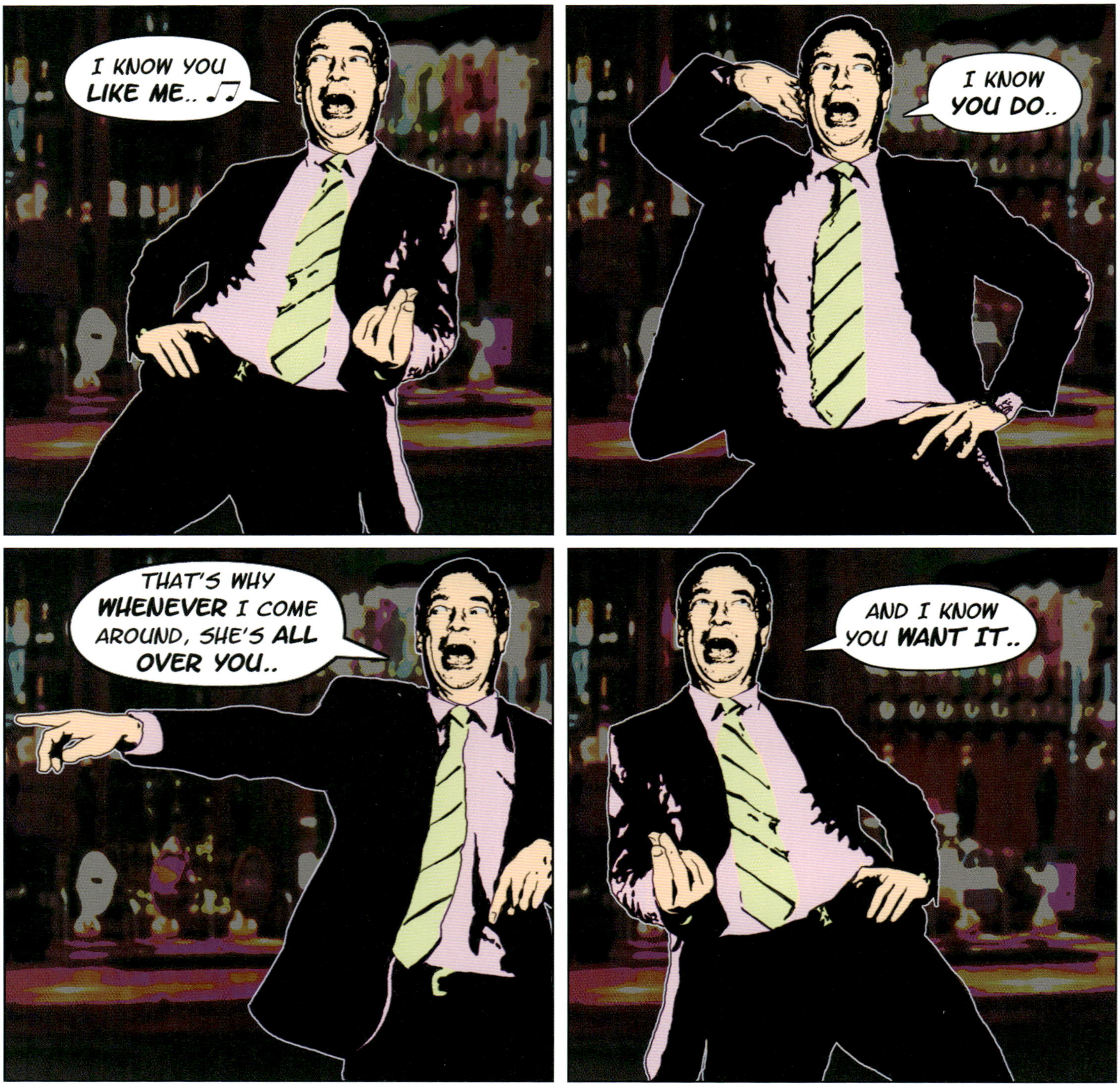

I KNOW YOU LIKE ME.. ♫
I KNOW YOU DO..
THAT'S WHY WHENEVER I COME AROUND, SHE'S ALL OVER YOU..
AND I KNOW YOU WANT IT..

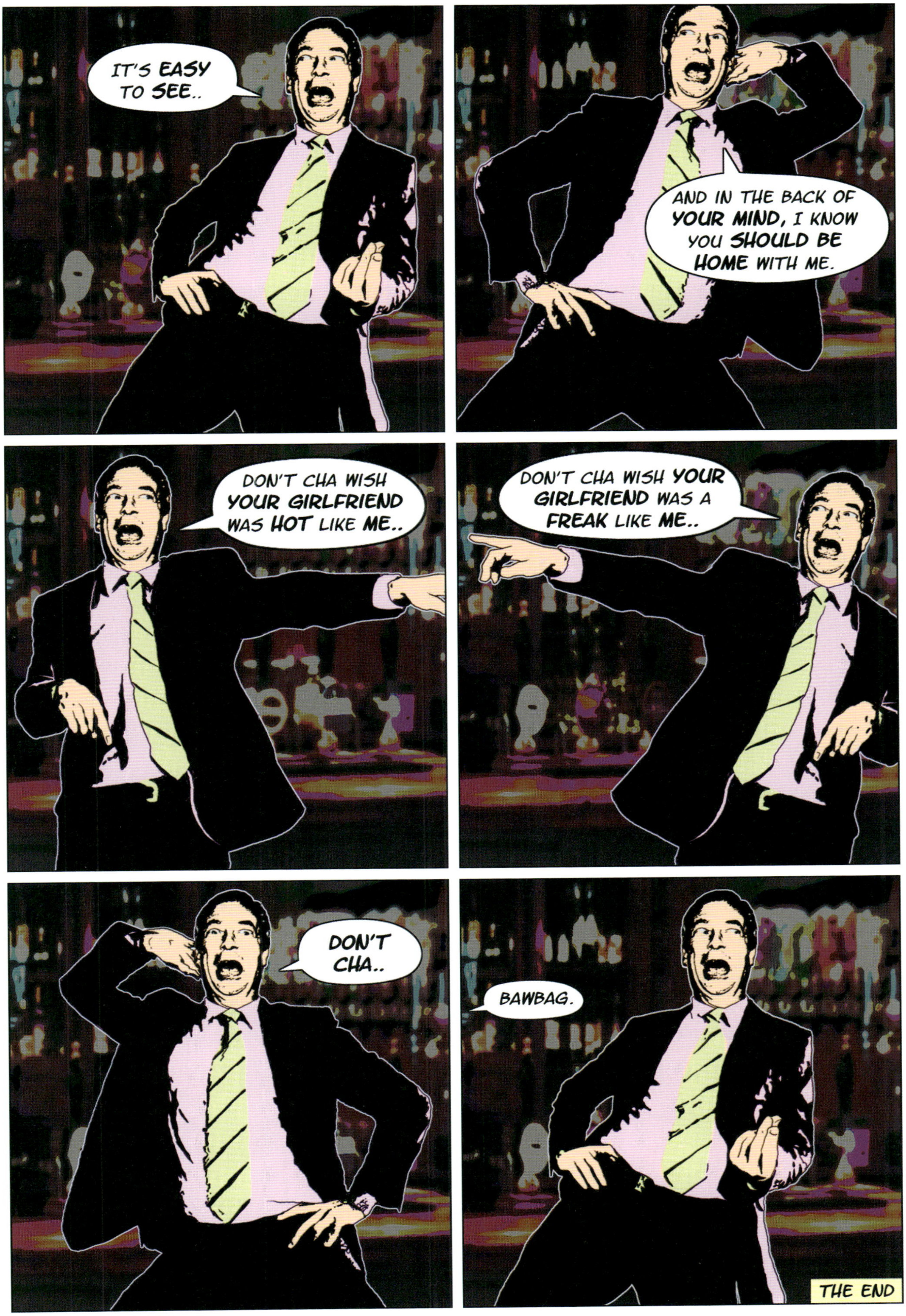
IT'S EASY TO SEE..
AND IN THE BACK OF YOUR MIND, I KNOW YOU SHOULD BE HOME WITH ME.
DON'T CHA WISH YOUR GIRLFRIEND WAS HOT LIKE ME..
DON'T CHA WISH YOUR GIRLFRIEND WAS A FREAK LIKE ME..
DON'T CHA..
BAWBAG.
THE END

MARGARET CURRAN IN SPACE

MAY 26TH 2013

Margaret Curran MP said she was "uncomfortable" that her son living in England would become "a foreigner". In the same week she practically denied all knowledge of former chancellor Denis Healey when he admitted the Labour government had misled Scots over the value of oil.

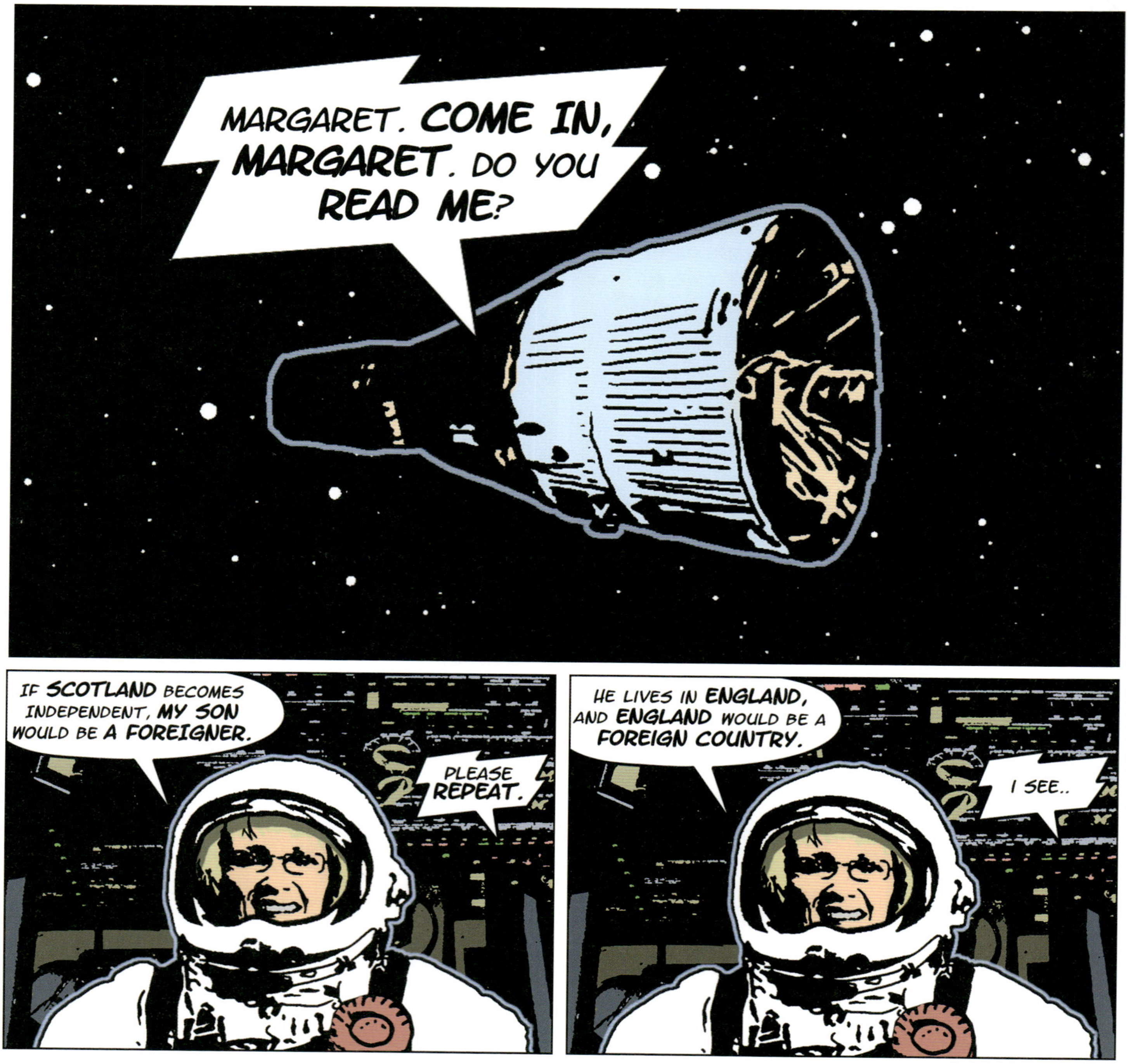
MARGARET. COME IN, MARGARET. DO YOU READ ME?
IF SCOTLAND BECOMES INDEPENDENT, MY SON WOULD BE A FOREIGNER.
PLEASE REPEAT.
HE LIVES IN ENGLAND, AND ENGLAND WOULD BE A FOREIGN COUNTRY.
I SEE..

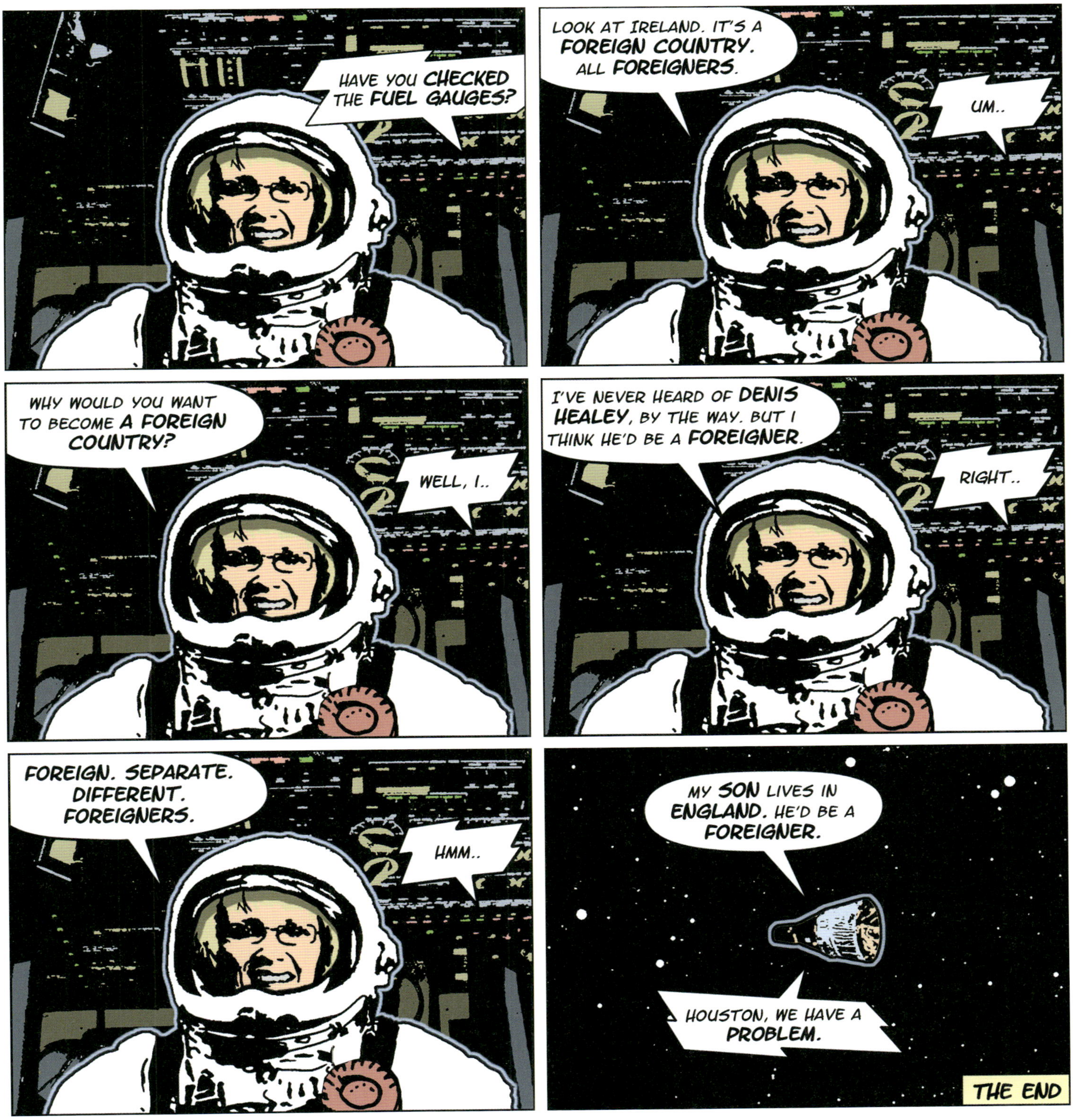
HAVE YOU CHECKED THE FUEL GAUGES?
LOOK AT IRELAND. IT'S A FOREIGN COUNTRY. ALL FOREIGNERS.
UM..
WHY WOULD YOU WANT TO BECOME A FOREIGN COUNTRY?
WELL, I..
I'VE NEVER HEARD OF DENIS HEALEY, BY THE WAY. BUT I THINK HE'D BE A FOREIGNER.
RIGHT..
FOREIGN. SEPARATE. DIFFERENT. FOREIGNERS.
HMM..
MY SON LIVES IN ENGLAND. HE'D BE A FOREIGNER.
HOUSTON, WE HAVE A PROBLEM.
THE END

LORD ROBERTSON PREDICTS

JUNE 2ND 2013

Lord Robertson of Port Ellen is truly the gift that keeps on giving. He'd already made the worst prediction ever and at this stage he began warming up his apocalypse globe. But the 'balkanisation of Europe' was just the beginning. There was much more to come.

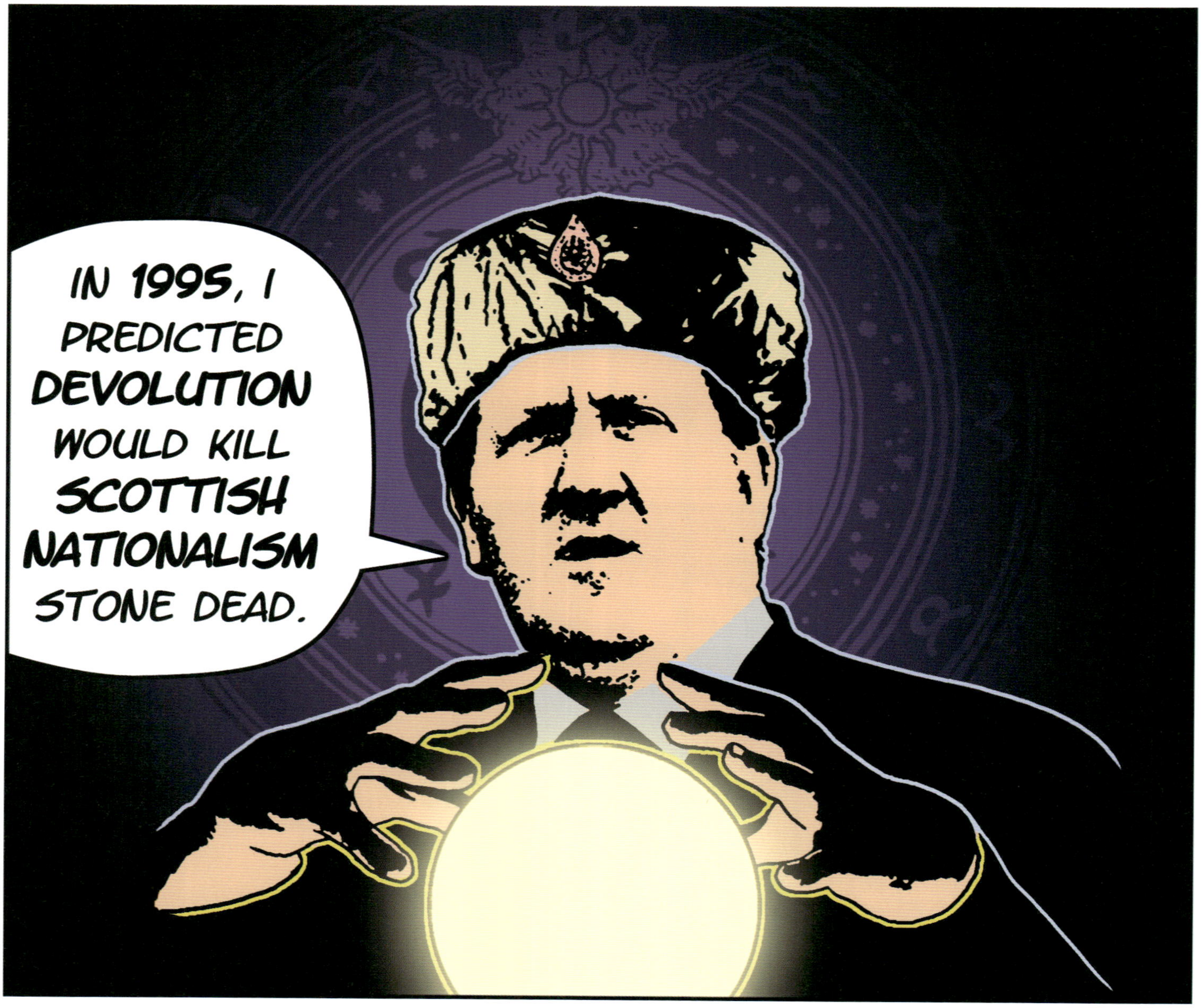
IN 1995, I PREDICTED DEVOLUTION WOULD KILL SCOTTISH NATIONALISM STONE DEAD.

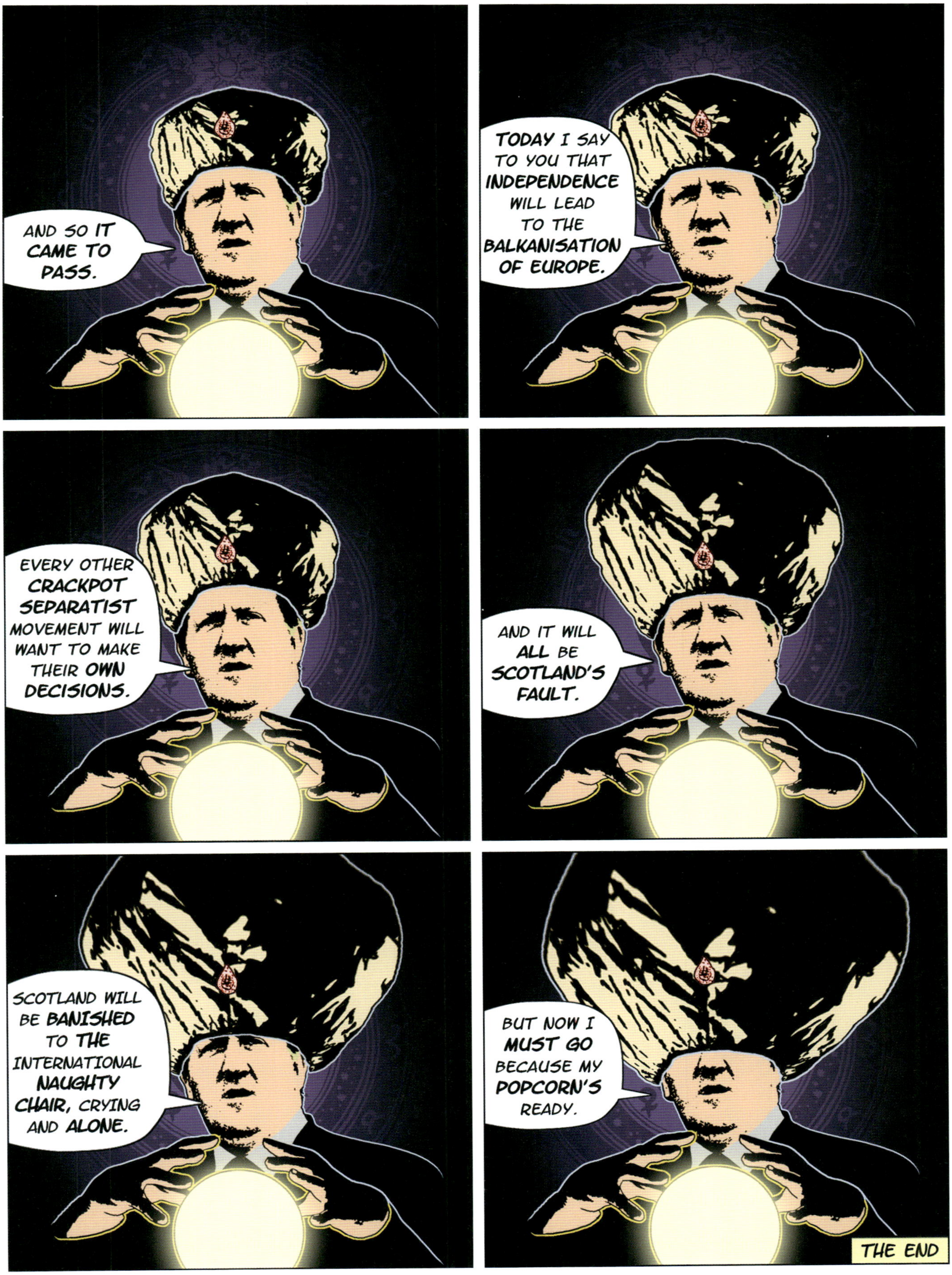
AND SO IT CAME TO PASS.
TODAY I SAY TO YOU THAT INDEPENDENCE WILL LEAD TO THE BALKANISATION OF EUROPE.
EVERY OTHER CRACKPOT SEPARATIST MOVEMENT WILL WANT TO MAKE THEIR OWN DECISIONS.
AND IT WILL ALL BE SCOTLAND'S FAULT.
SCOTLAND WILL BE BANISHED TO THE INTERNATIONAL NAUGHTY CHAIR, CRYING AND ALONE.
BUT NOW I MUST GO BECAUSE MY POPCORN'S READY.
THE END

LORD FOULKES IN A BOX

JUNE 9TH 2013

Ah, the lords. What would we do without them? Well, I guess we'd be ok. The TV programme that Lord Foulkes of Cumnock didn't see but complained about in the strongest terms was Iain MacWhirter's three-part series on the history of the independence debate, 'Road to Referendum'.

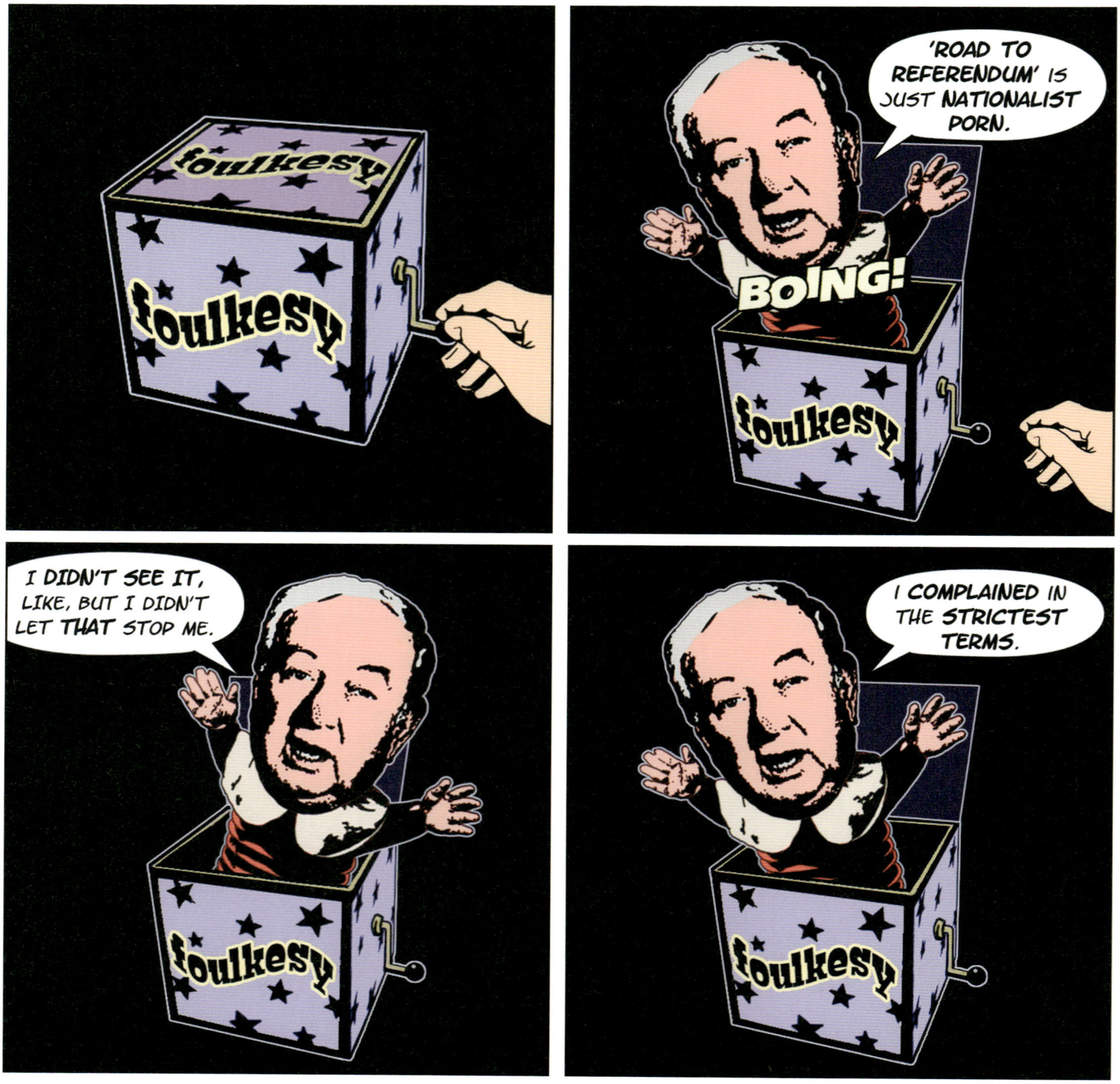

foulkesy
foulkesy
'ROAD TO REFERENDUM' IS JUST NATIONALIST PORN.
BOING!
foulkesy
I DIDN'T SEE IT, LIKE, BUT I DIDN'T LET THAT STOP ME.
foulkesy
I COMPLAINED IN THE STRICTEST TERMS.
foulkesy

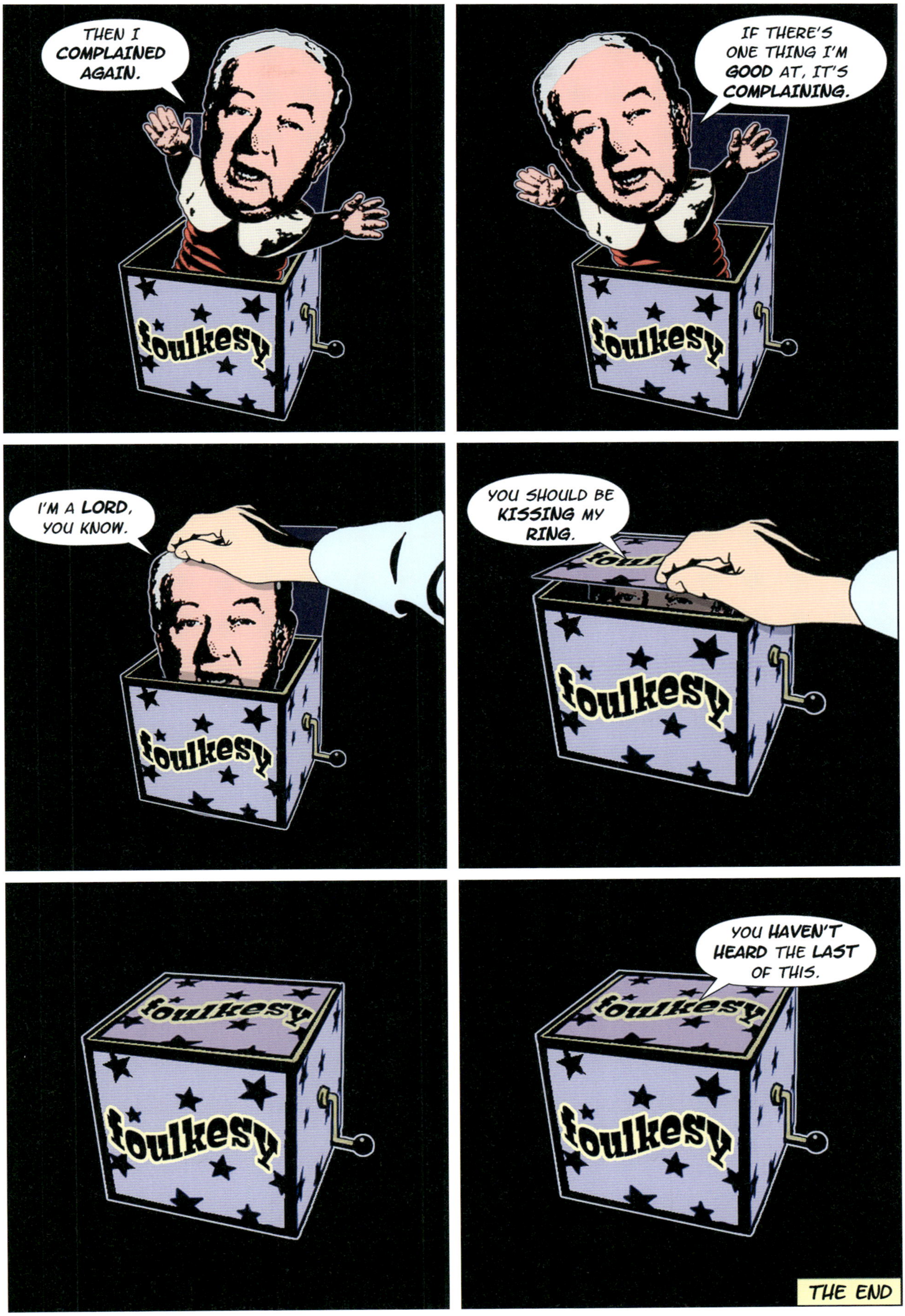
THEN I COMPLAINED AGAIN.
IF THERE'S ONE THING I'M GOOD AT, IT'S COMPLAINING.
foulkesy
I'M A LORD, YOU KNOW.
foulkesy
YOU SHOULD BE KISSING MY RING.
foulkesy
foulkesy
foulkesy
YOU HAVEN'T HEARD THE LAST OF THIS.
foulkesy
foulkesy
THE END

QUESTION TIME: NORTH BRITAIN SPECIAL!

JUNE 16TH 2013

The BBC has had a unique take on the word 'balanced' throughout the campaign. I don't recall exactly what irked me on this occasion but I believe it was not so much 'bias by omission' as 'bias by inclusion of guests who don't know the first thing about Scotland'.

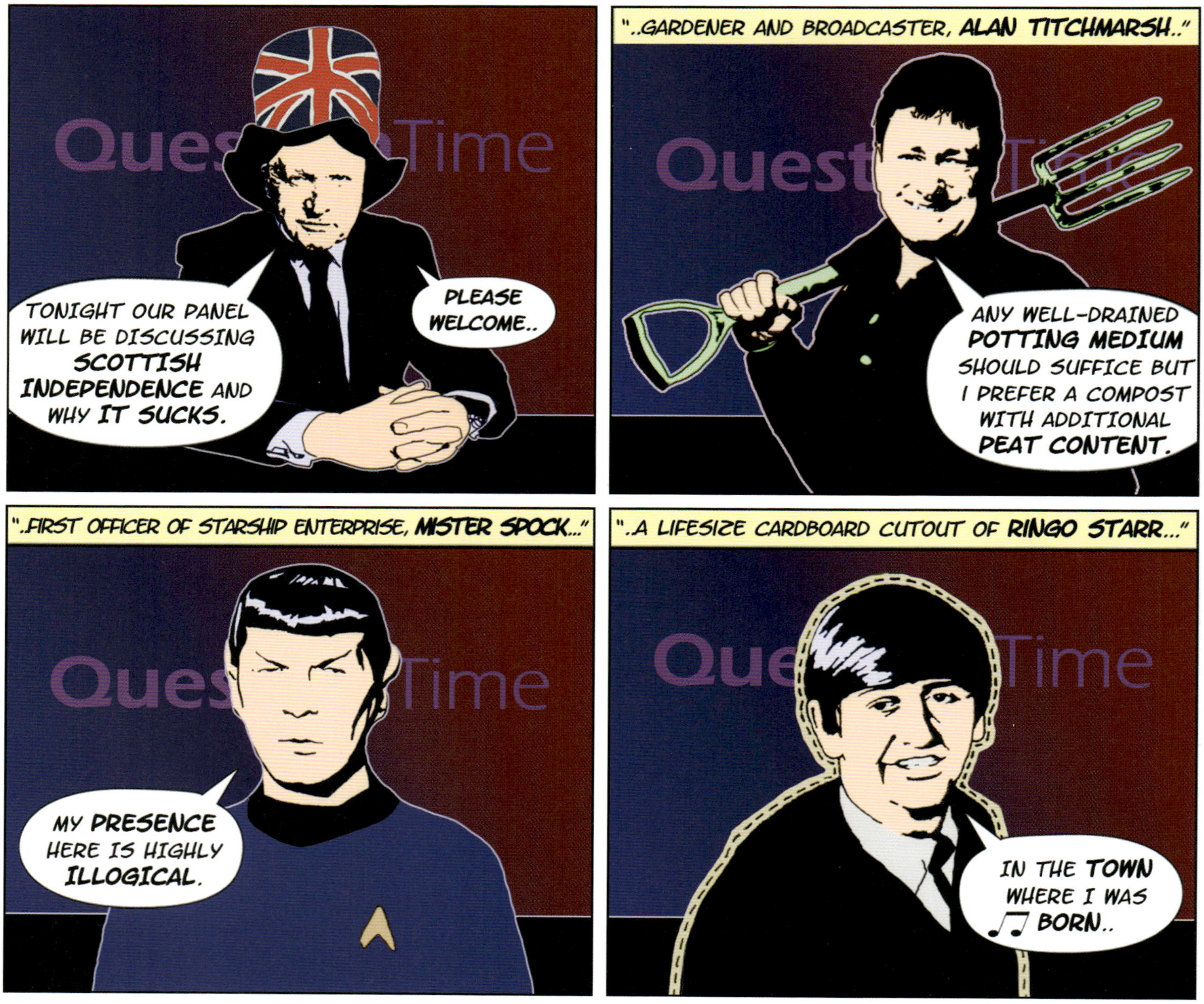

TONIGHT OUR PANEL WILL BE DISCUSSING SCOTTISH INDEPENDENCE AND WHY IT SUCKS.
PLEASE WELCOME..
"..GARDENER AND BROADCASTER, ALAN TITCHMARSH.."
ANY WELL-DRAINED POTTING MEDIUM SHOULD SUFFICE BUT I PREFER A COMPOST WITH ADDITIONAL PEAT CONTENT.
"..FIRST OFFICER OF STARSHIP ENTERPRISE, MISTER SPOCK..."
MY PRESENCE HERE IS HIGHLY ILLOGICAL.
"..A LIFESIZE CARDBOARD CUTOUT OF RINGO STARR..."
IN THE TOWN WHERE I WAS BORN..

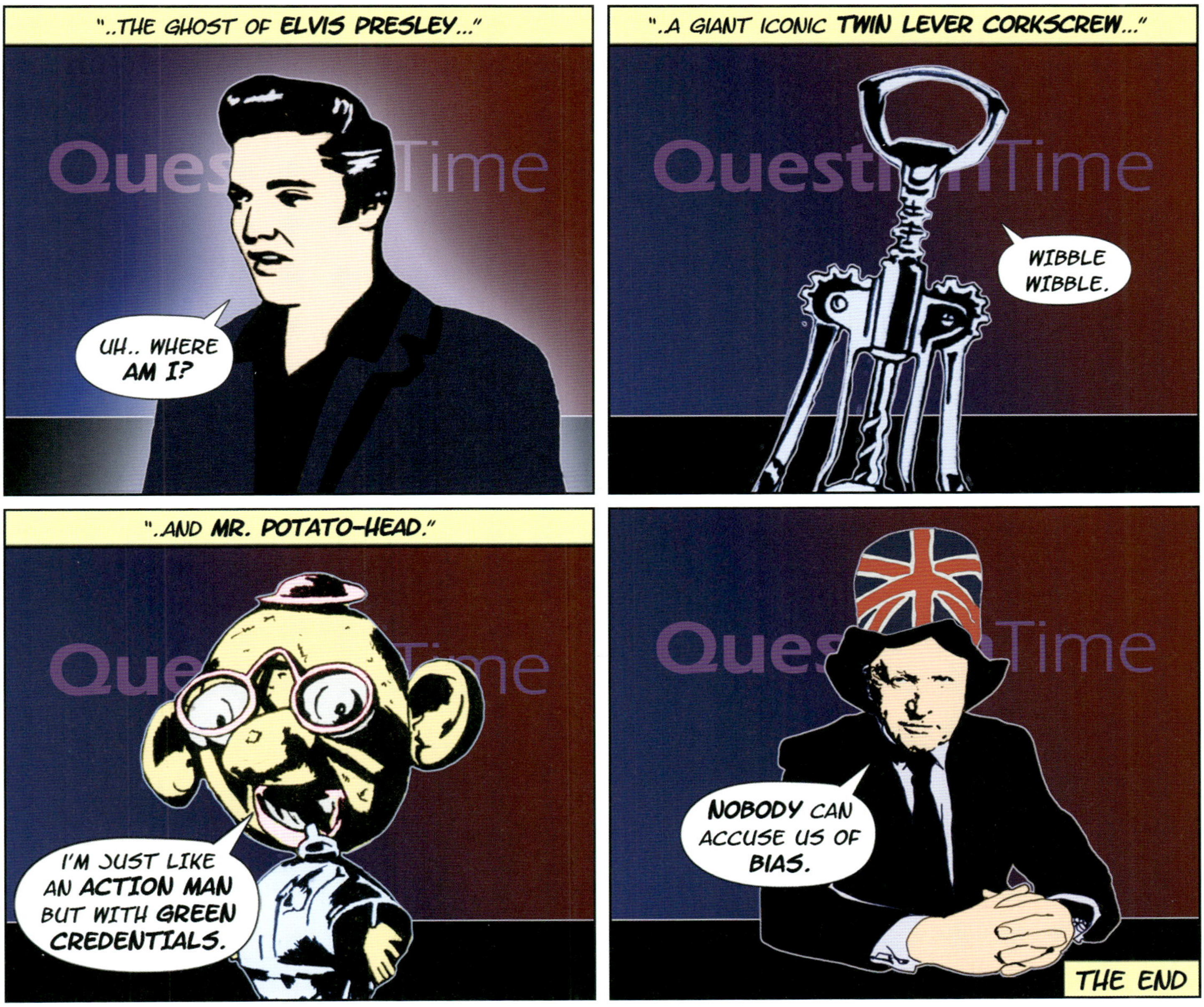
"..THE GHOST OF ELVIS PRESLEY..."
UH.. WHERE AM I?
"..A GIANT ICONIC TWIN LEVER CORKSCREW..."
WIBBLE WIBBLE.
"..AND MR. POTATO-HEAD."
I'M JUST LIKE AN ACTION MAN BUT WITH GREEN CREDENTIALS.
NOBODY CAN ACCUSE US OF BIAS.
THE END

THE STRANGE CASE OF ED MILIBAND

JUNE 23RD 2013

I wondered if the leader of the Labour Party might have some rogue special adviser dishing out thoroughly dubious guidance and making himself indispensible to one who in reality may be a little fragile. Enter Corky. Think of me whenever you see him.

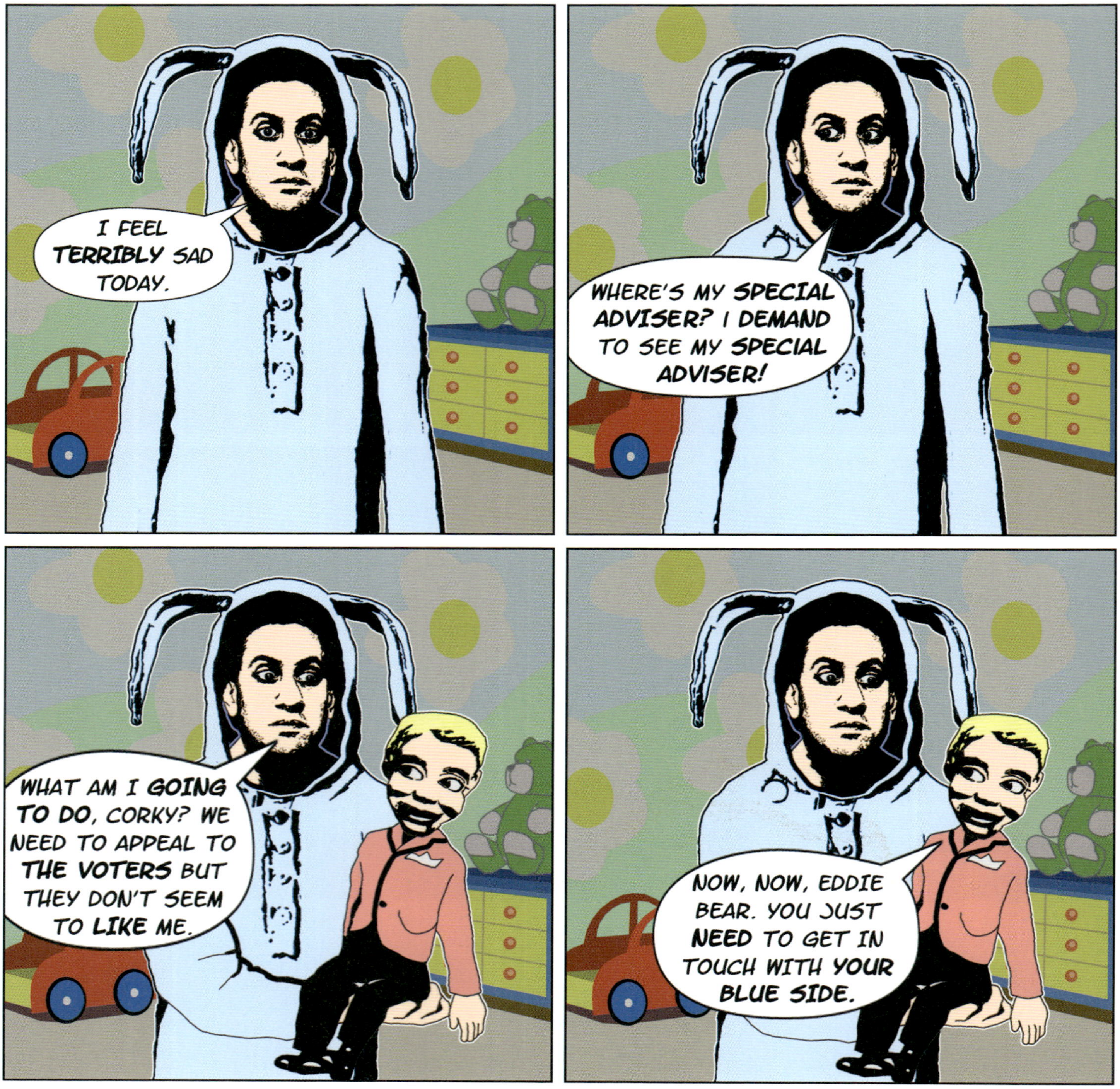
I FEEL TERRIBLY SAD TODAY.
WHERE'S MY SPECIAL ADVISER? I DEMAND TO SEE MY SPECIAL ADVISER!
WHAT AM I GOING TO DO, CORKY? WE NEED TO APPEAL TO THE VOTERS BUT THEY DON'T SEEM TO LIKE ME.
NOW, NOW, EDDIE BEAR. YOU JUST NEED TO GET IN TOUCH WITH YOUR BLUE SIDE.

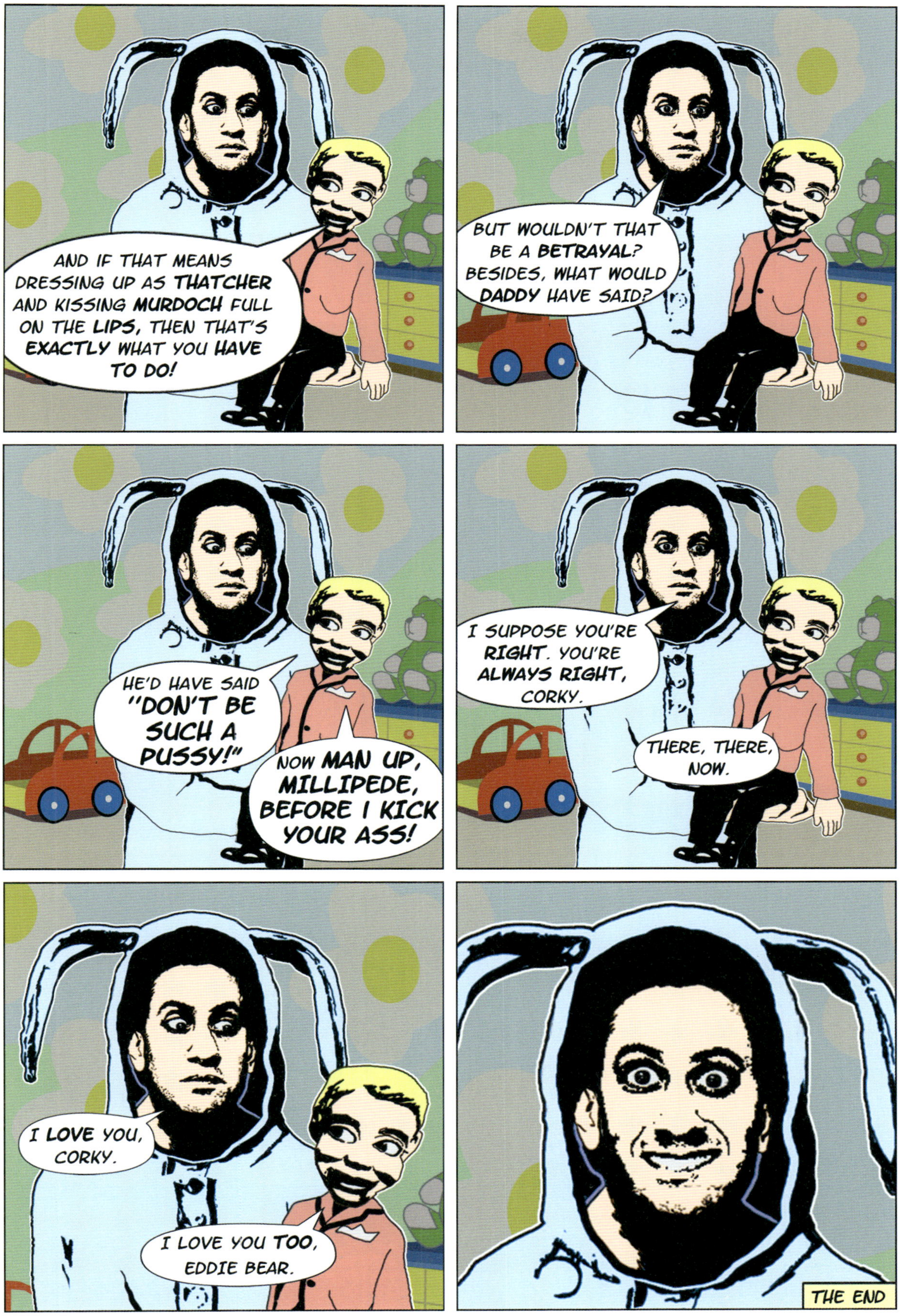

AND IF THAT MEANS DRESSING UP AS THATCHER AND KISSING MURDOCH FULL ON THE LIPS, THEN THAT'S EXACTLY WHAT YOU HAVE TO DO!
BUT WOULDN'T THAT BE A BETRAYAL? BESIDES, WHAT WOULD DADDY HAVE SAID?
HE'D HAVE SAID "DON'T BE SUCH A PUSSY!"
NOW MAN UP, MILLIPEDE, BEFORE I KICK YOUR ASS!
I SUPPOSE YOU'RE RIGHT. YOU'RE ALWAYS RIGHT, CORKY.
THERE, THERE, NOW.
I LOVE YOU, CORKY.
I LOVE YOU TOO, EDDIE BEAR.
THE END

THE STRANGE CASE OF ED MILIBAND - PART TWO

JULY 7TH 2013

Ed Miliband had a problem. He didn't want to look soft on the unions whilst trying to win over the right, but the unions were the ones responsible for getting him elected. "The hand that feeds bleeds" is very much a Rose Garnett line. *With Rose Garnett.*

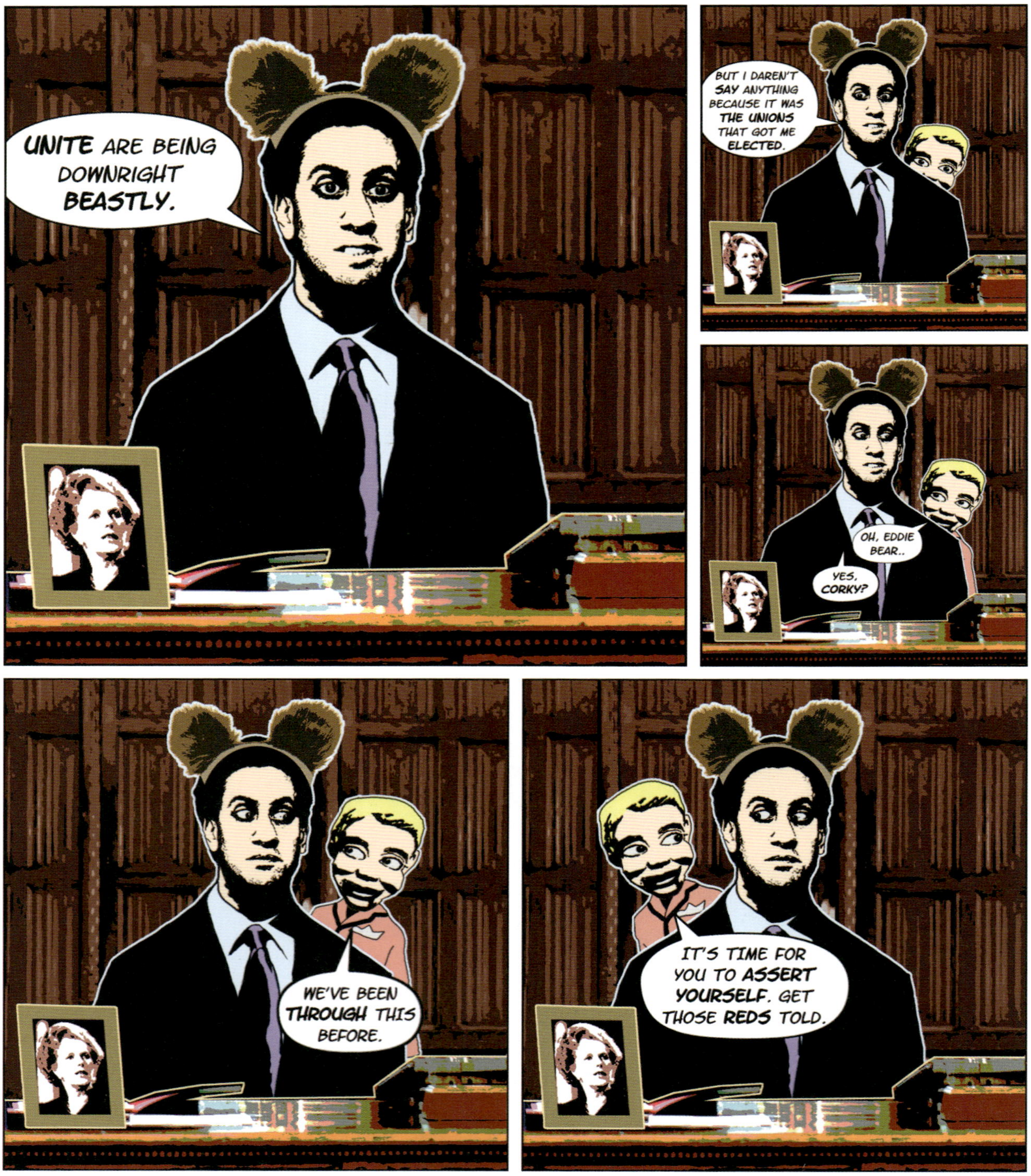
UNITE ARE BEING DOWNRIGHT BEASTLY.
BUT I DAREN'T SAY ANYTHING BECAUSE IT WAS THE UNIONS THAT GOT ME ELECTED.
OH, EDDIE BEAR..
YES, CORKY?
WE'VE BEEN THROUGH THIS BEFORE.
IT'S TIME FOR YOU TO ASSERT YOURSELF. GET THOSE REDS TOLD.

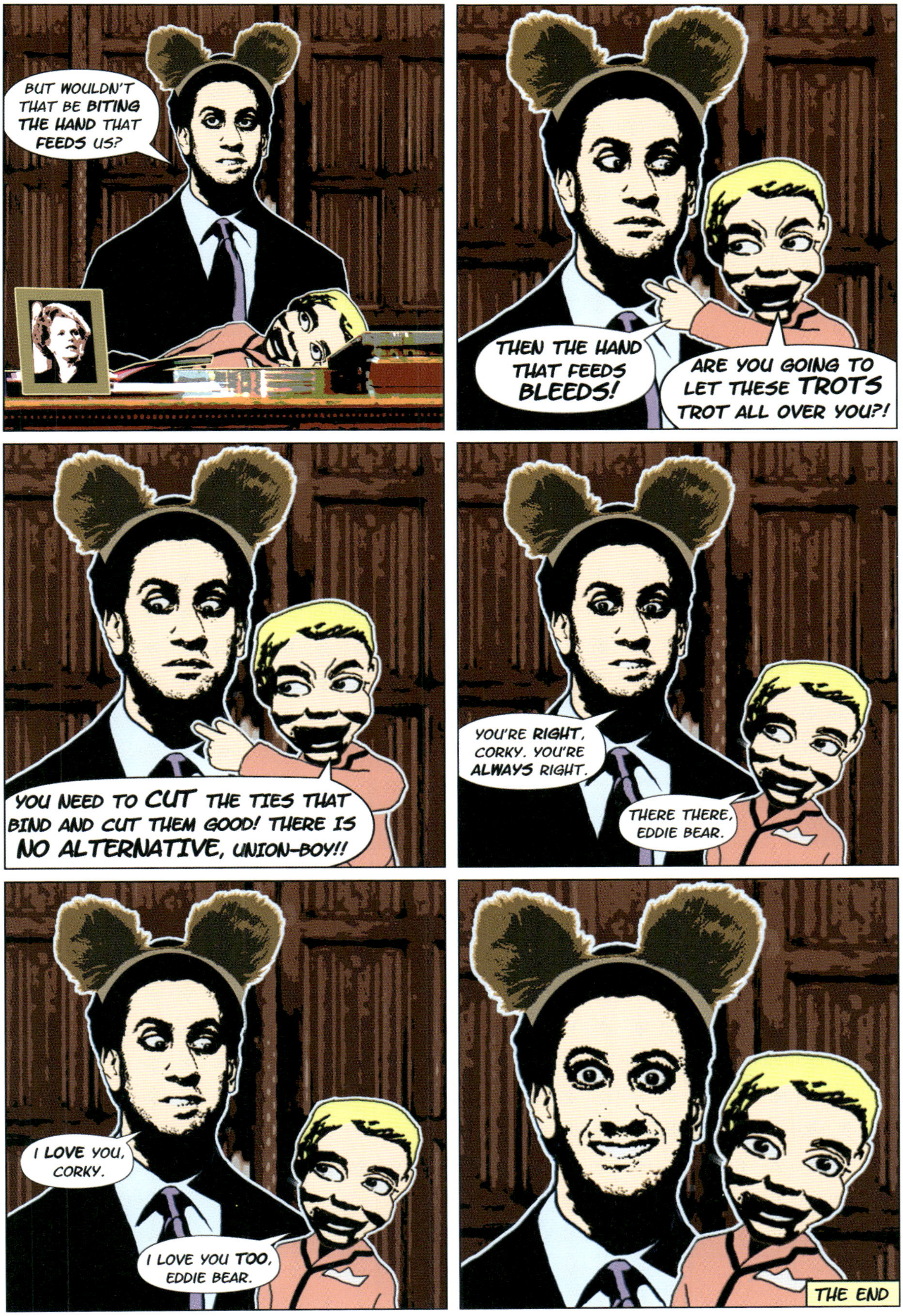

BUT WOULDN'T THAT BE BITING THE HAND THAT FEEDS US?
THEN THE HAND THAT FEEDS BLEEDS!
ARE YOU GOING TO LET THESE TROTS TROT ALL OVER YOU?!
YOU NEED TO CUT THE TIES THAT BIND AND CUT THEM GOOD! THERE IS NO ALTERNATIVE, UNION-BOY!!
YOU'RE RIGHT, CORKY. YOU'RE ALWAYS RIGHT.
THERE THERE, EDDIE BEAR.
I LOVE YOU, CORKY.
I LOVE YOU TOO, EDDIE BEAR.
THE END

ALISTAIR DARLING ACCENTUATES THE POSITIVE

JULY 14TH 2013

'Westminster could annex Clyde nuclear bases,' ran the headlines. We may laugh about it now, but it appears to have been seriously considered. This followed hot on the heels of Project Fear (Better Together's own nickname for its campaign) promising to be more positive.

project fear
LOOK CAMMY, WHAT THE DEVIL ARE YOU PLAYING AT?
project fear
ONE MINUTE MY FEAR-FIGHTERS ARE WORKING ON A POSITIVE CASE FOR THE UNION, THE NEXT WE'RE ANNEXING ARGYLL.
project fear
ARGYLL, CAMMY. IT'S WHERE WE KEEP THE BLOODY NUKES!
project fear
THIS IS AN EFFING DISASTER, BUT LUCKILY FOR YOU I'VE GOT A NEW IDEA.

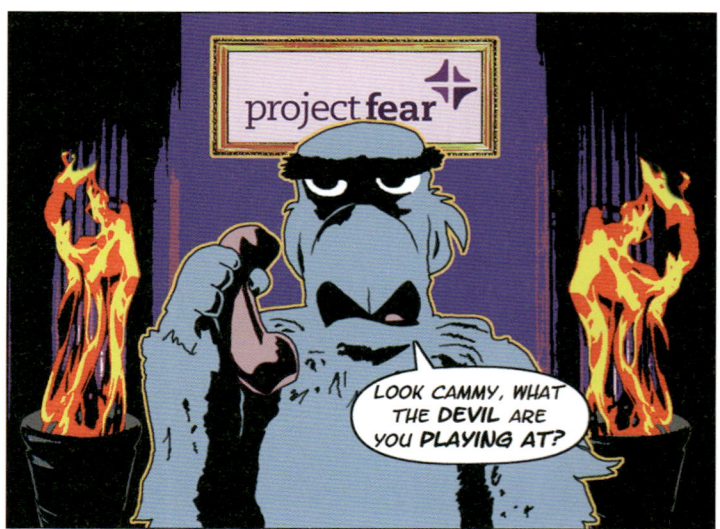

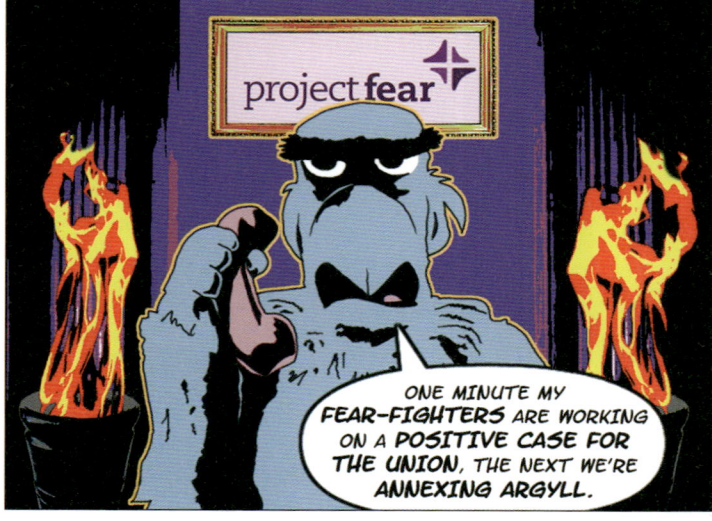

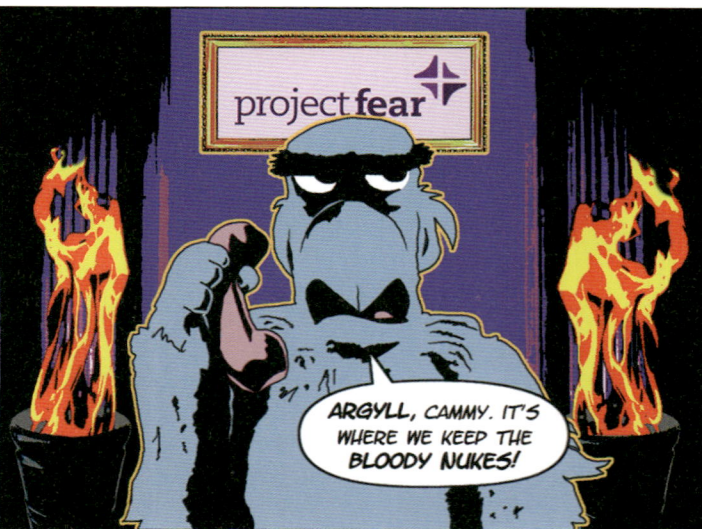

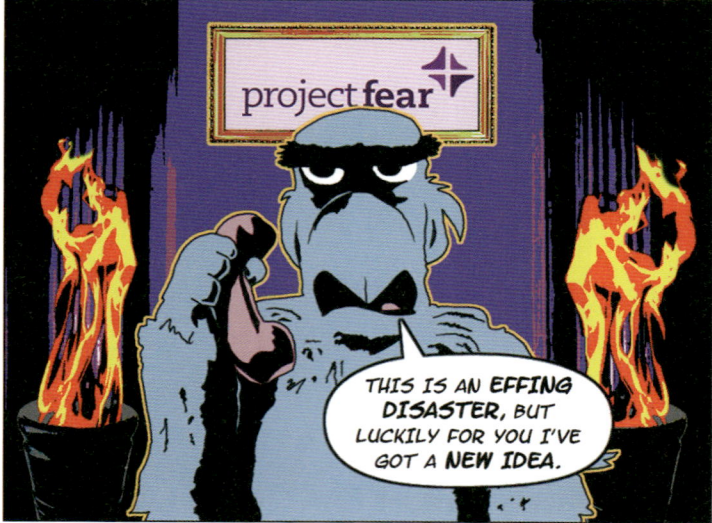

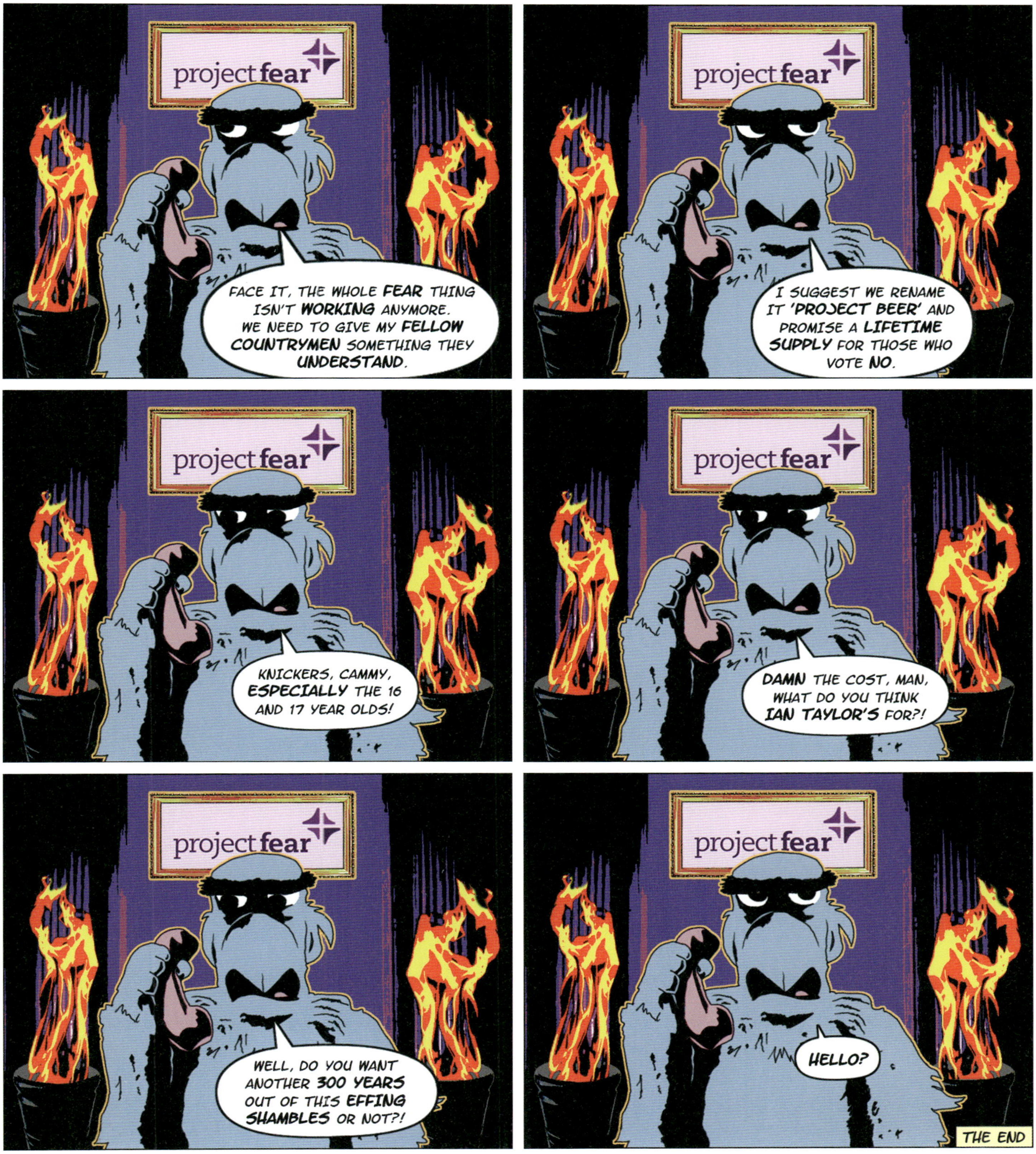
project fear
FACE IT, THE WHOLE FEAR THING ISN'T WORKING ANYMORE. WE NEED TO GIVE MY FELLOW COUNTRYMEN SOMETHING THEY UNDERSTAND.
I SUGGEST WE RENAME IT 'PROJECT BEER' AND PROMISE A LIFETIME SUPPLY FOR THOSE WHO VOTE NO.
KNICKERS, CAMMY, ESPECIALLY THE 16 AND 17 YEAR OLDS!
DAMN THE COST, MAN, WHAT DO YOU THINK IAN TAYLOR'S FOR?!
WELL, DO YOU WANT ANOTHER 300 YEARS OUT OF THIS EFFING SHAMBLES OR NOT?!
HELLO?
THE END

DAVID CAMERON PAINTS IT BLACK

JULY 21ST 2013

As the Conservative party delighted in carrying out a programme of brutal austerity cuts - idealogical measures dressed up as good housekeeping - it became clear that the Scottish question was nothing but a minor inconvenience. One for Alistair to deal with.

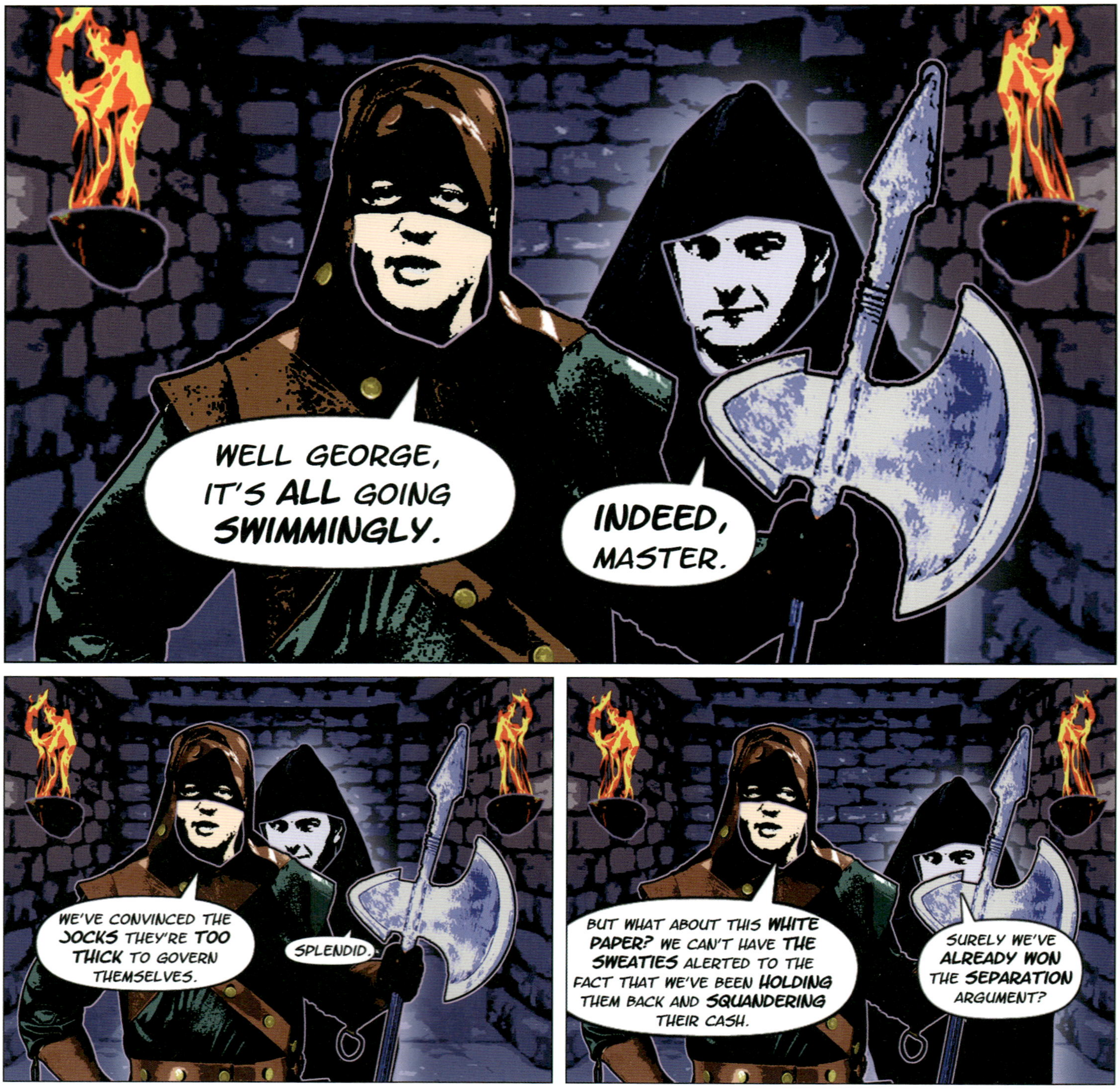

WELL GEORGE, IT'S ALL GOING SWIMMINGLY.
INDEED, MASTER.
WE'VE CONVINCED THE JOCKS THEY'RE TOO THICK TO GOVERN THEMSELVES.
SPLENDID.
BUT WHAT ABOUT THIS WHITE PAPER? WE CAN'T HAVE THE SWEATIES ALERTED TO THE FACT THAT WE'VE BEEN HOLDING THEM BACK AND SQUANDERING THEIR CASH.
SURELY WE'VE ALREADY WON THE SEPARATION ARGUMENT?

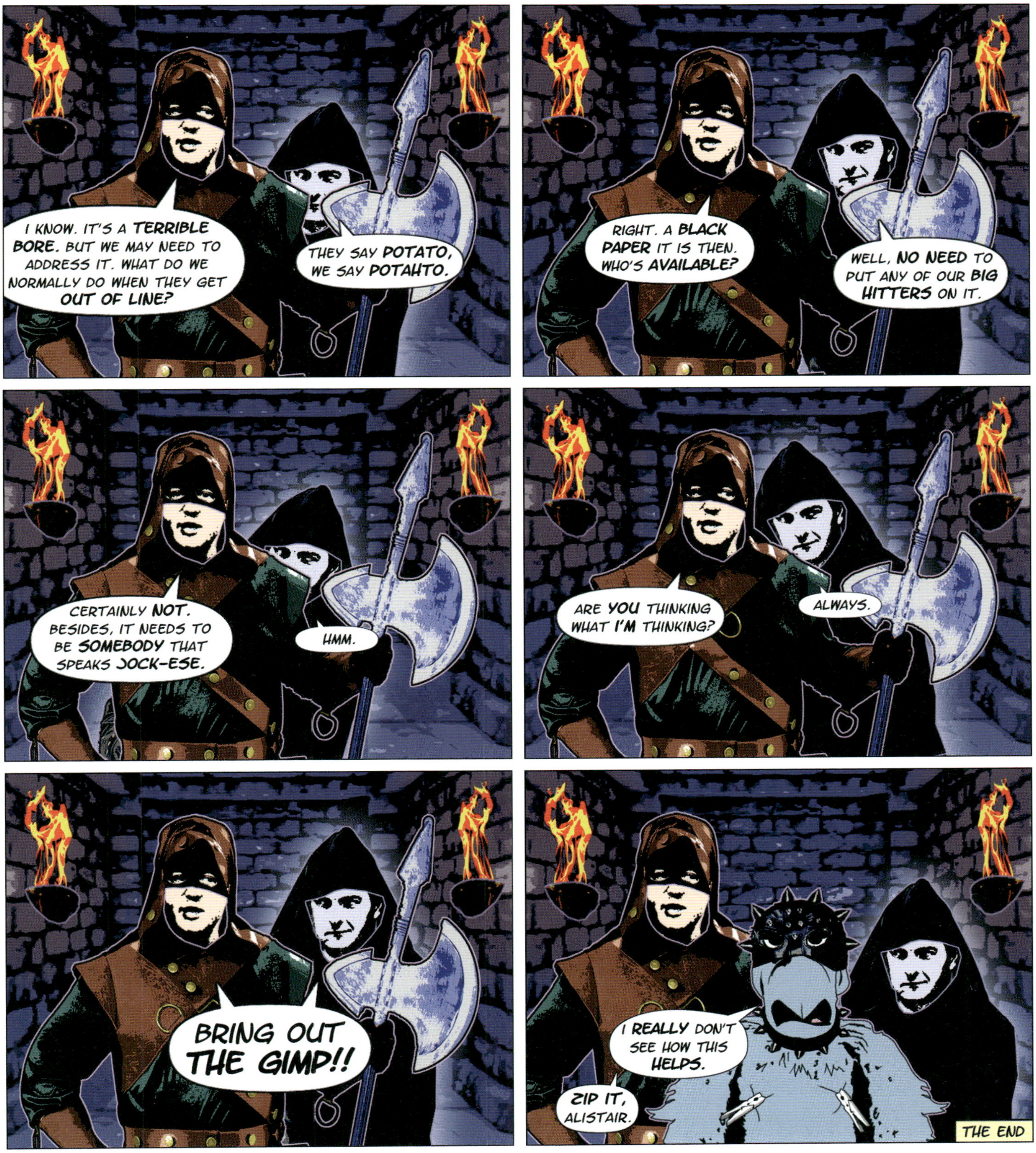
I KNOW. IT'S A TERRIBLE BORE. BUT WE MAY NEED TO ADDRESS IT. WHAT DO WE NORMALLY DO WHEN THEY GET OUT OF LINE?
THEY SAY POTATO, WE SAY POTAHTO.
RIGHT. A BLACK PAPER IT IS THEN. WHO'S AVAILABLE?
WELL, NO NEED TO PUT ANY OF OUR BIG HITTERS ON IT.
CERTAINLY NOT. BESIDES, IT NEEDS TO BE SOMEBODY THAT SPEAKS JOCK-ESE.
HMM.
ARE YOU THINKING WHAT I'M THINKING?
ALWAYS.
BRING OUT THE GIMP!!
I REALLY DON'T SEE HOW THIS HELPS.
ZIP IT, ALISTAIR.
THE END

THE BLAIR FEAR PROJECT

JULY 28TH 2013

Better Together's campaign director Blair McDougall held a public meeting in Bathgate, West Lothian. There were Yes voters present and one of them filmed the proceedings. This is pretty much what happened. *With Rose Garnett.*

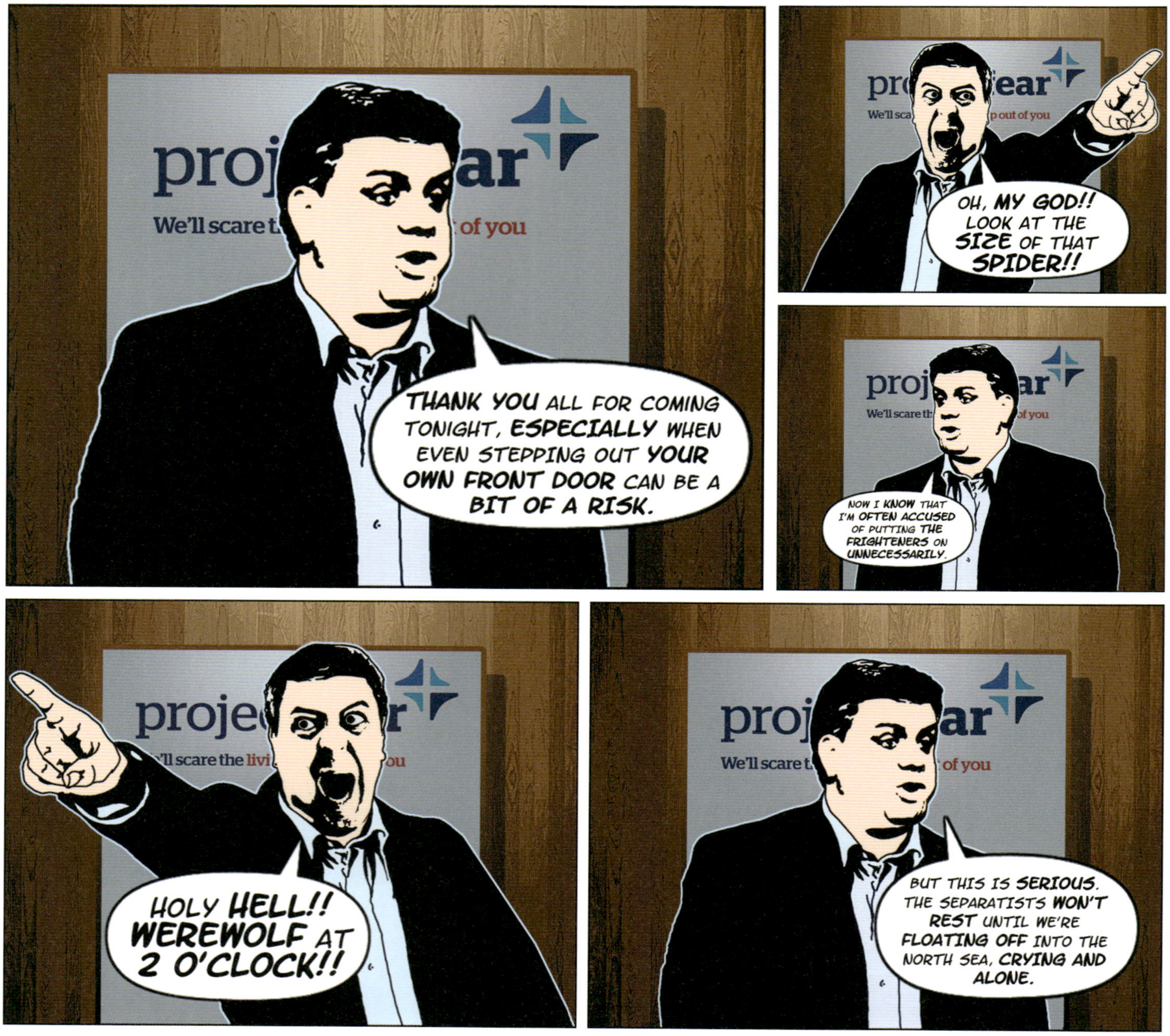

THANK YOU ALL FOR COMING TONIGHT, ESPECIALLY WHEN EVEN STEPPING OUT YOUR OWN FRONT DOOR CAN BE A BIT OF A RISK.
OH, MY GOD!! LOOK AT THE SIZE OF THAT SPIDER!!
NOW I KNOW THAT I'M OFTEN ACCUSED OF PUTTING THE FRIGHTENERS ON UNNECESSARILY.
HOLY HELL!! WEREWOLF AT 2 O'CLOCK!!
BUT THIS IS SERIOUS. THE SEPARATISTS WON'T REST UNTIL WE'RE FLOATING OFF INTO THE NORTH SEA, CRYING AND ALONE.

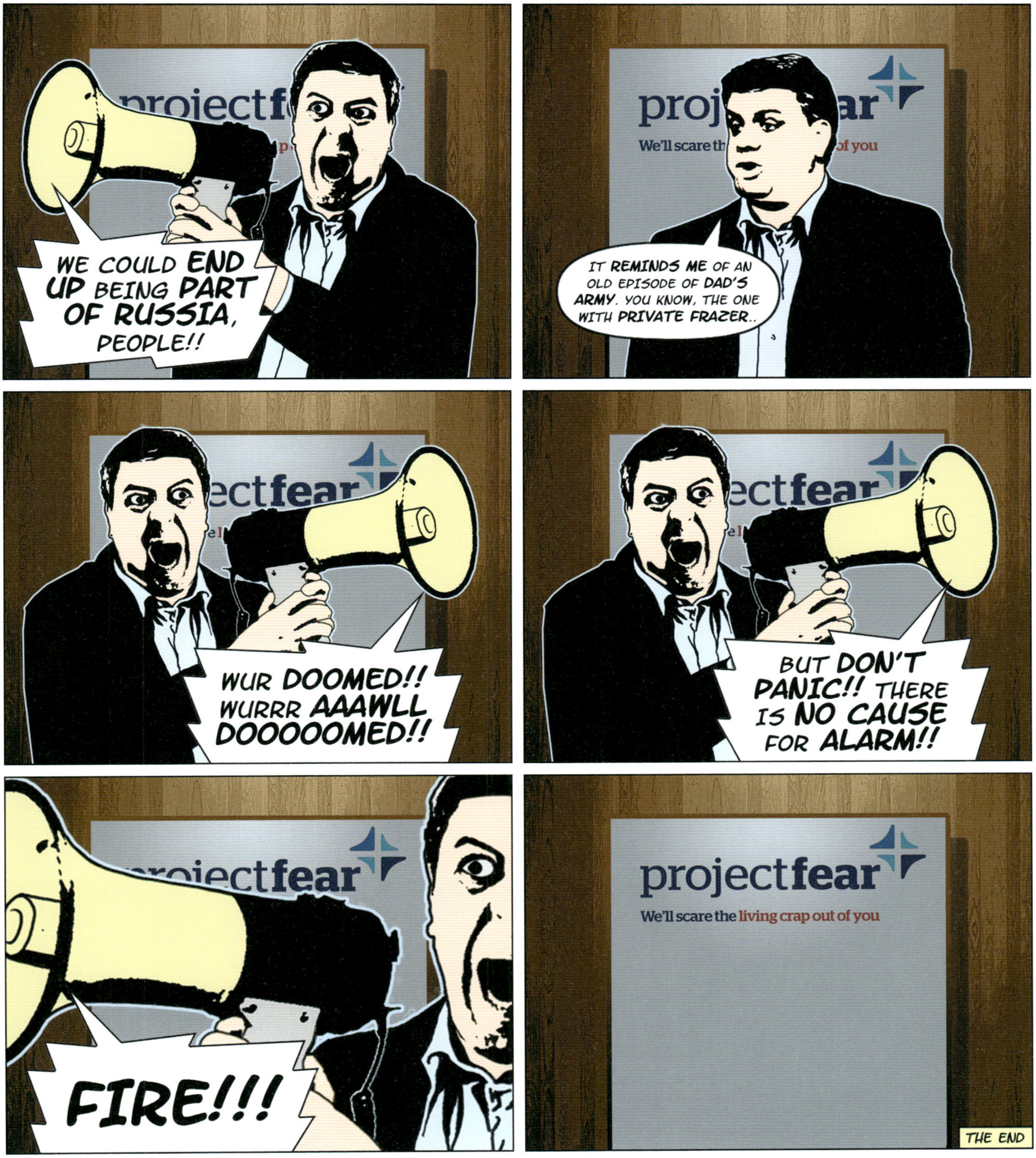
projectfear
WE COULD END UP BEING PART OF RUSSIA, PEOPLE!!
We'll scare th of you
IT REMINDS ME OF AN OLD EPISODE OF DAD'S ARMY. YOU KNOW, THE ONE WITH PRIVATE FRAZER..
WUR DOOMED!! WURRR AAAWLL DOOOOOMED!!
BUT DON'T PANIC!! THERE IS NO CAUSE FOR ALARM!!
FIRE!!!
projectfear
We'll scare the living crap out of you
THE END

BLAIR MCDOUGALL: NAT-FINDER GENERAL

AUGUST 4TH 2013

The No campaign were starting to get a tad over-zealous in their pursuit of 'Nats' and 'Cybernats'. Here, Blair gets more than he bargained for when he meets Labour party member, founder of Labour For Independence and former wrestler Allan Grogan. *With Rose Garnett.*

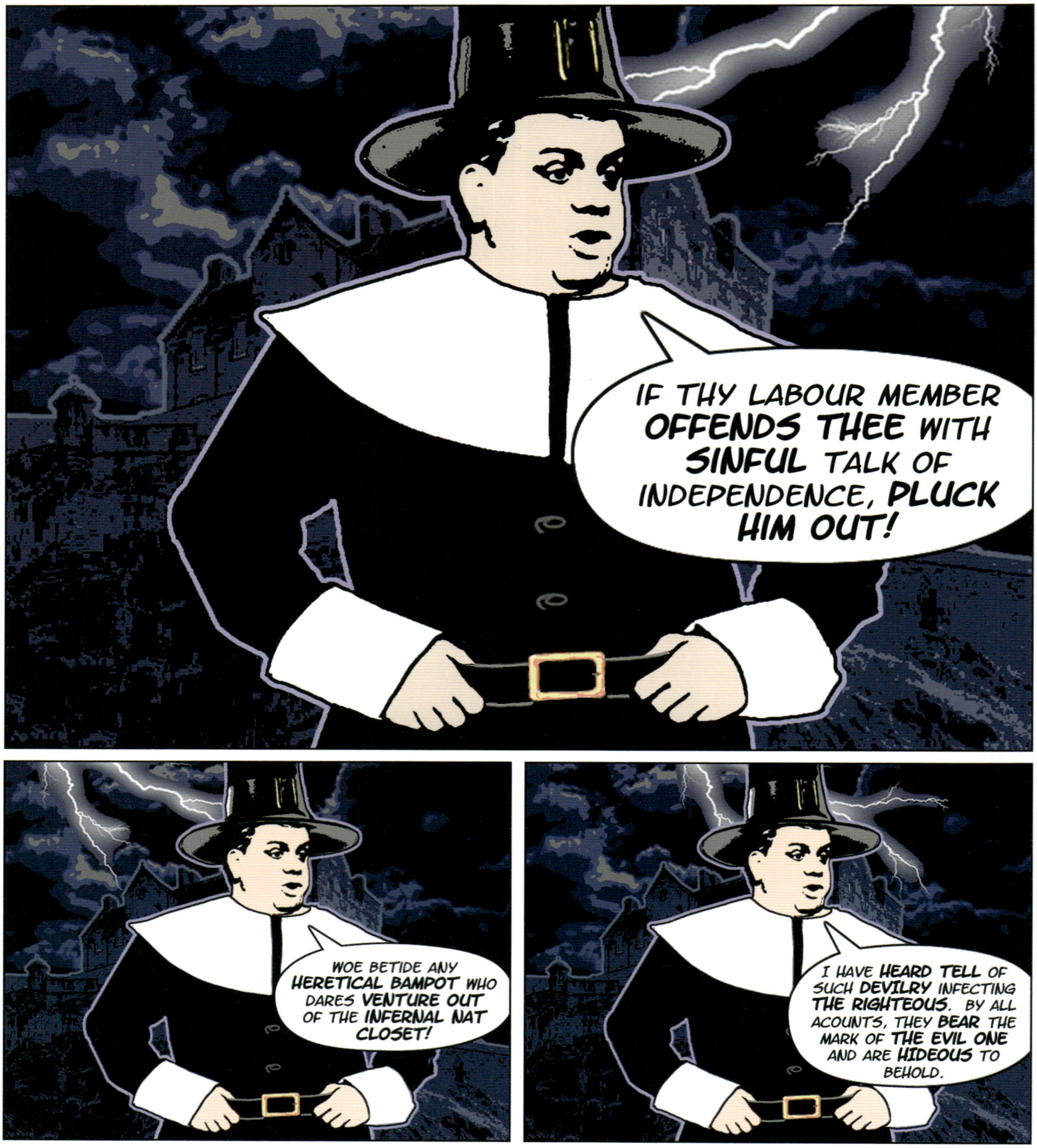
IF THY LABOUR MEMBER OFFENDS THEE WITH SINFUL TALK OF INDEPENDENCE, PLUCK HIM OUT!
WOE BETIDE ANY HERETICAL BAMPOT WHO DARES VENTURE OUT OF THE INFERNAL NAT CLOSET!
I HAVE HEARD TELL OF SUCH DEVILRY INFECTING THE RIGHTEOUS. BY ALL ACOUNTS, THEY BEAR THE MARK OF THE EVIL ONE AND ARE HIDEOUS TO BEHOLD.

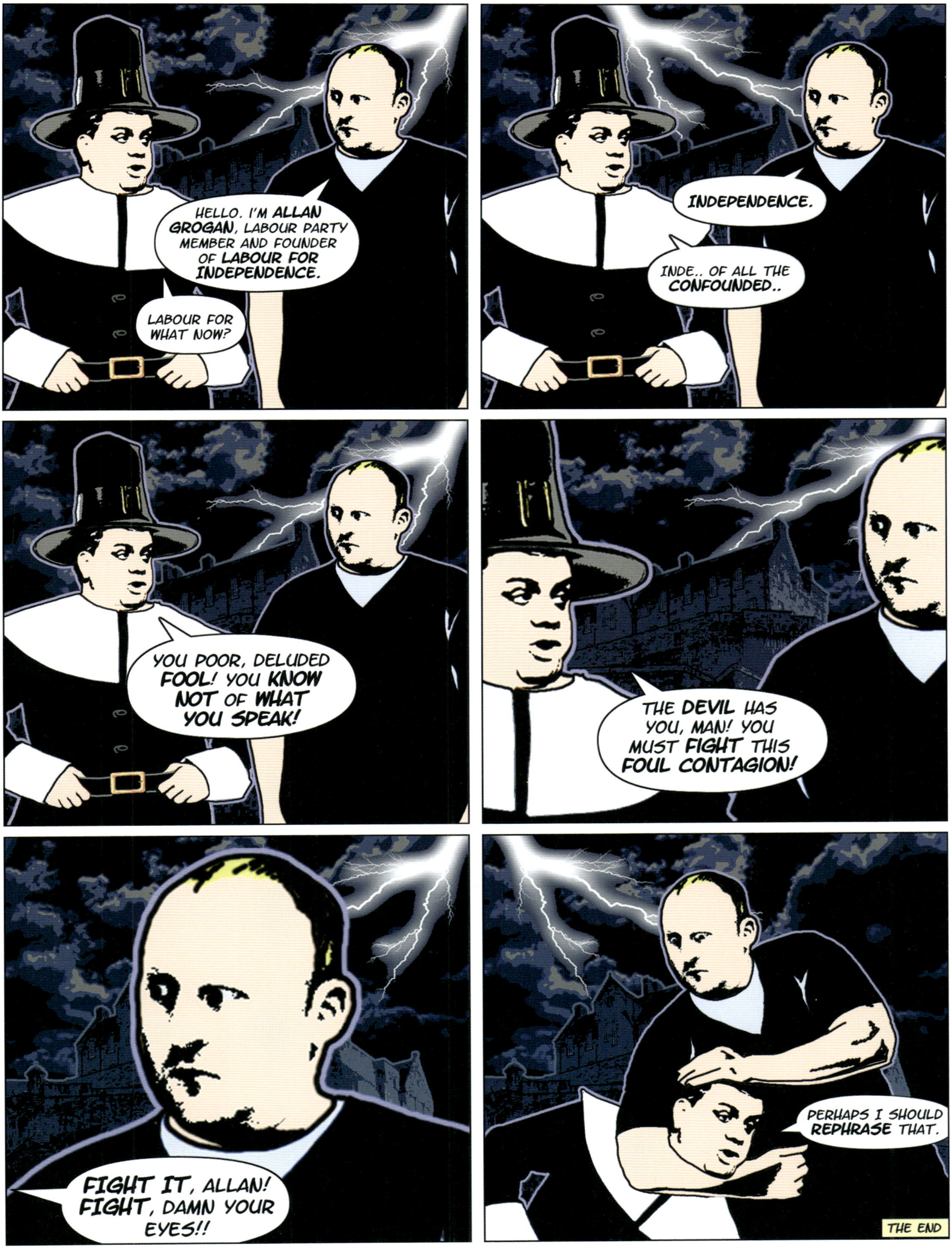
HELLO. I'M ALLAN GROGAN, LABOUR PARTY MEMBER AND FOUNDER OF LABOUR FOR INDEPENDENCE.
LABOUR FOR WHAT NOW?
INDEPENDENCE.
INDE.. OF ALL THE CONFOUNDED..
YOU POOR, DELUDED FOOL! YOU KNOW NOT OF WHAT YOU SPEAK!
THE DEVIL HAS YOU, MAN! YOU MUST FIGHT THIS FOUL CONTAGION!
FIGHT IT, ALLAN! FIGHT, DAMN YOUR EYES!!
PERHAPS I SHOULD REPHRASE THAT.
THE END

BLAIR: THERE CAN BE ONLY ONE

AUGUST 11TH 2013

The majority of Scotland's artists were backing independence and here Blair tries to redress the balance. Regarding 'stolen language', someone from the Yes camp used the phrase 'best of both worlds' or something. I don't know. It's not important. *With Rose Garnett.*

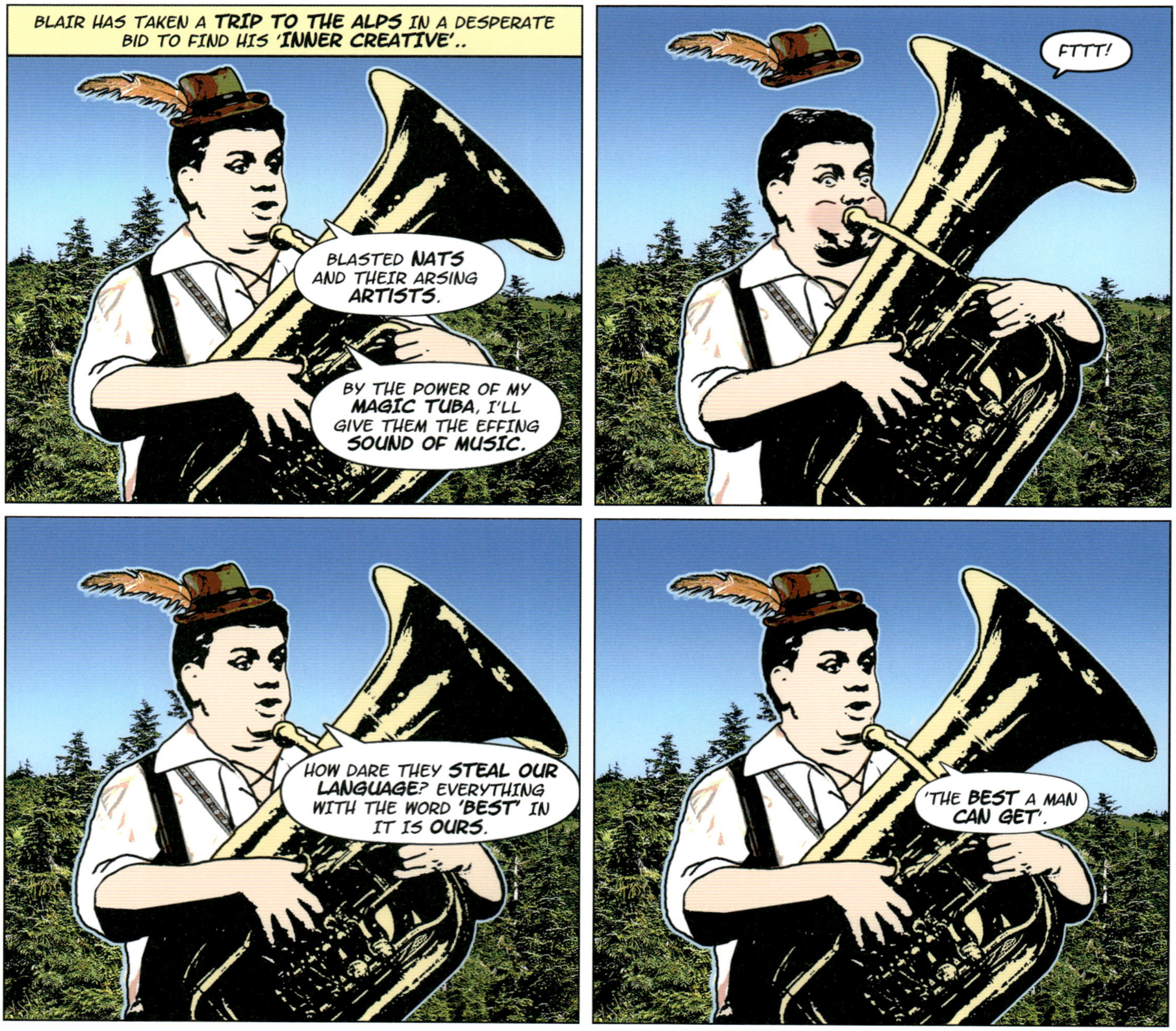

BLAIR HAS TAKEN A TRIP TO THE ALPS IN A DESPERATE BID TO FIND HIS 'INNER CREATIVE'..
BLASTED NATS AND THEIR ARSING ARTISTS.
BY THE POWER OF MY MAGIC TUBA, I'LL GIVE THEM THE EFFING SOUND OF MUSIC.
FTTT!
HOW DARE THEY STEAL OUR LANGUAGE? EVERYTHING WITH THE WORD 'BEST' IN IT IS OURS.
'THE BEST A MAN CAN GET'.

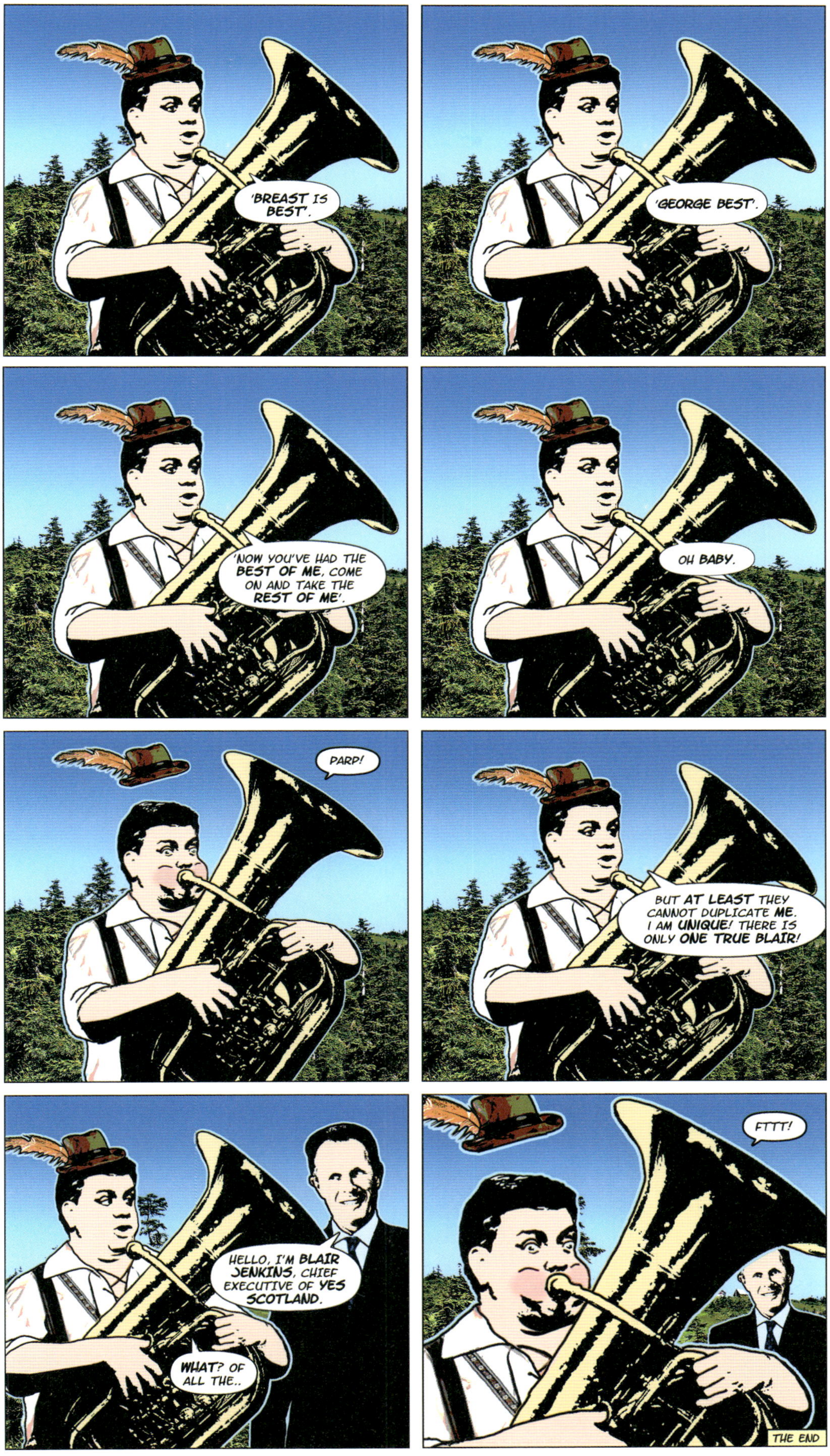

'BREAST IS BEST'.
'GEORGE BEST'.
'NOW YOU'VE HAD THE BEST OF ME, COME ON AND TAKE THE REST OF ME'.
OH BABY.
PARP!
BUT AT LEAST THEY CANNOT DUPLICATE ME. I AM UNIQUE! THERE IS ONLY ONE TRUE BLAIR!
HELLO, I'M BLAIR JENKINS, CHIEF EXECUTIVE OF YES SCOTLAND.
WHAT? OF ALL THE..
FTTT!
THE END

POLL-DENYING ACTIVITY

AUGUST 13TH 2013

Wings Over Scotland commissioned several polls, the first of which was entirely ignored by the press. The fact that it had been crowd-funded was newsworthy in itself, but the poll also found that only 6% of Scots trusted the mainstream media's coverage of the independence debate. *With Rose Garnett.*

THE FOLLOWING HAS BEEN ASSEMBLED FROM FOOTAGE DISCOVERED IN THE RUINS OF CASTLE HACKULA.
THE GENTLEMEN OF THE PRESS DISCUSS TOMORROW'S HEADLINES..
FITBA.
MURDER.
TOO WEE.
TOO POOR.
'FAT KIDS' ALWAYS SELLS.
WAS SALMOND A FAT KID? WE COULD CALL IT 'FAT NATS'.
NEDS.
'ECK'S FACTOR'.
'BLEEDIN ECK'.
IS IT PUB O'CLOCK YET?
LET'S JUST GO WITH OLD RELIABLE.
THURRR'S BIN A MURDURRRRR..
SUDDENLY, THERE IS A CHILL IN THE AIR..
DON'T TELL ME IT'S ANDREW NEIL..

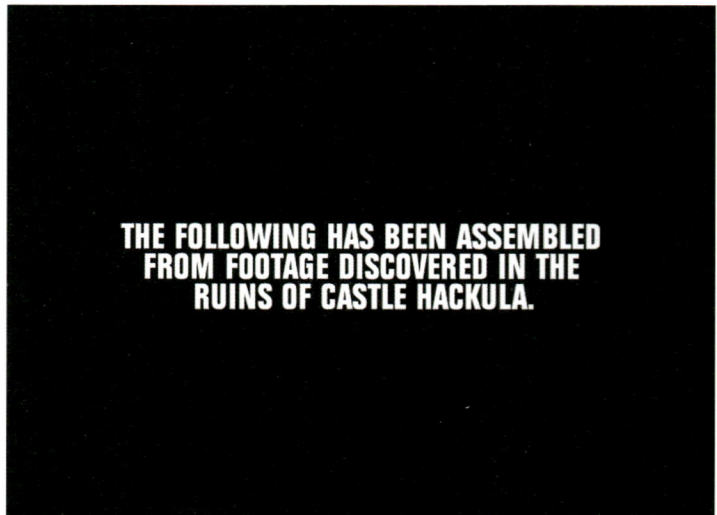

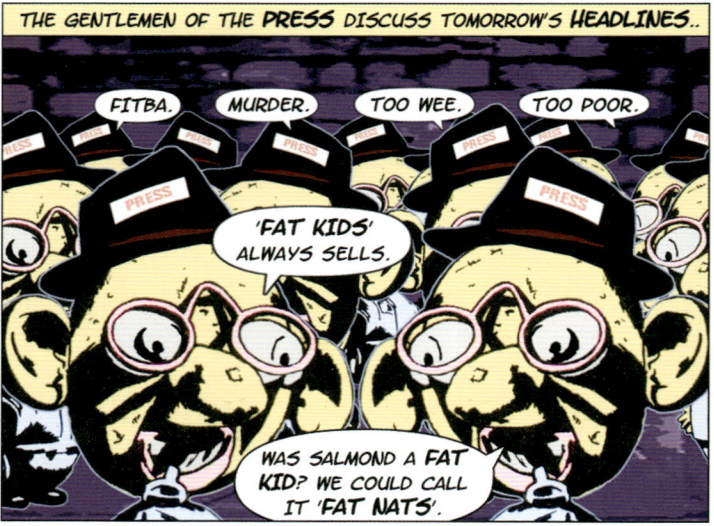

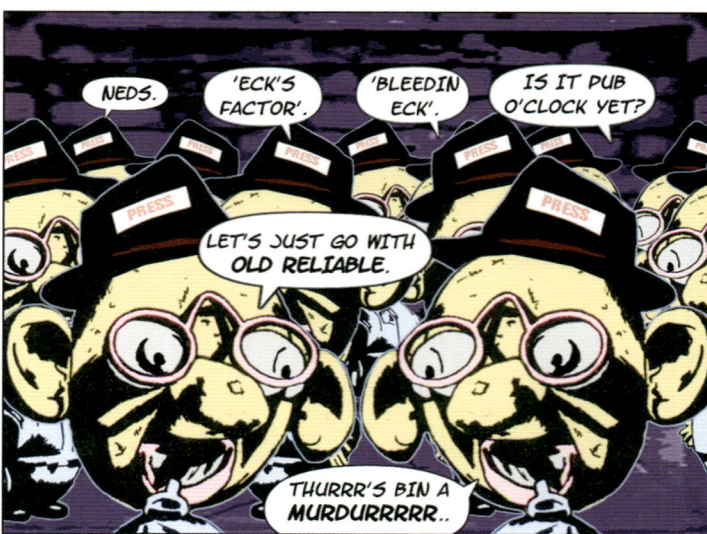

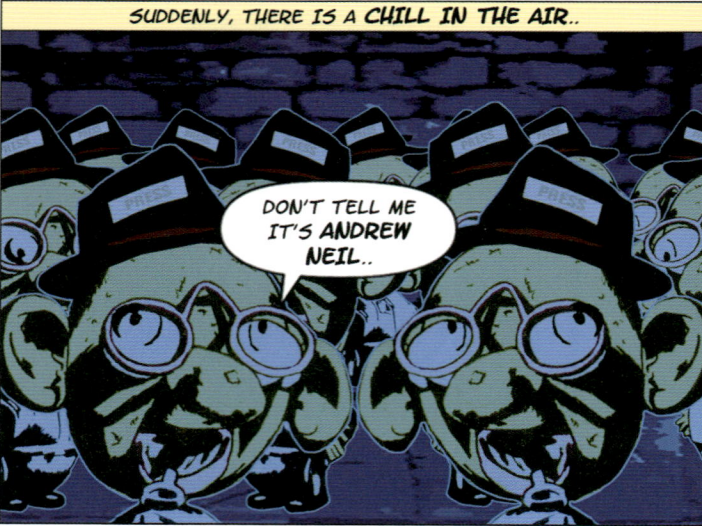

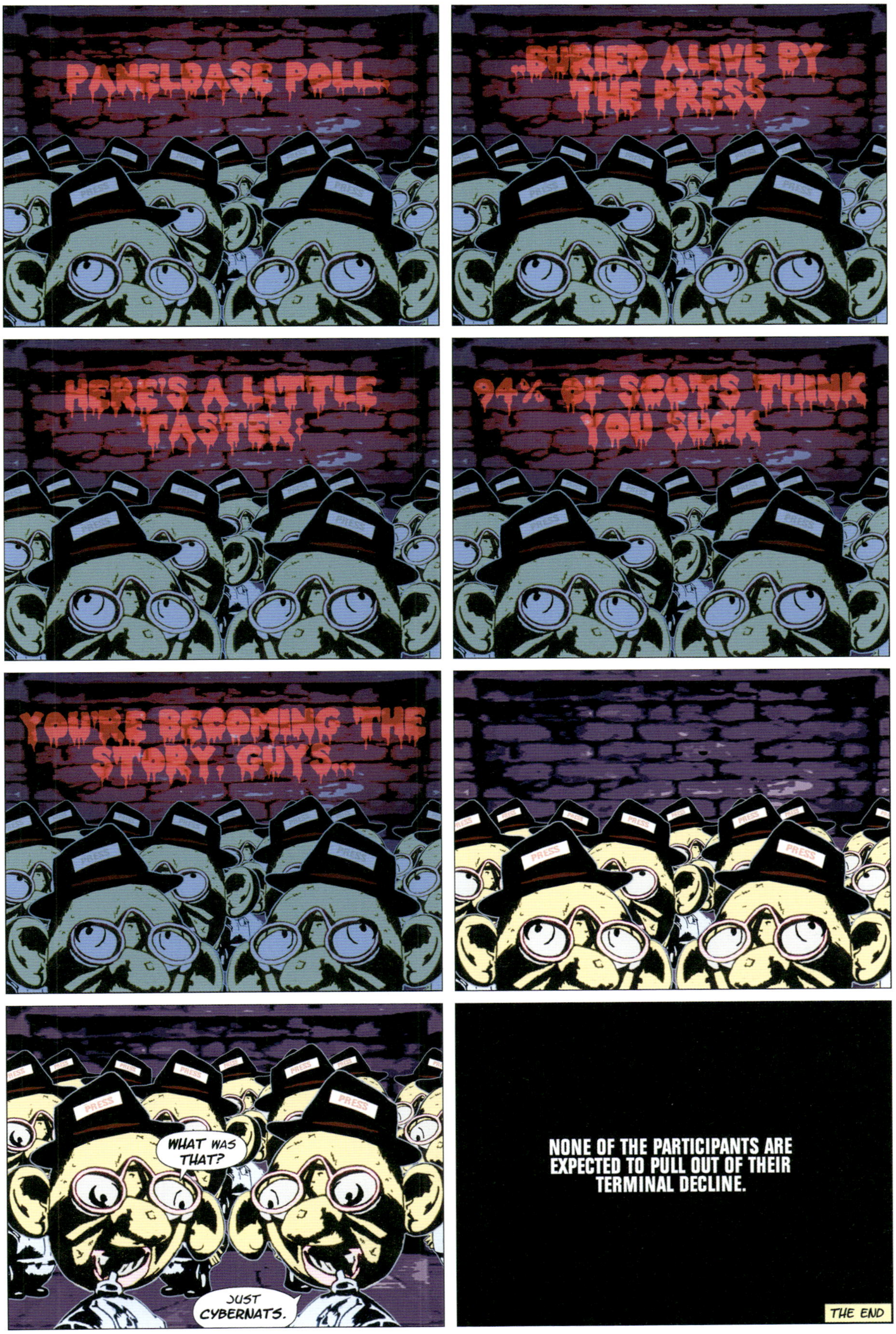
PANELBASE POLL...
...BURIED ALIVE BY THE PRESS
HERE'S A LITTLE TASTER:
94% OF SCOTS THINK YOU SUCK
YOU'RE BECOMING THE STORY, GUYS...
WHAT WAS THAT?
JUST CYBERNATS.
NONE OF THE PARTICIPANTS ARE EXPECTED TO PULL OUT OF THEIR TERMINAL DECLINE.
THE END

ALL QUIET ON THE 1966 FRONT

AUGUST 18TH 2013

There was some Scotland-England game. I don't know, I wasn't paying attention. But anecdotal evidence suggests the Scotland fans chanted 'I'd rather have a panda than a prince'. It went completely unreported in the media. *With Rose Garnett.*

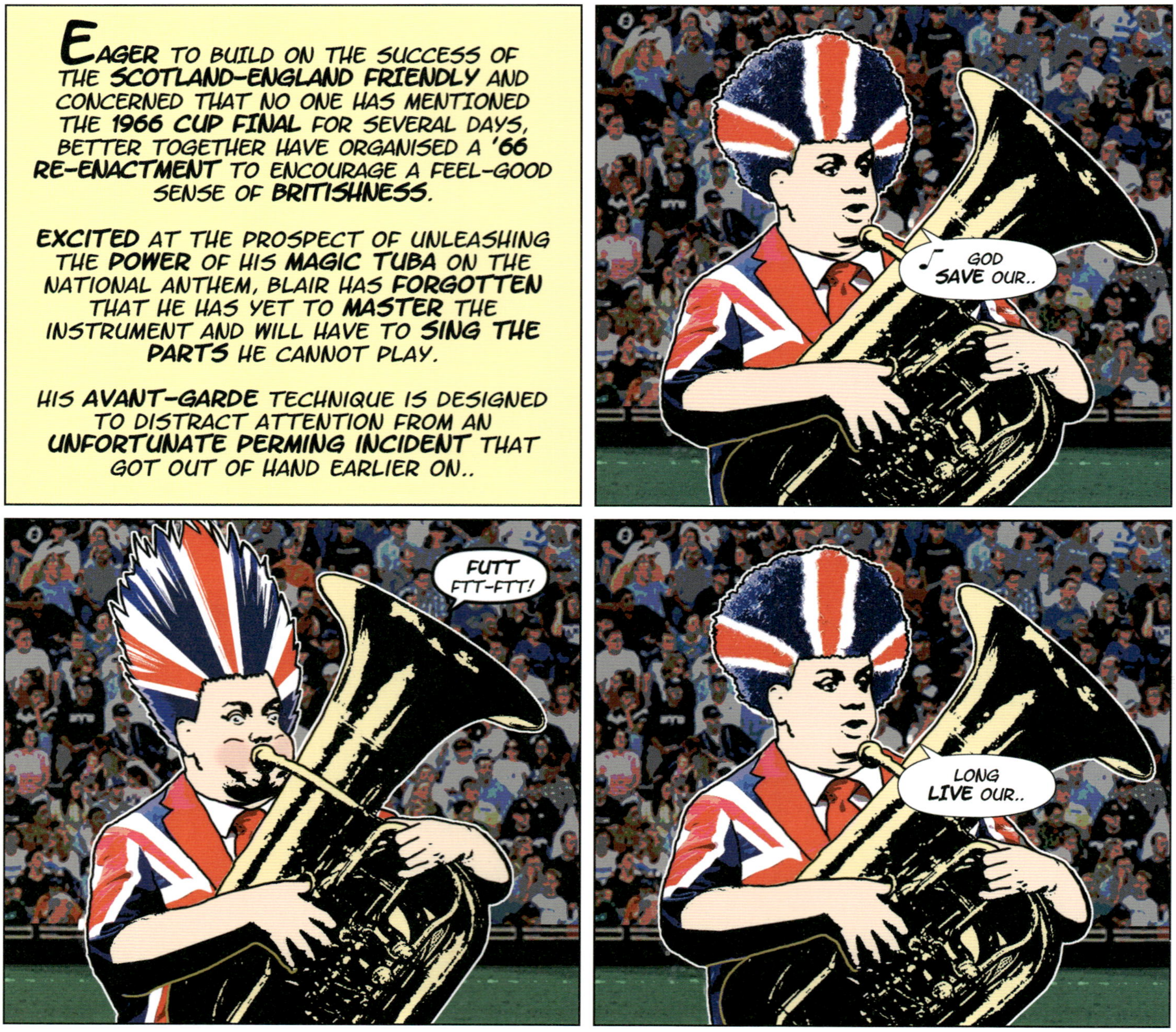
EAGER TO BUILD ON THE SUCCESS OF THE SCOTLAND-ENGLAND FRIENDLY AND CONCERNED THAT NO ONE HAS MENTIONED THE 1966 CUP FINAL FOR SEVERAL DAYS, BETTER TOGETHER HAVE ORGANISED A '66 RE-ENACTMENT TO ENCOURAGE A FEEL-GOOD SENSE OF BRITISHNESS.
EXCITED AT THE PROSPECT OF UNLEASHING THE POWER OF HIS MAGIC TUBA ON THE NATIONAL ANTHEM, BLAIR HAS FORGOTTEN THAT HE HAS YET TO MASTER THE INSTRUMENT AND WILL HAVE TO SING THE PARTS HE CANNOT PLAY.
HIS AVANT-GARDE TECHNIQUE IS DESIGNED TO DISTRACT ATTENTION FROM AN UNFORTUNATE PERMING INCIDENT THAT GOT OUT OF HAND EARLIER ON..
GOD SAVE OUR..
FUTT FTT-FTT!
LONG LIVE OUR..

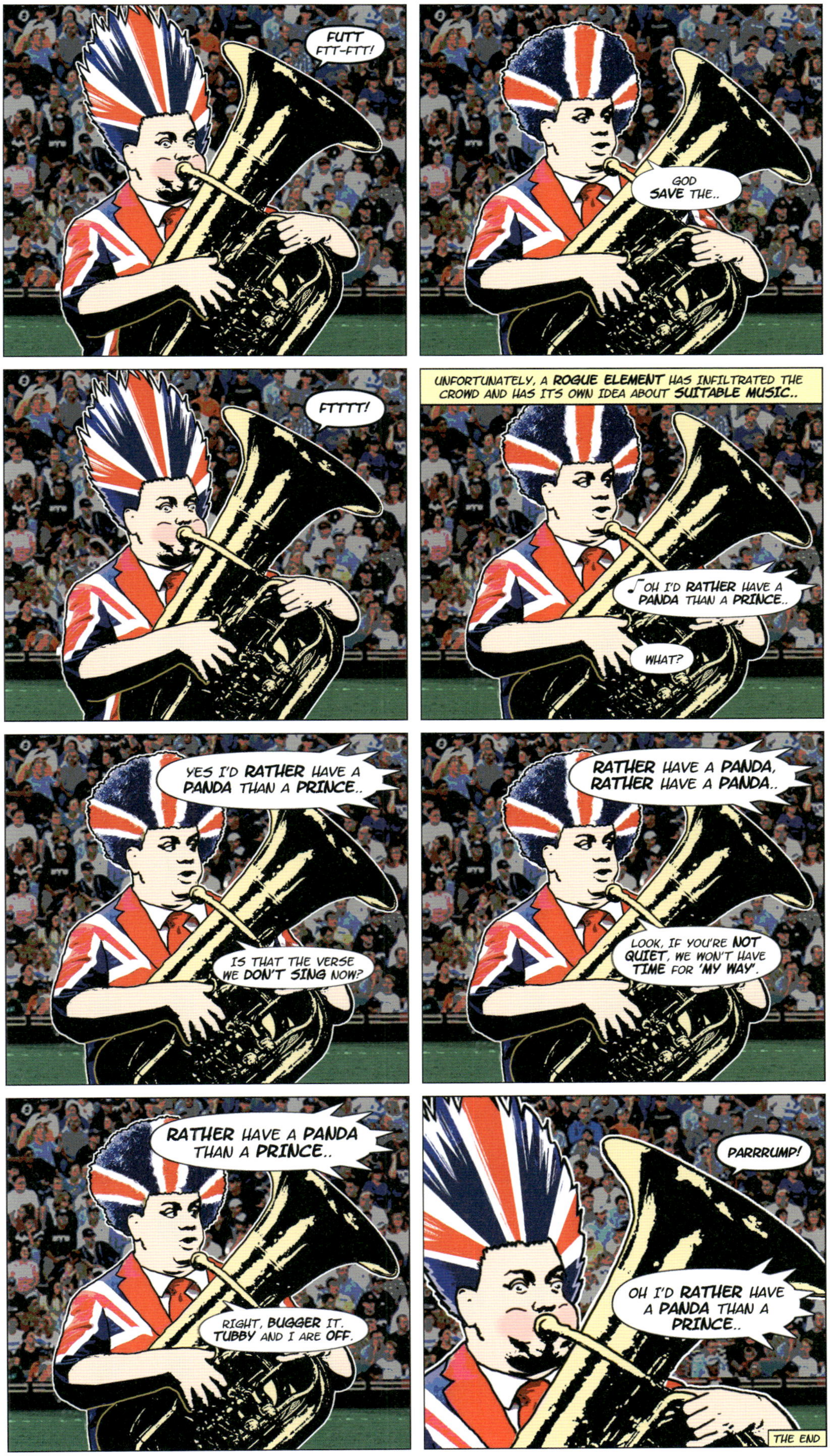
FUTT FTT-FTT!
GOD SAVE THE..
FTTTT!
UNFORTUNATELY, A ROGUE ELEMENT HAS INFILTRATED THE CROWD AND HAS ITS OWN IDEA ABOUT SUITABLE MUSIC..
♪OH I'D RATHER HAVE A PANDA THAN A PRINCE..
WHAT?
YES I'D RATHER HAVE A PANDA THAN A PRINCE..
IS THAT THE VERSE WE DON'T SING NOW?
RATHER HAVE A PANDA, RATHER HAVE A PANDA..
LOOK, IF YOU'RE NOT QUIET, WE WON'T HAVE TIME FOR 'MY WAY'.
RATHER HAVE A PANDA THAN A PRINCE..
RIGHT, BUGGER IT. TUBBY AND I ARE OFF.
PARRRUMP!
OH I'D RATHER HAVE A PANDA THAN A PRINCE..
THE END

CONFORMITY IN THE UK

AUGUST 24TH 2013

Better Together were sharing a version of the 'Anarchy in the UK' artwork, altered to read 'Unity in the UK'. It was supposed to be used as a freshers week pack, presumably because preserving the established order of the state would sit well with young people. *With Rose Garnett.*

IN AN ATTEMPT TO 'GET DOWN WITH THE KIDS', BLAIR ANNOUNCES THE LAUNCH OF A BETTER TOGETHER FRESHERS' WEEK PACK WITH AN 'EDGY' NEW DESIGN..
NOW I ADMIT I'M A LITTLE APPREHENSIVE ABOUT THIS..
I SAID I'D PREFER TO GO WITH A DISCO THEME, BUT IN THE SPIRIT OF TRYING TO BE COOL ON SOMEONE ELSE'S COAT-TAILS, HERE'S WHAT THE TEAM CAME UP WITH..
CONFORMITY IN THE U.K.
etter Together
AHEM..
CONFORMITY IN THE U.K.
etter Together
I DON'T MIND THE LOOK SO MUCH AS THE SLOGAN. IF ANYONE HAS ANY ALTERNATIVES, I'D WELCOME THE INPUT.

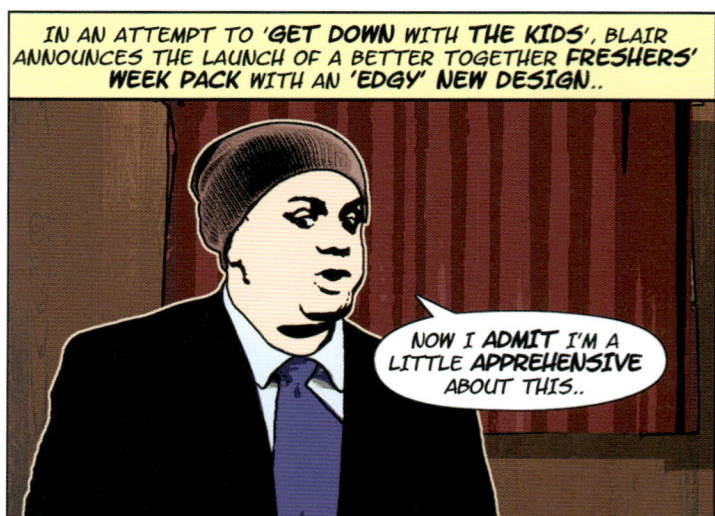

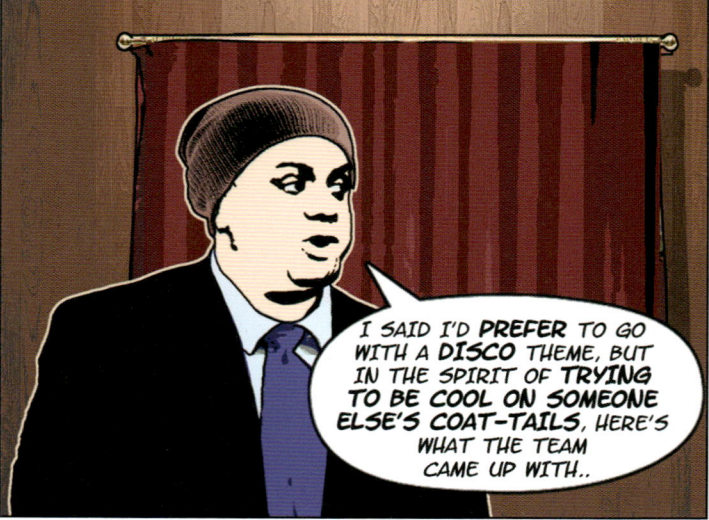

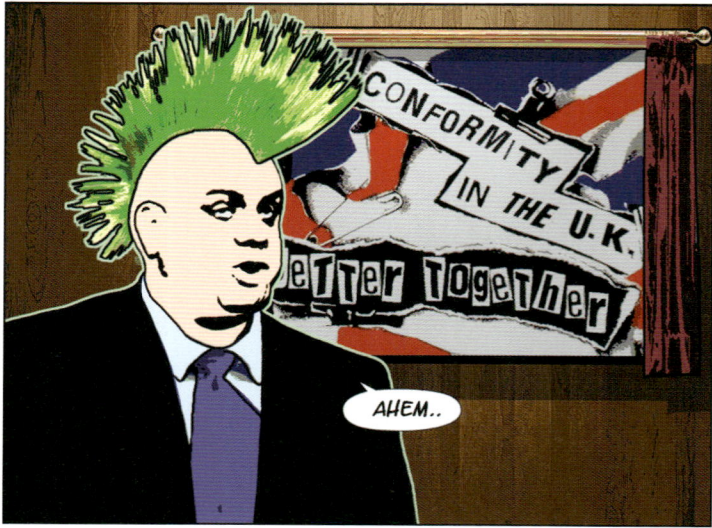

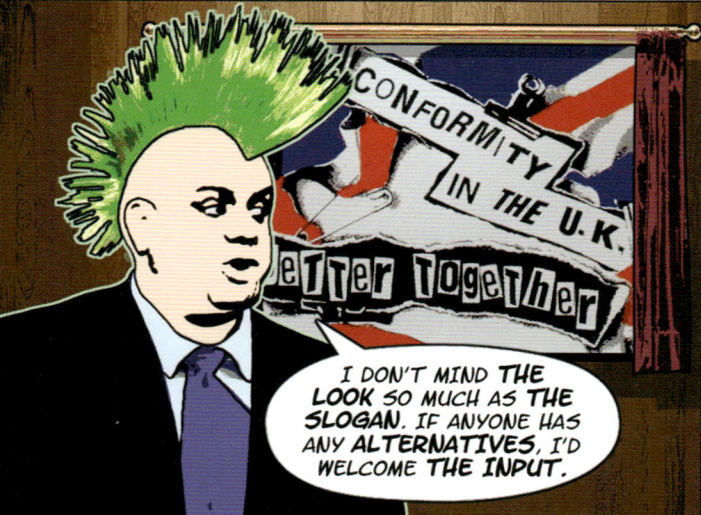

POVERTY IN THE UK.
WELL, I..
AUSTERITY IN THE UK.
THAT'S NOT QUITE..
LOBOTOMY IN THE UK.
CHIROPODY IN THE UK.
CHIR-WHAT NOW?
A NICE CUP OF TEA IN THE UK.
WILLY-WAVING IN THE UK.
WHO'S WILLY? IS THAT A FILM?
PRETTY VACANT!
I'M BEGINNING TO SUSPECT NAT INFILTRATION..
NEVER MIND THE McCRONE REPORT
HERE'S
BLAIR McDOUGALL
..IN WHICH CASE THE ACCOMPANYING TUBA-TASTIC ALBUM MAY NOT BE ENTIRELY APPROPRIATE..
THE END

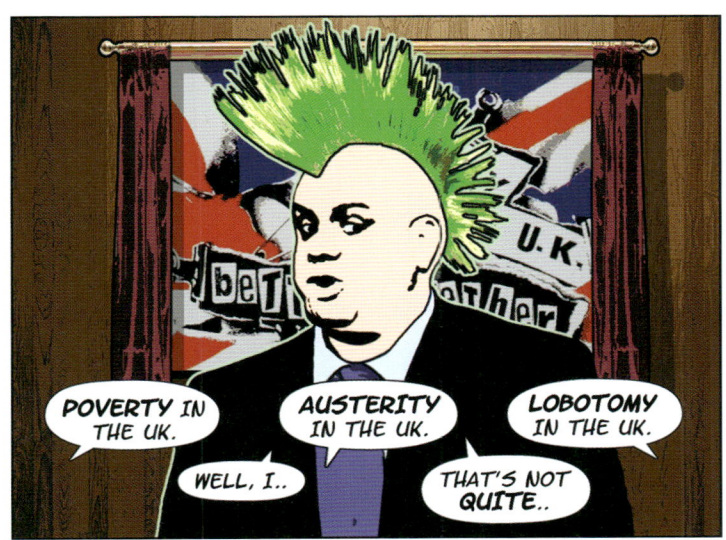

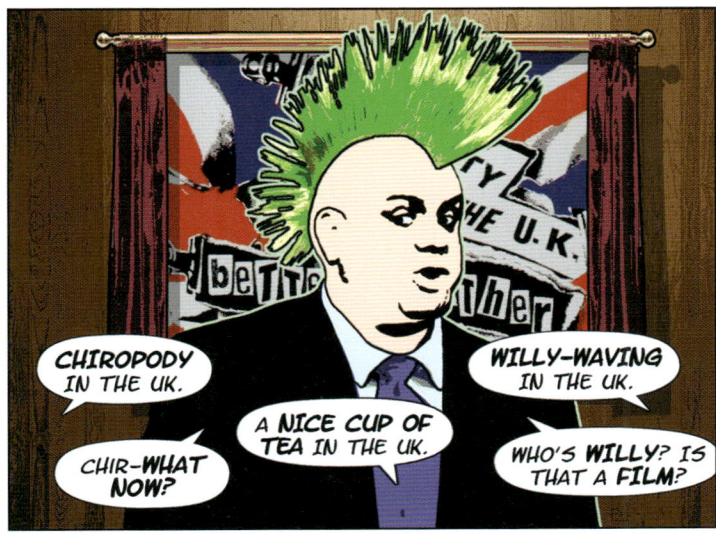

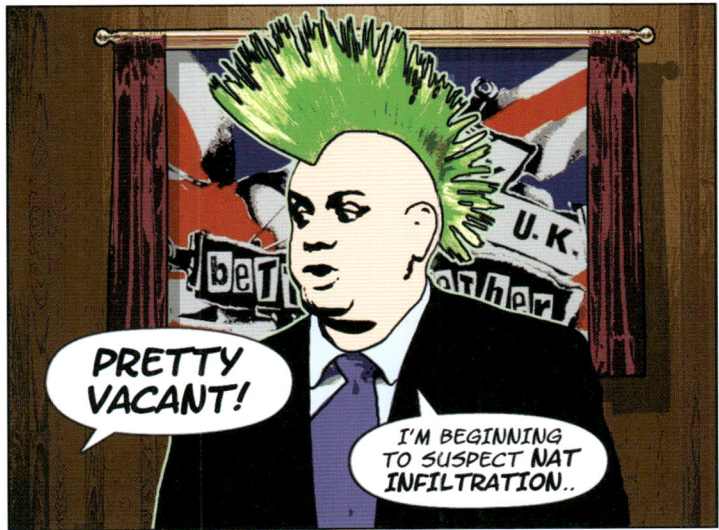

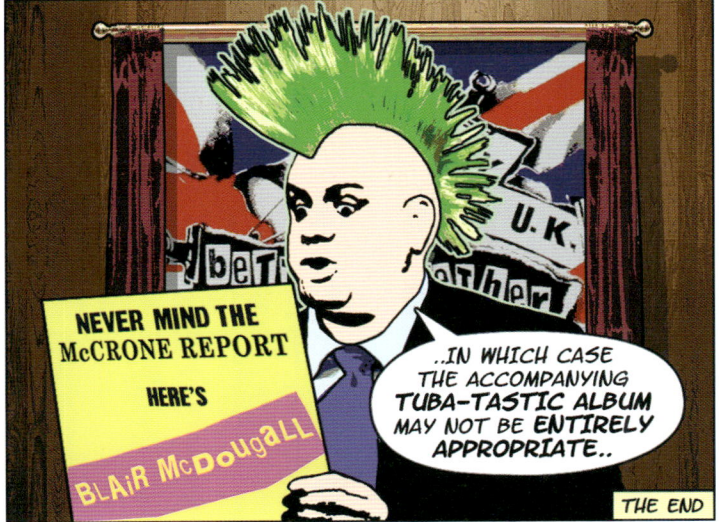

THE TENNENT'S SPECIAL RELATIONSHIP

AUGUST 31ST 2013

It's taken the UK government quite a while to realise that they're not particularly high on the American President's list of priorities. But when nobody from the Obama administration attended Lady Thatcher's funeral, the Prime Minister took it hard. *With Rose Garnett.*

FOLLOWING THE BREAKUP OF HIS SPECIAL RELATIONSHIP WITH BARACK OBAMA, DAVID CAMERON IS TAKING TIME OUT WITH SOME CONFISCATED SUPPLIES FROM 'PROJECT BEER'..
WE'VE BROKEN THE SACRED BOND. HOW CAN WE PUNCH ABOVE OUR WEIGHT NOW?
WE'VE BECOME THE CHEESE-EATING SURRENDER MONKEYS. AND IN BRITAIN, THAT'S CHEDDAR OF THE POOREST KIND.

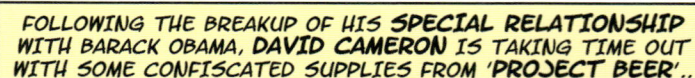

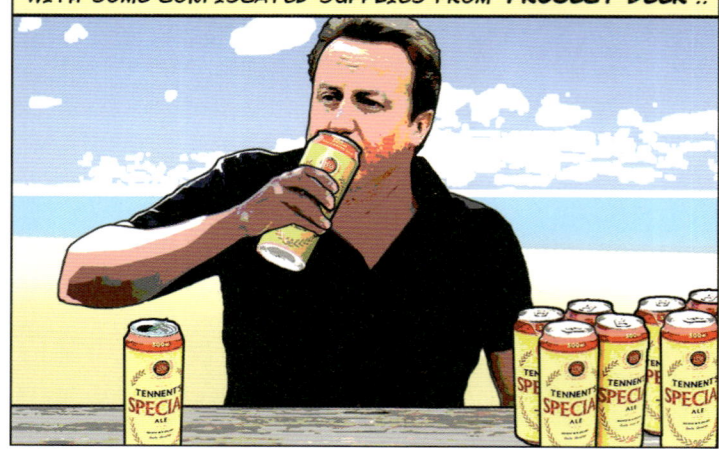

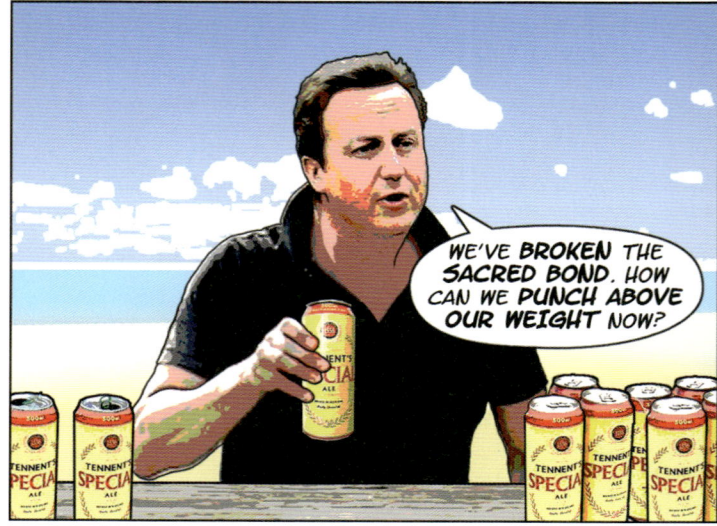

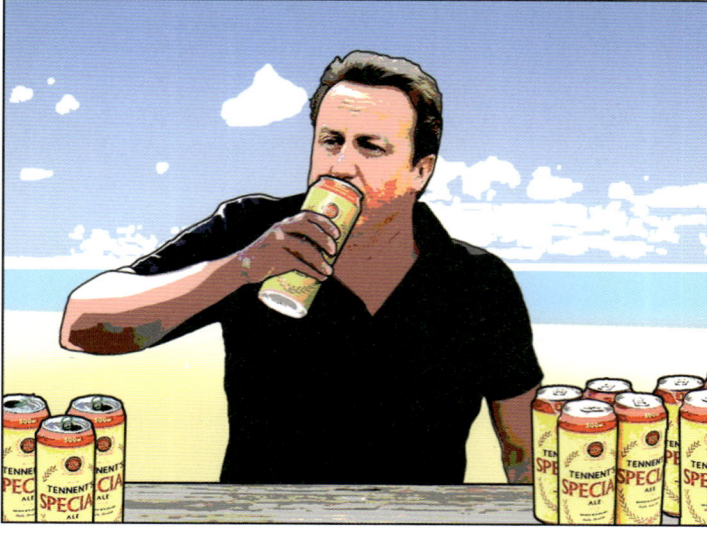

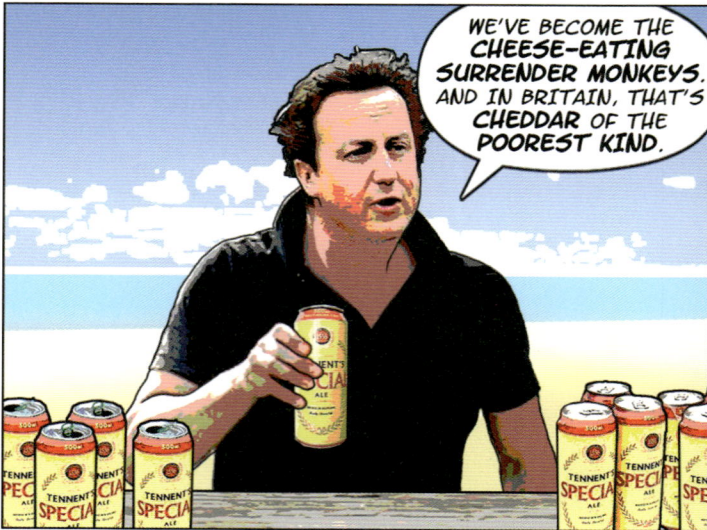

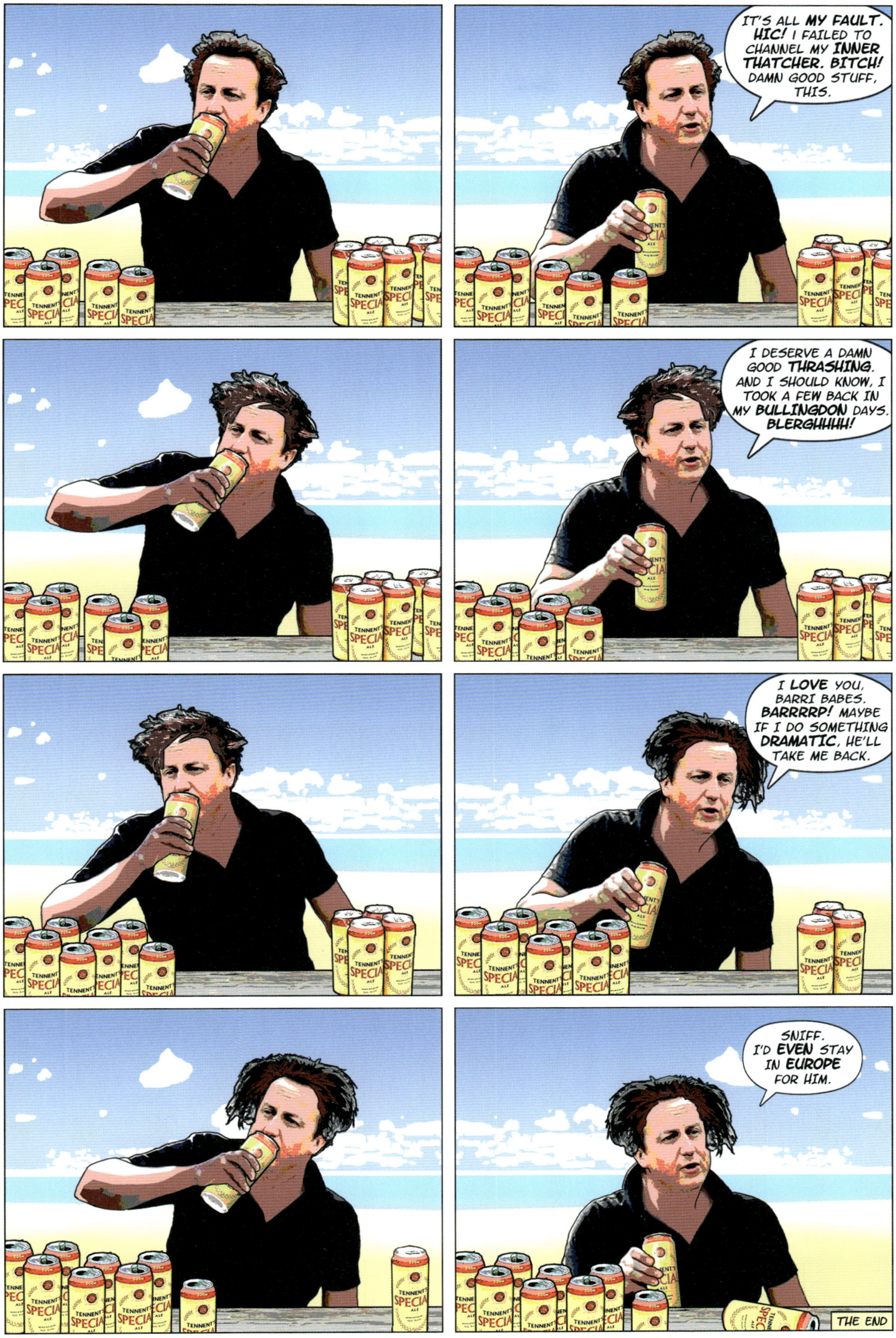
IT'S ALL MY FAULT. HIC! I FAILED TO CHANNEL MY INNER THATCHER. BITCH! DAMN GOOD STUFF, THIS.
I DESERVE A DAMN GOOD THRASHING. AND I SHOULD KNOW, I TOOK A FEW BACK IN MY BULLINGDON DAYS. BLERGHHHH!
I LOVE YOU, BARRI BABES. BARRRRP! MAYBE IF I DO SOMETHING DRAMATIC, HE'LL TAKE ME BACK.
SNIFF. I'D EVEN STAY IN EUROPE FOR HIM.
THE END

ANAS SARWAR BUYS A PINT OF MILK

SEPTEMBER 7TH 2013

Anas Sarwar, the turbo-waffling deputy leader of the Labour Party in Scotland, faced Nicola Sturgeon in an STV televised debate. Afterwards, he carried out some routine chores in a similar fashion. *With Rose Garnett.*

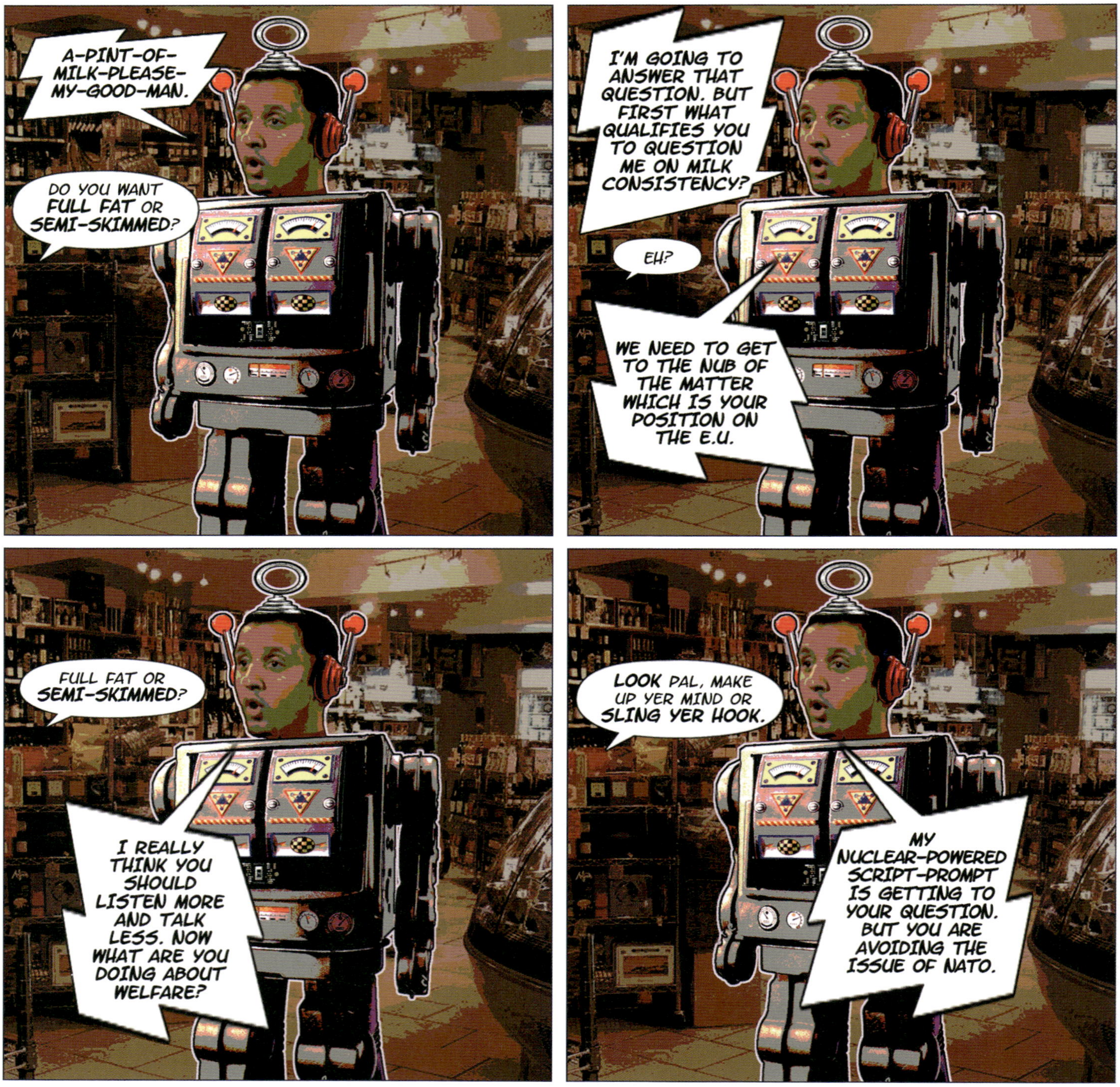

A-PINT-OF-MILK-PLEASE-MY-GOOD-MAN.
DO YOU WANT FULL FAT OR SEMI-SKIMMED?
I'M GOING TO ANSWER THAT QUESTION. BUT FIRST WHAT QUALIFIES YOU TO QUESTION ME ON MILK CONSISTENCY?
EH?
WE NEED TO GET TO THE NUB OF THE MATTER WHICH IS YOUR POSITION ON THE E.U.
FULL FAT OR SEMI-SKIMMED?
I REALLY THINK YOU SHOULD LISTEN MORE AND TALK LESS. NOW WHAT ARE YOU DOING ABOUT WELFARE?
LOOK PAL, MAKE UP YER MIND OR SLING YER HOOK.
MY NUCLEAR-POWERED SCRIPT-PROMPT IS GETTING TO YOUR QUESTION. BUT YOU ARE AVOIDING THE ISSUE OF NATO.

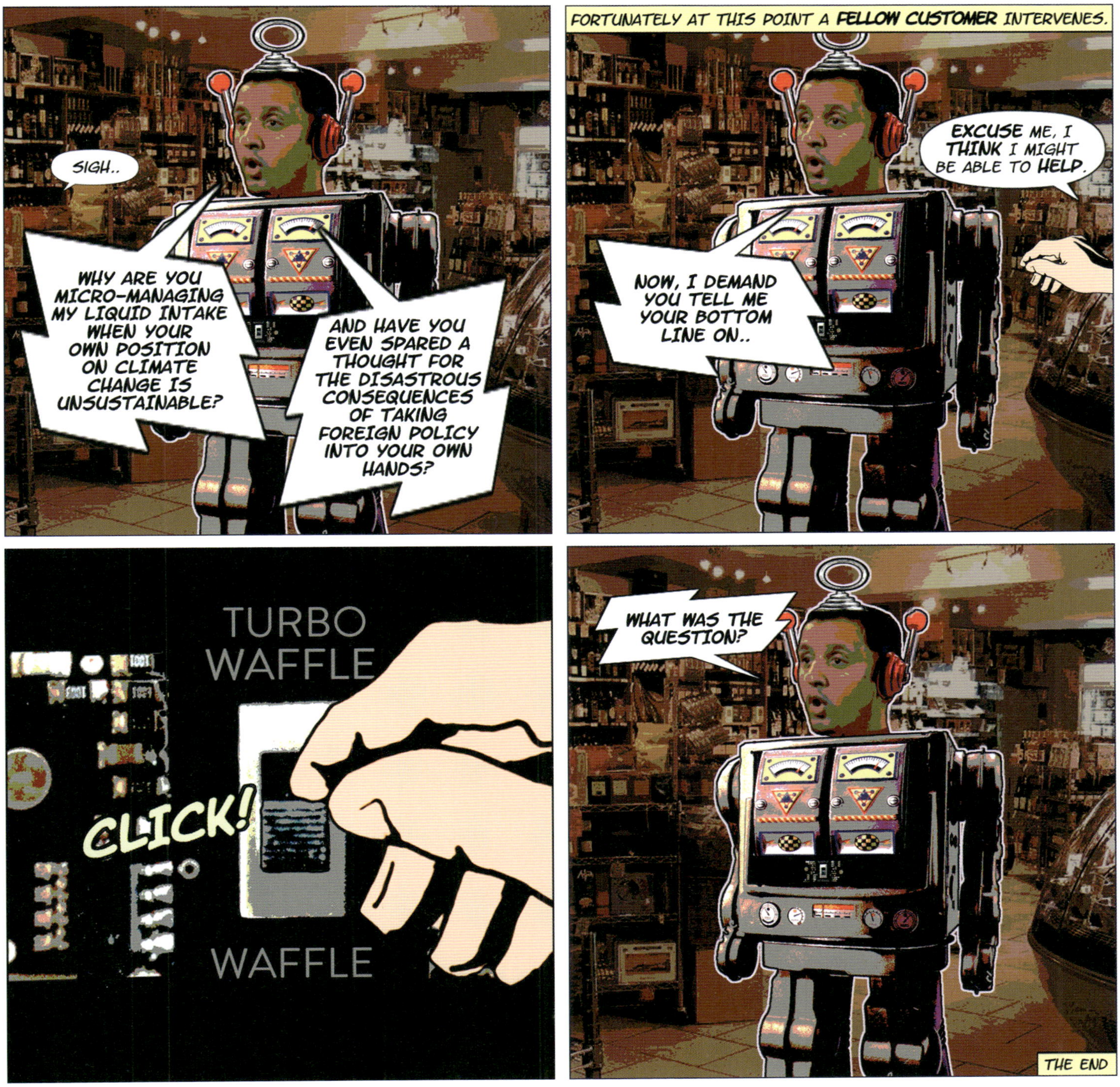
SIGH..
WHY ARE YOU MICRO-MANAGING MY LIQUID INTAKE WHEN YOUR OWN POSITION ON CLIMATE CHANGE IS UNSUSTAINABLE?
AND HAVE YOU EVEN SPARED A THOUGHT FOR THE DISASTROUS CONSEQUENCES OF TAKING FOREIGN POLICY INTO YOUR OWN HANDS?
FORTUNATELY AT THIS POINT A FELLOW CUSTOMER INTERVENES.
NOW, I DEMAND YOU TELL ME YOUR BOTTOM LINE ON..
EXCUSE ME, I THINK I MIGHT BE ABLE TO HELP.
TURBO WAFFLE
CLICK!
WAFFLE
WHAT WAS THE QUESTION?
THE END

CREDIT WHERE CREDIT'S DUE

SEPTEMBER 15TH 2013

The Telegraph's headline read "Danny Alexander: The Tories couldn't have done it without us." Not only was the LibDem Chief Secretary to the Treasury happy to be a part of a government presiding over zero-hours contracts, the bedroom tax and the dismantling of the NHS, he also wanted credit. *With Rose Garnett.*

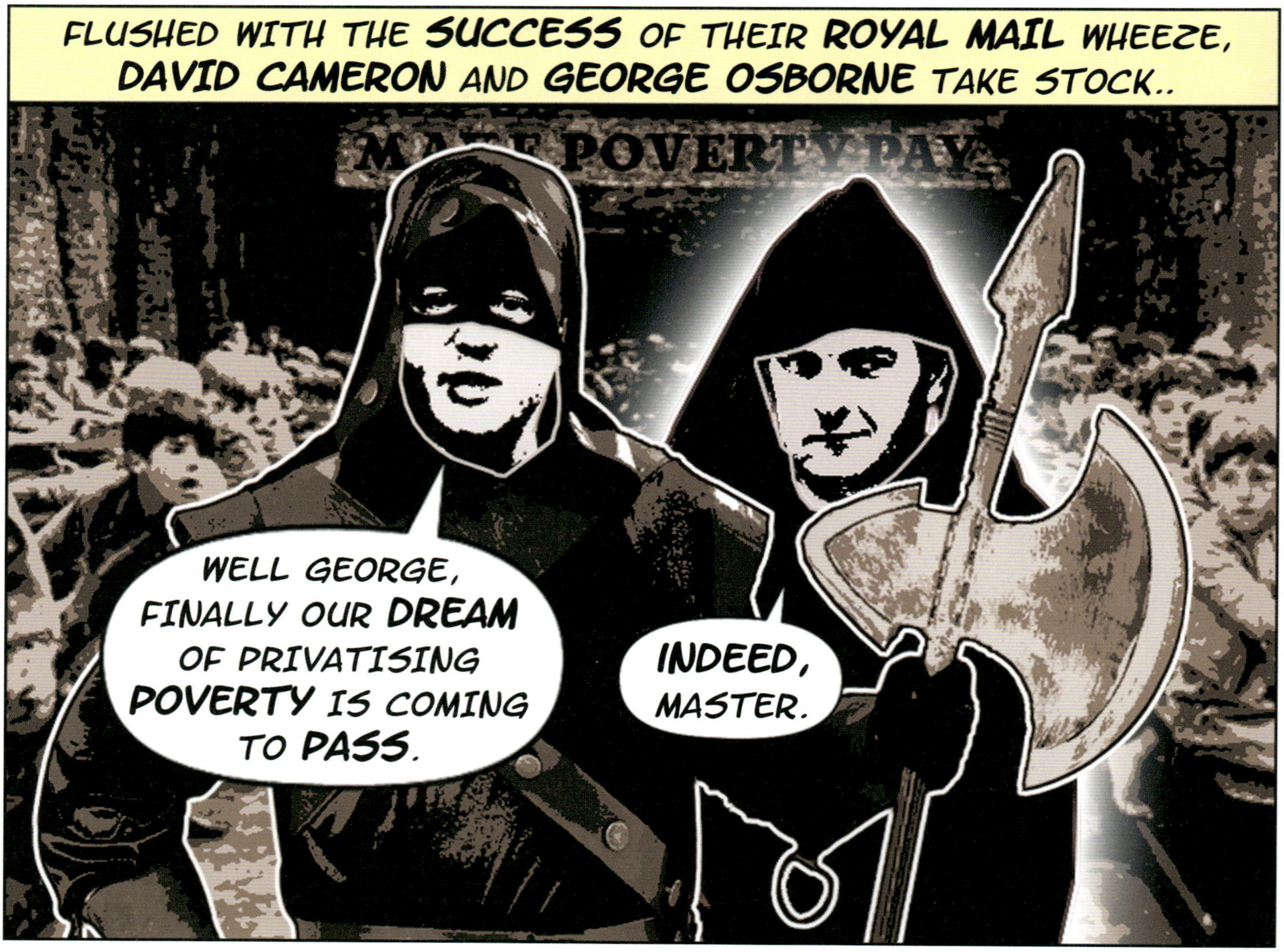
FLUSHED WITH THE **SUCCESS** OF THEIR **ROYAL MAIL** WHEEZE, **DAVID CAMERON** AND **GEORGE OSBORNE** TAKE STOCK..
WELL GEORGE, FINALLY OUR **DREAM** OF PRIVATISING **POVERTY** IS COMING TO **PASS**.
INDEED, MASTER.

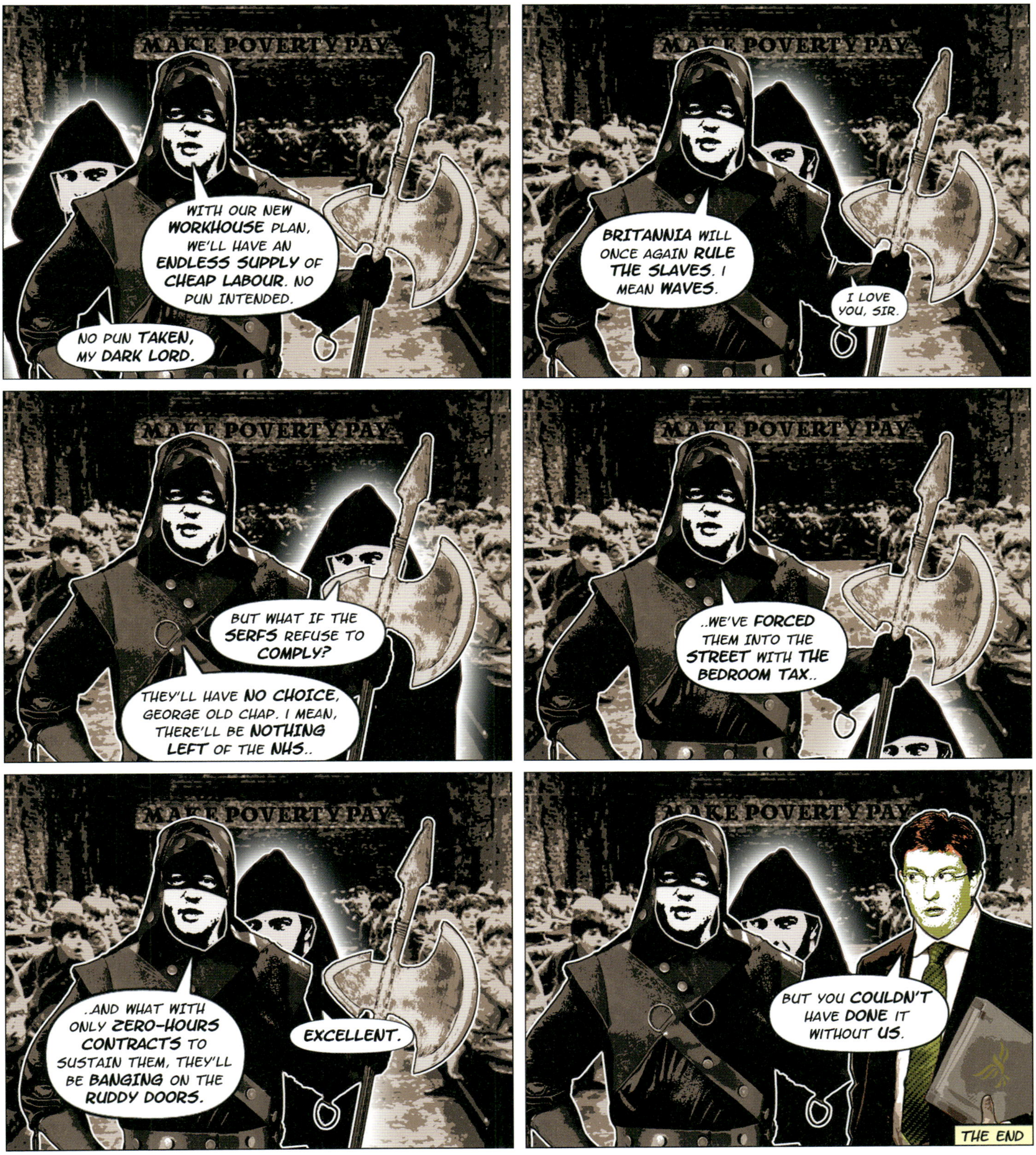
MAKE POVERTY PAY
WITH OUR NEW WORKHOUSE PLAN, WE'LL HAVE AN ENDLESS SUPPLY OF CHEAP LABOUR. NO PUN INTENDED.
NO PUN TAKEN, MY DARK LORD.
MAKE POVERTY PAY
BRITANNIA WILL ONCE AGAIN RULE THE SLAVES. I MEAN WAVES.
I LOVE YOU, SIR.
MAKE POVERTY PAY
BUT WHAT IF THE SERFS REFUSE TO COMPLY?
THEY'LL HAVE NO CHOICE, GEORGE OLD CHAP. I MEAN, THERE'LL BE NOTHING LEFT OF THE NHS..
MAKE POVERTY PAY
..WE'VE FORCED THEM INTO THE STREET WITH THE BEDROOM TAX..
MAKE POVERTY PAY
..AND WHAT WITH ONLY ZERO-HOURS CONTRACTS TO SUSTAIN THEM, THEY'LL BE BANGING ON THE RUDDY DOORS.
EXCELLENT.
MAKE POVERTY PAY
BUT YOU COULDN'T HAVE DONE IT WITHOUT US.
THE END

CALTON CALLING

SEPTEMBER 22ND 2013

The Calton Hill independence rally of September 2013 was a memorable day for all of us there. While I was listening to one of the speakers, a hot-air balloon circled high above and I couldn't help wondering if certain members of the No campaign might be aboard. *With Rose Garnett.*

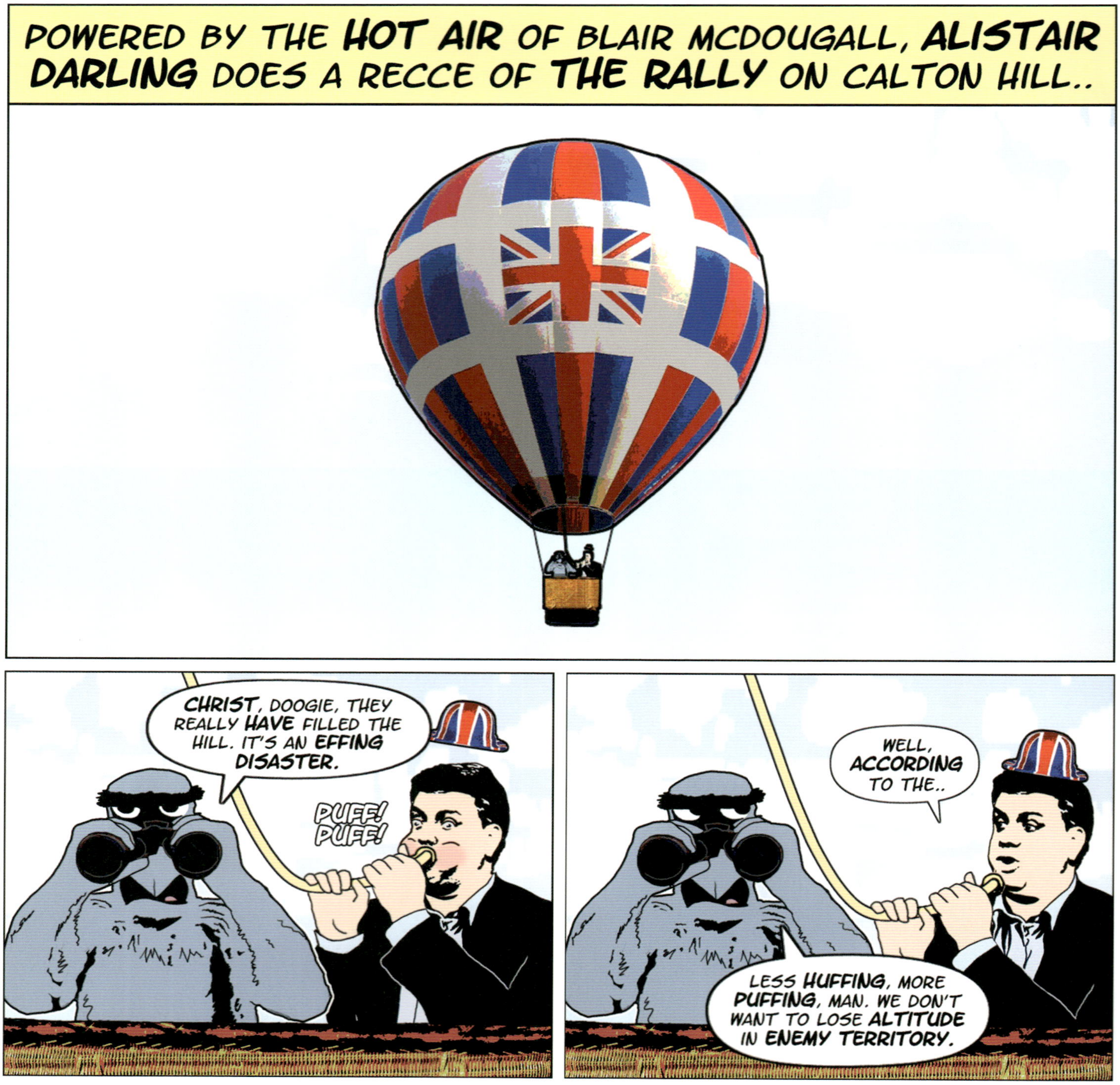

POWERED BY THE HOT AIR OF BLAIR MCDOUGALL, ALISTAIR DARLING DOES A RECCE OF THE RALLY ON CALTON HILL..
CHRIST, DOOGIE, THEY REALLY HAVE FILLED THE HILL. IT'S AN EFFING DISASTER.
PUFF! PUFF!
WELL, ACCORDING TO THE..
LESS HUFFING, MORE PUFFING, MAN. WE DON'T WANT TO LOSE ALTITUDE IN ENEMY TERRITORY.

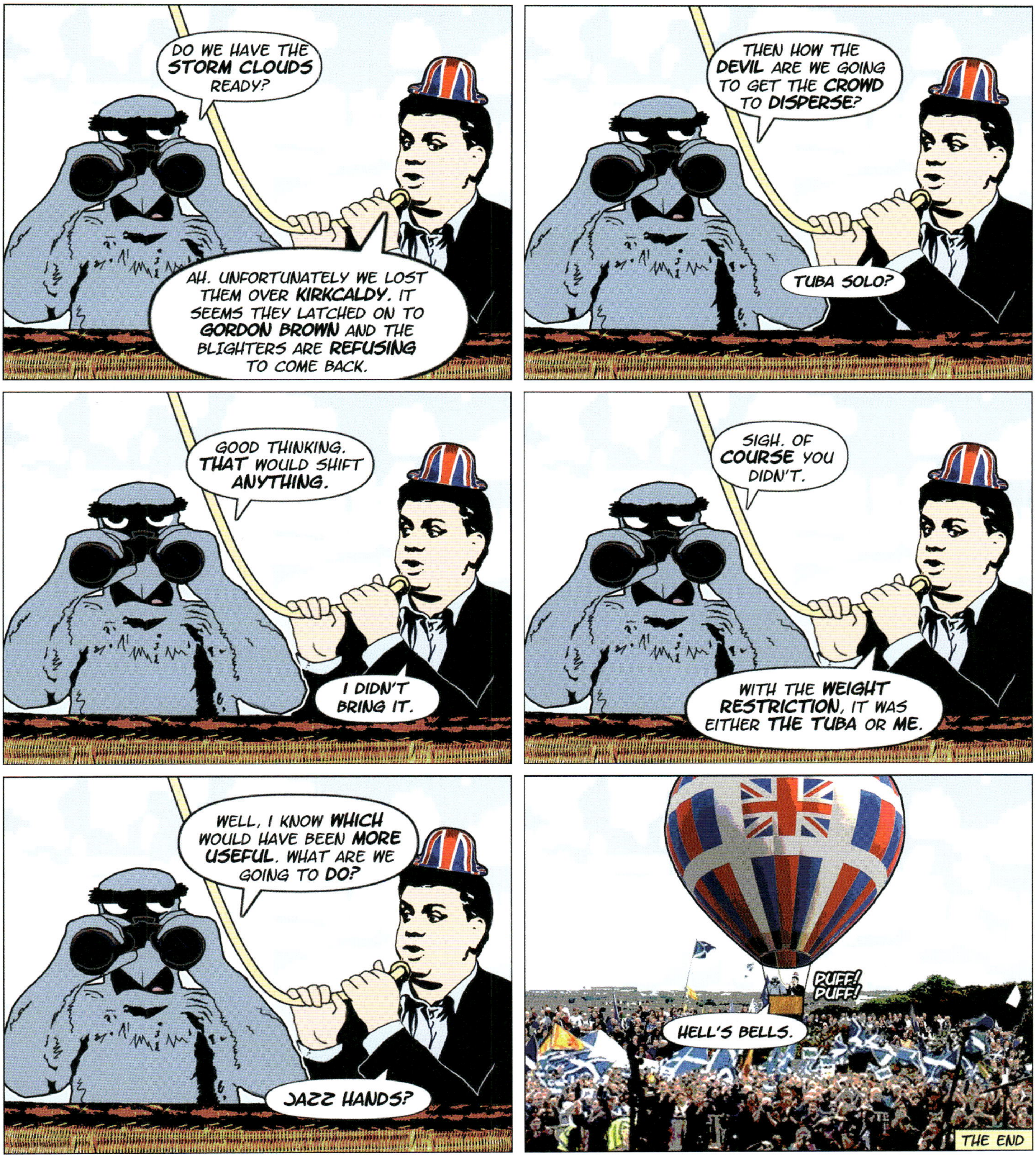
DO WE HAVE THE STORM CLOUDS READY?
AH. UNFORTUNATELY WE LOST THEM OVER KIRKCALDY. IT SEEMS THEY LATCHED ON TO GORDON BROWN AND THE BLIGHTERS ARE REFUSING TO COME BACK.
THEN HOW THE DEVIL ARE WE GOING TO GET THE CROWD TO DISPERSE?
TUBA SOLO?
GOOD THINKING. THAT WOULD SHIFT ANYTHING.
I DIDN'T BRING IT.
SIGH. OF COURSE YOU DIDN'T.
WITH THE WEIGHT RESTRICTION, IT WAS EITHER THE TUBA OR ME.
WELL, I KNOW WHICH WOULD HAVE BEEN MORE USEFUL. WHAT ARE WE GOING TO DO?
JAZZ HANDS?
PUFF! PUFF!
HELL'S BELLS.
THE END

THE EMPIRE STRIKES OUT

SEPTEMBER 29TH 2013

The Prime Minister flatly refused to debate with Alex Salmond, saying he was not getting involved and that the issue was for Scots alone. On this occasion he was photographed 'not getting involved' aboard a nuclear submarine on the Clyde. *With Rose Garnett.*

TAKE A LETTER TO THE FIRST MINISTER, GIDDY..
YES, MASTER.
IN BLOOD.
OF COURSE, YOUR ROYAL MIGHTINESS.
DEAR FATBOY, A DEBATE WITH ME IS AS LIKELY AS MY GIVING UP THE DINNERS FOR DONORS WHEEZE.
I LOVE IT WHEN YOU'RE STRICT, SIR. PLEASE BEAT ME LATER.
YOU KNOW VERY WELL THAT THE GIMP IS IN CHARGE OF PROJECT FEAR AND WE WILL RELEASE HIM FOR ANY TELEVISED SHOWDOWN.
WITH FIRM INSTRUCTIONS THAT HE RETURN TO HIS CUPBOARD WHEN IT'S OVER?
NATURALLY.
BUT LET ME TAKE THIS OPPORTUNITY TO SAY THAT YOUR PENSIONS POLICY IS PANTS..
DIRTY PANTIES..

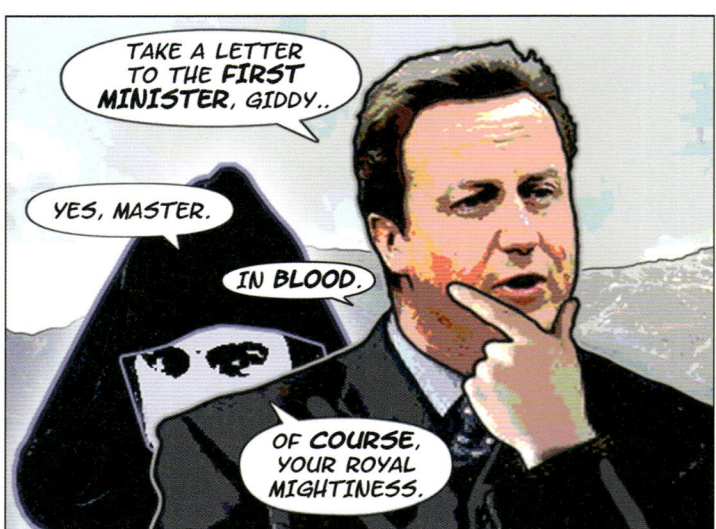

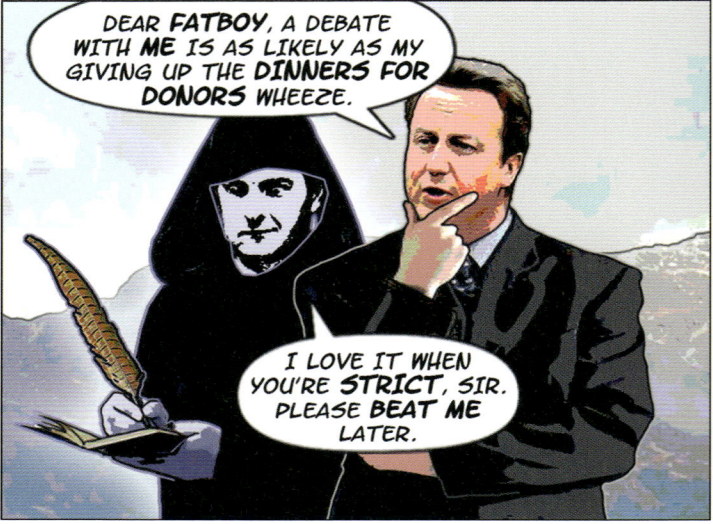

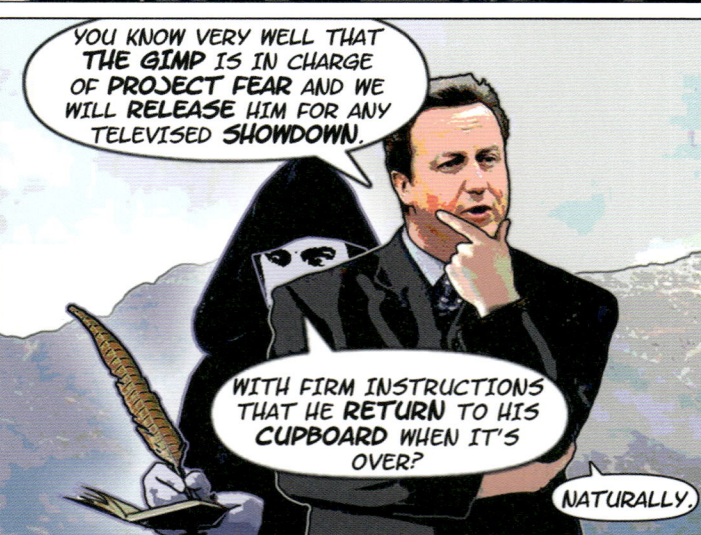

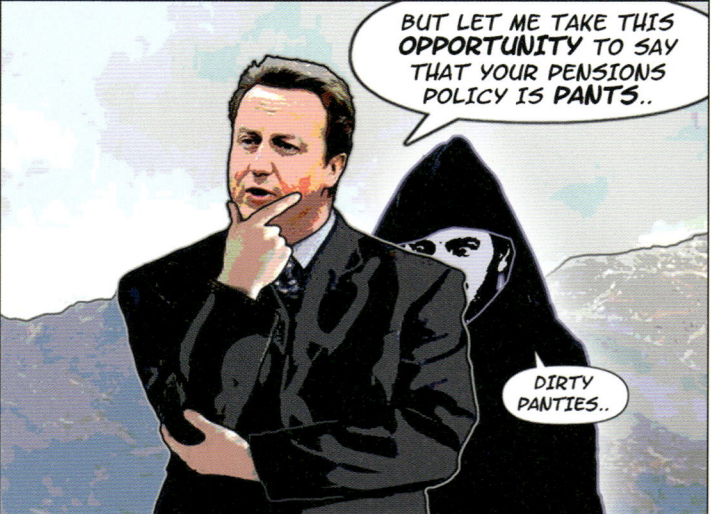

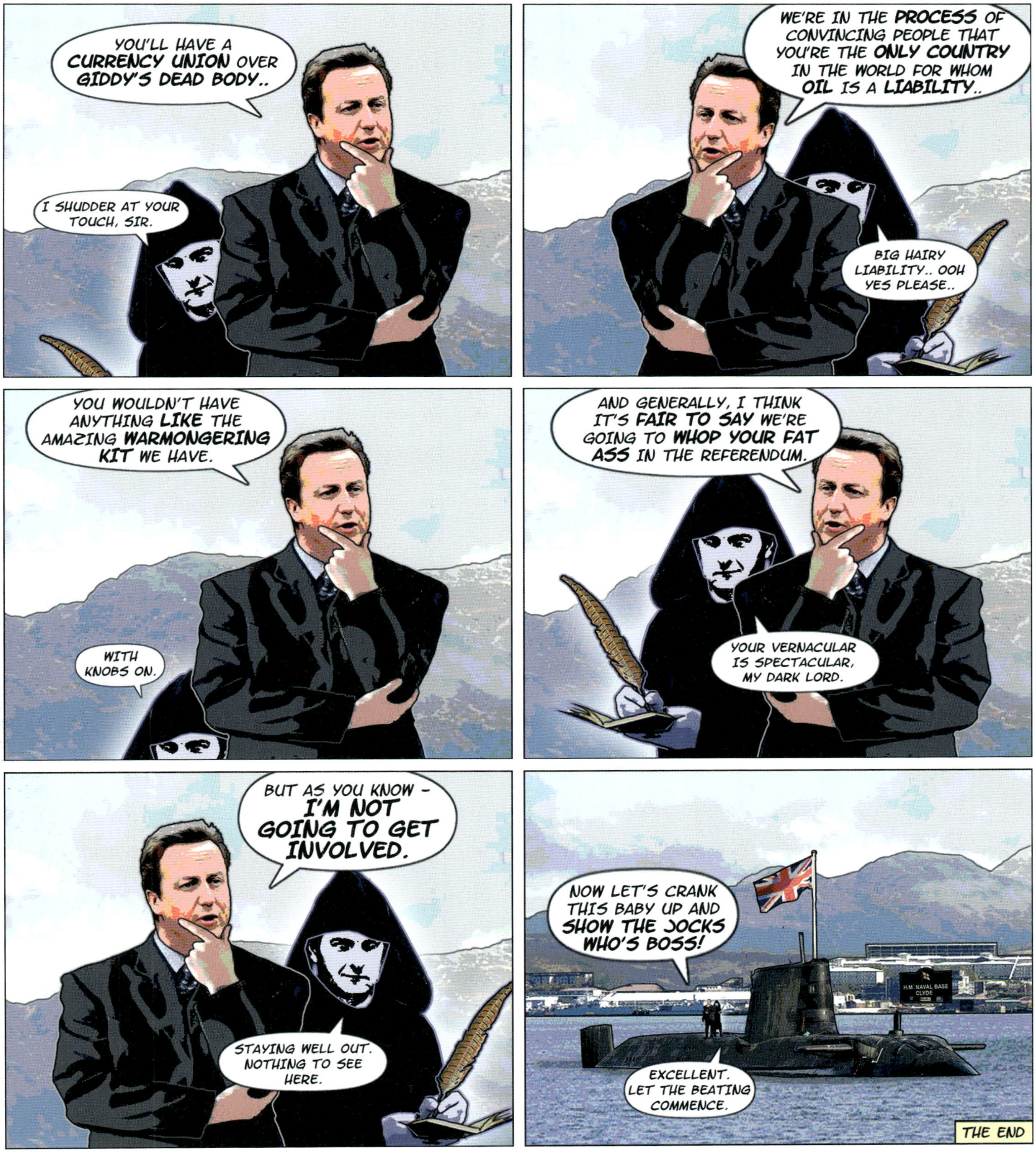
YOU'LL HAVE A CURRENCY UNION OVER GIDDY'S DEAD BODY..
I SHUDDER AT YOUR TOUCH, SIR.
WE'RE IN THE PROCESS OF CONVINCING PEOPLE THAT YOU'RE THE ONLY COUNTRY IN THE WORLD FOR WHOM OIL IS A LIABILITY..
BIG HAIRY LIABILITY.. OOH YES PLEASE..
YOU WOULDN'T HAVE ANYTHING LIKE THE AMAZING WARMONGERING KIT WE HAVE.
WITH KNOBS ON.
AND GENERALLY, I THINK IT'S FAIR TO SAY WE'RE GOING TO WHOP YOUR FAT ASS IN THE REFERENDUM.
YOUR VERNACULAR IS SPECTACULAR, MY DARK LORD.
BUT AS YOU KNOW - I'M NOT GOING TO GET INVOLVED.
STAYING WELL OUT. NOTHING TO SEE HERE.
NOW LET'S CRANK THIS BABY UP AND SHOW THE JOCKS WHO'S BOSS!
H.M. NAVAL BASE CLYDE
EXCELLENT. LET THE BEATING COMMENCE.
THE END

DAVID CAMERON'S GRAND GESTURE

OCTOBER 5TH 2013

"We want you to stay," said David Cameron in one of his first attempts at lovebombing Scotland. At this point the No campaign still thought they couldn't lose the referendum, so he spent just 54 seconds on the subject in his party conference speech. *With Rose Garnett.*

NOW LOOK HERE, JOCKLAND, WE ALL KNOW YOU DON'T HAVE THE GUMPTION TO GO IT ALONE AND THAT IT'LL BE A POKE IN THE EYE FOR FATBOY COME SEPTEMBER 2014..
BUT NEVERTHELESS, I HAVE TO GO THROUGH THE MOTIONS AND MAKE AN APPEAL FOR YOU TO STAY.
BIG FAT PLOPPIES.
FRANKLY, THIS ISN'T WORTH AN ENTIRE MINUTE OF MY TIME, WHICH IS WHY I'M ONLY GOING TO GIVE YOU 54 SECONDS.
LUCKY SWINES.
FACE IT, YOU'D BE LOST WITHOUT ENDLESS FOREIGN WARS.
OOH, JOHNNY FOREIGNER.

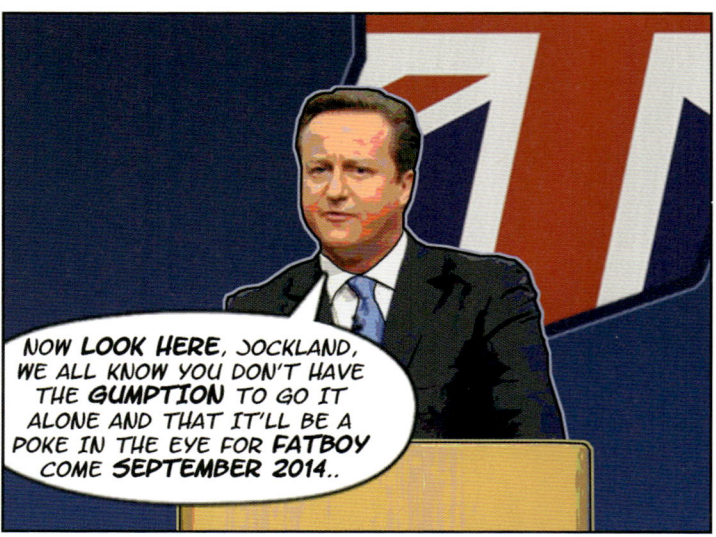

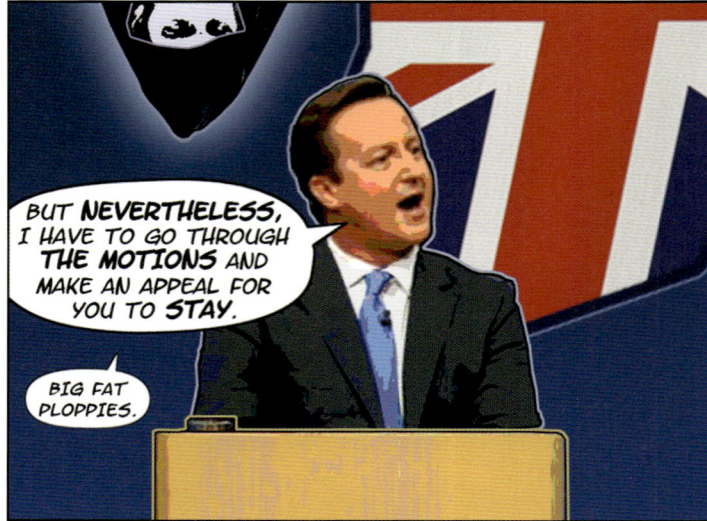

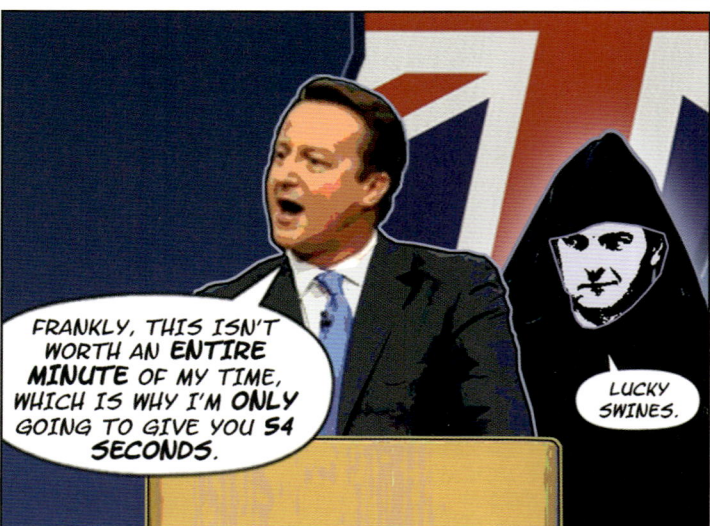

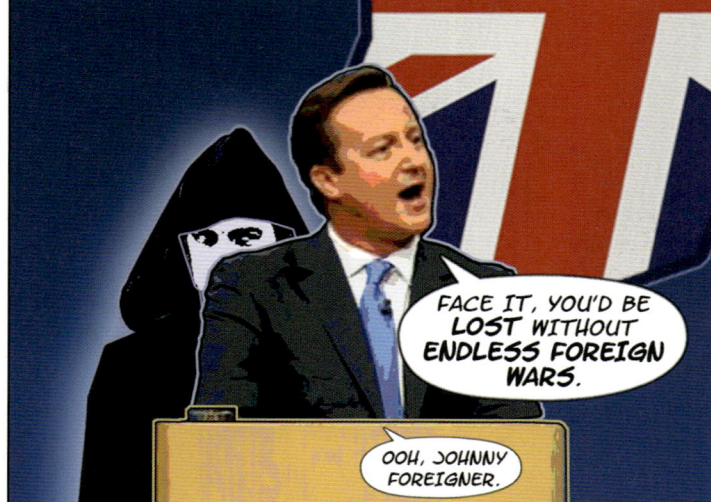

YOU KNOW YOU SECRETLY LOVE HAVING EUROPE'S BIGGEST STOCKPILE OF NUCLEAR WEAPONS SHOVED UP YOUR JACKSIE.
RIGHT UP THE TAILPIPE, MY DARK LIEGE.
AND WHY WOULD YOU NOT WANT TO SPEND YOUR OIL REVENUE ON PROPPING UP THE FOURTH MOST UNEQUAL SOCIETY IN THE DEVELOPED WORLD?
YOU GO, GIRL.
SO LET ME FINISH WITH A SIMPLE GESTURE THAT SUMS UP MY POSITION.
YOU'RE ALWAYS TOP WITH ME, SIRE.
YOU HAD ME AT JOCKLAND, MY SAUCY SOVEREIGN.
THE END

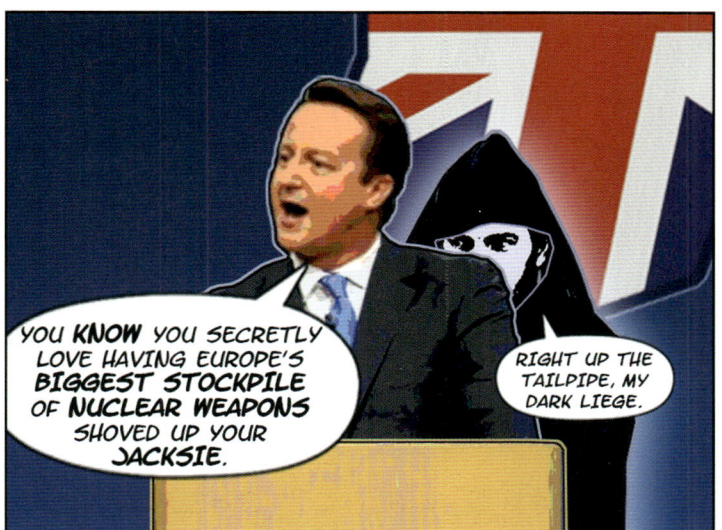

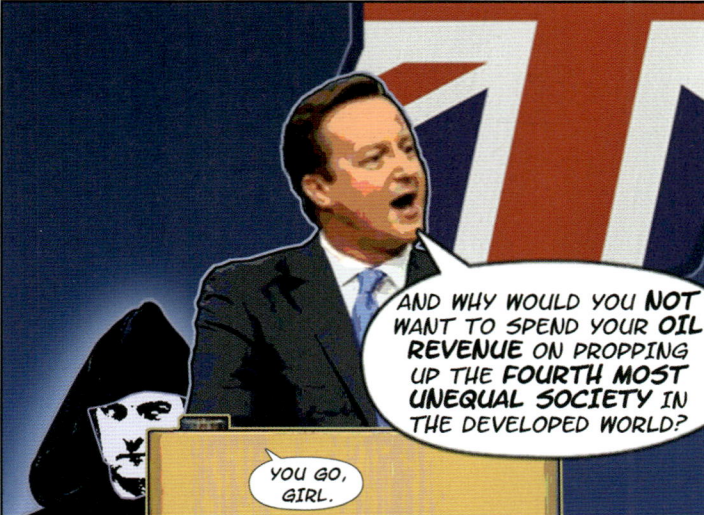

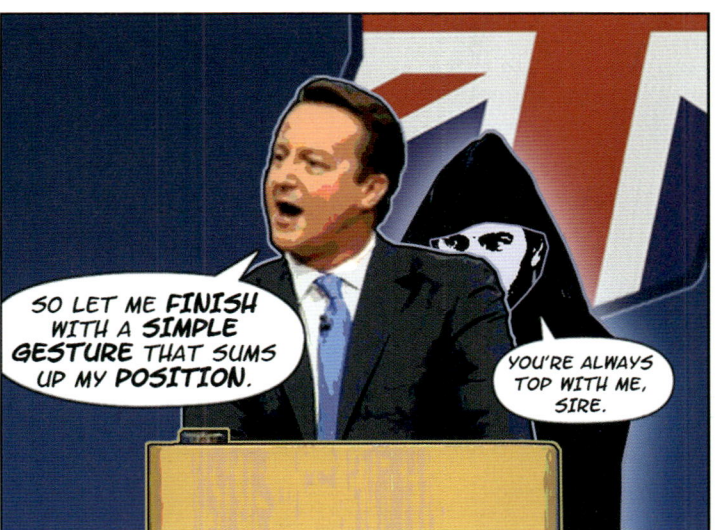

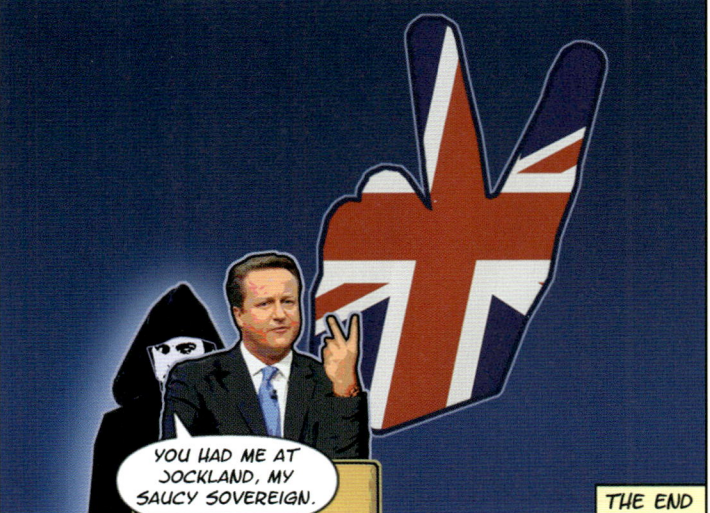

DAVID CAMERON'S SWEATER SOLUTIONS

OCTOBER 19TH 2013

David Cameron suggested combating the outrageous energy price rises by donning an extra jumper over the coming winter. Here he leads by example with some other practical solutions to UK problems. *With Rose Garnett.*

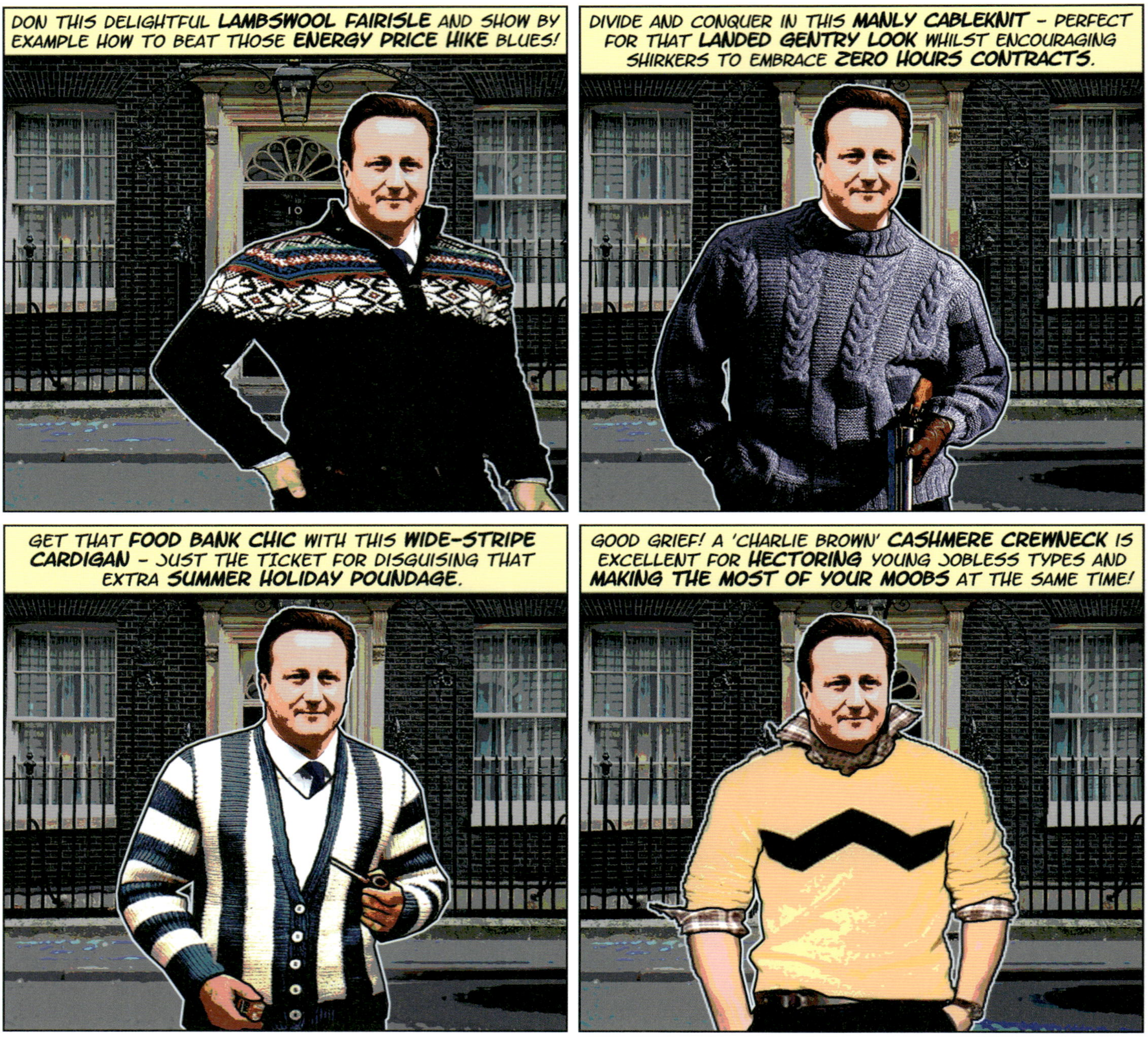
DON THIS DELIGHTFUL LAMBSWOOL FAIRISLE AND SHOW BY EXAMPLE HOW TO BEAT THOSE ENERGY PRICE HIKE BLUES!
DIVIDE AND CONQUER IN THIS MANLY CABLEKNIT - PERFECT FOR THAT LANDED GENTRY LOOK WHILST ENCOURAGING SHIRKERS TO EMBRACE ZERO HOURS CONTRACTS.
GET THAT FOOD BANK CHIC WITH THIS WIDE-STRIPE CARDIGAN - JUST THE TICKET FOR DISGUISING THAT EXTRA SUMMER HOLIDAY POUNDAGE.
GOOD GRIEF! A 'CHARLIE BROWN' CASHMERE CREWNECK IS EXCELLENT FOR HECTORING YOUNG JOBLESS TYPES AND MAKING THE MOST OF YOUR MOOBS AT THE SAME TIME!

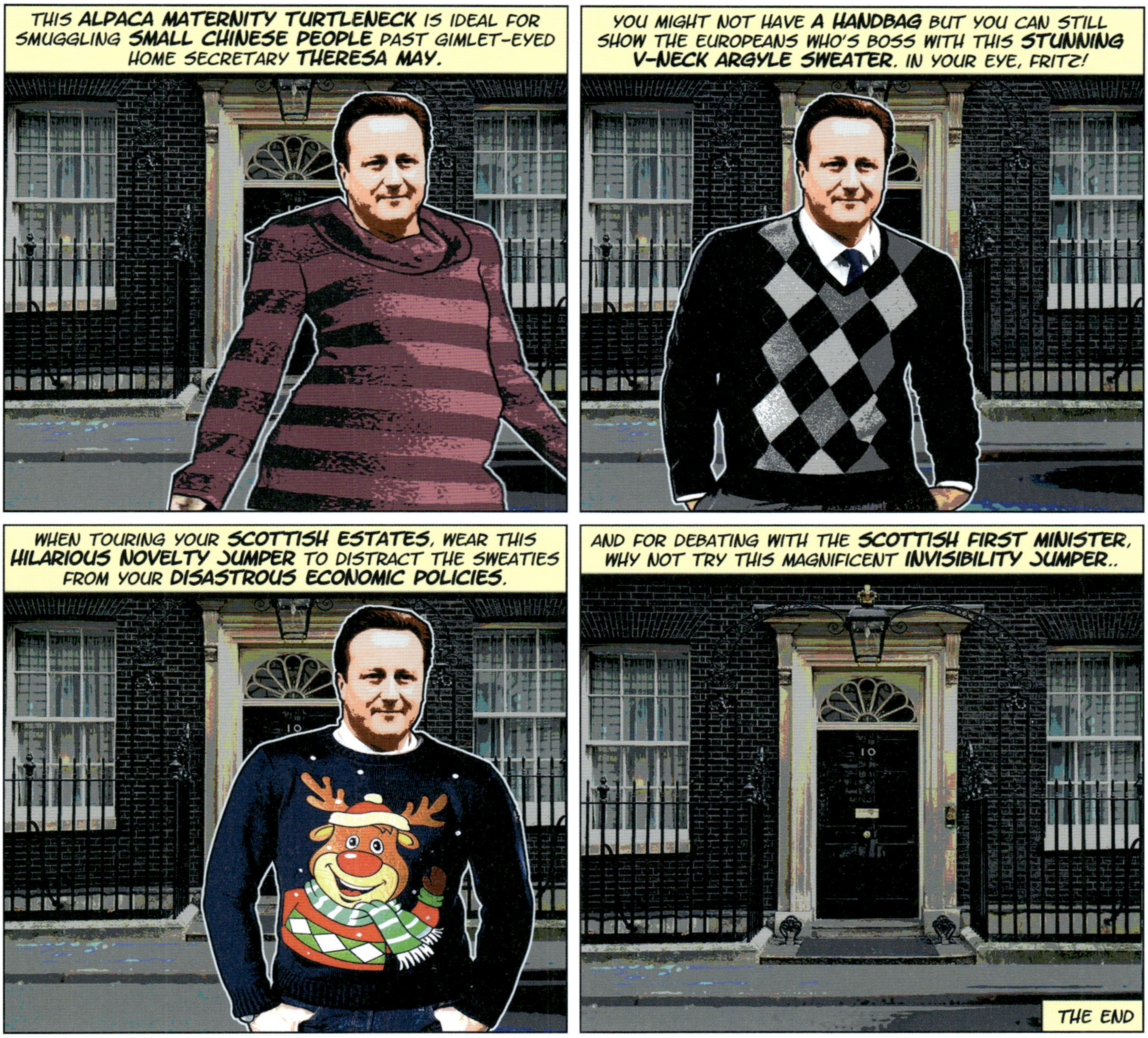
THIS ALPACA MATERNITY TURTLENECK IS IDEAL FOR SMUGGLING SMALL CHINESE PEOPLE PAST GIMLET-EYED HOME SECRETARY THERESA MAY.
YOU MIGHT NOT HAVE A HANDBAG BUT YOU CAN STILL SHOW THE EUROPEANS WHO'S BOSS WITH THIS STUNNING V-NECK ARGYLE SWEATER. IN YOUR EYE, FRITZ!
WHEN TOURING YOUR SCOTTISH ESTATES, WEAR THIS HILARIOUS NOVELTY JUMPER TO DISTRACT THE SWEATIES FROM YOUR DISASTROUS ECONOMIC POLICIES.
AND FOR DEBATING WITH THE SCOTTISH FIRST MINISTER, WHY NOT TRY THIS MAGNIFICENT INVISIBILITY JUMPER..
THE END

ONE MAN AND HIS PETROCHEMICAL PLANT

OCTOBER 26TH 2013

The Ineos petrochemical plant in Grangemouth was threatened with closure after union members rejected a survival plan. Ineos chairman Jim Ratcliffe walked away and 800 workers were left hanging until the union backed down. It wasn't normally the sort of thing I would tackle but it was a big story at the time, and a complex one. I thought I could tell a simplified version of it in pictures alone. It's the only cartoon in this collection where there literally are no words.

INEOS
THE END

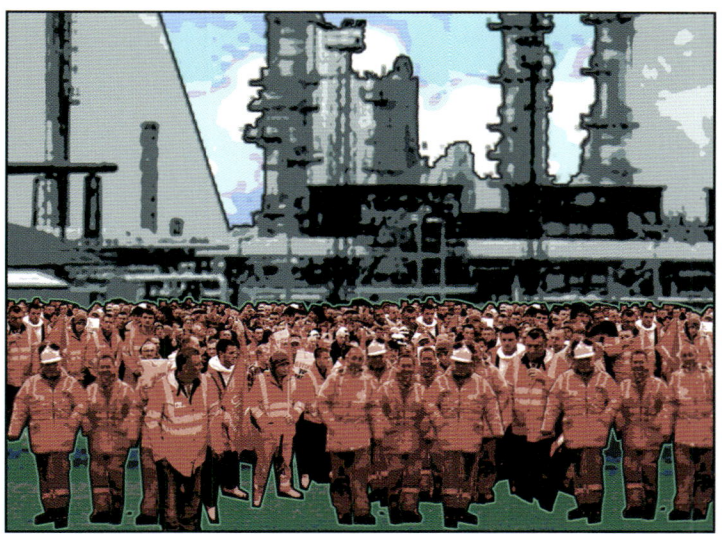

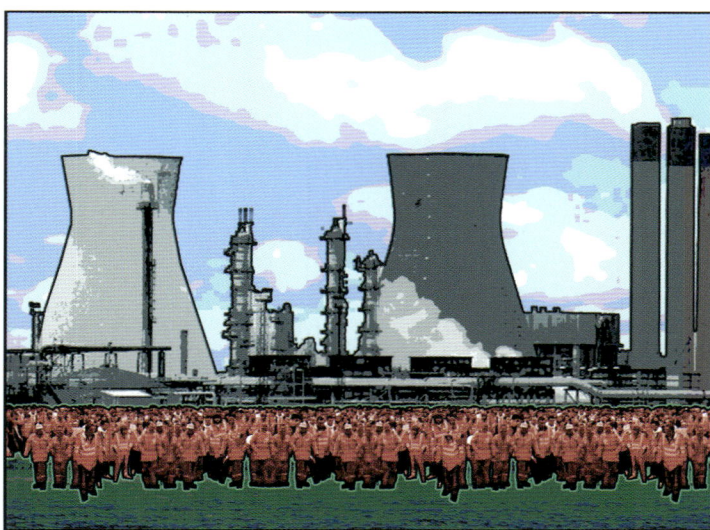

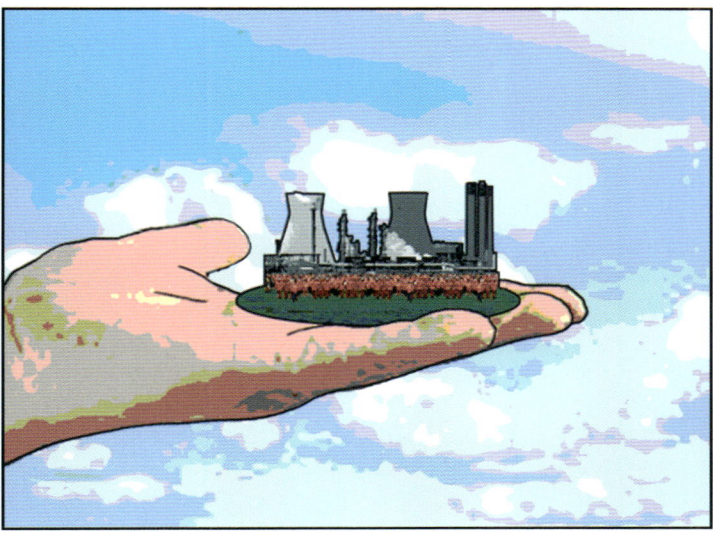

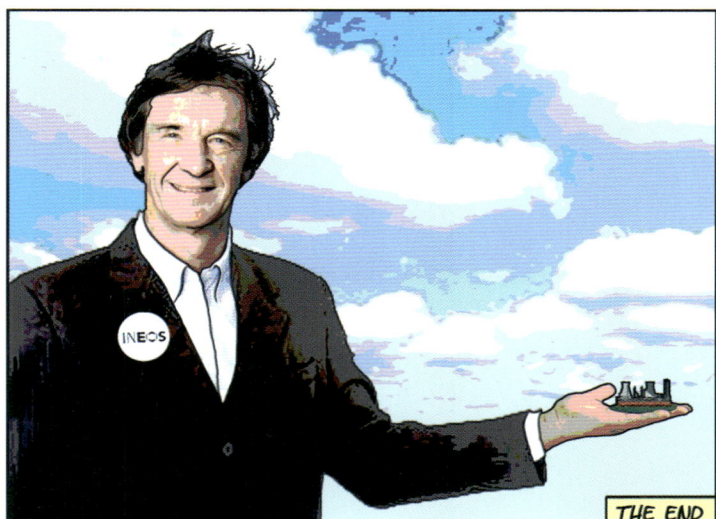

HS2 – EXCEPT FOR VIEWERS IN SCOTLAND

NOVEMBER 2ND 2013

Michael Moore was removed from his post as Secretary of State for Scotland and I wasted no time in christening his replacement 'The Cardboard Cutout Scottish Secretary'. One of his first tasks was to explain the benefits of the high speed rail link to Scotland.

INTRODUCING WESTMINSTER'S NEW MAN IN SCOTLAND, THE CARDBOARD CUTOUT SCOTTISH SECRETARY, ALISTAIR CARMICHAEL..
THE HIGH SPEED RAIL PROJECT IS GREAT NEWS FOR SCOTLAND.
HEATHROW
LONDON
PHASE ONE, DUE IN 2026, WILL RUN FROM LONDON TO HEATHROW AND BIRMINGHAM AT A COST OF £42.6BN.
BIRMINGHAM
HEATHROW
LONDON
A SECOND PHASE, PLANNED FOR 2033, WILL REACH LEEDS AND MANCHESTER.
LONDON
NOW, I KNOW WHAT YOU'RE THINKING. WHY DON'T WE START IN INVERNESS AND MOVE SOUTH?
LONDON

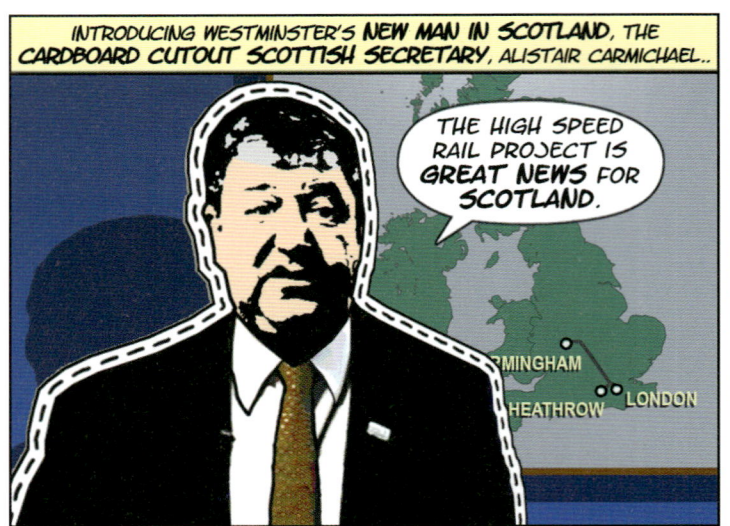

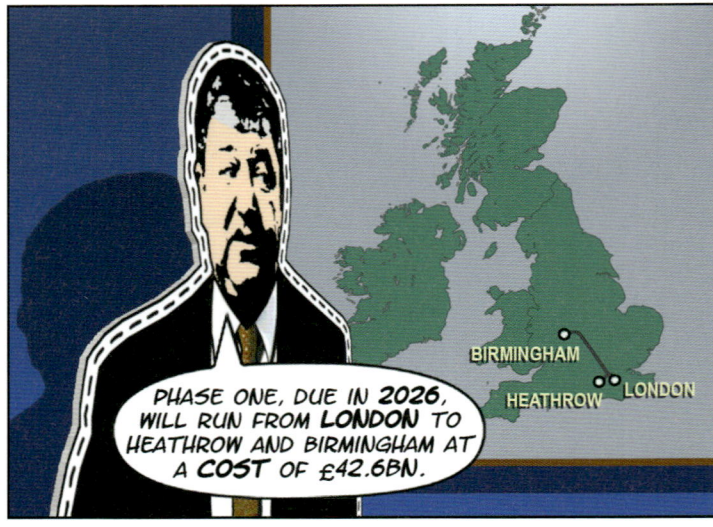

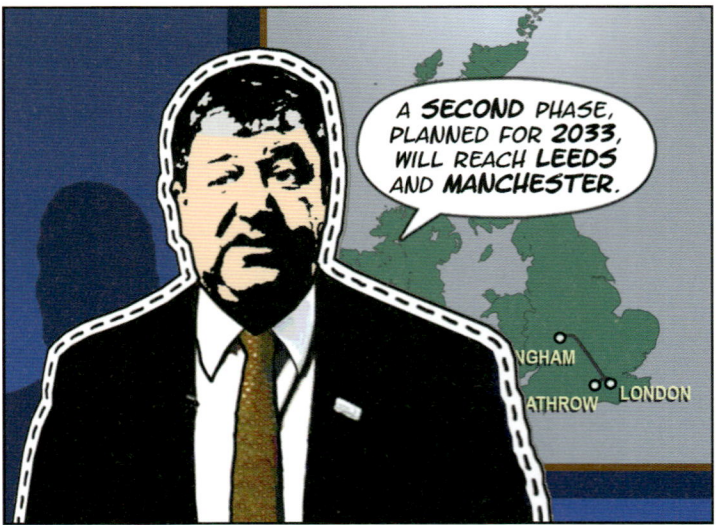

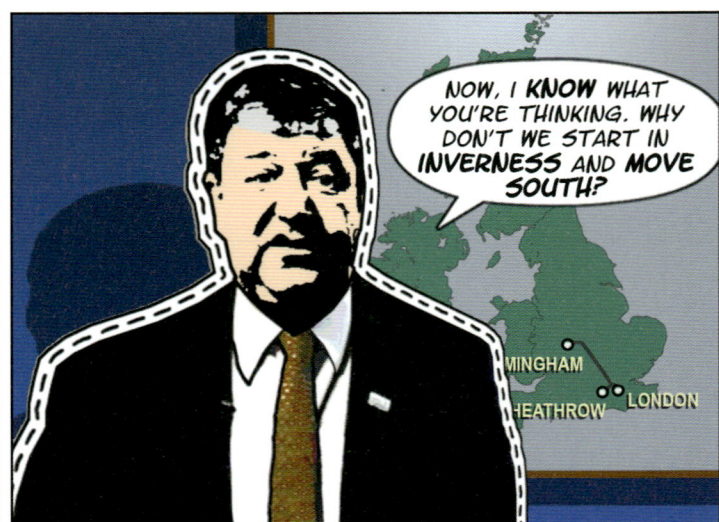

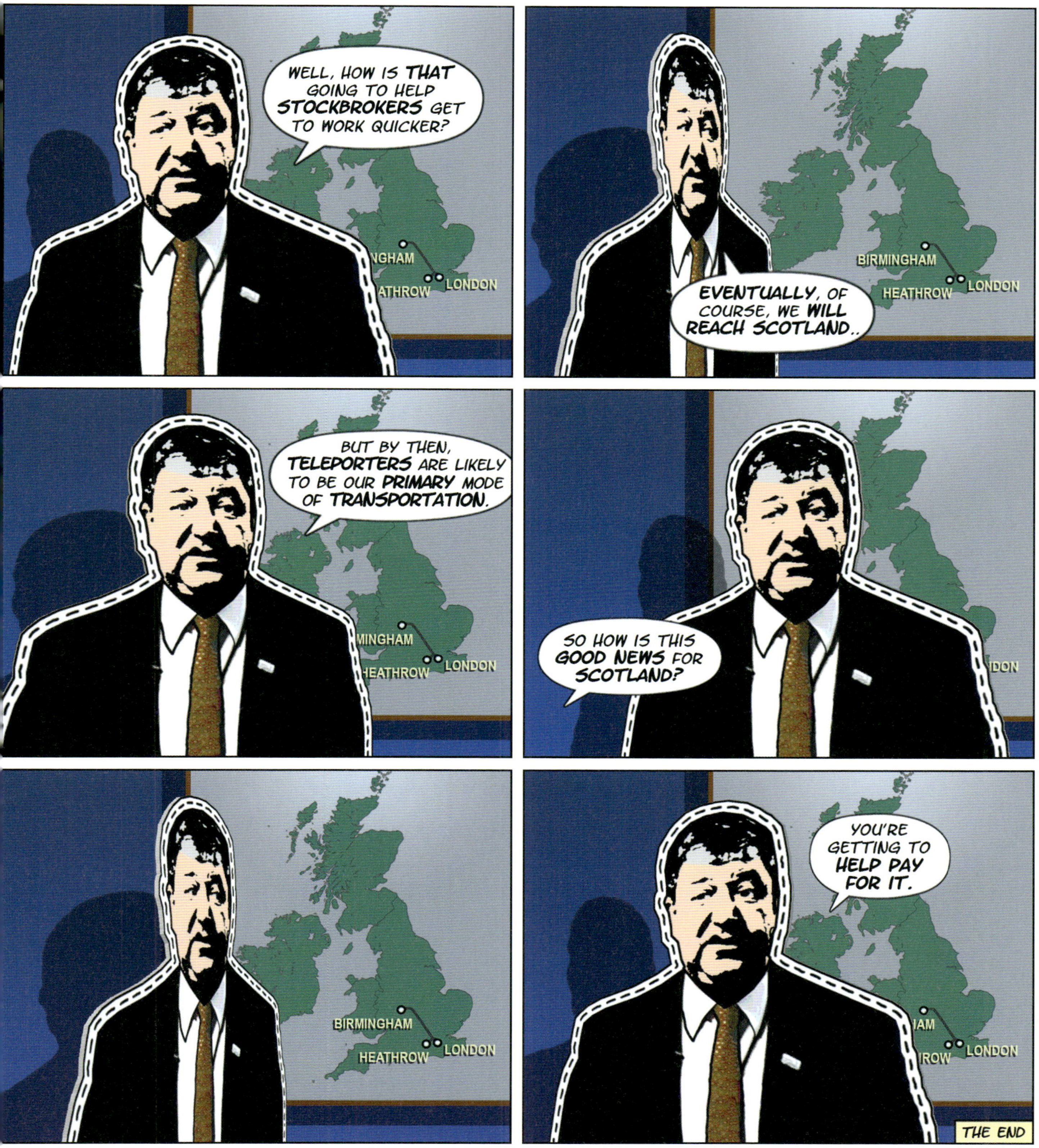
WELL, HOW IS THAT GOING TO HELP STOCKBROKERS GET TO WORK QUICKER?
NGHAM
ATHROW
LONDON
BIRMINGHAM
HEATHROW
LONDON
EVENTUALLY, OF COURSE, WE WILL REACH SCOTLAND..
BUT BY THEN, TELEPORTERS ARE LIKELY TO BE OUR PRIMARY MODE OF TRANSPORTATION.
MINGHAM
HEATHROW
LONDON
SO HOW IS THIS GOOD NEWS FOR SCOTLAND?
IDON
BIRMINGHAM
HEATHROW
LONDON
YOU'RE GETTING TO HELP PAY FOR IT.
IAM
IROW
LONDON
THE END

ALISTAIR CARMICHAEL: OUR MAN IN WESTMINSTER

NOVEMBER 9TH 2013

BAE Systems made a commercial decision and called an end to shipbuilding in Portsmouth, in favour of Scotland's two Clyde shipyards. Alistair Carmichael claimed this was a good reason to remain in the UK; that shipbuilding was the UK's gift to Scotland. *With Rose Garnett.*

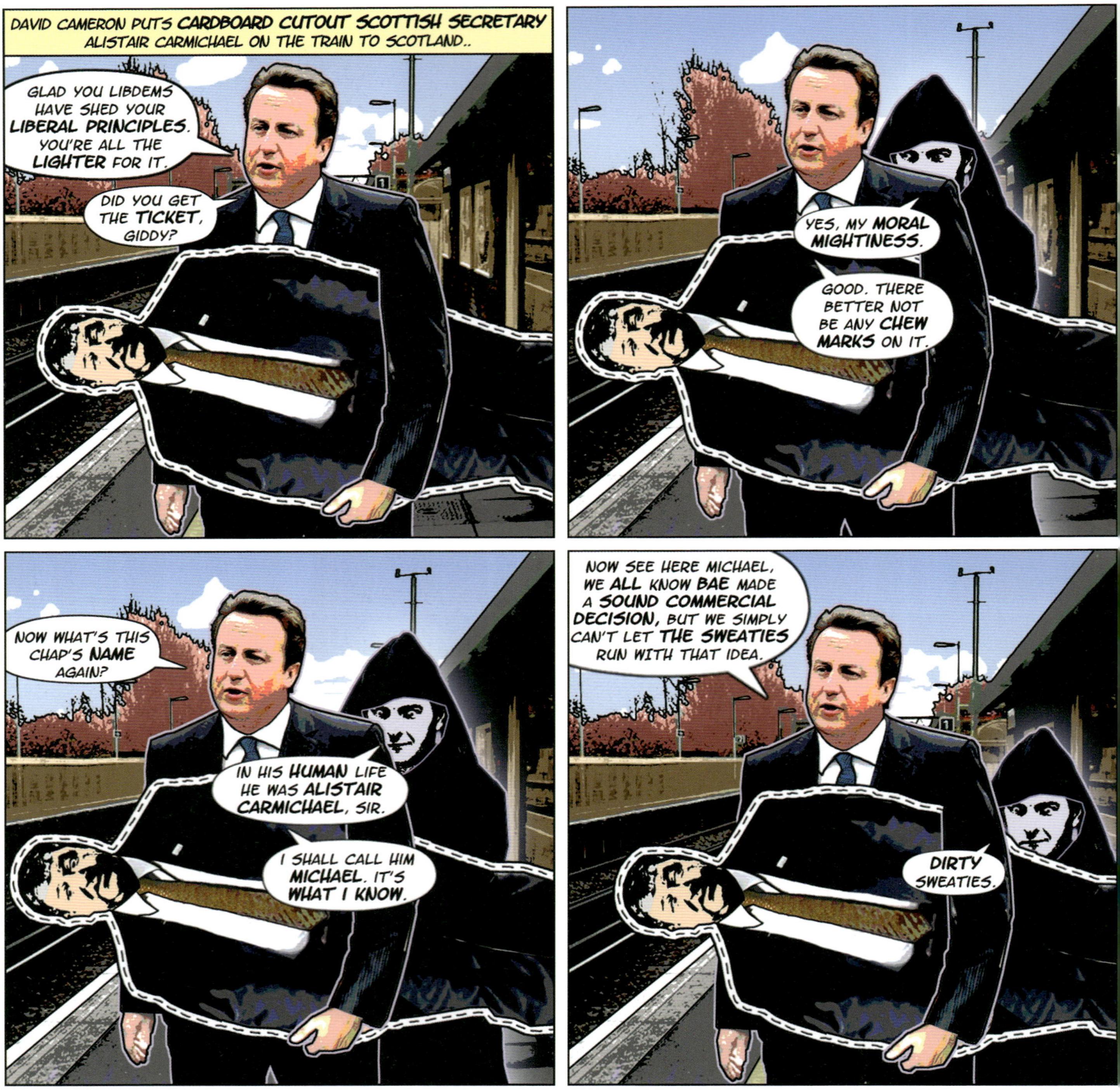

DAVID CAMERON PUTS CARDBOARD CUTOUT SCOTTISH SECRETARY ALISTAIR CARMICHAEL ON THE TRAIN TO SCOTLAND..
GLAD YOU LIBDEMS HAVE SHED YOUR LIBERAL PRINCIPLES. YOU'RE ALL THE LIGHTER FOR IT.
DID YOU GET THE TICKET, GIDDY?
YES, MY MORAL MIGHTINESS.
GOOD. THERE BETTER NOT BE ANY CHEW MARKS ON IT.
NOW WHAT'S THIS CHAP'S NAME AGAIN?
IN HIS HUMAN LIFE HE WAS ALISTAIR CARMICHAEL, SIR.
I SHALL CALL HIM MICHAEL. IT'S WHAT I KNOW.
NOW SEE HERE MICHAEL, WE ALL KNOW BAE MADE A SOUND COMMERCIAL DECISION, BUT WE SIMPLY CAN'T LET THE SWEATIES RUN WITH THAT IDEA.
DIRTY SWEATIES.

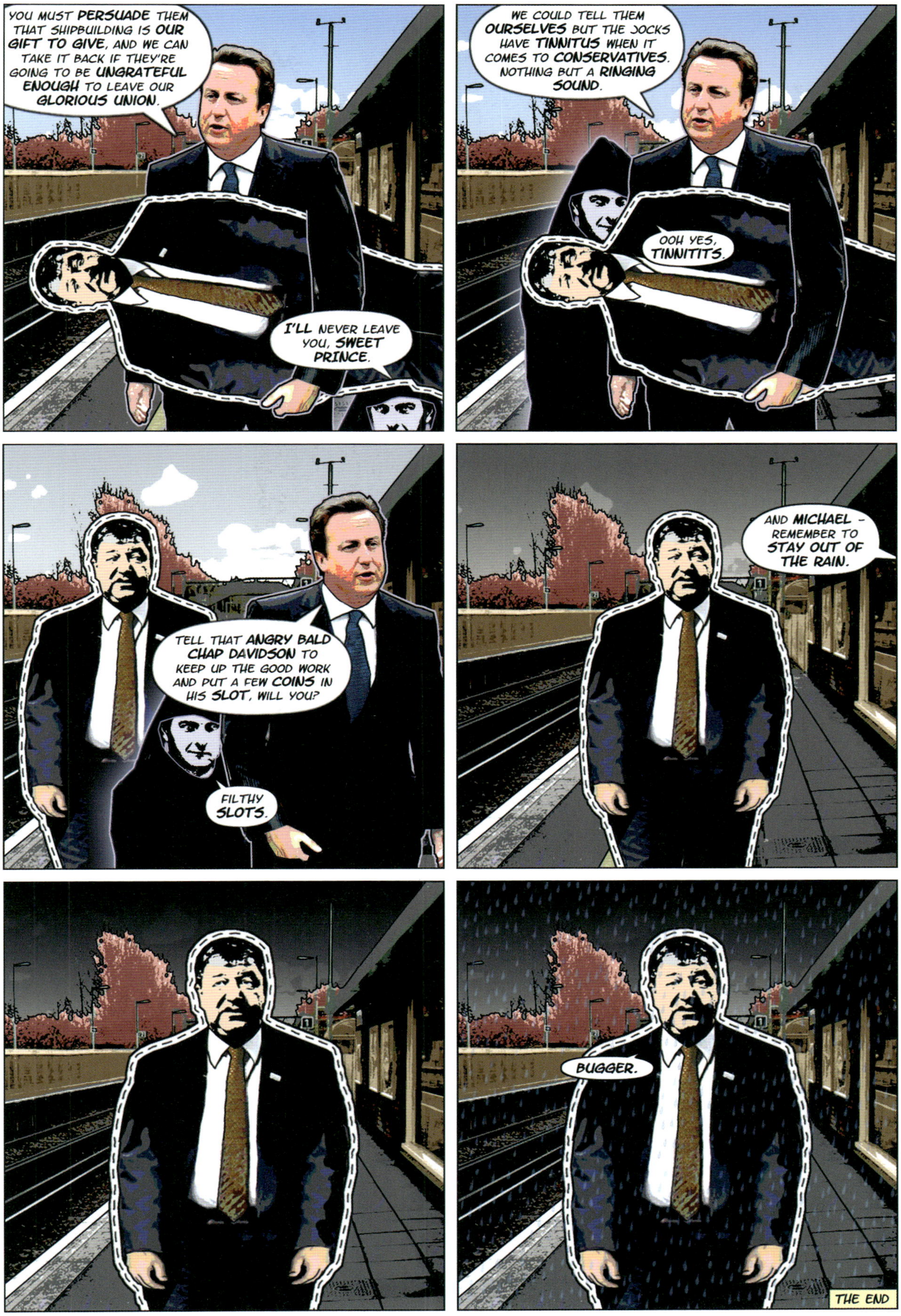
YOU MUST PERSUADE THEM THAT SHIPBUILDING IS OUR GIFT TO GIVE, AND WE CAN TAKE IT BACK IF THEY'RE GOING TO BE UNGRATEFUL ENOUGH TO LEAVE OUR GLORIOUS UNION.
I'LL NEVER LEAVE YOU, SWEET PRINCE.
WE COULD TELL THEM OURSELVES BUT THE JOCKS HAVE TINNITUS WHEN IT COMES TO CONSERVATIVES. NOTHING BUT A RINGING SOUND.
OOH YES, TINNITITS.
TELL THAT ANGRY BALD CHAP DAVIDSON TO KEEP UP THE GOOD WORK AND PUT A FEW COINS IN HIS SLOT, WILL YOU?
FILTHY SLOTS.
AND MICHAEL - REMEMBER TO STAY OUT OF THE RAIN.
BUGGER.
THE END

DEBATER OF THE YEAR

NOVEMBER 16TH 2013

Johann Lamont won the Herald's Debater of the Year award. The same week, Glasgow City Council caused an uproar by trying to remove the cone from the Duke of Wellington statue in the city centre, where it had been for years. Here I combined the two, for no particular reason.

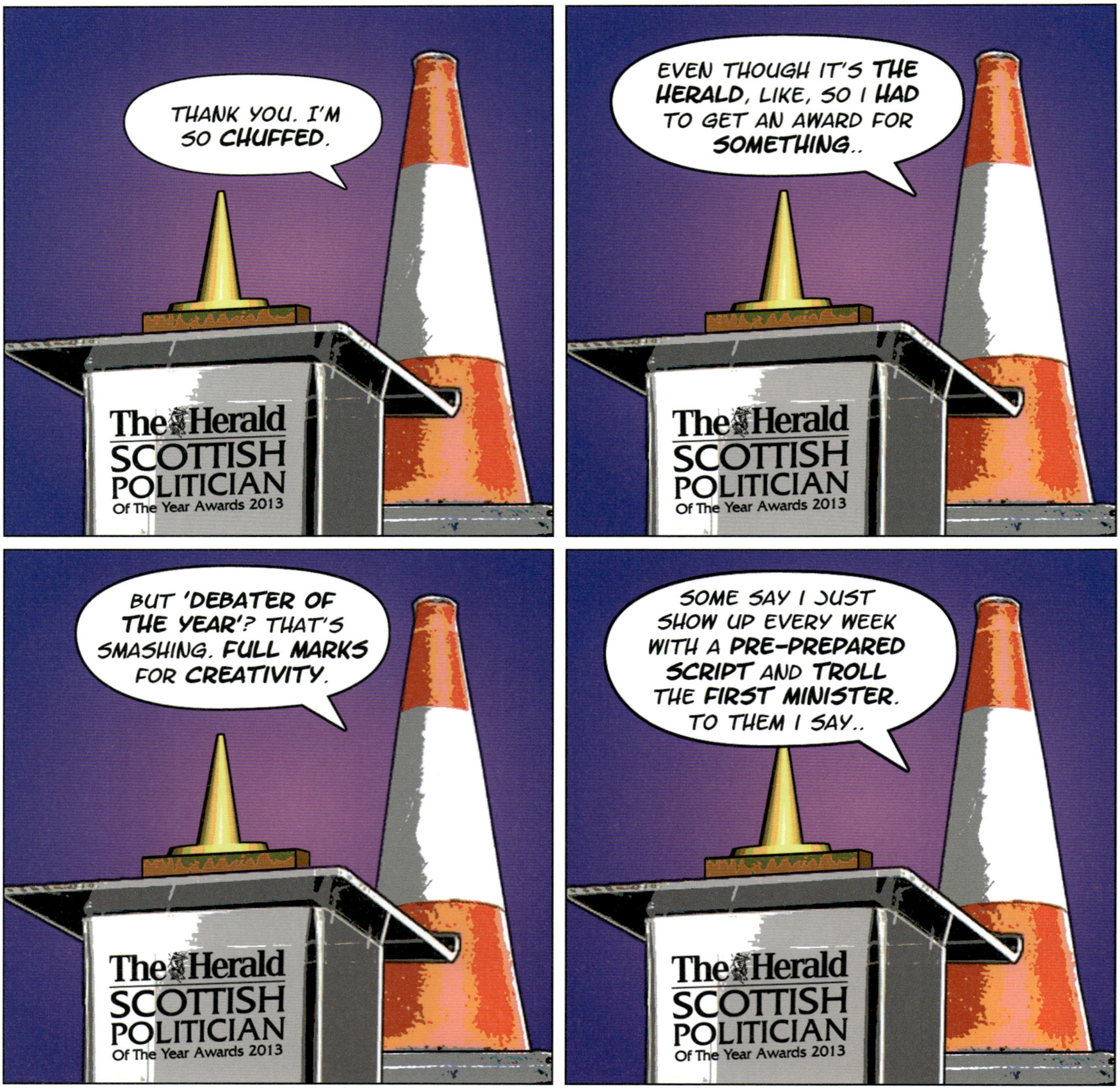

THANK YOU. I'M SO CHUFFED.
The Herald SCOTTISH POLITICIAN Of The Year Awards 2013
EVEN THOUGH IT'S THE HERALD, LIKE, SO I HAD TO GET AN AWARD FOR SOMETHING..
The Herald SCOTTISH POLITICIAN Of The Year Awards 2013
BUT 'DEBATER OF THE YEAR'? THAT'S SMASHING. FULL MARKS FOR CREATIVITY.
The Herald SCOTTISH POLITICIAN Of The Year Awards 2013
SOME SAY I JUST SHOW UP EVERY WEEK WITH A PRE-PREPARED SCRIPT AND TROLL THE FIRST MINISTER. TO THEM I SAY..
The Herald SCOTTISH POLITICIAN Of The Year Awards 2013

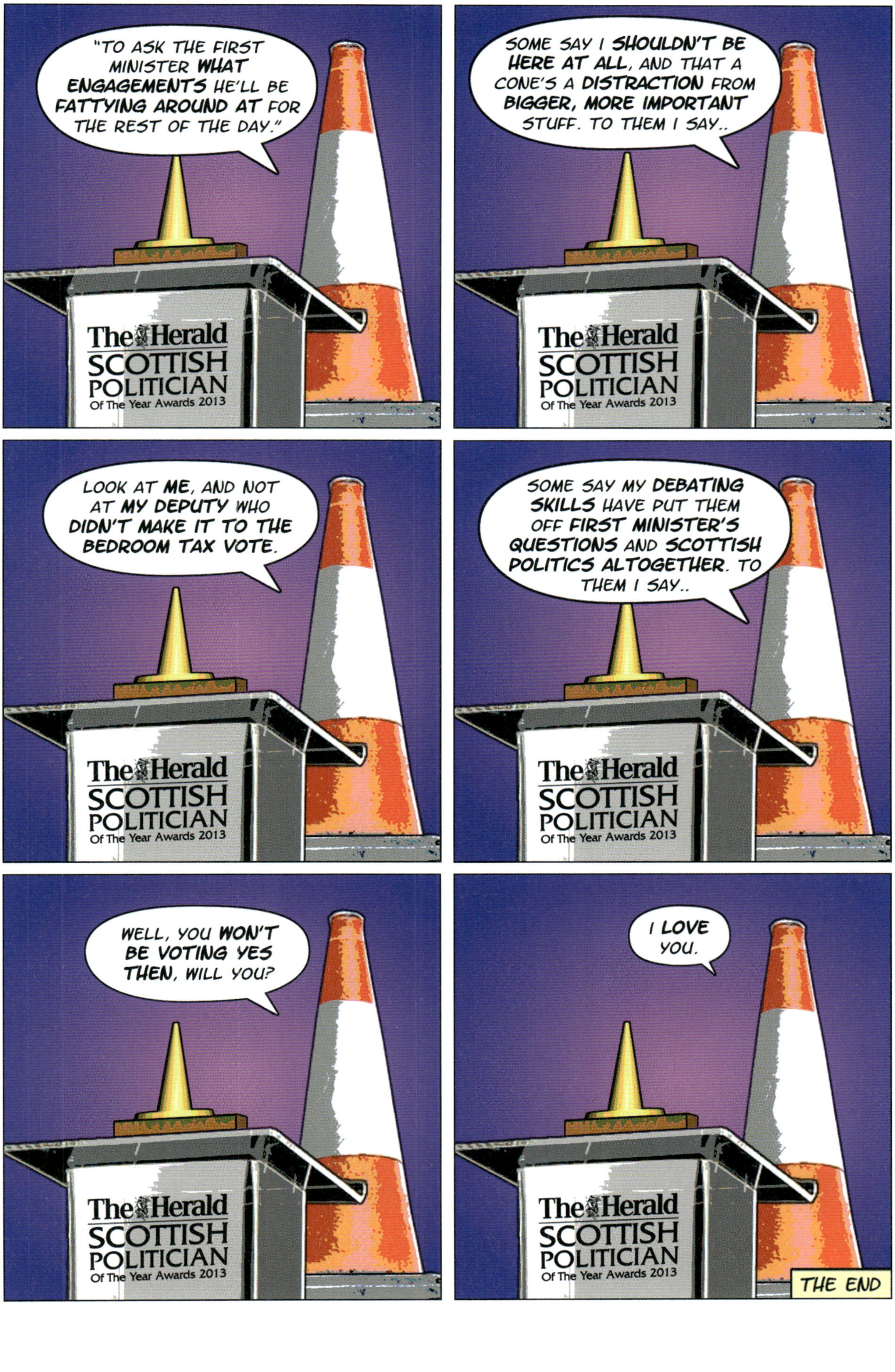
"TO ASK THE FIRST MINISTER WHAT ENGAGEMENTS HE'LL BE FATTYING AROUND AT FOR THE REST OF THE DAY."
SOME SAY I SHOULDN'T BE HERE AT ALL, AND THAT A CONE'S A DISTRACTION FROM BIGGER, MORE IMPORTANT STUFF. TO THEM I SAY..
LOOK AT ME, AND NOT AT MY DEPUTY WHO DIDN'T MAKE IT TO THE BEDROOM TAX VOTE.
SOME SAY MY DEBATING SKILLS HAVE PUT THEM OFF FIRST MINISTER'S QUESTIONS AND SCOTTISH POLITICS ALTOGETHER. TO THEM I SAY..
WELL, YOU WON'T BE VOTING YES THEN, WILL YOU?
I LOVE YOU.
The Herald SCOTTISH POLITICIAN Of The Year Awards 2013
THE END

6 THINGS MORE USEFUL THAN TRIDENT

NOVEMBER 3RD 2012

This post was originally to be called '3 Things More Useful Than Trident' but when I found out Trident was pointless, I changed it to '100 Things More Useful Than Trident.' That was going well until I had to go and buy milk.

This week, when the Westminster government announced an initial £350 million spend on a new generation of nuclear weapons whilst simultaneously telling us we were broke, I couldn't help but wonder what was so special about them. It wasn't so much the price tag that bothered me, even when I discovered £350m was a fraction of the overall £100bn required. It was more to do with being a stickler for symmetry in the exchange of goods – usually when I'm going to spend £100bn on something, I want to know I'm going to get £100bn of useful stuff back.

However, having conducted some research, I can confirm that the following objects are each in their own way more useful than Trident.

1. A Bucket With A Hole In It

Depending on the cargo you mean to transport, a bucket with a hole in it can be put to far greater use than a submarine-launched ballistic missile system. Stones for example, if chosen correctly, can be carried from one end of the garden to another. Bread rolls too can be stacked in such a manner so as to negate the effects of any hole. Once transported, the stones and bread rolls can be employed as missiles in the event of an invasion by ground troops, something that could never be said of Trident. And remember, a bucket with a hole in it can be made even more effective with the addition of a newspaper to line it. I recommend The Scotsman.

2. A Cardboard Sink

New advances in production mean that cardboard sinks can be quite robust. They can withstand several litres of soapy water and, given sufficient interim drying time, can be used many times before becoming ineffective. This is something that could never be said of Trident as just a single use would devastate half the planet, leaving a dusty crater where only the Mars rover might feel at home. Cardboard is also recyclable, unlike Trident which is currently festering on our doorstep without any means of disposal. Additional notes: Trident's green credentials are negative and are effectively purple; a cardboard sink is unlikely to be deployed accidentally.

3. My Old Socks

They've turned a strange charcoal grey, have been breeched in both heels and are quite threadbare. But they've been in my life for as long as I can remember and I've grown quite fond of them. I think of them as my comfort socks as the elastic has wilted and therefore won't contribute to any future varicose veins. Trident is similar in that it too has been in my life for as long as I can remember. The idea of it deteriorating so close to home however, does not inspire a similar affection. It's also more expensive to replace. I plan to get another winter out of my comfort socks and when I buy a new pair I'm hoping they will come in under £100bn.

4. A Betamax Video Recorder

Betamax is much maligned but was actually far superior technologically to VHS. If you happen to have inherited a working Betamax, you're likely to also have a library of movies taped sometime in the 1980's, as well as some video store cast-offs such as 'Microwave Massacre.' This is a huge source of entertainment and is unlikely to give you leukaemia. A Betamax in good condition can still be used to record your favourite TV moments. Providing you have the strength to press its huge buttons you can watch Michael Gove behaving like a knob whenever you please. Highlights from Philip Hammond's thrill-packed term as defence secretary alas do not make good television.

5. A Stick

Sticks are incredibly useful. I keep a collection in the garden in case of unforeseen circumstances. Once I had to use a stick to get my keys off the roof. You might wonder what my keys were doing on the roof. I put them there with a stick. Another time, LaFlamme brought me a pot plant. It started to grow and I used a stick to support it. Soon I needed a bigger stick and then a bigger one. I asked LaFlamme what kind of a plant it was and she said 'oak.' Soon it took over the flat and began producing little sticks of its own for future generations to get their keys off the roof. This is all in stark contrast to Trident, which is likely to only ever produce universal death.

6. Garbage

One of the main reasons cited for keeping Trident is that it's a major employer. Aside from the fact that it's a twisted individual who thinks weapons of mass destruction would make a fine job creation scheme, it turns out only two jobs would be at stake – one guy regularly taps it with a screwdriver and another checks if we're all still alive. Garbage on the other hand is a major employer. It takes many thousands of people up and down the country to administer and physically deal with the collection and disposal of garbage, as well as to sort through the recycling and figure out what you're meant to do with Tetrapaks. If we didn't have garbage, unemployment would soar. Once Trident is dismantled it too will become garbage, creating even more employment opportunities.

Let's face it, even soldiers don't have any use for Trident.

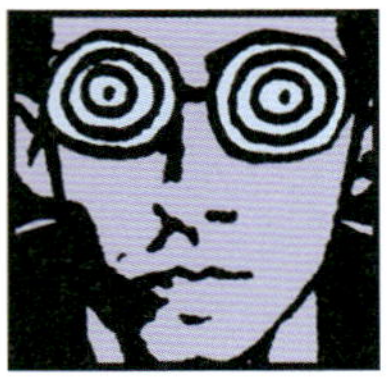

STRANGE INTERLUDE

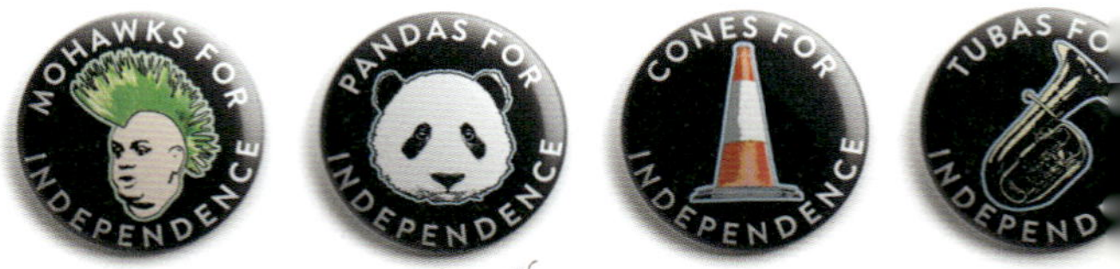
MOHAWKS FOR INDEPENDENCE
PANDAS FOR INDEPENDENCE
CONES FOR INDEPENDENCE

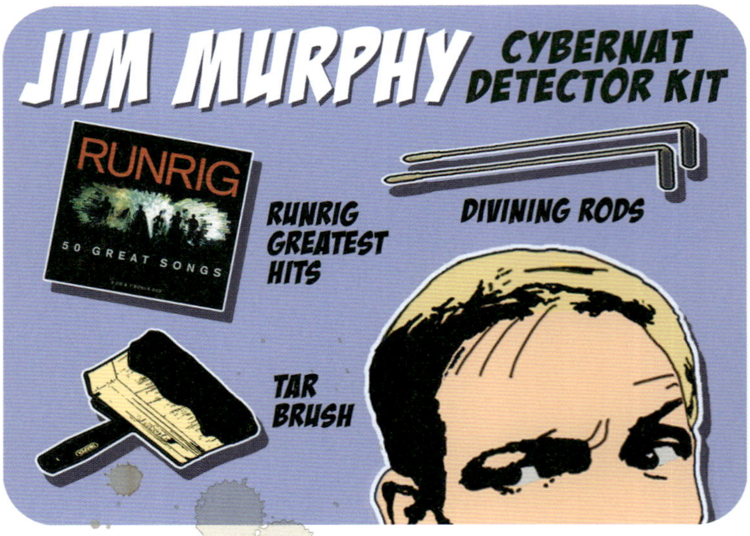
JIM MURPHY
CYBERNAT DETECTOR KIT
RUNRIG
50 GREAT SONGS
RUNRIG GREATEST HITS
DIVINING RODS
TAR BRUSH

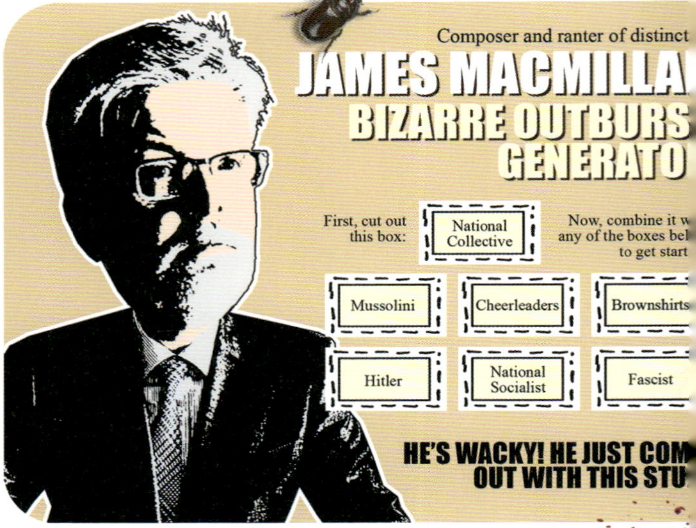
Composer and ranter of distinct
JAMES MACMILLA
BIZARRE OUTBURS
GENERATO
First, cut out this box:
National Collective
Now, combine it w
any of the boxes bel
to get start
Mussolini
Cheerleaders
Brownshirts
Hitler
National Socialist
Fascist
HE'S WACKY! HE JUST COM
OUT WITH THIS STU

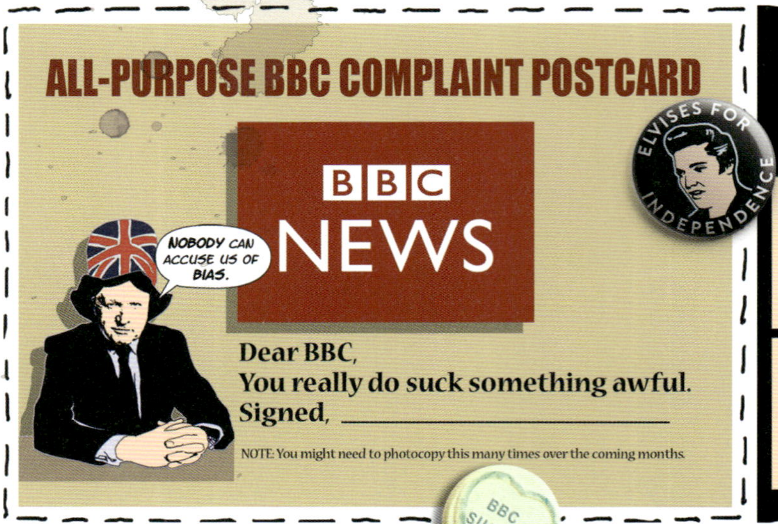
ALL-PURPOSE BBC COMPLAINT POSTCARD
BBC NEWS
NOBODY CAN ACCUSE US OF BIAS.
ELVISES FOR INDEPENDENCE
Dear BBC,
You really do suck something awful.
Signed, ______________________
NOTE: You might need to photocopy this many times over the coming months.
BBC SUCKS

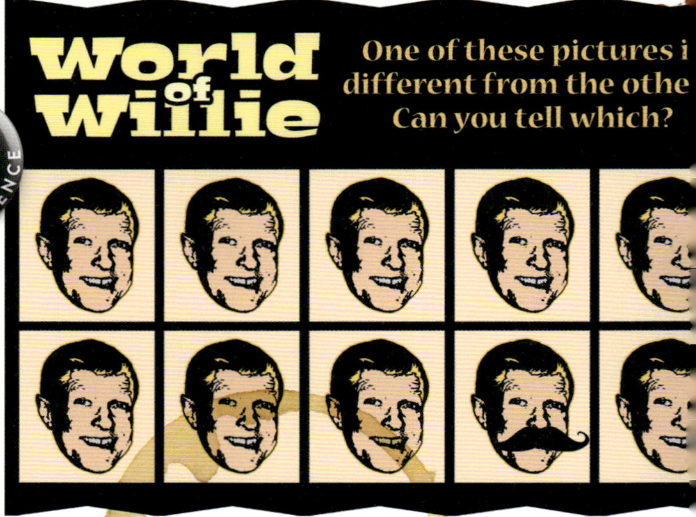
World of Willie
One of these pictures i
different from the othe
Can you tell which?

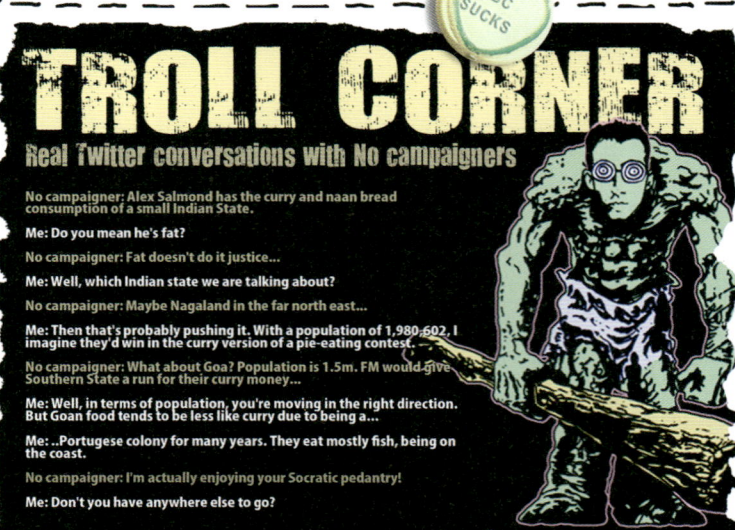

TROLL CORNER

Real Twitter conversations with No campaigners

No campaigner: Alex Salmond has the curry and naan bread consumption of a small Indian State.

Me: Do you mean he's fat?

No campaigner: Fat doesn't do it justice...

Me: Well, which Indian state we are talking about?

No campaigner: Maybe Nagaland in the far north east...

Me: Then that's probably pushing it. With a population of 1,980,602, I imagine they'd win in the curry version of a pie-eating contest.

No campaigner: What about Goa? Population is 1.5m. FM would give Southern State a run for their curry money...

Me: Well, in terms of population, you're moving in the right direction. But Goan food tends to be less like curry due to being a...

Me: ..Portugese colony for many years. They eat mostly fish, being on the coast.

No campaigner: I'm actually enjoying your Socratic pedantry!

Me: Don't you have anywhere else to go?

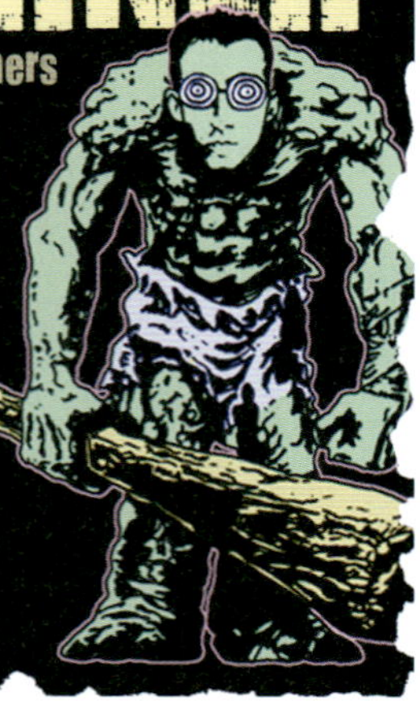

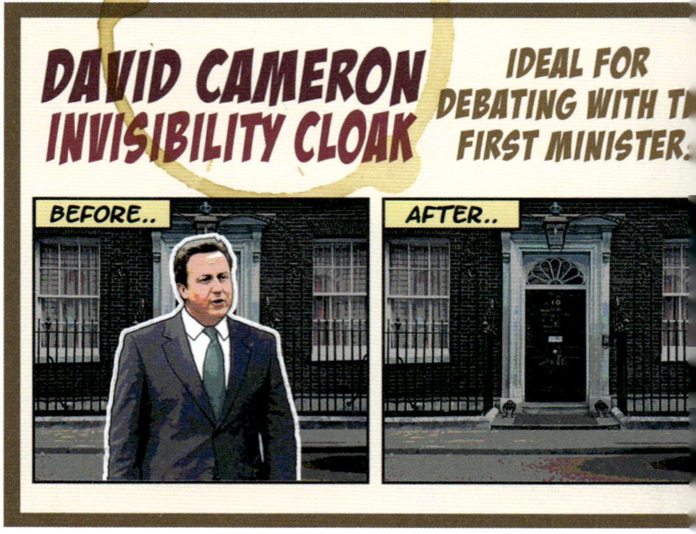
DAVID CAMERON INVISIBILITY CLOAK
IDEAL FOR DEBATING WITH TI
FIRST MINISTER.
BEFORE..
AFTER..

EU FEAR
CURRENCY FEAR
THE OIL IS RUNNING OUT
TUBA
FEAR
CALM
BLAIR MCDOUGALL PHRENOLOGY BUST

BLAIR McDOUGALL PHRENOLOGY BUST

We've all wondered from time to time what goes on in the minds of brilliant individuals such as Better Together campaign director, Blair McDougall. Well, with this lifelike, solid porcelain phrenology bust, you can see for yourself. It's all mapped out and take my word for it, Blair is more, so much more, than a gifted tuba virtuoso! But he's that too!

Special Bawheid edition - massive 32" circumference!

STUDY THE BONCE OF A GENIUS!

NICK CLEGG PROMISES THE EARTH

I'm Nick Clegg and if you vote 'No' on the 18th of September I can promise you this very earth. Not just the earth, but the sun, moon, stars and all the little planets in God's universe.

You might say I'm in no position to promise much of anything, what with our disastrous performance in government and the total collapse of our support base. Then there's Lord Rennard! Sheesh! But look on the bright side. I'm Nick Clegg! Vote 'No'!

PLEDGE NOW!

LORD ROBERTSON FORTUNE-TELLING KIT

First, cut out the squares below. Then close your eyes and ask yourself a question about the future. Grab whichever square comes to hand and there you have it - you can predict at least as well as Mystic Dode and his throbbing orb.

TIP: Try asking yourself if the forces of darkness will be unleashed in an independent Scotland!

YES	NO	AM I BEING PAID TO ANSWER THIS?

COUPONS FOR NO CAMPAIGNERS

CUT OUT AND GIVE TO POOR MISGUIDED SOULS

This coupon entitles you to broaden your horizons.	This coupon entitles you to renounce fear.
This coupon entitles you to demand more of your politicians.	This coupon entitles you to imagine being governed by a Tory/Ukip coalition.

YOUR SECRET WORD IS: YES

DEPENDENCE IS FOR KIDS

AN APPEAL ON BEHALF OF THE CARDBOARD CUTOUT SCOTTISH SECRETARY

Friends, the cardboard cutout Scottish Secretary needs your help. Due to 2-dimensionality and the total absence of a spine, he finds standing up for Scotland nigh on impossible.

We're looking into reinforcing him with some kind of inner corrugated medium and compressed paperboard backing, or maybe just a metal pole thing. Then we can prop him up against the wall or something. I don't know.

TOTALLY SPINELESS! SEND CASH NOW!

LIVE TUBA CHAT

121 PARPING!

ONLY **36p** per min

0981 987 6543

UNELECTED BUFFOONS

LIVE ERMINE

36p per min

0981 987 6543

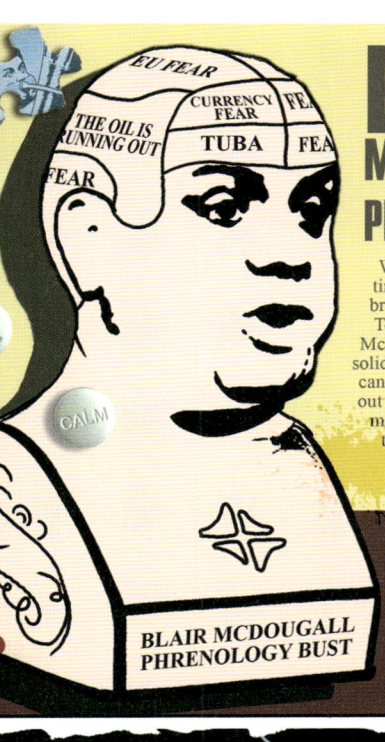

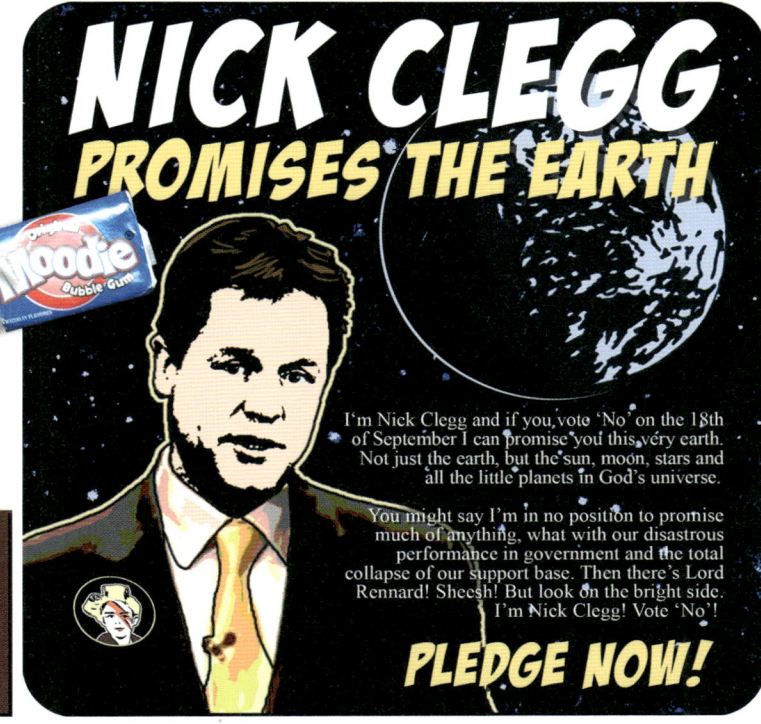

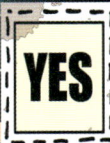

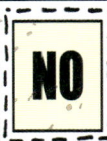

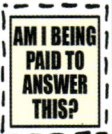

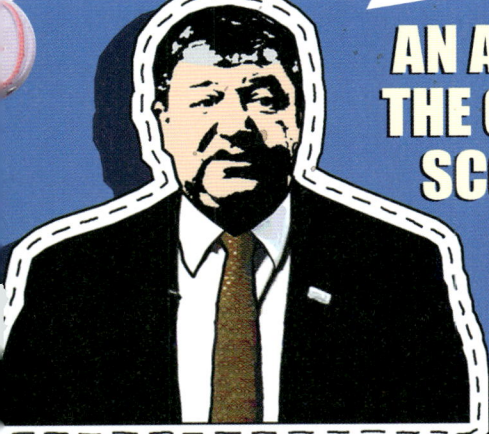

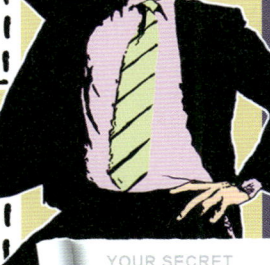

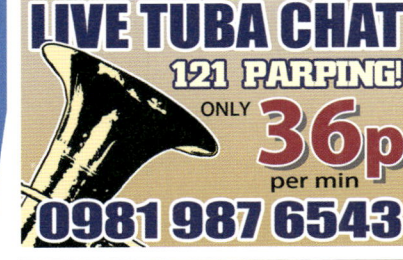

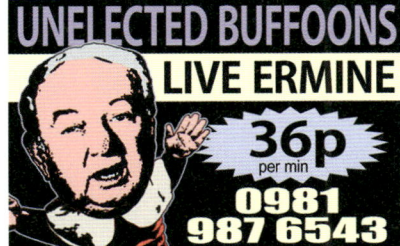

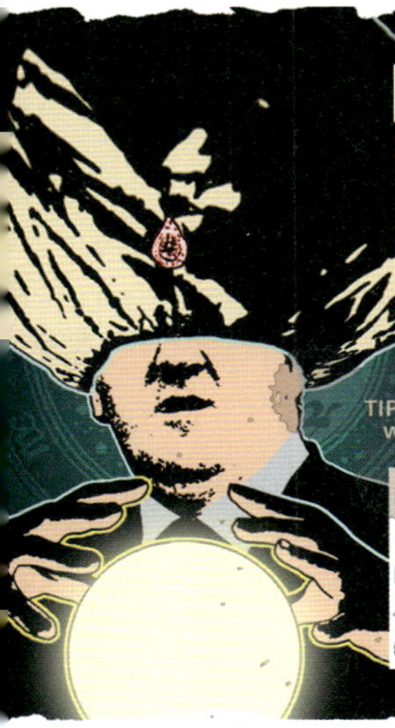

REGIONAL COLLECTIVE by Alistair Darling

JUNE 28TH 2013

Now look. I only got into this because of that Joyce McMillan and her 'all the artists are voting Yes' nonsense. This may or may not be true, but if it is, it's because Alex Salmond promised them a washing-free independent Scotland. If he'd said independence meant getting out of bed sober before noon and looking presentable, they'd very soon come around to Better Together.

Of course there are Scottish artists who support the UK. There must be. Just because I haven't met any doesn't mean they don't exist. Admittedly we're lacking any equivalent of that dreadful National Collective and their woeful bleatings about wishing trees and Icelandic goat herders. Even their cartoons are poor. I haven't been in a single one of them. Better Together's lack in this regard may not necessarily be a bad thing. Do you really want 500 Questions dressed up as an extended prose poem? Or a demolition of the SNP's currency plans in rap?

REGIONAL COLLECTIVE
ARTISTS AND CREATIVES AGAINST SCOTTISH INDEPENDENCE

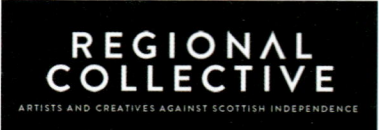

But not to be outdone, I have taken the initiative and set up a new website, Regional Collective – Artists and Creatives Against Scottish Independence, as a platform for No-voting artistic types. You know who you are, even if I don't. Let this be a starting point for a new flourishing of anti-independence bile in the creative arts.

Why me, I hear you ask. Well, somebody has to do it. I may not be much of an artist but I'm certainly creative. As Chancellor of the Exchequer, I was the one who bailed out the banks with your money, a hugely imaginative act which I'm sure would never have occurred to any of you; I've flipped for Britain, having designated four properties as my second home in four years; and I claimed parliamentary expenses for a flat that I let out whilst also claiming living allowances for Downing Street. I'd like to see Alan Bissett try that.

Regional Collective
ARTISTS AND CREATIVES AGAINST SCOTTI-SH INDEPENDENCE
An Alistair Darling Joint

So, on to the website. My first challenge was to design a logo. Now, my understanding of typesetting is that you should use as many different colours and styles as possible but stick to well-known fonts such as Comic Sans and Brush Script for maximum effect. Hence, my first effort.

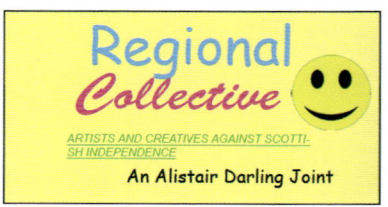

The result of this was that I had to get Ian Taylor to pay National Collective for the logo opposite. We may not have any design sense but we certainly have a truckload of cash, and in politics that's what counts.

What about the actual content of the site? Well, let's start with photography. And just to show we can do Icelandic goat-herders as well as any secessionists bent on breaking up Britain, here's a man with a bucket:

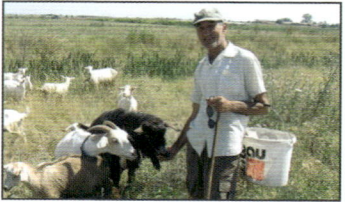

I'm not seeing any ice in this particular shot but I'm

led to believe the most amazing results can be achieved with Photoshop. Whether that extends to painting in a grassroots artists' collective that doesn't exist remains to be seen.

Next – a poem in the Scots tongue:

But pith and power, till my last hour, I'll mak this declaration;
We're bought and sold for English gold, Such a parcel of incredibly dedicated and hard-working public servants in a nation.

Perhaps the biggest challenge for the website would be in the field of illustration as, unlike photography and poetry, it requires some skill. I set out with pencil and paper, thinking a self-portrait might give the site a little character:

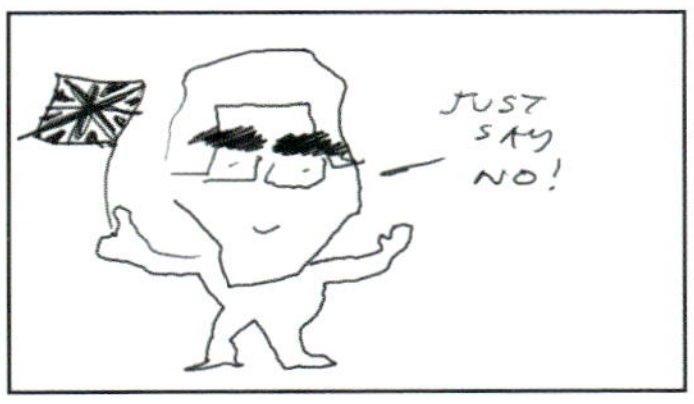
JUST SAY NO!

And so it did. It gave it a little character with bushy eyebrows waving a flag. Once again, I had to get Ian Taylor to pay National Collective for the portrait below, even though I'm not convinced it's a particularly true likeness.

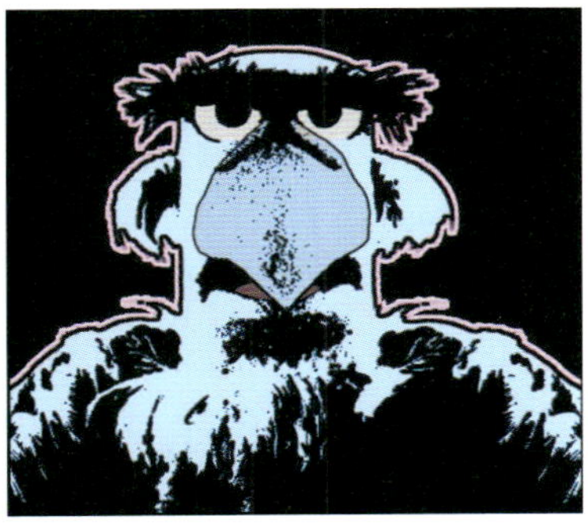

If this exercise proves nothing else, we've shown we can keep National Collective in work.
One final point. Let it never be said that Better Together are offering a politics of fear rather than any kind of positive vision. Of course we're offering a positive vision – if you vote Yes, you're positively screwed.

Now, calling all No-supporting artists. Are you there? Hello? Ok, call me.

VOTE NO OR THE TIME LORD GETS IT

NOVEMBER 23RD 2013

"The SNP simply cannot guarantee that we'd still get Doctor Who after independence," said Ruth Davidson. The story was then backed up by the Scotland Office. Doctor Who is seen in dozens of countries around the world, but apparently Scotland is uniquely incapable of hooking this up.

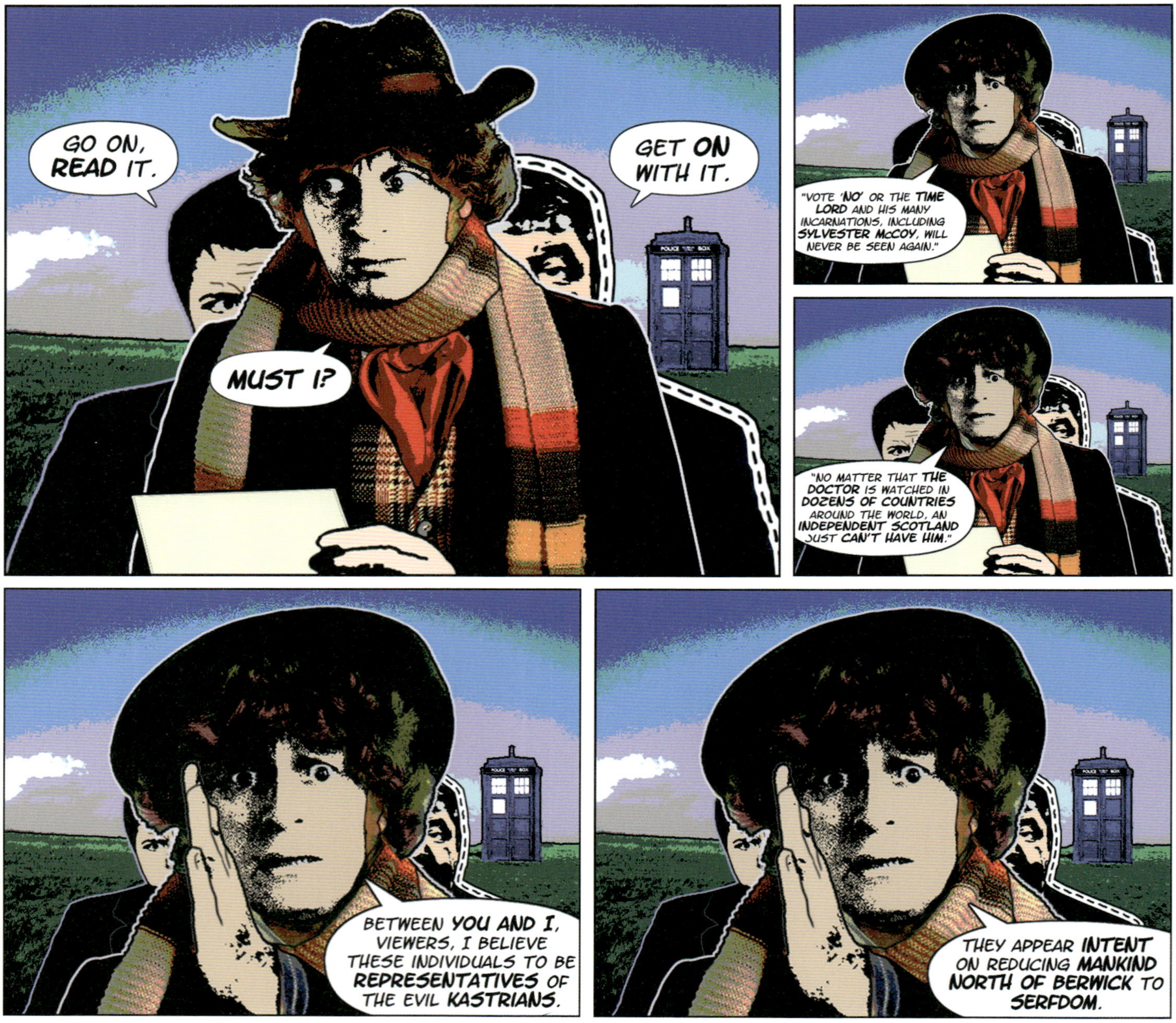

GO ON, READ IT.
GET ON WITH IT.
MUST I?
"VOTE 'NO' OR THE TIME LORD AND HIS MANY INCARNATIONS, INCLUDING SYLVESTER McCOY, WILL NEVER BE SEEN AGAIN."
"NO MATTER THAT THE DOCTOR IS WATCHED IN DOZENS OF COUNTRIES AROUND THE WORLD, AN INDEPENDENT SCOTLAND JUST CAN'T HAVE HIM."
BETWEEN YOU AND I, VIEWERS, I BELIEVE THESE INDIVIDUALS TO BE REPRESENTATIVES OF THE EVIL KASTRIANS.
THEY APPEAR INTENT ON REDUCING MANKIND NORTH OF BERWICK TO SERFDOM.

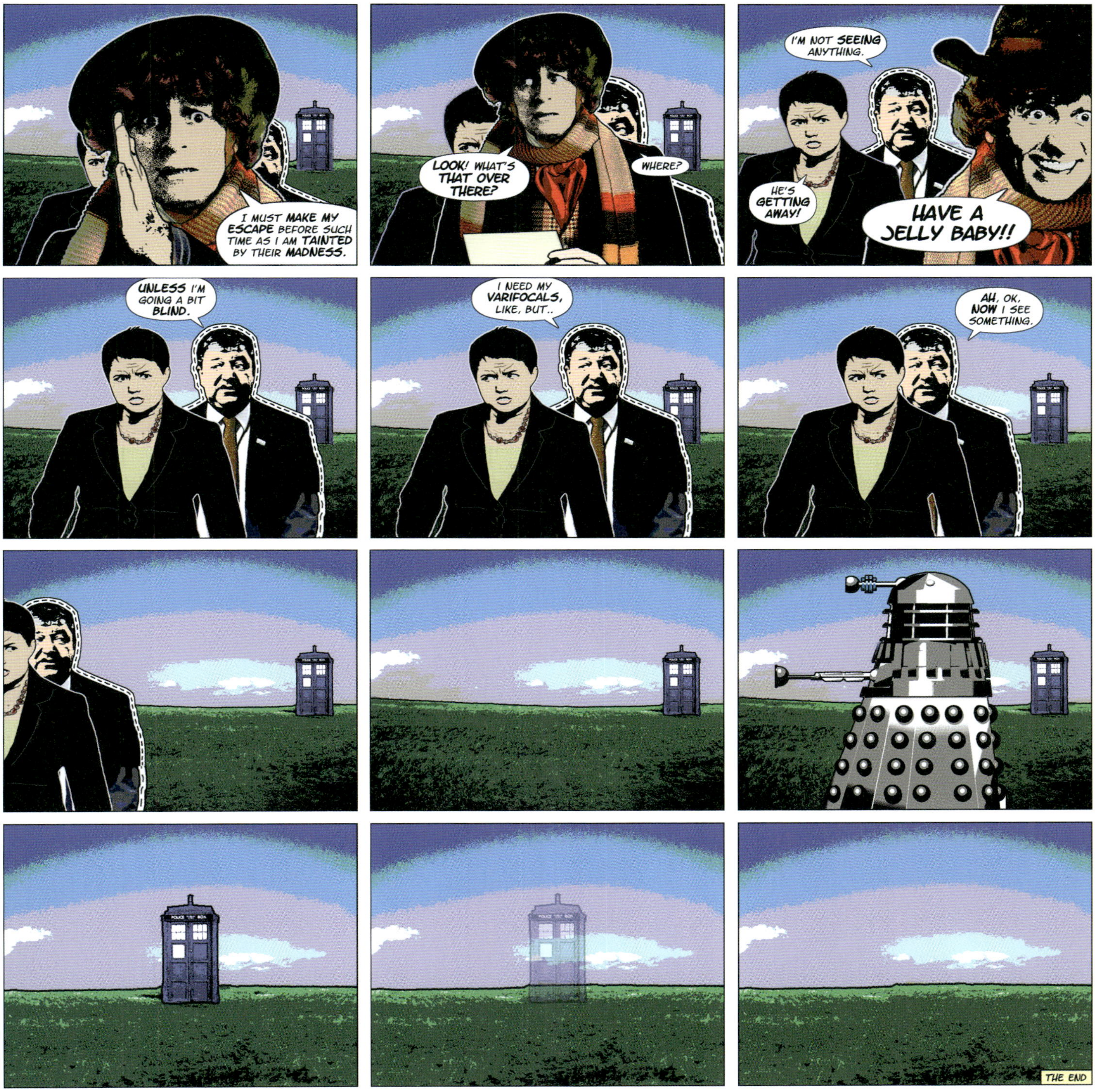

I MUST MAKE MY ESCAPE BEFORE SUCH TIME AS I AM TAINTED BY THEIR MADNESS.
LOOK! WHAT'S THAT OVER THERE?
WHERE?
I'M NOT SEEING ANYTHING.
HE'S GETTING AWAY!
HAVE A JELLY BABY!!
UNLESS I'M GOING A BIT BLIND.
I NEED MY VARIFOCALS, LIKE, BUT..
AH, OK, NOW I SEE SOMETHING.
THE END

ALISTAIR CARMICHAEL STANDS UP FOR SCOTLAND

NOVEMBER 29TH 2013

Alistair Carmichael had often been described as a 'political bruiser', without anything much to back it up. In a televised debate with Nicola Sturgeon, we were able to see this heavyweight in action. It was not pretty. He actually used the words "be quiet" at one point.

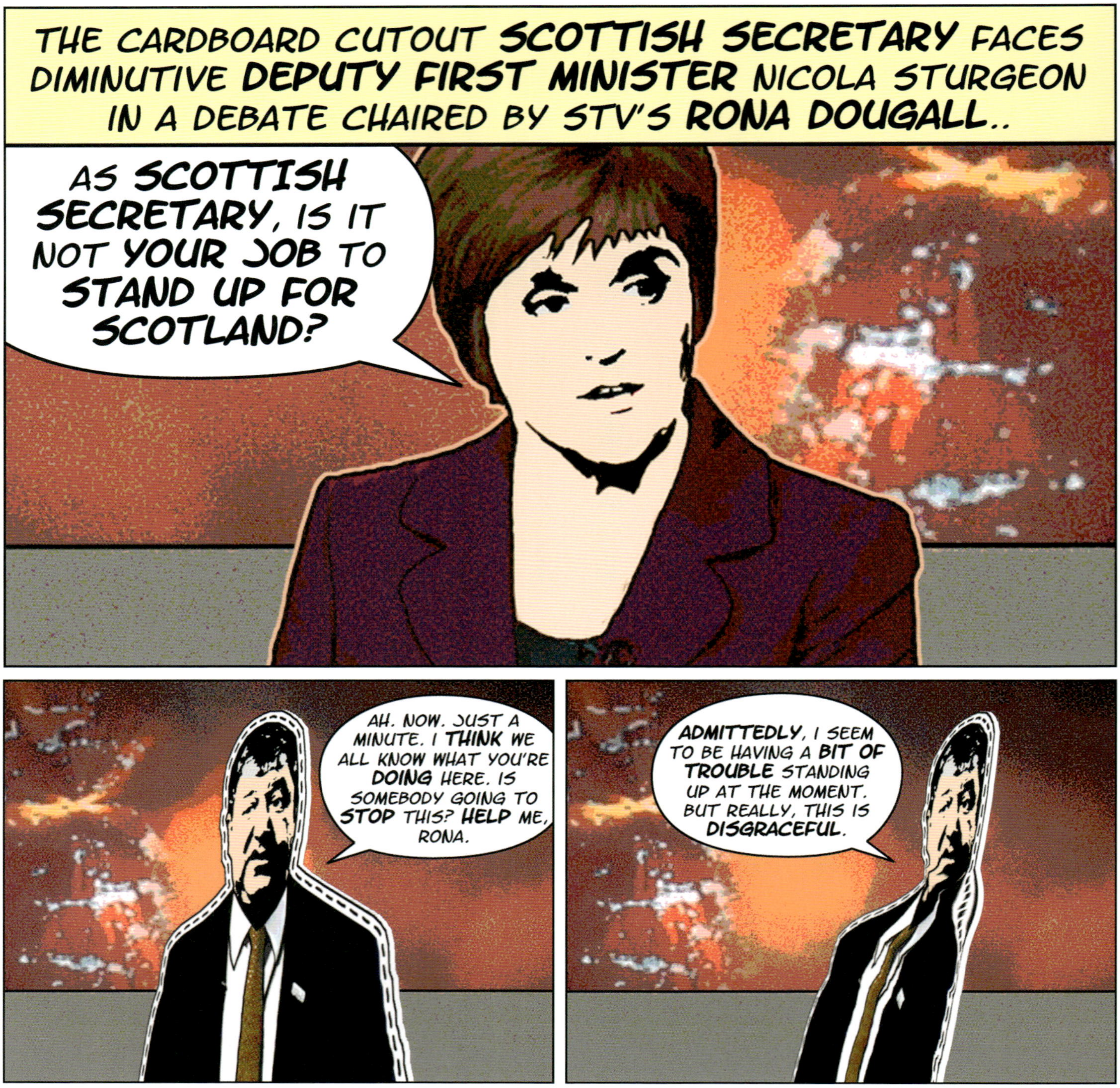

THE CARDBOARD CUTOUT SCOTTISH SECRETARY FACES DIMINUTIVE DEPUTY FIRST MINISTER NICOLA STURGEON IN A DEBATE CHAIRED BY STV'S RONA DOUGALL..
AS SCOTTISH SECRETARY, IS IT NOT YOUR JOB TO STAND UP FOR SCOTLAND?
AH. NOW. JUST A MINUTE. I THINK WE ALL KNOW WHAT YOU'RE DOING HERE. IS SOMEBODY GOING TO STOP THIS? HELP ME, RONA.
ADMITTEDLY, I SEEM TO BE HAVING A BIT OF TROUBLE STANDING UP AT THE MOMENT. BUT REALLY, THIS IS DISGRACEFUL.

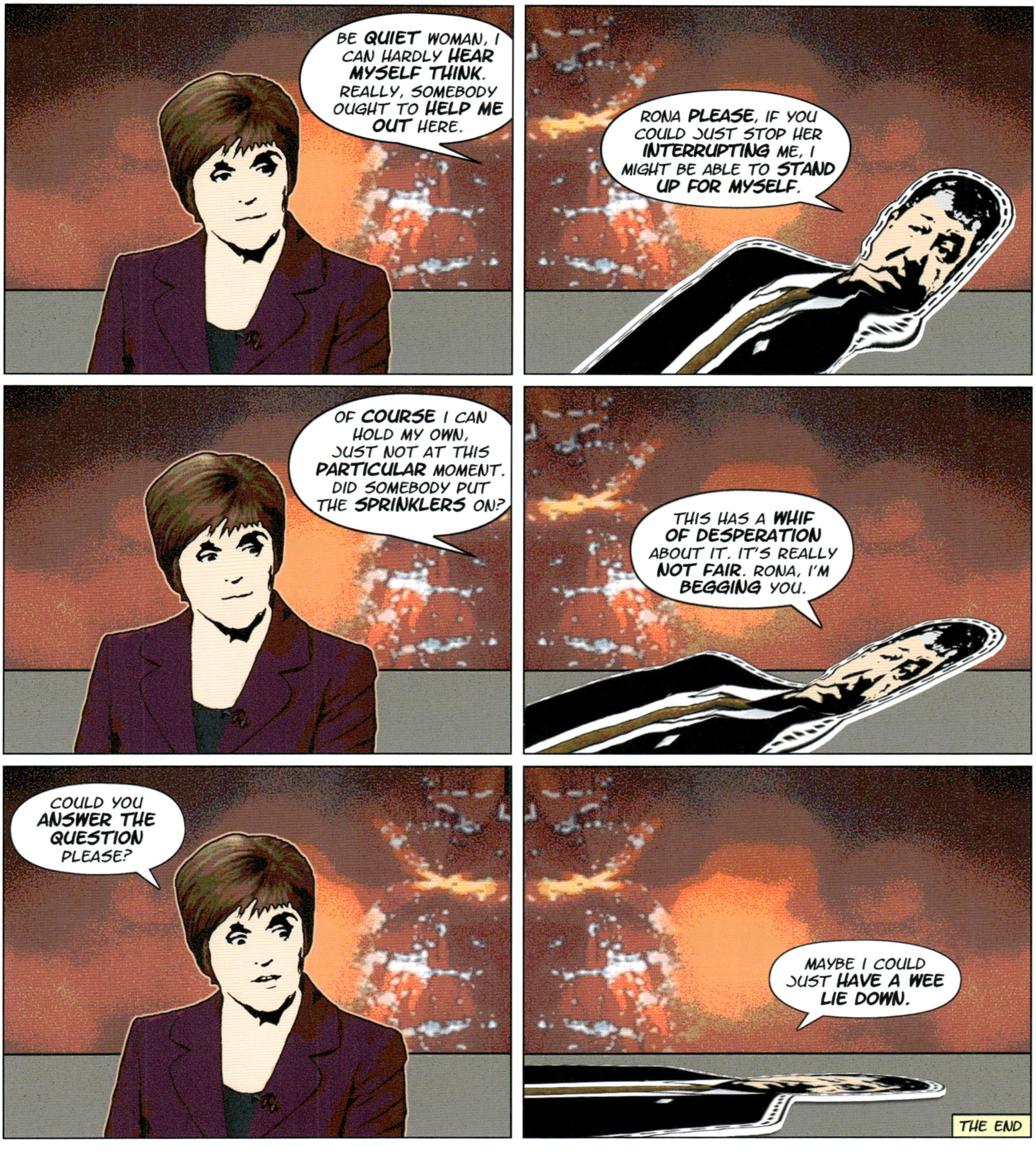
BE QUIET WOMAN, I CAN HARDLY HEAR MYSELF THINK. REALLY, SOMEBODY OUGHT TO HELP ME OUT HERE.
RONA PLEASE, IF YOU COULD JUST STOP HER INTERRUPTING ME, I MIGHT BE ABLE TO STAND UP FOR MYSELF.
OF COURSE I CAN HOLD MY OWN, JUST NOT AT THIS PARTICULAR MOMENT. DID SOMEBODY PUT THE SPRINKLERS ON?
THIS HAS A WHIF OF DESPERATION ABOUT IT. IT'S REALLY NOT FAIR. RONA, I'M BEGGING YOU.
COULD YOU ANSWER THE QUESTION PLEASE?
MAYBE I COULD JUST HAVE A WEE LIE DOWN.
THE END

NATIONALIST PORN

DECEMBER 7TH 2013

Alistair Darling was getting a hard time about his leadership of Better Together and Michael Gove - please god, make it happen - was suggested as a replacement. 'That ANC terrorist chap' was of course Nelson Mandela who died that week. *With Rose Garnett.*

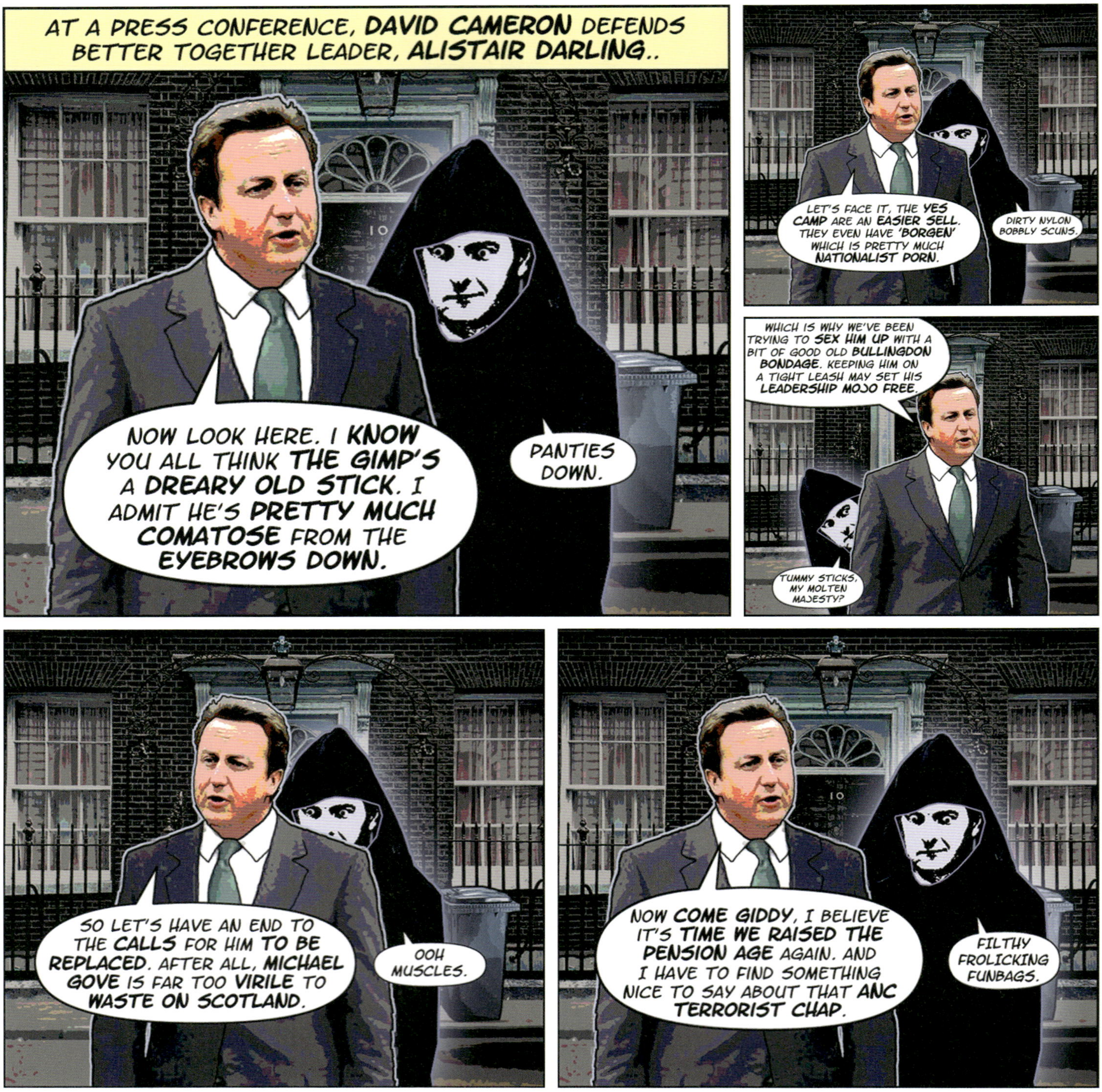

AT A PRESS CONFERENCE, DAVID CAMERON DEFENDS BETTER TOGETHER LEADER, ALISTAIR DARLING..
NOW LOOK HERE. I KNOW YOU ALL THINK THE GIMP'S A DREARY OLD STICK. I ADMIT HE'S PRETTY MUCH COMATOSE FROM THE EYEBROWS DOWN.
PANTIES DOWN.
LET'S FACE IT, THE YES CAMP ARE AN EASIER SELL. THEY EVEN HAVE 'BORGEN' WHICH IS PRETTY MUCH NATIONALIST PORN.
DIRTY NYLON BOBBLY SCUNS.
WHICH IS WHY WE'VE BEEN TRYING TO SEX HIM UP WITH A BIT OF GOOD OLD BULLINGDON BONDAGE. KEEPING HIM ON A TIGHT LEASH MAY SET HIS LEADERSHIP MOJO FREE.
TUMMY STICKS, MY MOLTEN MAJESTY?
SO LET'S HAVE AN END TO THE CALLS FOR HIM TO BE REPLACED. AFTER ALL, MICHAEL GOVE IS FAR TOO VIRILE TO WASTE ON SCOTLAND.
OOH MUSCLES.
NOW COME GIDDY, I BELIEVE IT'S TIME WE RAISED THE PENSION AGE AGAIN. AND I HAVE TO FIND SOMETHING NICE TO SAY ABOUT THAT ANC TERRORIST CHAP.
FILTHY FROLICKING FUNBAGS.

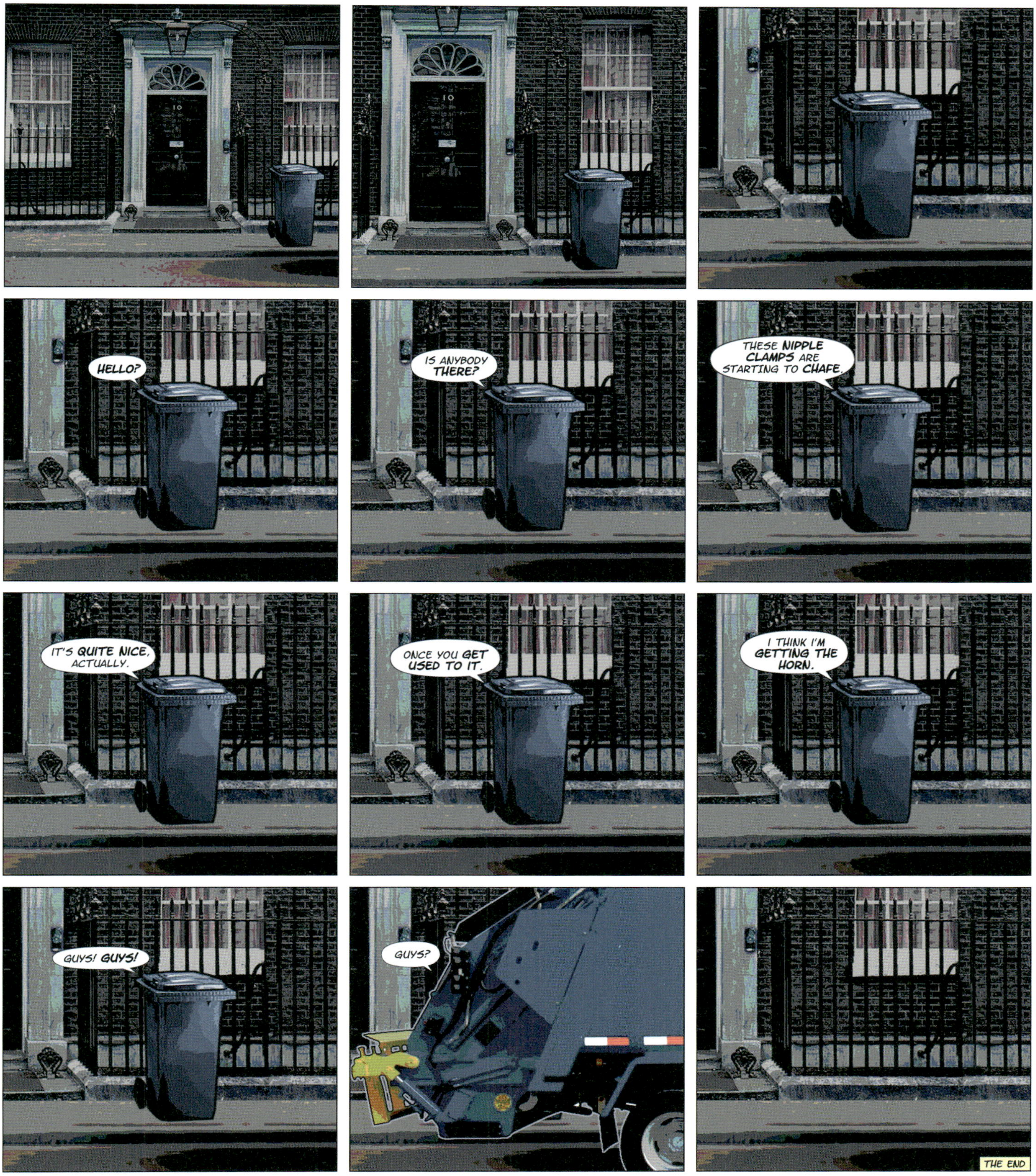
HELLO?
IS ANYBODY THERE?
THESE NIPPLE CLAMPS ARE STARTING TO CHAFE.
IT'S QUITE NICE, ACTUALLY.
ONCE YOU GET USED TO IT.
I THINK I'M GETTING THE HORN.
GUYS! GUYS!
GUYS?
THE END

GREG MOODIE REFUSES TO BE BORED INTO SUBMISSION

DECEMBER 14TH 2013

This was my last cartoon of 2013. I was depressed and exhausted, but it wasn't hard to spot a key tactic of the No campaign: get the debate bogged down in tedious technicalities until the undecideds simply switch off.

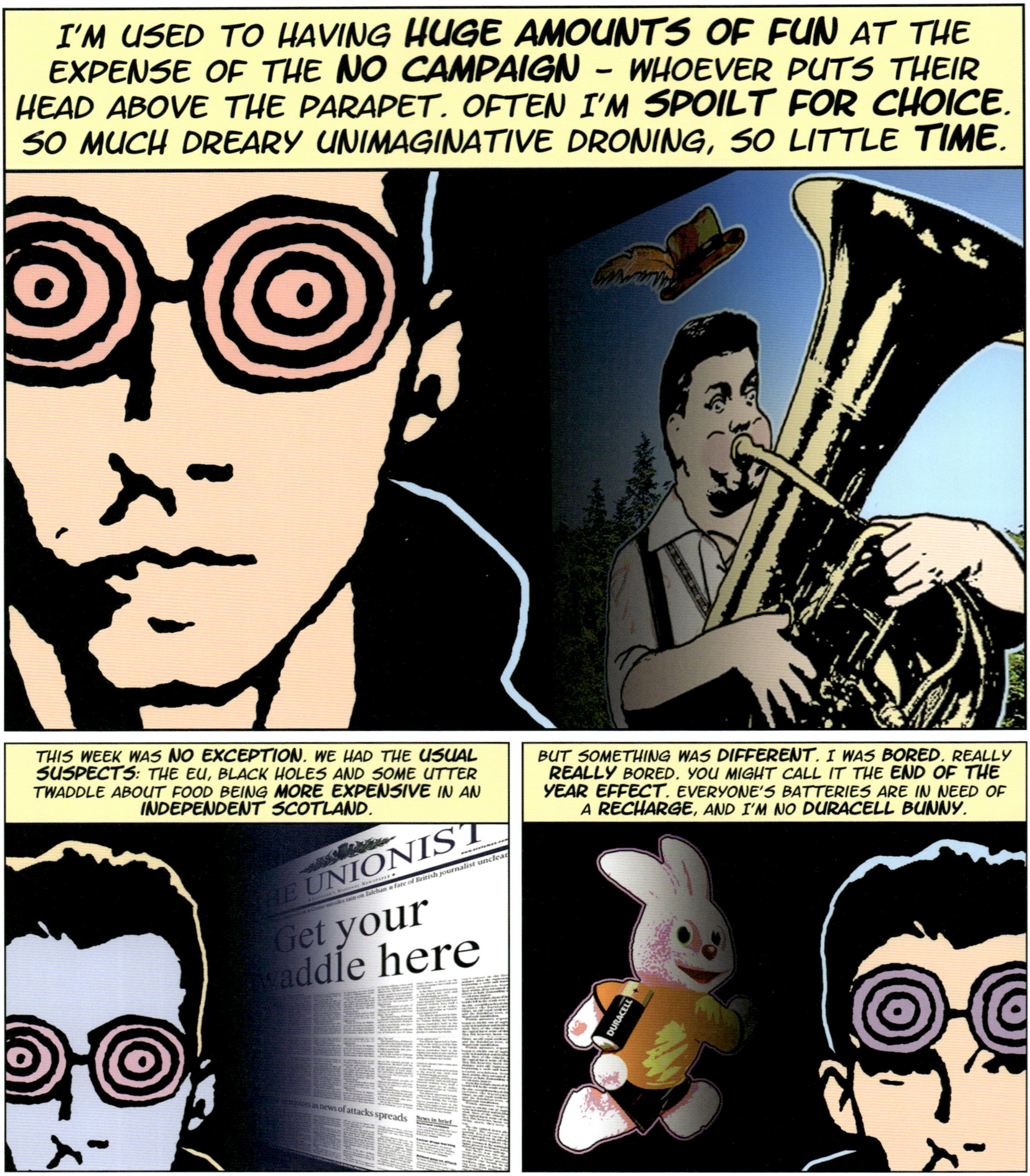
I'M USED TO HAVING HUGE AMOUNTS OF FUN AT THE EXPENSE OF THE NO CAMPAIGN - WHOEVER PUTS THEIR HEAD ABOVE THE PARAPET. OFTEN I'M SPOILT FOR CHOICE. SO MUCH DREARY UNIMAGINATIVE DRONING, SO LITTLE TIME.
THIS WEEK WAS NO EXCEPTION. WE HAD THE USUAL SUSPECTS: THE EU, BLACK HOLES AND SOME UTTER TWADDLE ABOUT FOOD BEING MORE EXPENSIVE IN AN INDEPENDENT SCOTLAND.
UNIONIST
Get your
waddle here
BUT SOMETHING WAS DIFFERENT. I WAS BORED. REALLY REALLY BORED. YOU MIGHT CALL IT THE END OF THE YEAR EFFECT. EVERYONE'S BATTERIES ARE IN NEED OF A RECHARGE, AND I'M NO DURACELL BUNNY.
DURACELL

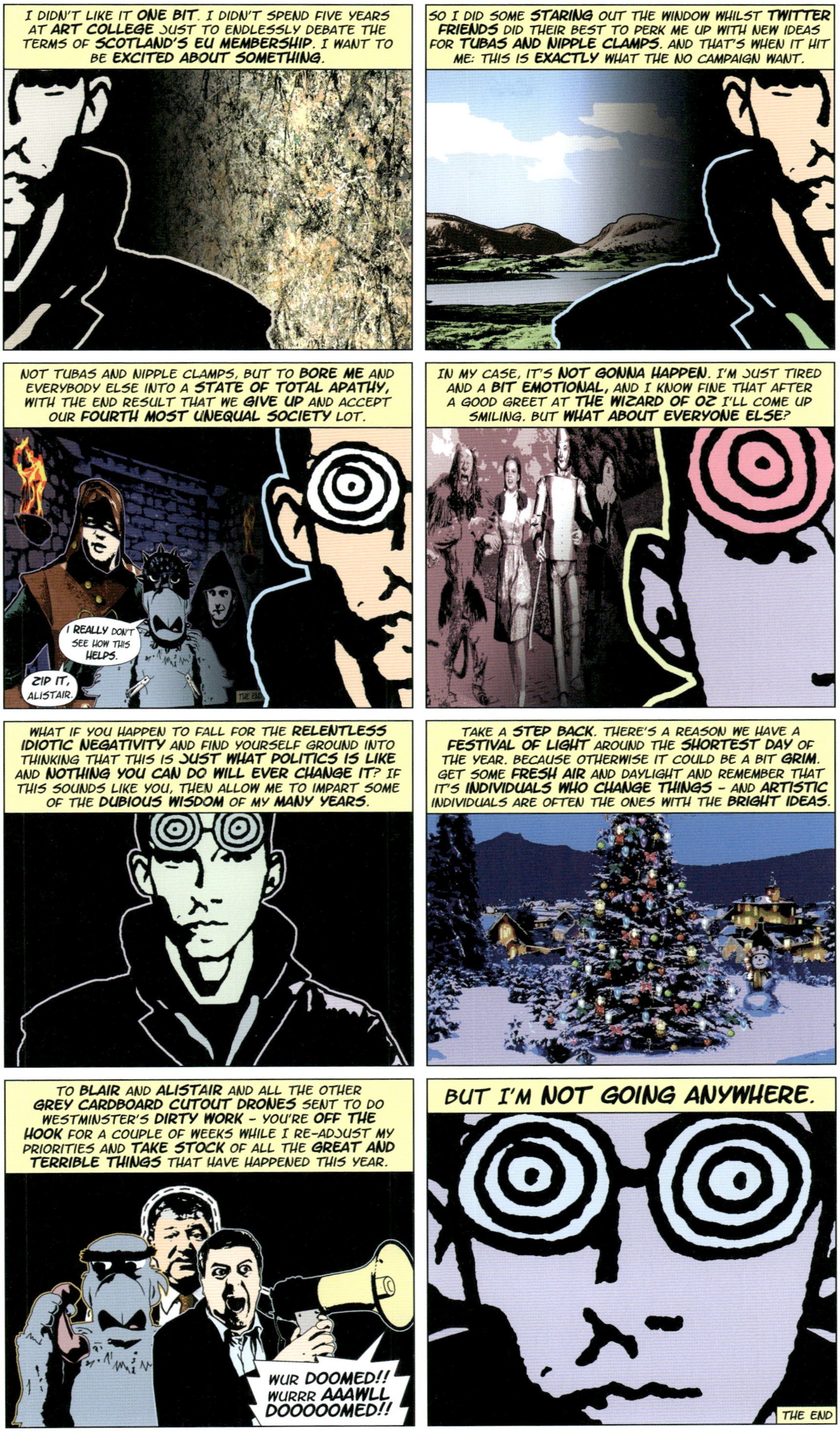
I DIDN'T LIKE IT ONE BIT. I DIDN'T SPEND FIVE YEARS AT ART COLLEGE JUST TO ENDLESSLY DEBATE THE TERMS OF SCOTLAND'S EU MEMBERSHIP. I WANT TO BE EXCITED ABOUT SOMETHING.
SO I DID SOME STARING OUT THE WINDOW WHILST TWITTER FRIENDS DID THEIR BEST TO PERK ME UP WITH NEW IDEAS FOR TUBAS AND NIPPLE CLAMPS. AND THAT'S WHEN IT HIT ME: THIS IS EXACTLY WHAT THE NO CAMPAIGN WANT.
NOT TUBAS AND NIPPLE CLAMPS, BUT TO BORE ME AND EVERYBODY ELSE INTO A STATE OF TOTAL APATHY, WITH THE END RESULT THAT WE GIVE UP AND ACCEPT OUR FOURTH MOST UNEQUAL SOCIETY LOT.
I REALLY DON'T SEE HOW THIS HELPS.
ZIP IT, ALISTAIR.
IN MY CASE, IT'S NOT GONNA HAPPEN. I'M JUST TIRED AND A BIT EMOTIONAL, AND I KNOW FINE THAT AFTER A GOOD GREET AT THE WIZARD OF OZ I'LL COME UP SMILING. BUT WHAT ABOUT EVERYONE ELSE?
WHAT IF YOU HAPPEN TO FALL FOR THE RELENTLESS IDIOTIC NEGATIVITY AND FIND YOURSELF GROUND INTO THINKING THAT THIS IS JUST WHAT POLITICS IS LIKE AND NOTHING YOU CAN DO WILL EVER CHANGE IT? IF THIS SOUNDS LIKE YOU, THEN ALLOW ME TO IMPART SOME OF THE DUBIOUS WISDOM OF MY MANY YEARS.
TAKE A STEP BACK. THERE'S A REASON WE HAVE A FESTIVAL OF LIGHT AROUND THE SHORTEST DAY OF THE YEAR. BECAUSE OTHERWISE IT COULD BE A BIT GRIM. GET SOME FRESH AIR AND DAYLIGHT AND REMEMBER THAT IT'S INDIVIDUALS WHO CHANGE THINGS - AND ARTISTIC INDIVIDUALS ARE OFTEN THE ONES WITH THE BRIGHT IDEAS.
TO BLAIR AND ALISTAIR AND ALL THE OTHER GREY CARDBOARD CUTOUT DRONES SENT TO DO WESTMINSTER'S DIRTY WORK - YOU'RE OFF THE HOOK FOR A COUPLE OF WEEKS WHILE I RE-ADJUST MY PRIORITIES AND TAKE STOCK OF ALL THE GREAT AND TERRIBLE THINGS THAT HAVE HAPPENED THIS YEAR.
WUR DOOMED!! WURRR AAAWLL DOOOOOMED!!
BUT I'M NOT GOING ANYWHERE.
THE END

PLAYING THE SPOONS ON WILLIAM HAGUE'S HEAD

JANUARY 18TH 2014

At the beginning of 2014, I felt so low that I wasn't sure I could go back to cartooning. But then the former UK foreign secretary paid a visit to Scotland, and all I could think of was what it would be like to play the spoons on his head.

GREG **STRUGGLES** TO FIND ANY POINT TO **WILLIAM HAGUE'S** VISIT TO **SCOTLAND**, OR INDEED TO **WILLIAM HAGUE**, AND DECIDES TO **PHOTOBOMB** THE UK FOREIGN SECRETARY IN A **MOST UNORTHODOX MANNER**..

..BLAH BLAH INDEPENDENT **SCOTLAND** WILL HAVE TO PAY BILLIONS TO **THE EU** JUST TO AVOID THE **NAUGHTY CHAIR**..

IN WILLY WE TRUST

MR. HAGUE HAS ALWAYS PREVIOUSLY BEEN CONSIDERED "**TOO IRRELEVANT FOR CARTOONS**," BUT GREG HAS NEVER BEEN ONE TO **SHY AWAY** FROM A CHALLENGE. HE **BEGINS** BY **TUNING HIS INSTRUMENTS**..

BONG!

..BLAH BLAH **SCHENGEN AGREEMENT**..

DECLARING THE SPOONS '**SLIGHTLY SHARP** BUT **GOOD ENOUGH FOR HIS PURPOSES**', HE SETS OFF AT A GENTLE PACE WITH THE **OPENING STANZAS** OF RAVEL'S '**BOLERO**'..

TAP-TAPPITY-TAP TAPPITY-TAP-TAP-TAP TAPPITY-TAP-TAPPITY TAPPITY-TAPPITY!

..BLAH BLAH **BORDER CONTROLS**..

ADOPTING A **SECOND SPOON** FOR THE ALTOGETHER MORE CHALLENGING '**MY OLD MAN'S A DUSTMAN**', HE BEGINS TO FIND HIS **RHYTHM** AND SUGGESTS THAT HE 'MAY BE PERFORMING AT THE **PEAK OF HIS POWERS**'..

RING-TACKA TACKA-TACKA!

..BLAH BLAH **WOULD HAVE TO REAPPLY**..

AT THIS POINT, THE **FOREIGN SECRETARY** BECOMES **SUSPICIOUS.** HE BELIEVES SOMEONE MIGHT BE **PLAYING THE SPOONS** ON HIS **HEAD,** BUT DECIDES TO CONTINUE, AS HE FEELS HE IS GETTING THROUGH TO THE **20–STRONG CROWD.**

RING-TACKA TACKA-TACKA!

IF I DIDN'T **KNOW** ANY **BETTER,** I MIGHT THINK SOMEONE WAS **PLAYING** THE **SPOONS** ON MY **HEAD.**

UNFORTUNATELY, AFTER A **STIRRING RENDITION** OF 'FLIGHT OF THE **BUMBLEBEE',** GREG BEGINS TO EXPERIENCE **NUMBNESS** – NOT IN HIS HANDS, BUT IN HIS **BRAIN,** AS THE **INCESSANT HAGUE DRONE** TAKES ITS TOLL..

DIDDLY-DIDDLY DIDDLY-DIDDLY!

..BLAH BLAH **SEPARATION..** UNCERTAINTY..

THE **CONSUMMATE MUSICIAN** RETIRES, EXHAUSTED FROM THE **SHEER TEDIUM,** HIS **INSTRUMENTS** BY NOW **SIZZLING HOT..**

..BLAH BLAH **RENEGOTIATED TERMS..**

APART FROM A **BIT** OF A **HEADACHE,** I THINK THAT WENT **QUITE WELL..**

THE END.

JIM MURPHY: CYBERNAT DETECTOR

JANUARY 25TH 2014

In a piece for the Daily Mail, Jim Murphy MP suggested that audiences at public meetings and television debates should be vetted in order to weed out so-called cybernats. The Daily Mail went on to write a semi-regular 'Cybernat Watch' column.

GREG TRIES TO ATTEND A LOCAL EDITION OF QUESTION TIME, BUT THE ALL-POWERFUL DAILY MAIL HAS FORCED BROADCASTERS TO EMPLOY JIM MURPHY MP TO WEED OUT 'CYBERNATS' FROM ALL TV DEBATE AUDIENCES..
JUST A MINUTE, SONNY..
YES?
HAVE YOU EVER WORN TARTAN TROUSERS?
CERTAINLY NOT. I'M FROM DUNDEE.
DO YOU OWN ANY RUNRIG RECORDS?
ONLY 'SMACK MY BITCH UP'.
DO YOU HAVE A RELIGIOUS TITLE AND A WEBSITE THAT RHYMES WITH 'PINGS OVER SCOTLAND'?
YOU'RE THINKING OF BELLA CALEDONIA.

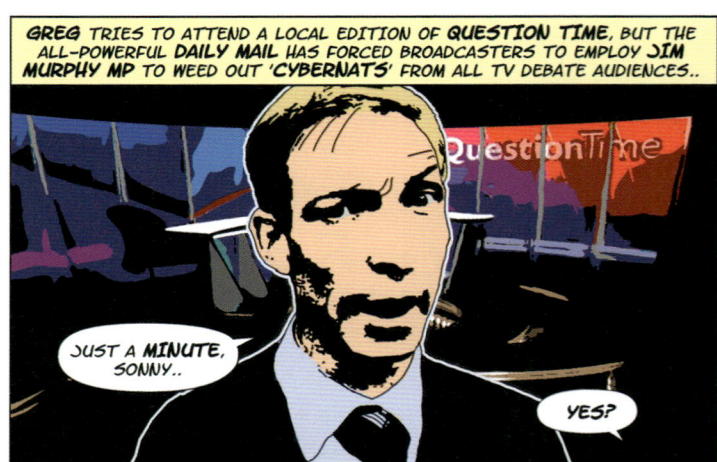

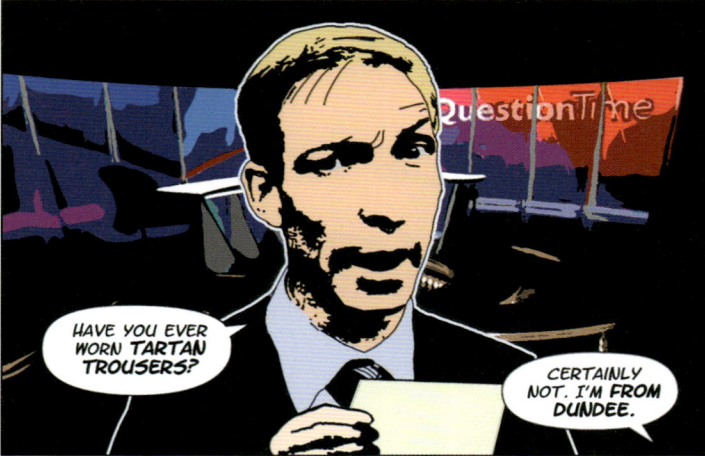

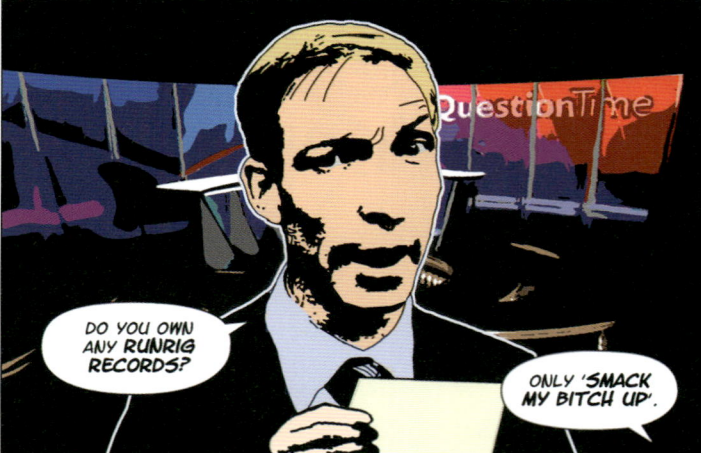

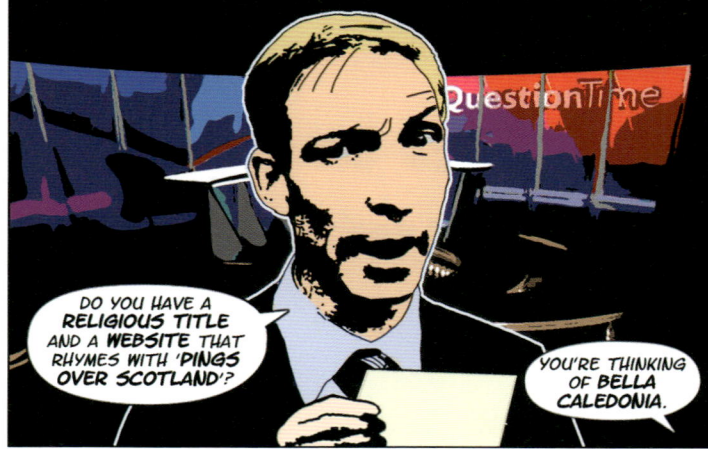

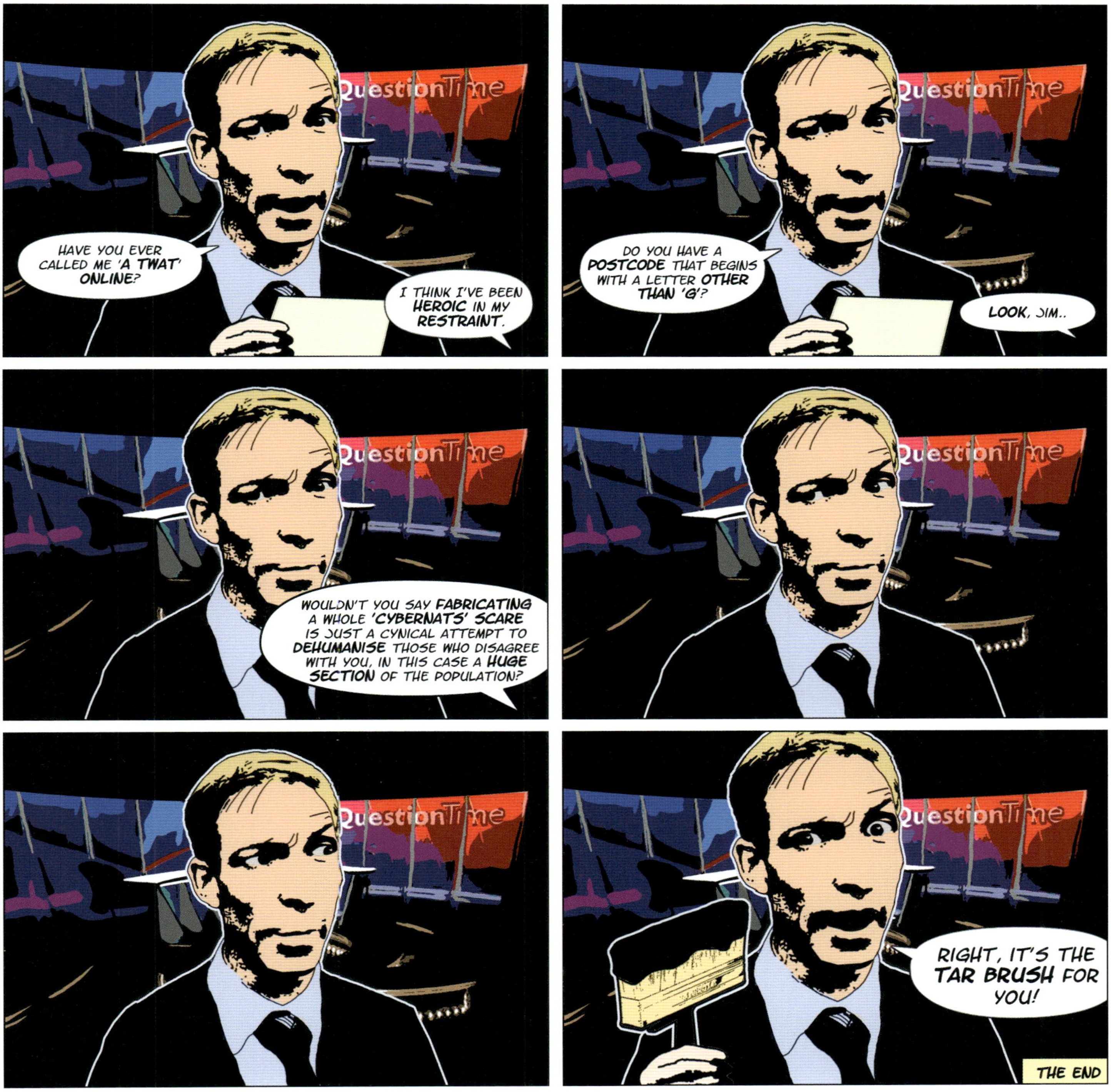
HAVE YOU EVER CALLED ME 'A TWAT' ONLINE?
I THINK I'VE BEEN HEROIC IN MY RESTRAINT.
DO YOU HAVE A POSTCODE THAT BEGINS WITH A LETTER OTHER THAN 'G'?
LOOK, JIM..
WOULDN'T YOU SAY FABRICATING A WHOLE 'CYBERNATS' SCARE IS JUST A CYNICAL ATTEMPT TO DEHUMANISE THOSE WHO DISAGREE WITH YOU, IN THIS CASE A HUGE SECTION OF THE POPULATION?
RIGHT, IT'S THE TAR BRUSH FOR YOU!
THE END

WEE THINGS WITH JOHANN LAMONT

FEBRUARY 1ST 2014

When Westminster ruled out a currency union, Johann had the chance to make things difficult for Alex Salmond at First Minister's Questions. Instead, she clutched defeat from the jaws of victory with 'wee things'. A Labour Party spokesman later described it as a 'slip of the tongue'.

JOHANN DESCRIBES THE CONTROL OF NUCLEAR WEAPONS, BEDROOM TAX, FOREIGN POLICY, CHILDCARE, MINIMUM WAGE AND A HUGE RAFT OF ECONOMIC LEVERS AS "WEE THINGS" OFFERED BY INDEPENDENCE. HERE, GREG INVITES THE LEADER OF THE LABOUR PARTY IN SCOTLAND TO EXTRAPOLATE FURTHER..
THIS IS AN ELEPHANT. IT'S NOT THAT BIG REALLY WHEN YOU THINK ABOUT IT. THEY USED TO HAVE ONE AT THE ZOO AND IT WASN'T ALL THAT IMPRESSIVE.
GIANT HAYSTACKS. A MERE SLIP OF A MAN. WRESTLERS NOWADAYS ARE MUCH BIGGER. I'VE SEEN THEM LIKE TWENTY FEET HIGH. I LIKE THE WRESTLING.
BUCKINGHAM PALACE. I SUPPOSE IT'S QUITE BIG FOR A HOUSE, BUT I THINK YOU'D PROBABLY GROW INTO IT IF YOU LIVED THERE. ONCE I'M QUEEN, I'LL LET YOU KNOW.
THE NORTH SEA'S TOTALLY OVER-RATED. I MEAN, SET IT ALONGSIDE THE ARABIAN OR EVEN THE MEDITERRANEAN AND YOU'LL SEE IT'S NO OCEAN. I SWAM IT ONCE.

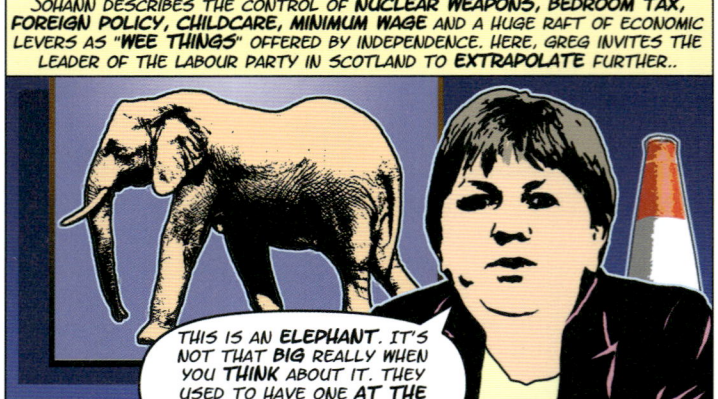

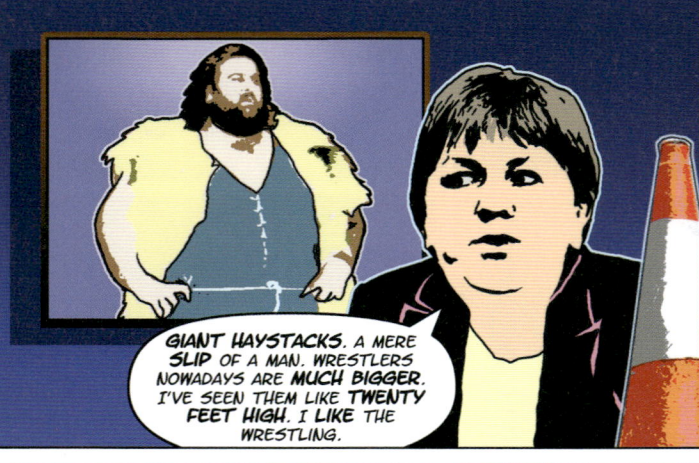

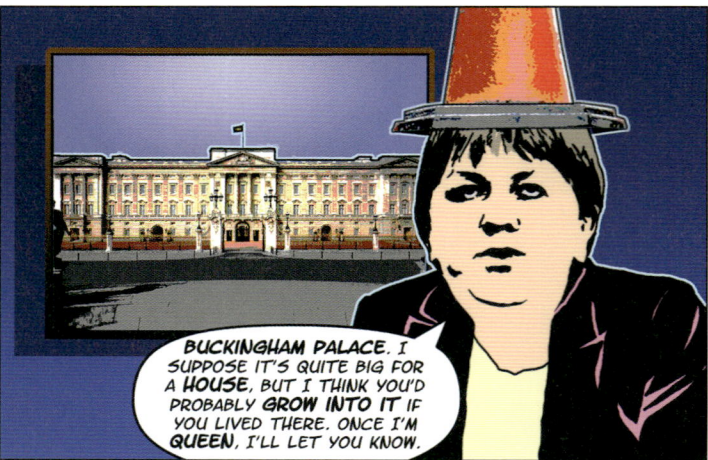

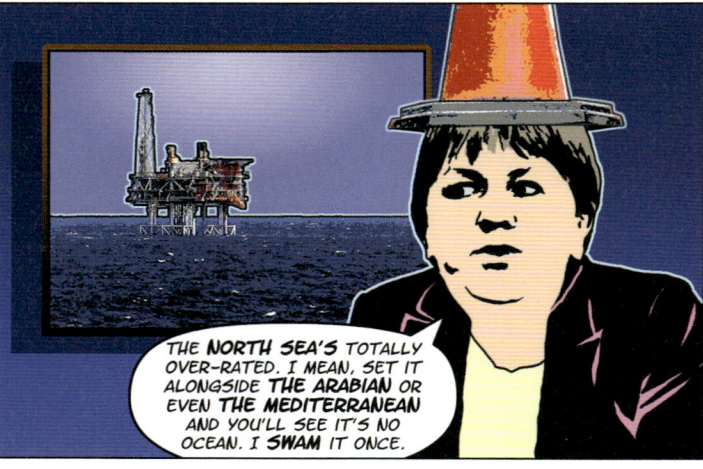

THE GRAND CANYON. IT MIGHT BE GRAND BUT IT'S ACTUALLY QUITE WEE. YOU COULD WALK IT IN ABOUT TEN MINUTES. I DID IT IN NINE, DOOR TO DOOR.
MOUNT EVEREST. SEE HOW THERE'S A MAN IN FRONT OF IT? IT'S ONLY A WEE BIT BIGGER THAN HIM. I COULD CLIMB IT TODAY IF I WANTED TO.
THE UNIVERSE. I DON'T REALLY SEE WHAT THE BIG HAIRY DEAL IS. ALL THESE PLANETS AND THINGS ARE TINY. EVEN IF IT IS EXPANDING, IT'S GOT A GOOD BIT TO GO YET.
THE LABOUR PARTY IN SCOTLAND HAVE SINCE INFORMED US THAT THIS ENTIRE SPEECH WAS A SLIP OF THE TONGUE.
THE END.

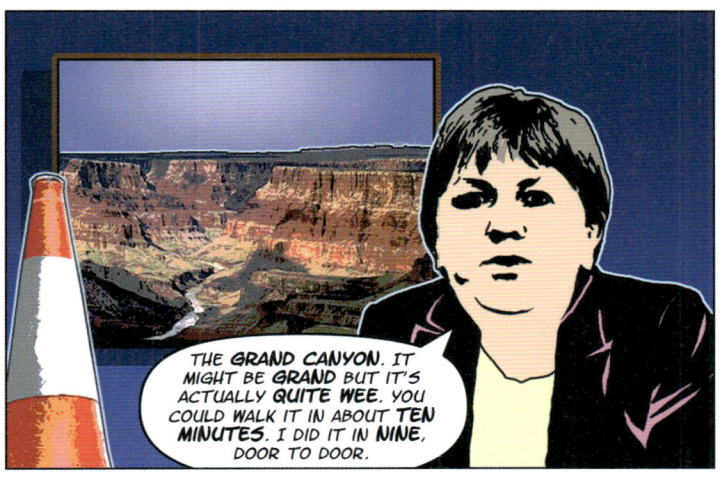

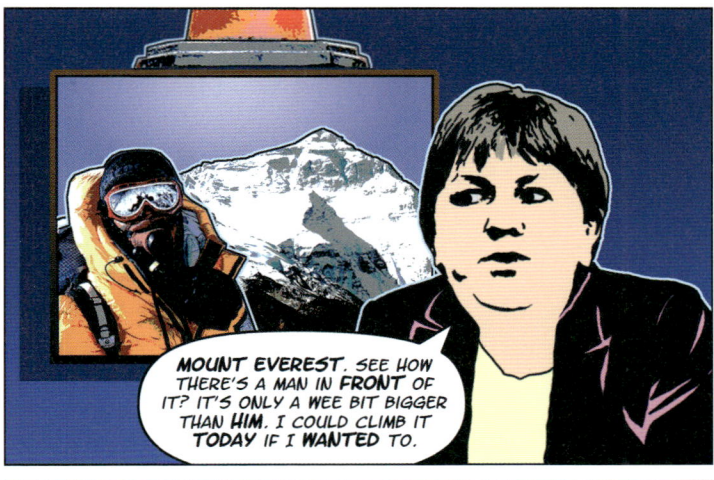

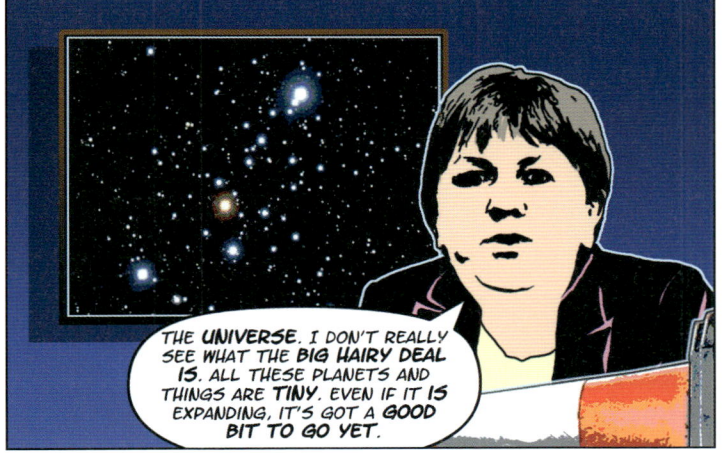

DAVID CAMERON APPEALS TO SCOTLAND. OR NOT.

FEBRUARY 8TH 2014

Cameron knew there was no economic argument for Scotland to remain in the UK, and playing heavy wasn't having the desired effect. So he decided to hark back to the Olympic Games. I thought he might as well have done it in verse, with Land of Hope and Glory in the background.

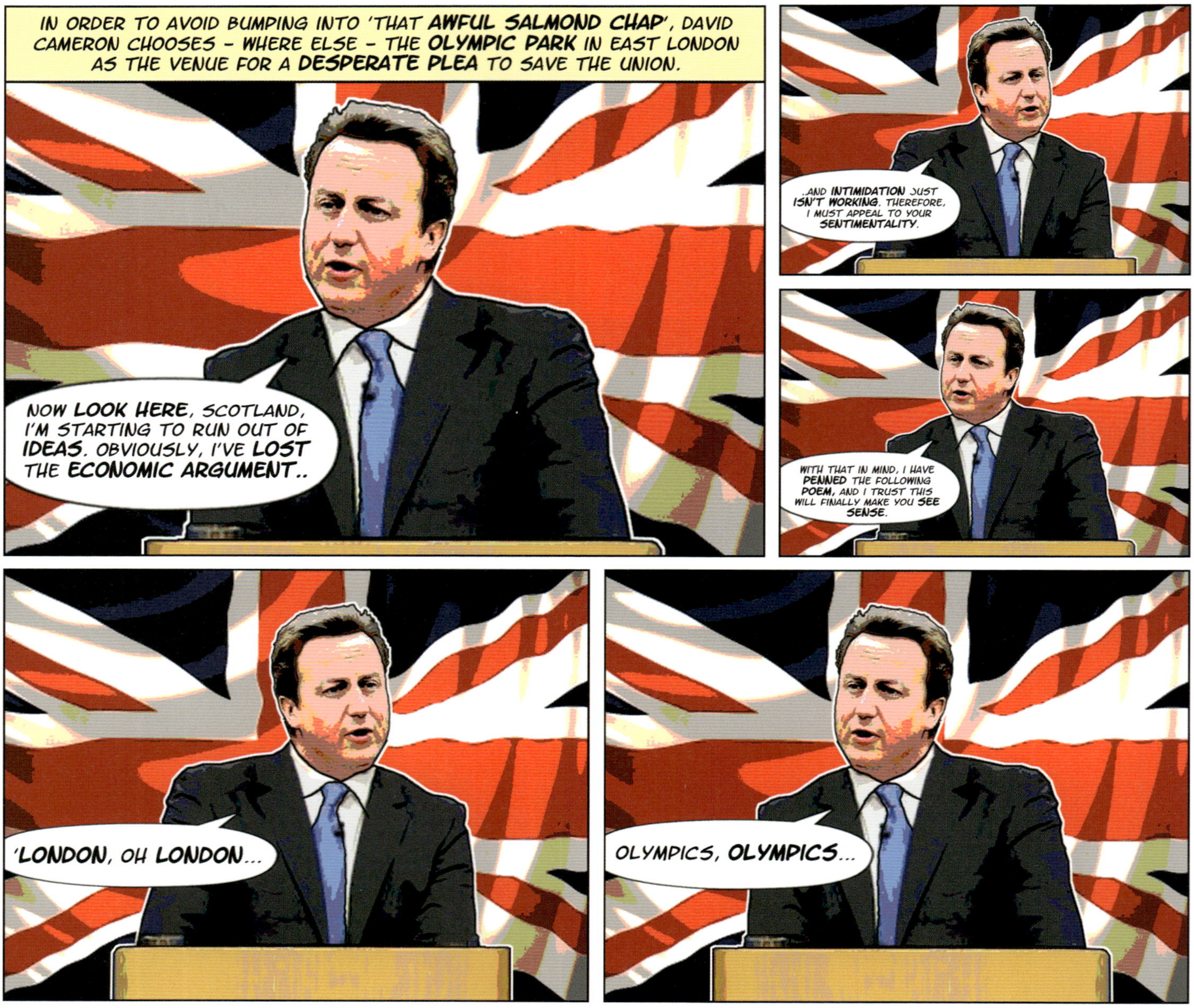

IN ORDER TO AVOID BUMPING INTO 'THAT AWFUL SALMOND CHAP', DAVID CAMERON CHOOSES – WHERE ELSE – THE OLYMPIC PARK IN EAST LONDON AS THE VENUE FOR A DESPERATE PLEA TO SAVE THE UNION.
NOW LOOK HERE, SCOTLAND, I'M STARTING TO RUN OUT OF IDEAS. OBVIOUSLY, I'VE LOST THE ECONOMIC ARGUMENT..
..AND INTIMIDATION JUST ISN'T WORKING. THEREFORE, I MUST APPEAL TO YOUR SENTIMENTALITY.
WITH THAT IN MIND, I HAVE PENNED THE FOLLOWING POEM, AND I TRUST THIS WILL FINALLY MAKE YOU SEE SENSE.
'LONDON, OH LONDON...
OLYMPICS, OLYMPICS...

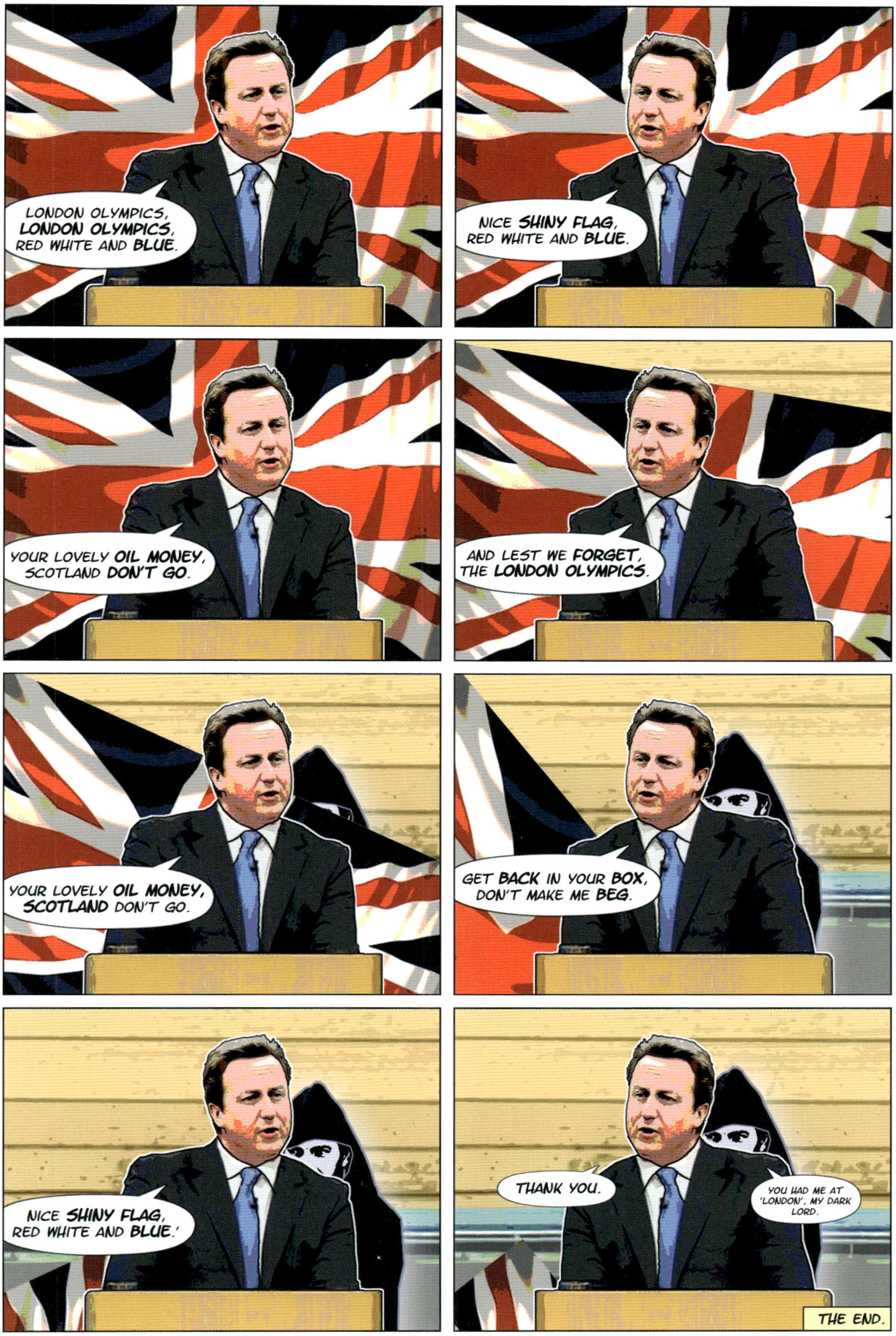
LONDON OLYMPICS, LONDON OLYMPICS, RED WHITE AND BLUE.
NICE SHINY FLAG, RED WHITE AND BLUE.
YOUR LOVELY OIL MONEY, SCOTLAND DON'T GO.
AND LEST WE FORGET, THE LONDON OLYMPICS.
YOUR LOVELY OIL MONEY, SCOTLAND DON'T GO.
GET BACK IN YOUR BOX, DON'T MAKE ME BEG.
NICE SHINY FLAG, RED WHITE AND BLUE.'
THANK YOU.
YOU HAD ME AT 'LONDON', MY DARK LORD.
THE END.

A VERY ODD CHANCELLOR

FEBRUARY 15TH 2014

"It would be a very odd chancellor that insisted on a course of action that cost their own businesses hundreds of millions of pounds, that blew a massive hole in their balance of payments and would potentially leave the rest of the UK shouldering the entirety of UK debt." – Nicola Sturgeon.

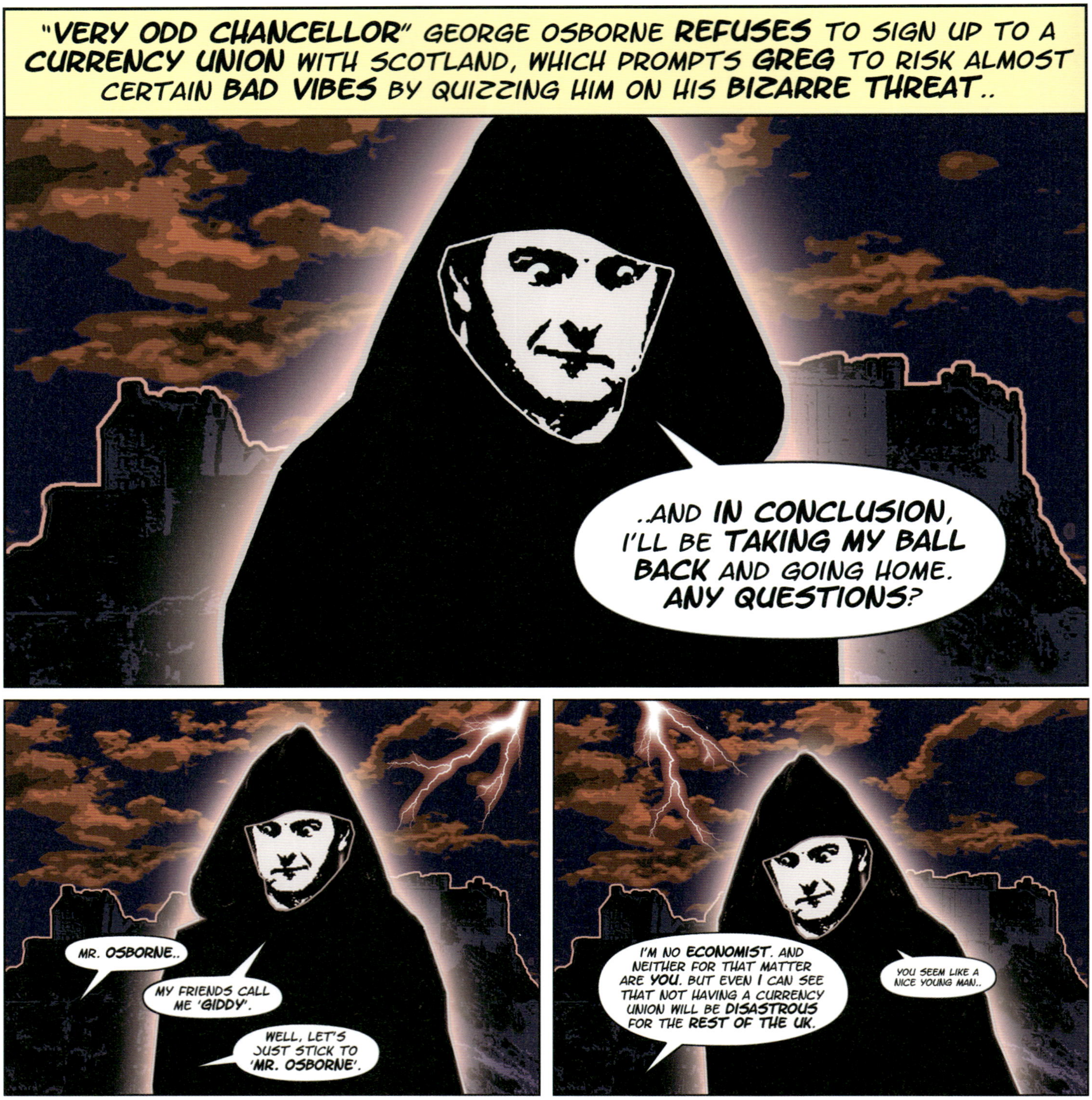

"VERY ODD CHANCELLOR" GEORGE OSBORNE REFUSES TO SIGN UP TO A CURRENCY UNION WITH SCOTLAND, WHICH PROMPTS GREG TO RISK ALMOST CERTAIN BAD VIBES BY QUIZZING HIM ON HIS BIZARRE THREAT..
..AND IN CONCLUSION, I'LL BE TAKING MY BALL BACK AND GOING HOME. ANY QUESTIONS?
MR. OSBORNE..
MY FRIENDS CALL ME 'GIDDY'.
WELL, LET'S JUST STICK TO 'MR. OSBORNE'.
I'M NO ECONOMIST. AND NEITHER FOR THAT MATTER ARE YOU. BUT EVEN I CAN SEE THAT NOT HAVING A CURRENCY UNION WILL BE DISASTROUS FOR THE REST OF THE UK.
YOU SEEM LIKE A NICE YOUNG MAN..

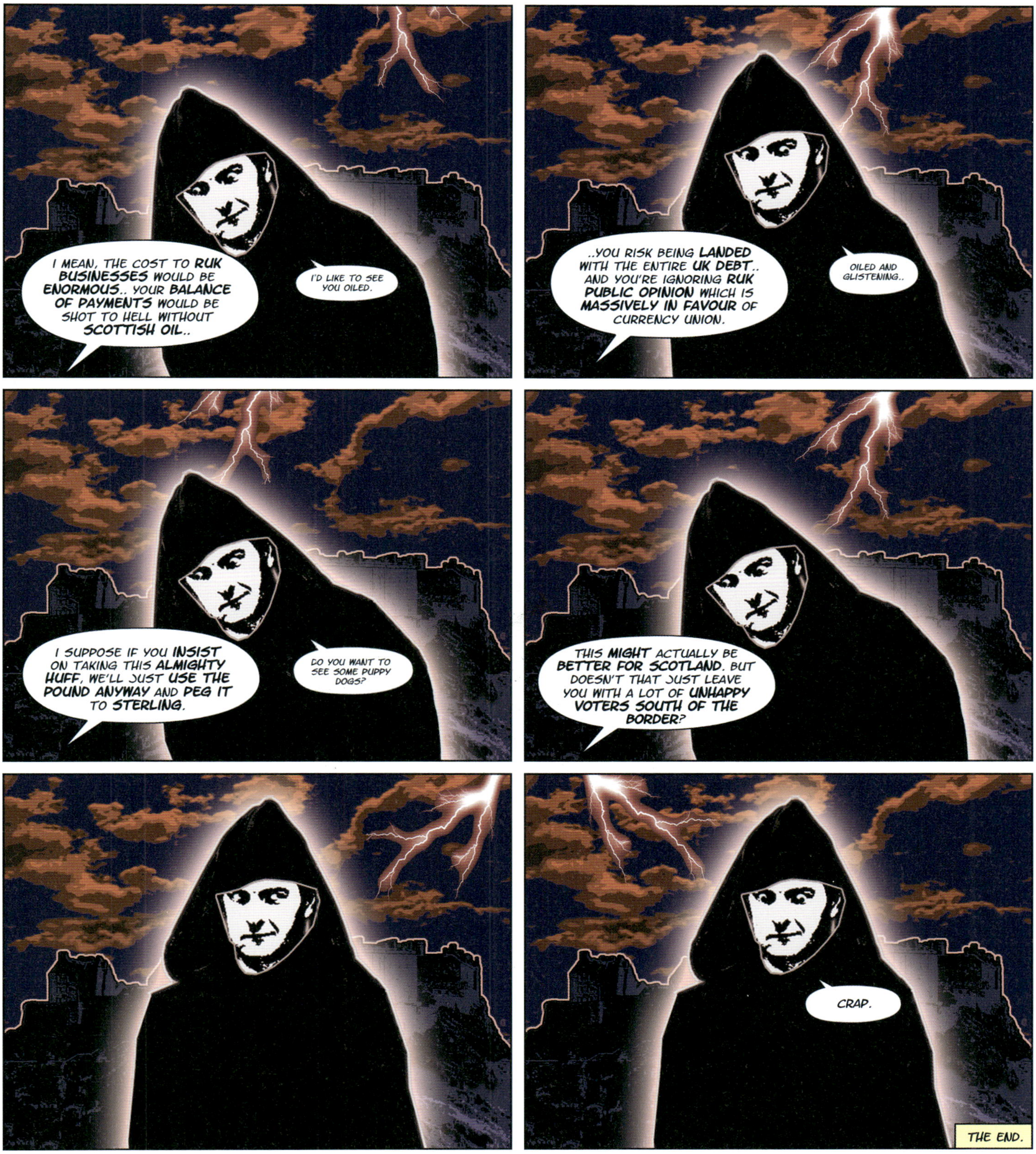

I MEAN, THE COST TO RUK BUSINESSES WOULD BE ENORMOUS.. YOUR BALANCE OF PAYMENTS WOULD BE SHOT TO HELL WITHOUT SCOTTISH OIL..
I'D LIKE TO SEE YOU OILED.
..YOU RISK BEING LANDED WITH THE ENTIRE UK DEBT.. AND YOU'RE IGNORING RUK PUBLIC OPINION WHICH IS MASSIVELY IN FAVOUR OF CURRENCY UNION.
OILED AND GLISTENING..
I SUPPOSE IF YOU INSIST ON TAKING THIS ALMIGHTY HUFF, WE'LL JUST USE THE POUND ANYWAY AND PEG IT TO STERLING.
DO YOU WANT TO SEE SOME PUPPY DOGS?
THIS MIGHT ACTUALLY BE BETTER FOR SCOTLAND. BUT DOESN'T THAT JUST LEAVE YOU WITH A LOT OF UNHAPPY VOTERS SOUTH OF THE BORDER?
CRAP.
THE END.

GROUND CONTROL TO MAJOR TOM

FEBRUARY 22ND 2014

When David Bowie relayed a message from his home in New York urging Scots to 'stay with us', I recalled the closing section of Space Oddity. Major Tom, already distant, loses contact with ground control altogether and gradually disappears into infinity.

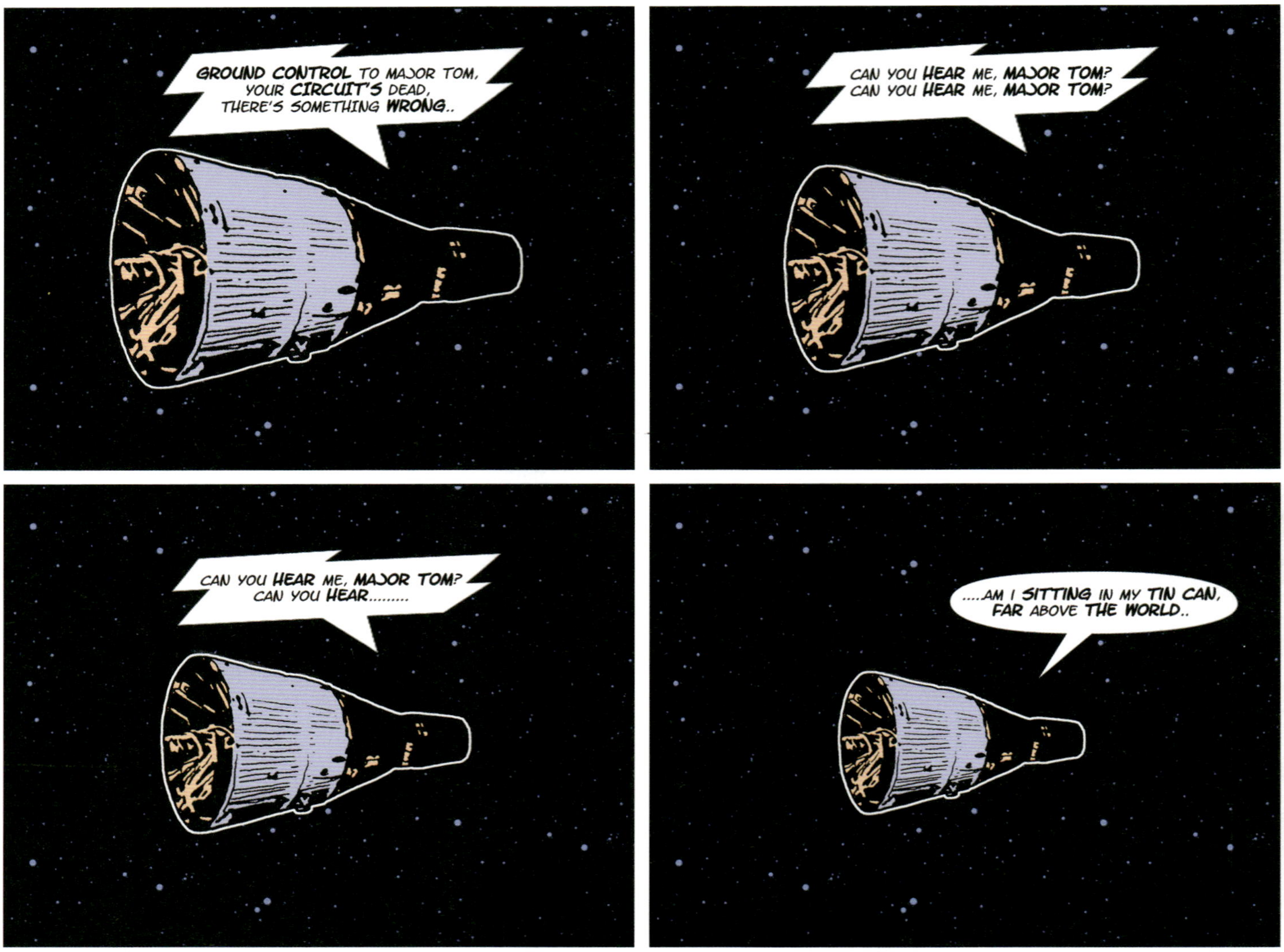
GROUND CONTROL TO MAJOR TOM, YOUR CIRCUIT'S DEAD, THERE'S SOMETHING WRONG..
CAN YOU HEAR ME, MAJOR TOM? CAN YOU HEAR ME, MAJOR TOM?
CAN YOU HEAR ME, MAJOR TOM? CAN YOU HEAR.........
....AM I SITTING IN MY TIN CAN, FAR ABOVE THE WORLD..

PLANET EARTH IS BLUE, AND THERE'S NOTHING I CAN DO..
CHING-A-CHING A-CHING A-CHING-CHING!*
* C, F, G, A. I KNEW MY PERFECT PITCH WOULD COME IN HANDY SOMEDAY.
CHING-A-CHING A-CHING A-CHING-CHING!
AT THIS POINT, DAVID REACHES FOR HIS STYLOPHONE..
WEEEEEE! WEEE WEEE WEEE!
IF I WAS DAVID BOWIE, I PROBABLY WOULDN'T KNOW ANYTHING ABOUT SCOTTISH INDEPENDENCE EITHER. IT'S OK, DAVID. I STILL LOVE YOU. THE END.

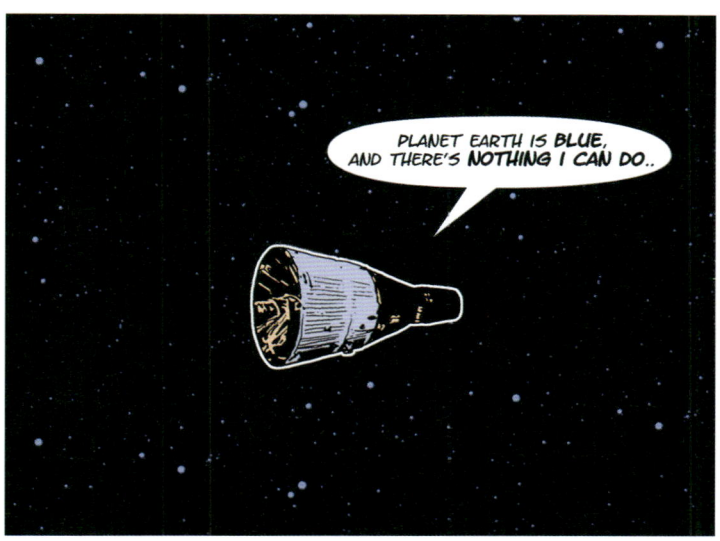

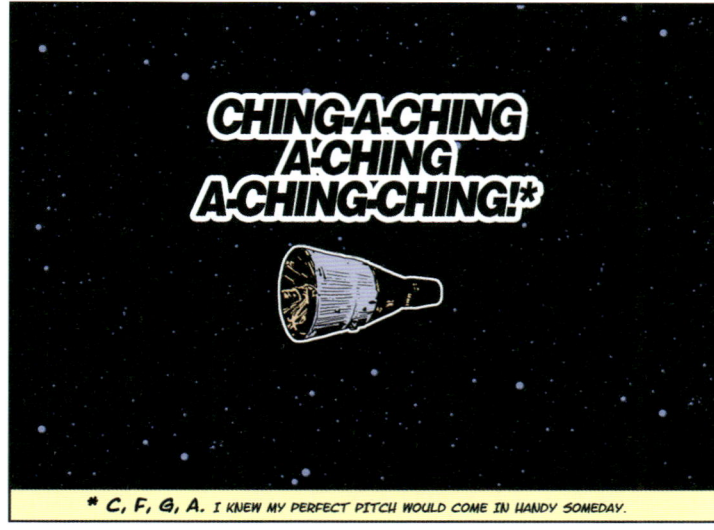

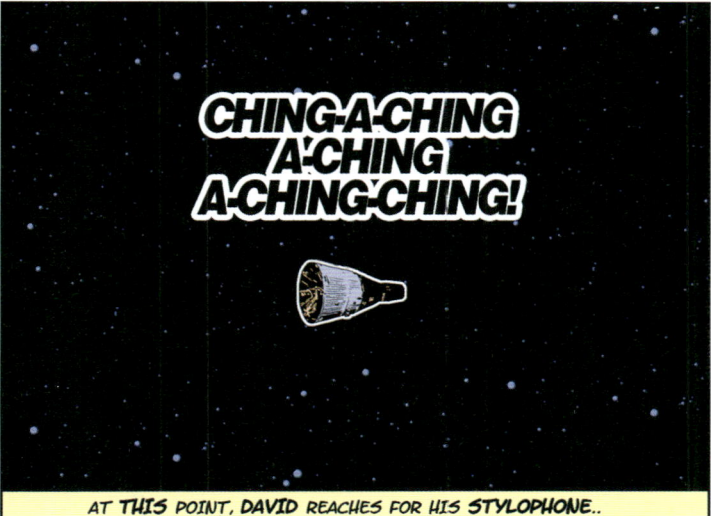

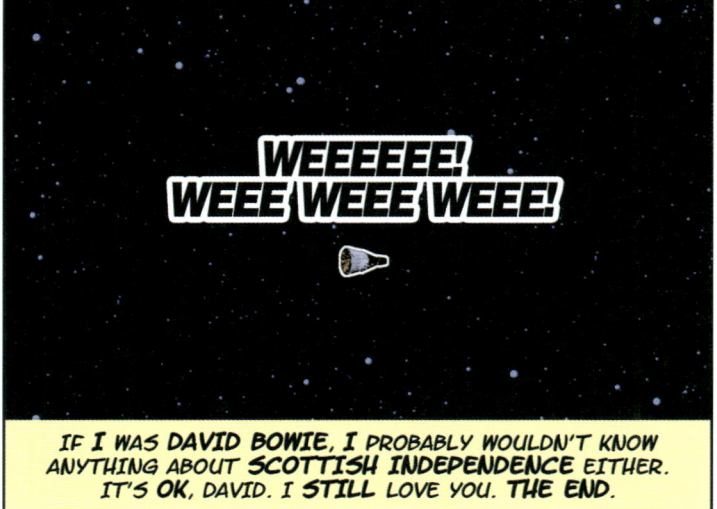

BLAIR MCDOUGALL INTRODUCES THE ZINE

MARCH 1ST 2014

I was largely responsible for the National Collective Zine, in that I commissioned most of the work and assembled it. The idea was to show a side of the artists' movement that hadn't really been seen - visual art and literature - as well as to introduce the Michael Gove punch bag.

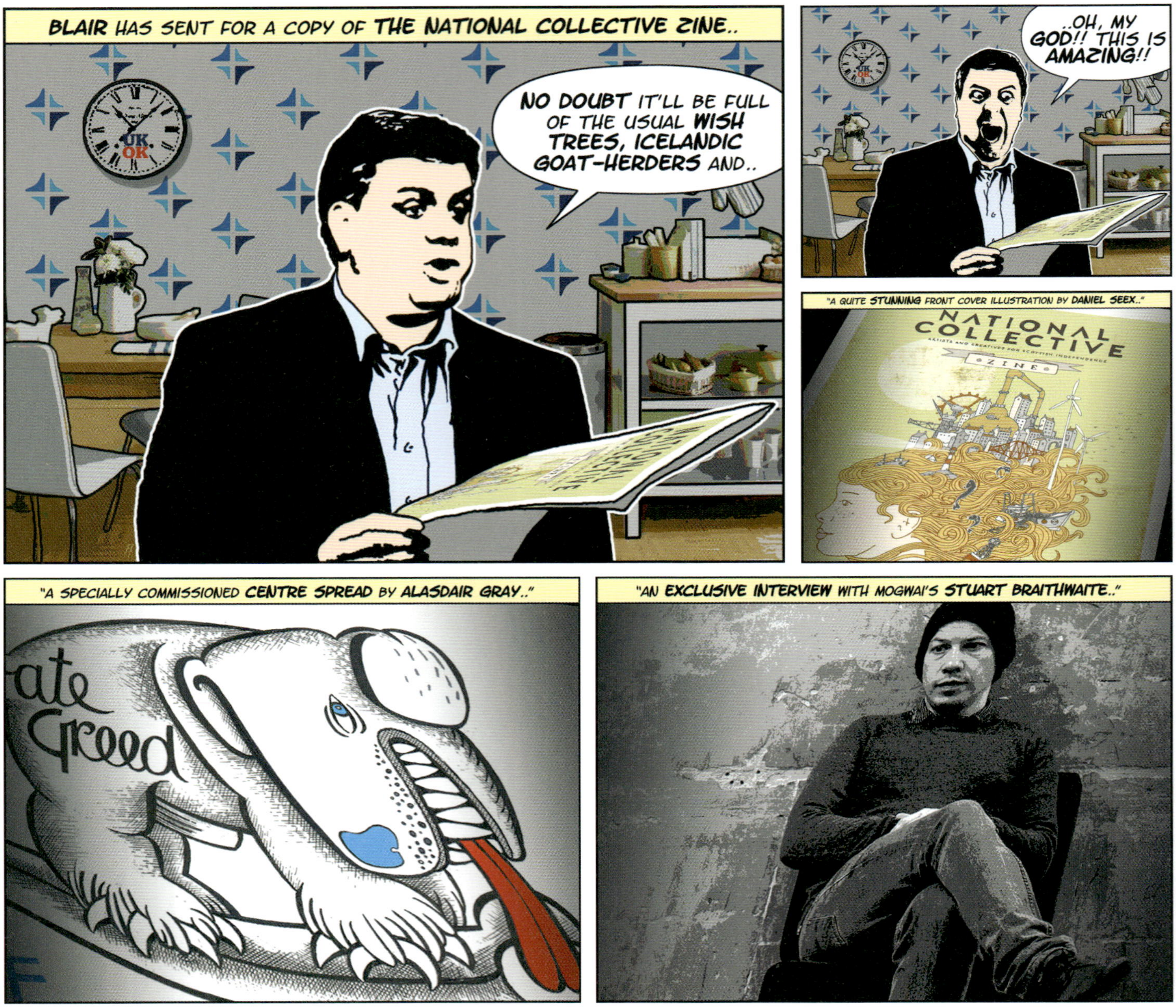

BLAIR HAS SENT FOR A COPY OF THE NATIONAL COLLECTIVE ZINE..
UK OK
NO DOUBT IT'LL BE FULL OF THE USUAL WISH TREES, ICELANDIC GOAT-HERDERS AND..
..OH, MY GOD!! THIS IS AMAZING!!
"A QUITE STUNNING FRONT COVER ILLUSTRATION BY DANIEL SEEX.."
NATIONAL COLLECTIVE
ZINE
"A SPECIALLY COMMISSIONED CENTRE SPREAD BY ALASDAIR GRAY.."
ate Greed
"AN EXCLUSIVE INTERVIEW WITH MOGWAI'S STUART BRAITHWAITE.."

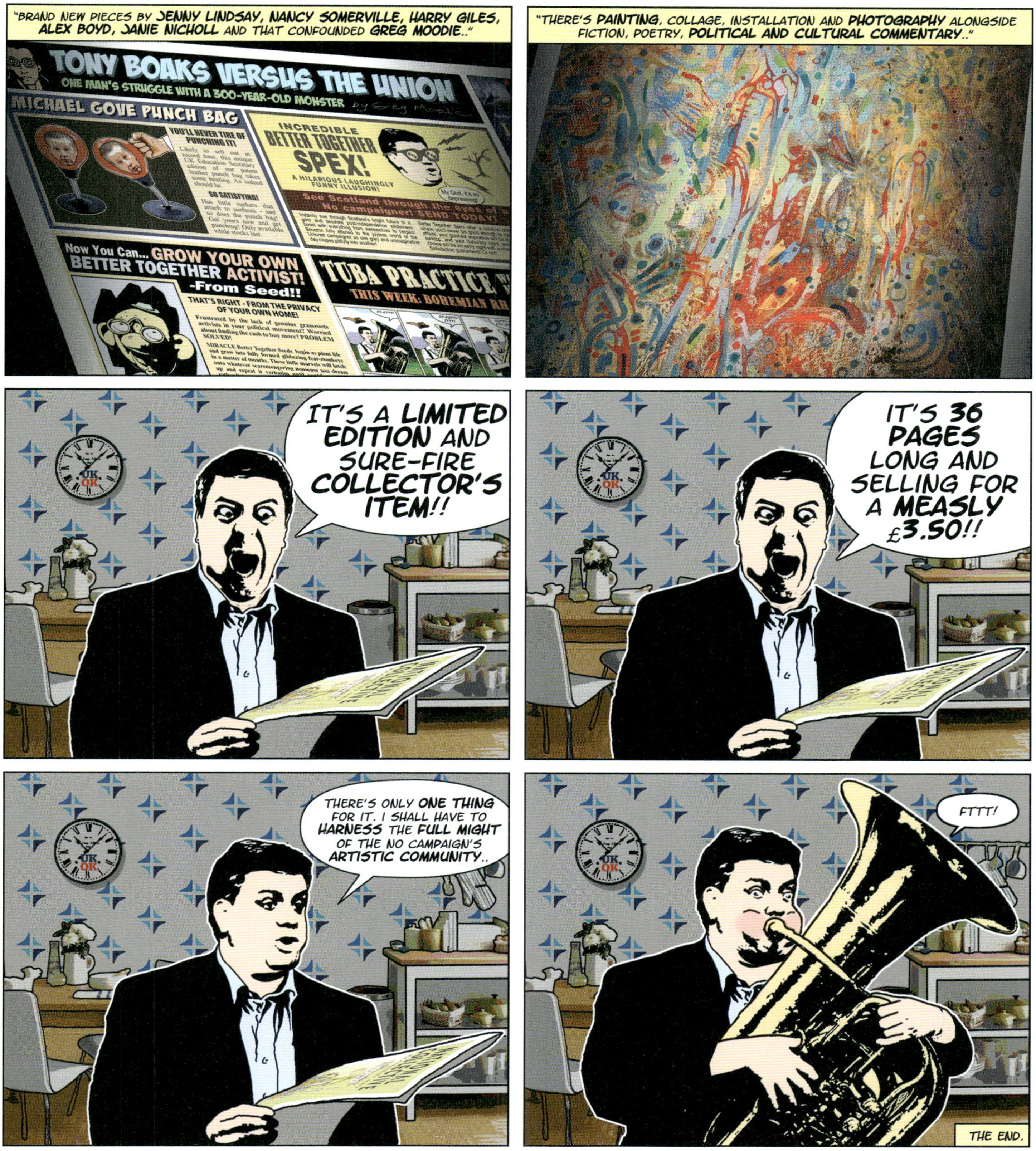
"BRAND NEW PIECES BY JENNY LINDSAY, NANCY SOMERVILLE, HARRY GILES, ALEX BOYD, JANIE NICHOLL AND THAT CONFOUNDED GREG MOODIE.."
TONY BOAKS VERSUS THE UNION
ONE MAN'S STRUGGLE WITH A 300-YEAR-OLD MONSTER
MICHAEL GOVE PUNCH BAG
INCREDIBLE BETTER TOGETHER SPEX!
Now You Can... GROW YOUR OWN BETTER TOGETHER ACTIVIST! -From Seed!!
TUBA PRACTICE
"THERE'S PAINTING, COLLAGE, INSTALLATION AND PHOTOGRAPHY ALONGSIDE FICTION, POETRY, POLITICAL AND CULTURAL COMMENTARY.."
IT'S A LIMITED EDITION AND SURE-FIRE COLLECTOR'S ITEM!!
IT'S 36 PAGES LONG AND SELLING FOR A MEASLY £3.50!!
THERE'S ONLY ONE THING FOR IT. I SHALL HAVE TO HARNESS THE FULL MIGHT OF THE NO CAMPAIGN'S ARTISTIC COMMUNITY..
FTTT!
THE END.

ABERDEEN CITY COUNCIL: THE NATION'S HINDQUARTERS

MARCH 8TH 2014

Mr. Potato-Head often comes in handy. Whenever I need to represent amorphous groups of people such as the press, or faceless individuals such as the two characters below, he's always reliable. (The 'hindquarters' quote was lifted from American painter Robert Indiana.)

JUST AS IN THE ANATOMY OF MAN, EVERY NATION HAS ITS HINDQUARTERS. SO CONTINUES THE SORRY SAGA OF SPECTACULARLY DYSFUNCTIONAL ABERDEEN CITY COUNCIL..
MUCH TWATTAGE
ABERDEEN CITY COUNCIL
COUNCILLOR WILLIE YOUNG (LAB), DRIVEN BY BLIND FUMING HATRED OF THE SCOTTISH GOVERNMENT, THE SNP IN PARTICULAR, AND ALEX SALMOND SPECIFICALLY, ANNOUNCED A BAN ON MINISTERS VISITING ALL COUNCIL PROPERTY.
NASTY, NASTY NATS. KEEP THEM OUT, I SAY.
THEN COUNCIL LEADER BARNEY CROCKETT (LAB) ANNOUNCED A CLIMBDOWN. NOT BECAUSE BLIND FUMING HATRED WAS UNBECOMING OF ELECTED OFFICIALS, OR BECAUSE THIS WOULD BE UNUSUAL BEHAVIOUR FOR ABERDEEN CITY COUNCIL, BUT BECAUSE PEOPLE BEGAN TO TAKE NOTICE.
IT'S NOT LOOKING GOOD IN THE PRESS, WILLIE, OLD BOY.
BOO.
HOWEVER, THIS DIDN'T STOP MR. CROCKETT FROM GOING ON TO PROMOTE A 'NO' VOTE IN THE REFERENDUM BY SENDING A HEAVY-HANDED LETTER WITH COUNCIL TAX BILLS TO ALL 200,000 ABERDEEN RESIDENTS.
"ABERDEEN IS STRONGER NOW AND WILL BE STRONGER IN THE FUTURE – ECONOMICALLY, POLITICALLY AND SOCIALLY – AS A PARTNER WITHIN THE UK."
GOOD JOB, BARNS.

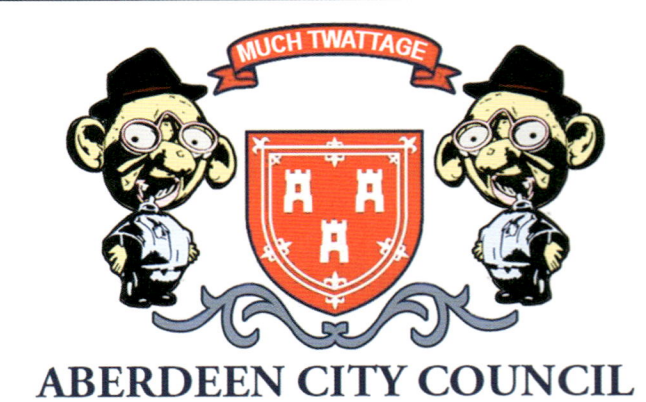

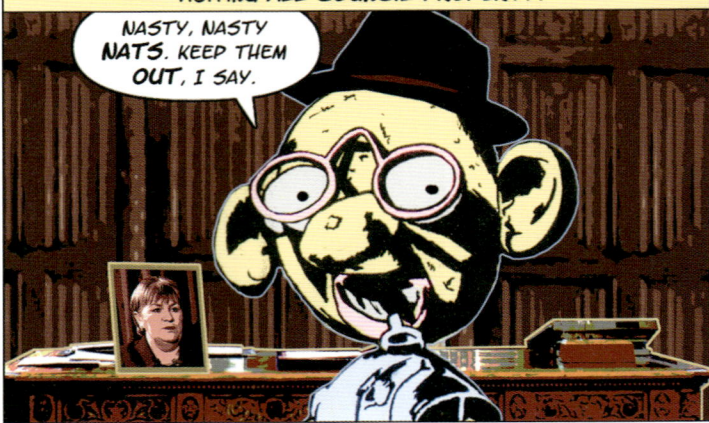

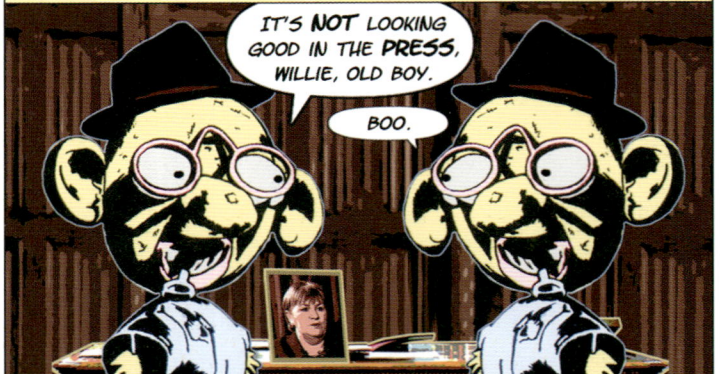

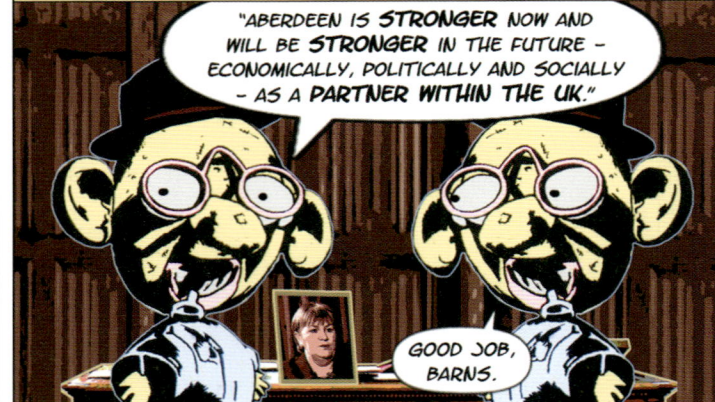

EXCUSE ME, BOYS. PROPAGANDA OF THE WORST KIND? AN APPALLING MISUSE OF POWER? A GROTESQUE WASTE OF COUNCIL RESOURCES?
NONSENSE, IT DOESN'T COST MUCH TO SEND A LETTER.
STANDARD LETTER. JUST WITH BIG BITS ABOUT VOTING 'NO'.
WELL, NO DOUBT YOU CONSIDER YOURSELVES MAVERICKS RAILING AGAINST A GOVERNMENT WHICH SUPPOSEDLY FAVOURS OTHER COUNCILS MORE, BUT IT MAY BE THAT VOTERS ARE MORE INCLINED TO SEE YOU AS BITTER TWISTED TWATS WHO ARE OUT OF CONTROL AND UNFIT FOR OFFICE. HAVE YOU THOUGHT ABOUT THAT?
CAN WE BE BITTER TWISTED MAVERICKS?
I DON'T MIND BEING A TWAT IF IT MEANS I GET TO HATE ALEX SALMOND.
THE END.

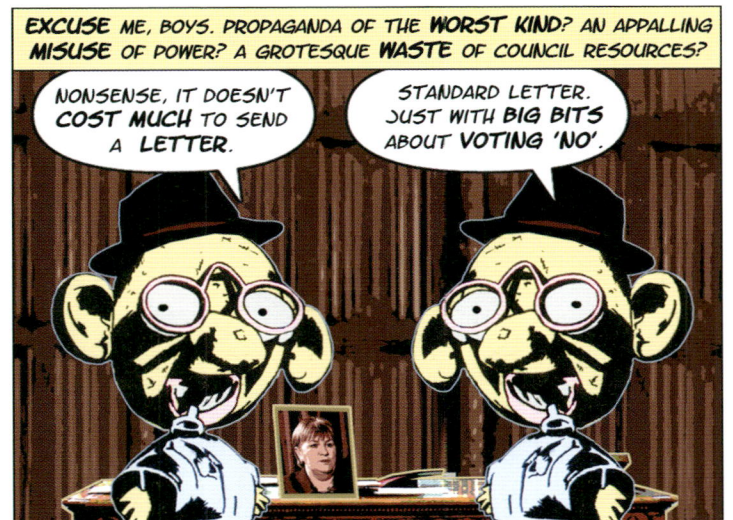

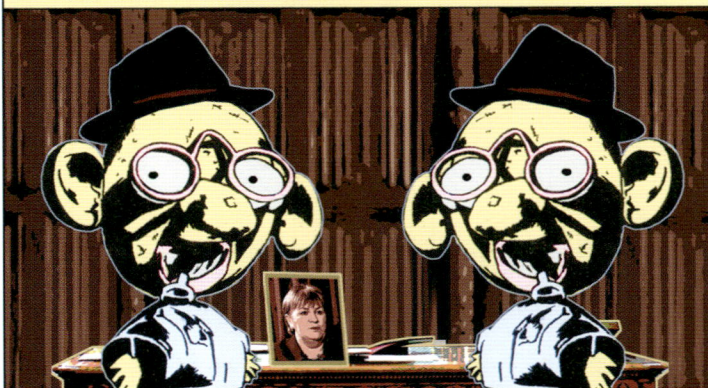

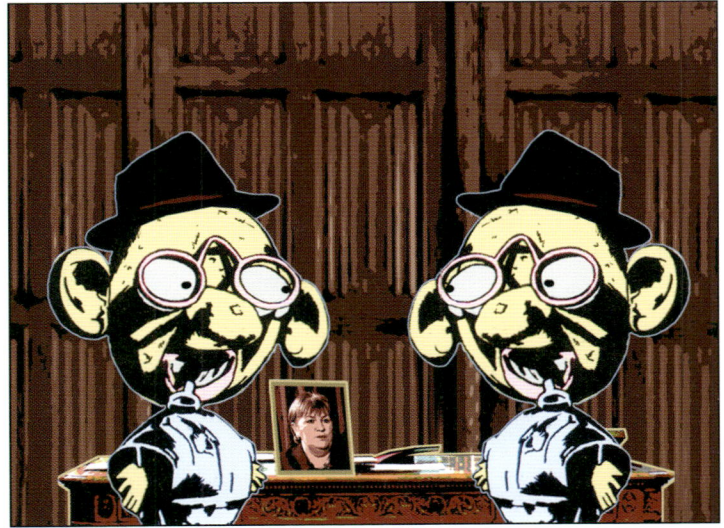

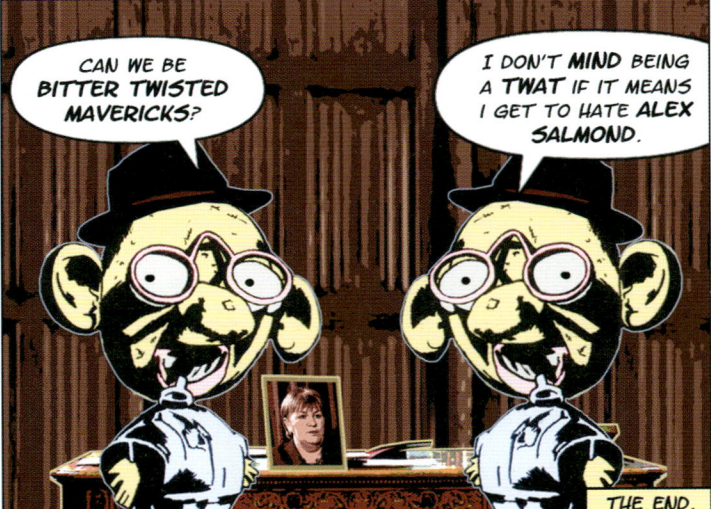

A FAMILY OF NATIONS

MARCH 15TH 2014

When David Cameron spoke at the Scottish Conservatives conference, banging on about the First World War and the curling, he was so out of touch with Scotland I thought he might as well promise to bring in Nigel Farage as a coalition partner. He might think we'd like that.

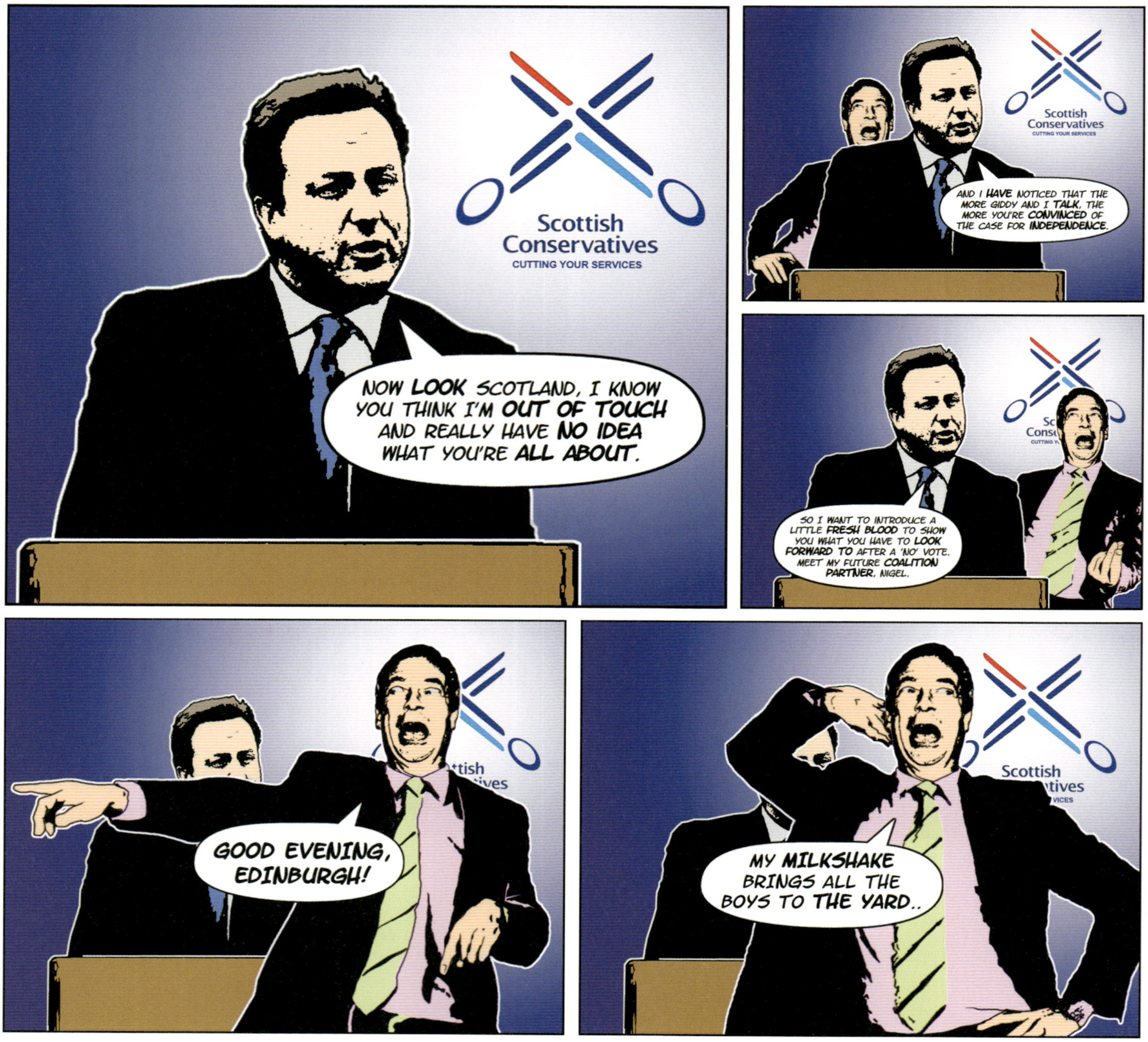

Scottish Conservatives
CUTTING YOUR SERVICES
NOW LOOK SCOTLAND, I KNOW YOU THINK I'M OUT OF TOUCH AND REALLY HAVE NO IDEA WHAT YOU'RE ALL ABOUT.
AND I HAVE NOTICED THAT THE MORE GIDDY AND I TALK, THE MORE YOU'RE CONVINCED OF THE CASE FOR INDEPENDENCE.
SO I WANT TO INTRODUCE A LITTLE FRESH BLOOD TO SHOW YOU WHAT YOU HAVE TO LOOK FORWARD TO AFTER A 'NO' VOTE. MEET MY FUTURE COALITION PARTNER, NIGEL.
GOOD EVENING, EDINBURGH!
MY MILKSHAKE BRINGS ALL THE BOYS TO THE YARD..

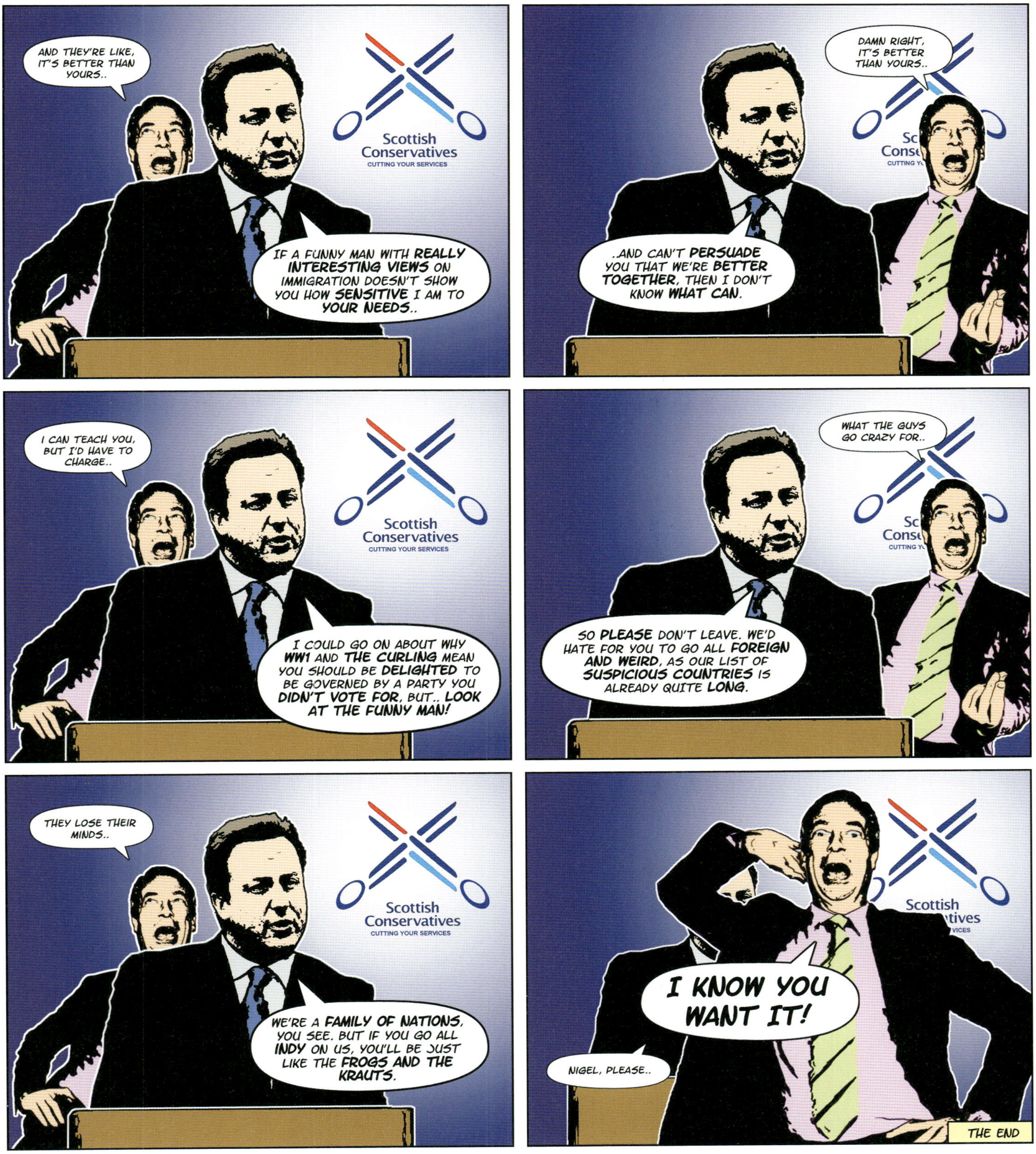
AND THEY'RE LIKE, IT'S BETTER THAN YOURS..
IF A FUNNY MAN WITH REALLY INTERESTING VIEWS ON IMMIGRATION DOESN'T SHOW YOU HOW SENSITIVE I AM TO YOUR NEEDS..
Scottish Conservatives
CUTTING YOUR SERVICES
DAMN RIGHT, IT'S BETTER THAN YOURS..
..AND CAN'T PERSUADE YOU THAT WE'RE BETTER TOGETHER, THEN I DON'T KNOW WHAT CAN.
I CAN TEACH YOU, BUT I'D HAVE TO CHARGE..
I COULD GO ON ABOUT WHY WW1 AND THE CURLING MEAN YOU SHOULD BE DELIGHTED TO BE GOVERNED BY A PARTY YOU DIDN'T VOTE FOR, BUT.. LOOK AT THE FUNNY MAN!
WHAT THE GUYS GO CRAZY FOR..
SO PLEASE DON'T LEAVE. WE'D HATE FOR YOU TO GO ALL FOREIGN AND WEIRD, AS OUR LIST OF SUSPICIOUS COUNTRIES IS ALREADY QUITE LONG.
THEY LOSE THEIR MINDS..
WE'RE A FAMILY OF NATIONS, YOU SEE. BUT IF YOU GO ALL INDY ON US, YOU'LL BE JUST LIKE THE FROGS AND THE KRAUTS.
I KNOW YOU WANT IT!
NIGEL, PLEASE..
THE END

UNTIED WITH LABOUR

MARCH 22ND 2014

I believe 'United With Labour' was set up purely to allow Gordon Brown to enter the debate without having to be in the same room as Alistair Darling. But after several launches and this plug from Ed Miliband, it fizzled out, possibly because Brown doesn't take much interest in politics these days.

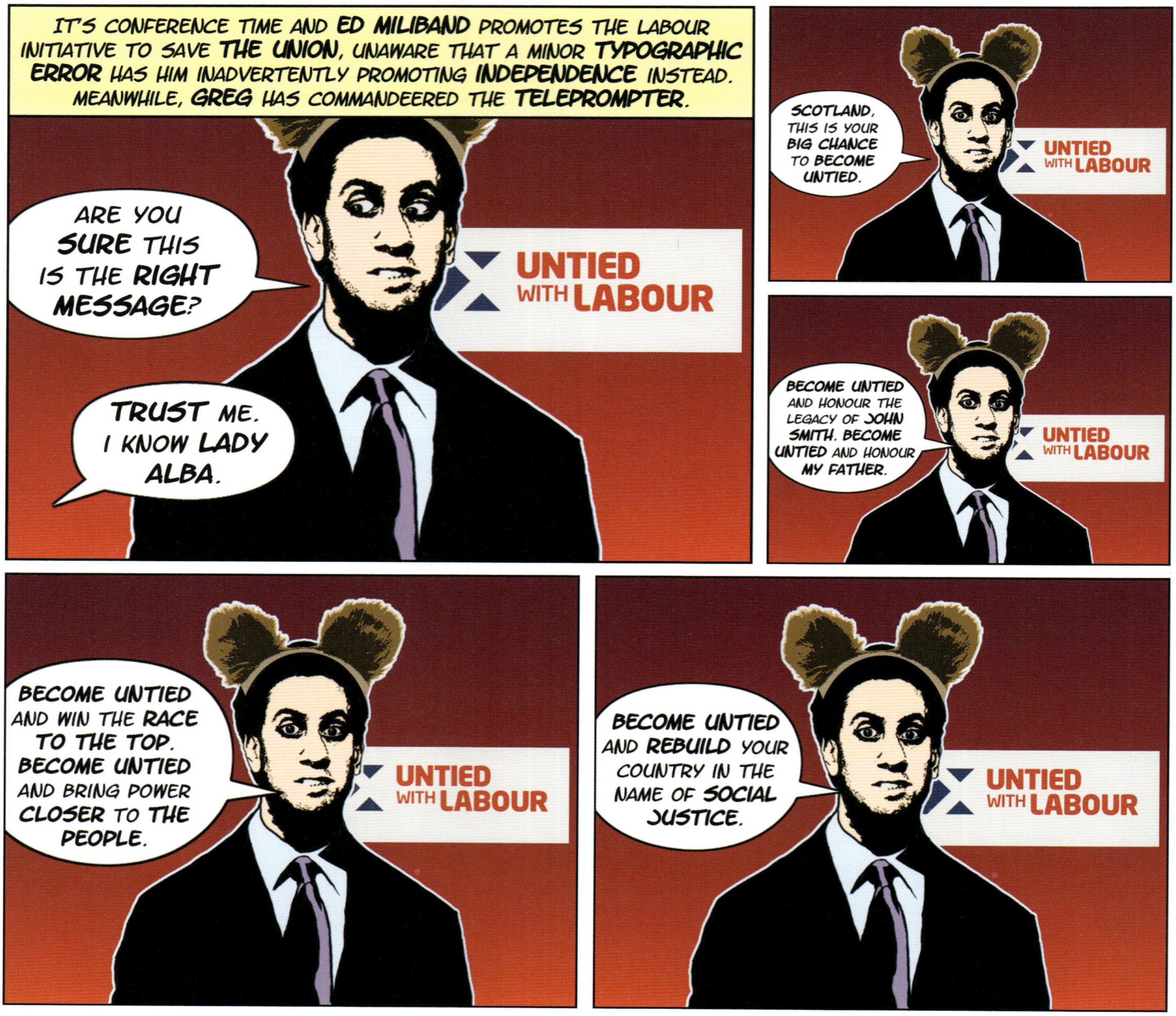

IT'S CONFERENCE TIME AND ED MILIBAND PROMOTES THE LABOUR INITIATIVE TO SAVE THE UNION, UNAWARE THAT A MINOR TYPOGRAPHIC ERROR HAS HIM INADVERTENTLY PROMOTING INDEPENDENCE INSTEAD. MEANWHILE, GREG HAS COMMANDEERED THE TELEPROMPTER.
ARE YOU SURE THIS IS THE RIGHT MESSAGE?
TRUST ME. I KNOW LADY ALBA.
UNTIED WITH LABOUR
SCOTLAND, THIS IS YOUR BIG CHANCE TO BECOME UNTIED.
UNTIED WITH LABOUR
BECOME UNTIED AND HONOUR THE LEGACY OF JOHN SMITH. BECOME UNTIED AND HONOUR MY FATHER.
UNTIED WITH LABOUR
BECOME UNTIED AND WIN THE RACE TO THE TOP. BECOME UNTIED AND BRING POWER CLOSER TO THE PEOPLE.
UNTIED WITH LABOUR
BECOME UNTIED AND REBUILD YOUR COUNTRY IN THE NAME OF SOCIAL JUSTICE.
UNTIED WITH LABOUR

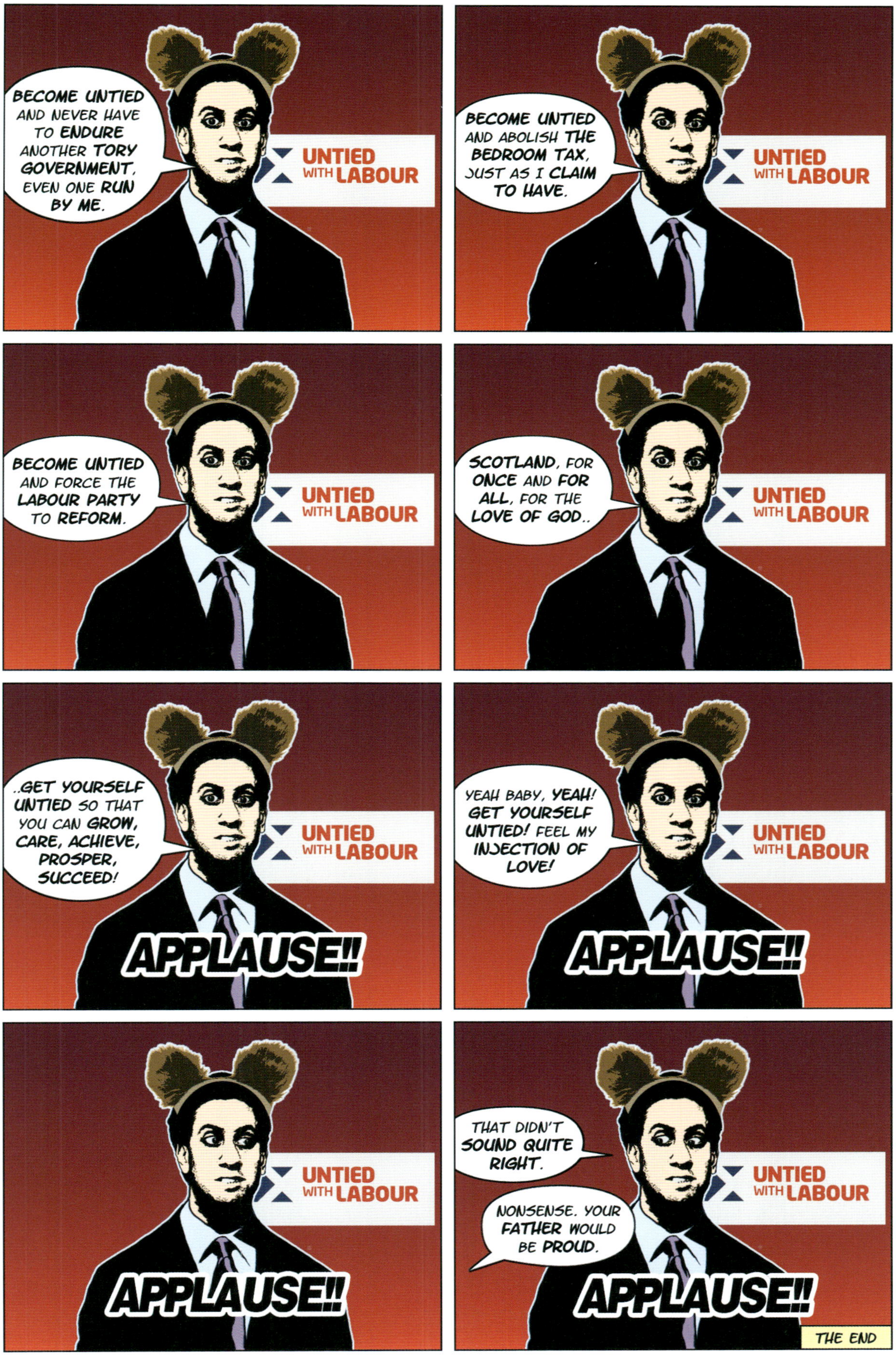

BECOME UNTIED AND NEVER HAVE TO ENDURE ANOTHER TORY GOVERNMENT, EVEN ONE RUN BY ME.
UNTIED WITH LABOUR
BECOME UNTIED AND ABOLISH THE BEDROOM TAX, JUST AS I CLAIM TO HAVE.
UNTIED WITH LABOUR
BECOME UNTIED AND FORCE THE LABOUR PARTY TO REFORM.
UNTIED WITH LABOUR
SCOTLAND, FOR ONCE AND FOR ALL, FOR THE LOVE OF GOD..
UNTIED WITH LABOUR
..GET YOURSELF UNTIED SO THAT YOU CAN GROW, CARE, ACHIEVE, PROSPER, SUCCEED!
UNTIED WITH LABOUR
APPLAUSE!!
YEAH BABY, YEAH! GET YOURSELF UNTIED! FEEL MY INJECTION OF LOVE!
UNTIED WITH LABOUR
APPLAUSE!!
UNTIED WITH LABOUR
APPLAUSE!!
THAT DIDN'T SOUND QUITE RIGHT.
NONSENSE. YOUR FATHER WOULD BE PROUD.
UNTIED WITH LABOUR
APPLAUSE!!
THE END

THE "THRILLING" CASE FOR THE UK

MARCH 29TH 2014

Nick Clegg urged the No campaign to make the case for the UK "just as thrilling as the drama of leaving it". He didn't suggest how to go about it, and seemed to be forgetting that Better Together were imagination-lite, so I tried to fill in a few of the blanks.

LIBERAL DEMOCRAT LEADER NICK CLEGG SAYS THE CASE FOR THE UK SHOULD BE AS "THRILLING" AS THE CASE FOR INDEPENDENCE. HERE HE EXPLAINS HOW HIS PARTY PLANS TO LEAD THE WAY IN THE THRILLS DEPARTMENT.
FIRST OF ALL LET ME SAY THAT AFTER A REBRANDING EXERCISE, 'PROJECT FEAR' WILL NOW BE KNOWN AS 'PROJECT ECSTATIC BRILLIANT SUNSHINE EXCITEMENT'.
NOW DON'T GO EXPECTING MIRACLES. WE'LL STILL BE WEIGHING YOU DOWN LIKE THE ANCHOR ON THE TITANIC. BUT..
..DANNY ALEXANDER'S FIGURED OUT HOW TO DO SMILEY EMOTICONS.
WE'VE ALSO REBRANDED SCOTTISH LEADER WILLIE RENNIE. FROM NOW ON HE'LL BE KNOWN AS 'CAPTAIN HERCULES FANTASTICAL BIGBALLS THE THIRD'.

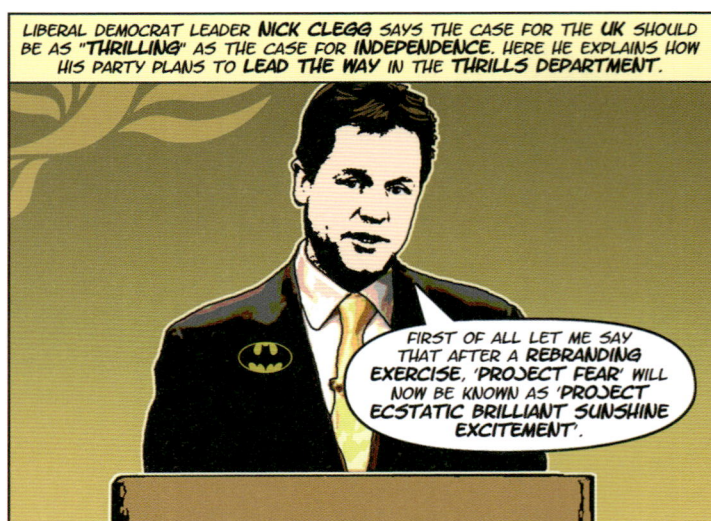

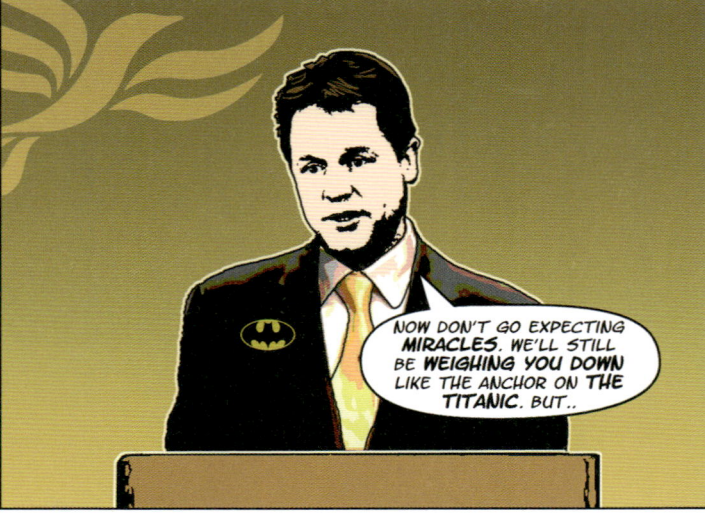

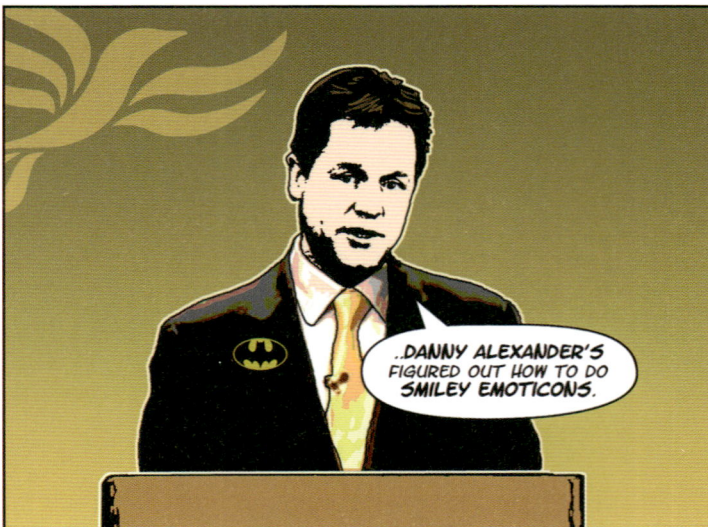

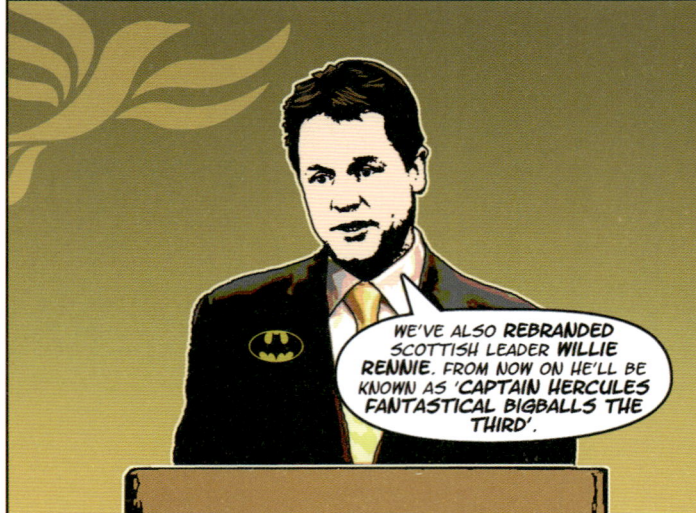

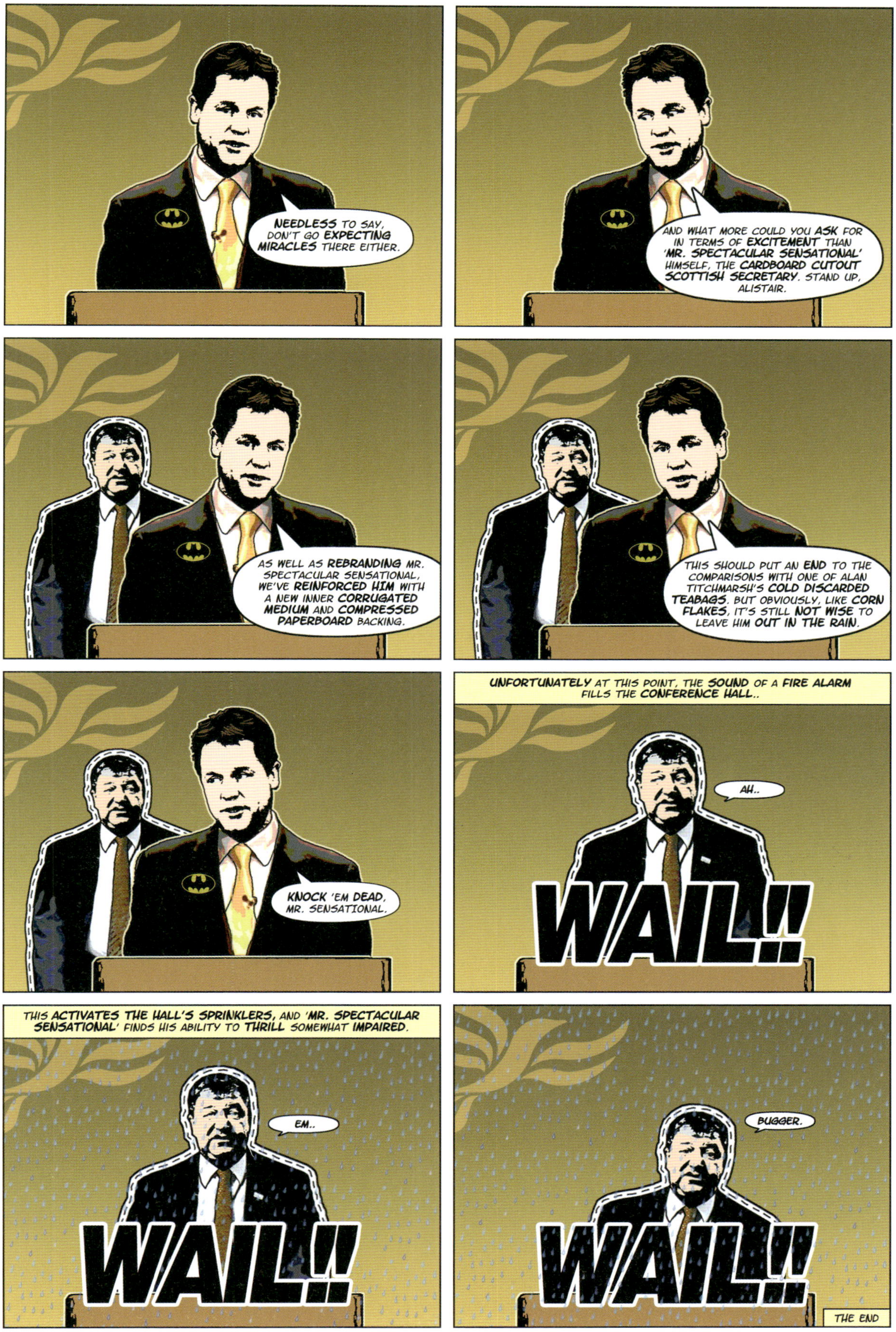
NEEDLESS TO SAY, DON'T GO EXPECTING MIRACLES THERE EITHER.
AND WHAT MORE COULD YOU ASK FOR IN TERMS OF EXCITEMENT THAN 'MR. SPECTACULAR SENSATIONAL' HIMSELF, THE CARDBOARD CUTOUT SCOTTISH SECRETARY. STAND UP, ALISTAIR.
AS WELL AS REBRANDING MR. SPECTACULAR SENSATIONAL, WE'VE REINFORCED HIM WITH A NEW INNER CORRUGATED MEDIUM AND COMPRESSED PAPERBOARD BACKING.
THIS SHOULD PUT AN END TO THE COMPARISONS WITH ONE OF ALAN TITCHMARSH'S COLD DISCARDED TEABAGS. BUT OBVIOUSLY, LIKE CORN FLAKES, IT'S STILL NOT WISE TO LEAVE HIM OUT IN THE RAIN.
KNOCK 'EM DEAD, MR. SENSATIONAL.
UNFORTUNATELY AT THIS POINT, THE SOUND OF A FIRE ALARM FILLS THE CONFERENCE HALL..
AH..
WAIL!!
THIS ACTIVATES THE HALL'S SPRINKLERS, AND 'MR. SPECTACULAR SENSATIONAL' FINDS HIS ABILITY TO THRILL SOMEWHAT IMPAIRED.
EM..
WAIL!!
BUGGER.
WAIL!!
THE END

DANCING TO UKIP'S TUNE

APRIL 5TH 2014

This is pretty much the current state of Westminster politics. There is virtually no difference between the three main parties and they're all courting this strange little man with his unpalatable views on Europe and immigration.

DESPITE HAVING ONLY EVER LOST THEIR DEPOSIT IN SCOTLAND, NIGEL FARAGE'S GRISLY HOBGOBLINS CONTINUE TO BE THE DRIVING FORCE IN UK POLITICS..
I'M TOO SEXY FOR MY SHIRT, TOO SEXY FOR MY SHIRT..
YOU GO, GIRL!
SO SEXY IT HURTS..
HE REALLY IS A TERRIFIC DANCER..
AND I'M TOO SEXY FOR YOUR PARTY, TOO SEXY FOR YOUR PARTY..
I COULD WATCH HIM FOR HOURS.
NO WAY I'M DISCO DANCING..
DIRTY DANCING..

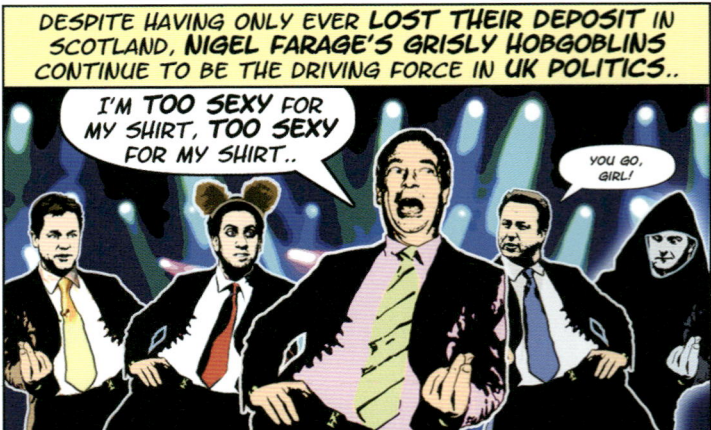

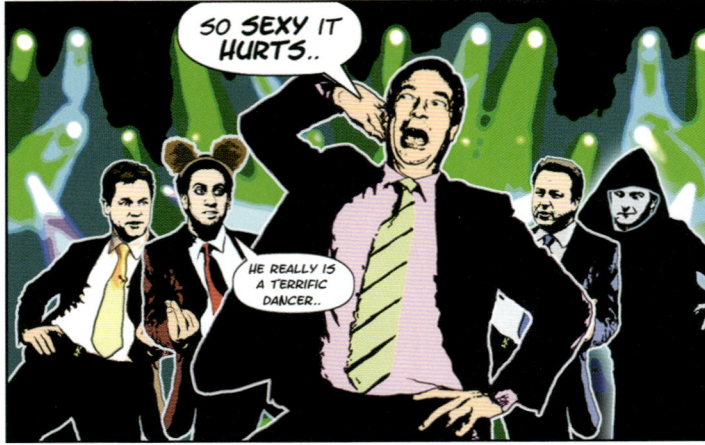

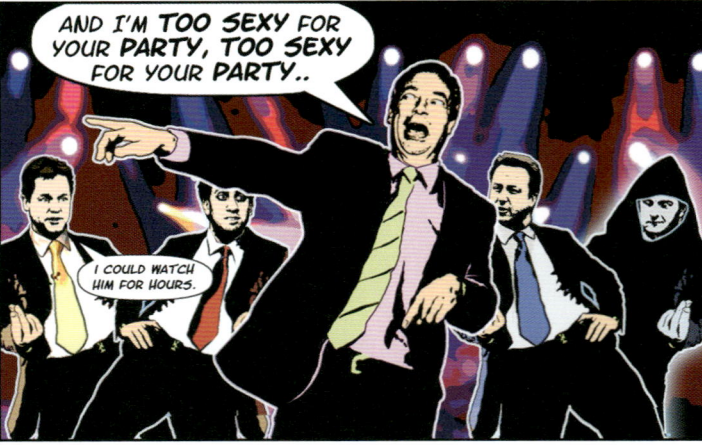

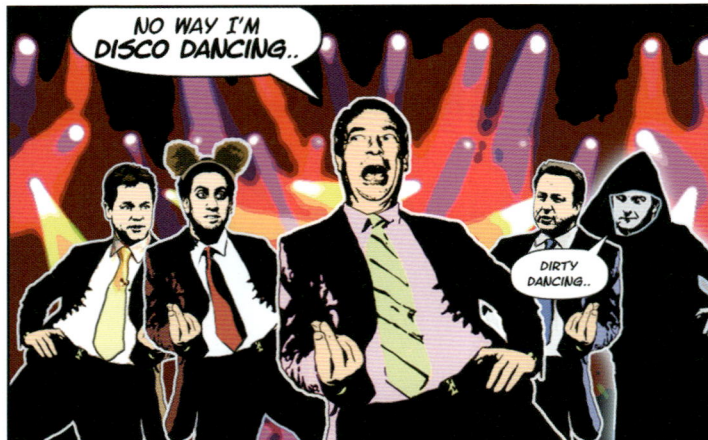

I'M A MODEL, YOU KNOW WHAT I MEAN, AND I DO MY LITTLE TURN ON THE CATWALK..
I'M GLAD I POPPED THAT 'E'.
YEAH ON THE CATWALK, ON THE CATWALK, YEAH I DO MY LITTLE TURN ON THE CATWALK..
THE COKE'S REALLY KICKING IN.
I'M TOO SEXY FOR MY CAR, TOO SEXY FOR MY CAR, TOO SEXY BY FAR..
THESE SHROOMS ARE AWESOME.
SEVERAL HOURS LATER..
I'M TOO SEXY FOR MY SHIRT, TOO SEXY FOR MY SHIRT..
TOTALLY OFF MY TITS.
ETC ETC. THE END.

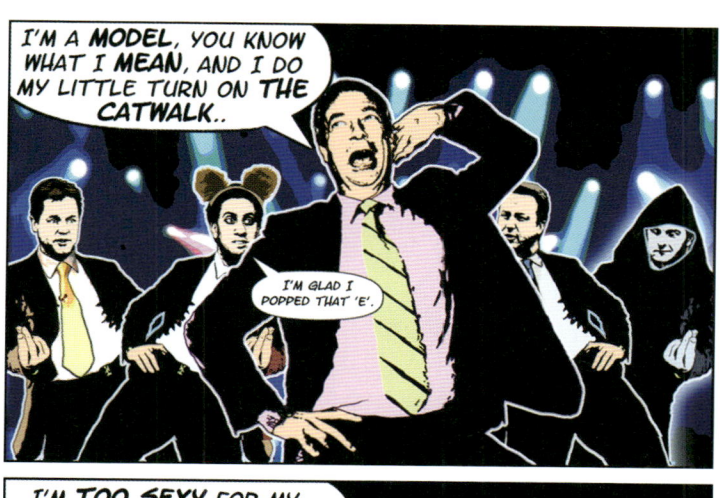

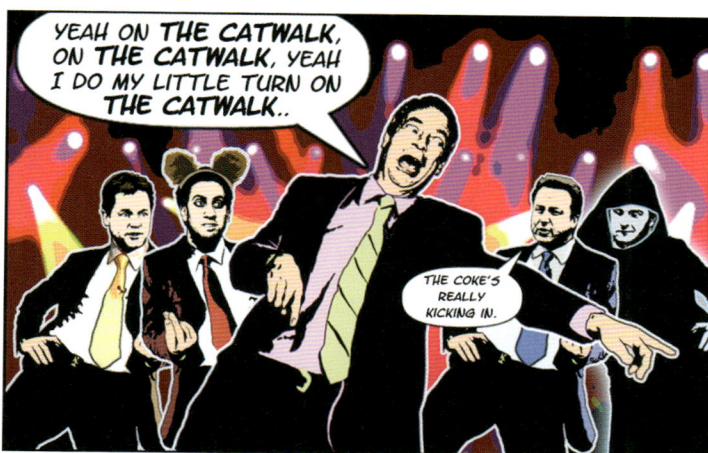

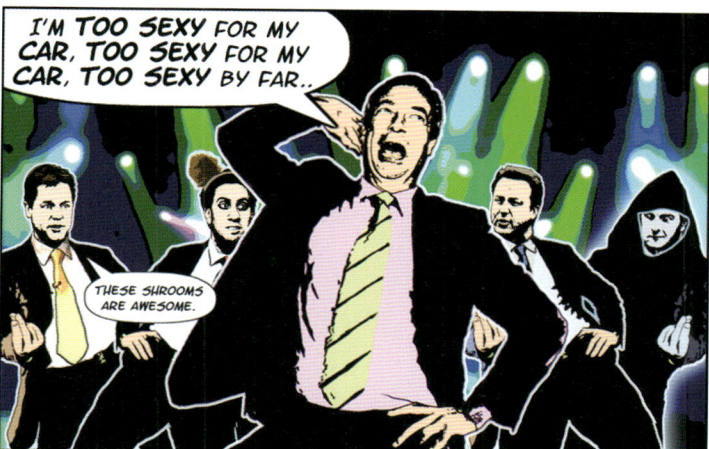

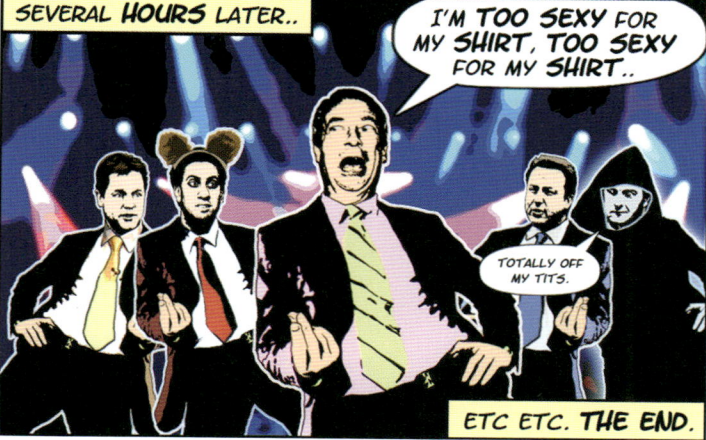

LORD ROBERTSON AND THE FORCES OF DARKNESS

APRIL 11TH 2014

A Yes vote would be "cataclysmic," said Lord Robertson. "The loudest cheers for the breakup of Britain would be from our adversaries and from our enemies. The forces of darkness would simply love it." The Scottish Government described the comments as "crass and offensive" but I prefer to congratulate His Lordship on having gotten so far on so little.

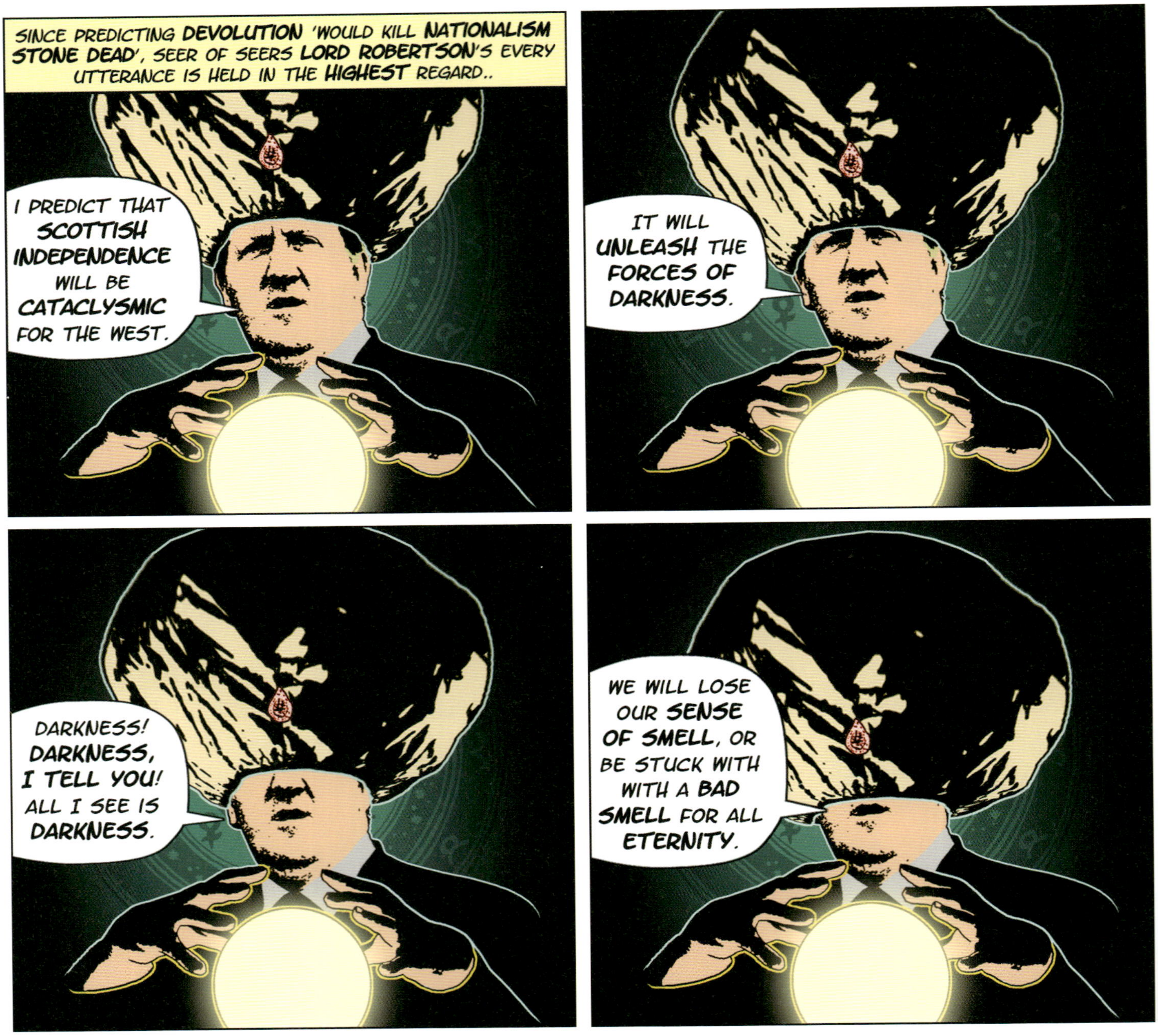

SINCE PREDICTING DEVOLUTION 'WOULD KILL NATIONALISM STONE DEAD', SEER OF SEERS LORD ROBERTSON'S EVERY UTTERANCE IS HELD IN THE HIGHEST REGARD..
I PREDICT THAT SCOTTISH INDEPENDENCE WILL BE CATACLYSMIC FOR THE WEST.
IT WILL UNLEASH THE FORCES OF DARKNESS.
DARKNESS! DARKNESS, I TELL YOU! ALL I SEE IS DARKNESS.
WE WILL LOSE OUR SENSE OF SMELL, OR BE STUCK WITH WITH A BAD SMELL FOR ALL ETERNITY.

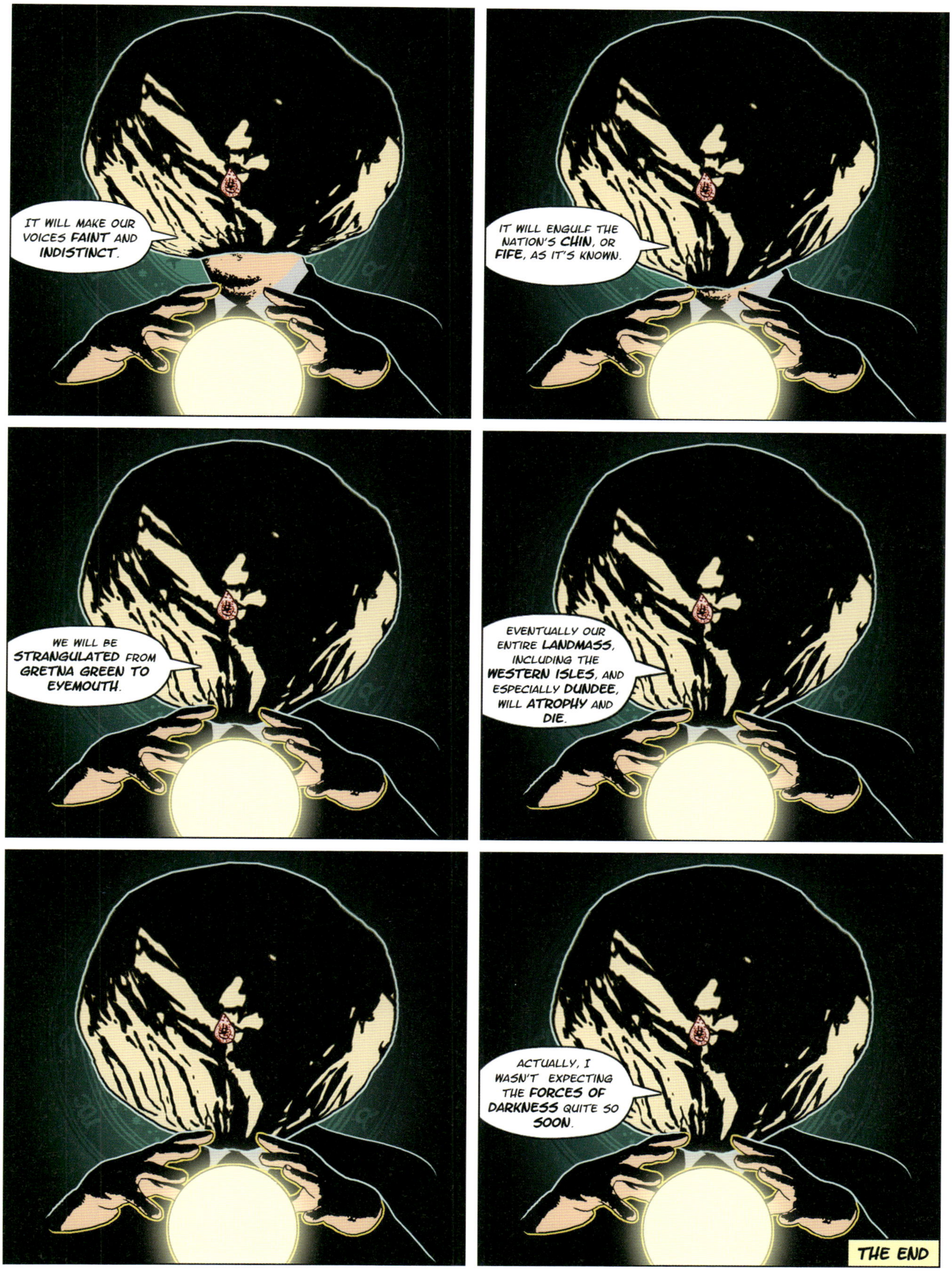
IT WILL MAKE OUR VOICES FAINT AND INDISTINCT.
IT WILL ENGULF THE NATION'S CHIN, OR FIFE, AS IT'S KNOWN.
WE WILL BE STRANGULATED FROM GRETNA GREEN TO EYEMOUTH.
EVENTUALLY OUR ENTIRE LANDMASS, INCLUDING THE WESTERN ISLES, AND ESPECIALLY DUNDEE, WILL ATROPHY AND DIE.
ACTUALLY, I WASN'T EXPECTING THE FORCES OF DARKNESS QUITE SO SOON.
THE END

DONORGATE: THE ANNIV*RSARY EDITION

APRIL 19TH 2014

Ian T*ylor and V*tol are back in the news. The Independent has just reported on how the oil giant paid an average of just 10.5% tax on profits of £9bn over the last nine years, with the blessing of the HMRC. Good to see the system works for somebody.

THIS IS IAN T*YLOR, HEAD OF THE WORLD'S LARGEST OIL COMPANY V*TOL. IAN IS A MAN WHO IS USED TO GETTING HIS WAY.
GREETINGS, PLEBSTERS!
WHEN SCOTLAND HAD THE TEMERITY TO SUGGEST THAT IT MAY WANT TO LEAVE THE UN*TED K*NGDOM, IAN WAS SWIFT TO ACT, MEETING WITH BETTER TOGETHER HEAD, ALISTAIR D*RLING (LAB).
SEE HERE ALISTAIR, GET THE SCOTS TO FALL INTO LINE, THERE'S A GOOD CHAP.
CERTAINLY, YOUR OILY-NESS. BUT HOW?
I'LL GET RIGHT ONTO IT.
WHEN N*TIONAL C*LLECTIVE POINTED OUT THAT THE 'NO' CAMPAIGN'S NEW BACKER HEADED A COMPANY THAT HAD LINKS TO SERBIAN WARLORD ARKAN, WAS CONVICTED OF GRAND LARCENY IN THE US, AVOIDED UK TAX AND SKIRTED SANCTIONS ON IRANIAN OIL, AGAIN IAN WASTED NO TIME.
LISTEN LAWYER MAN, GET THESE N*TIONAL C*LLECTIVE BLIGHTERS OUT OF MY WAY, WILL YOU?
OF COURSE. YOU'RE THE DUKE OF OIL. BUT FIRST..

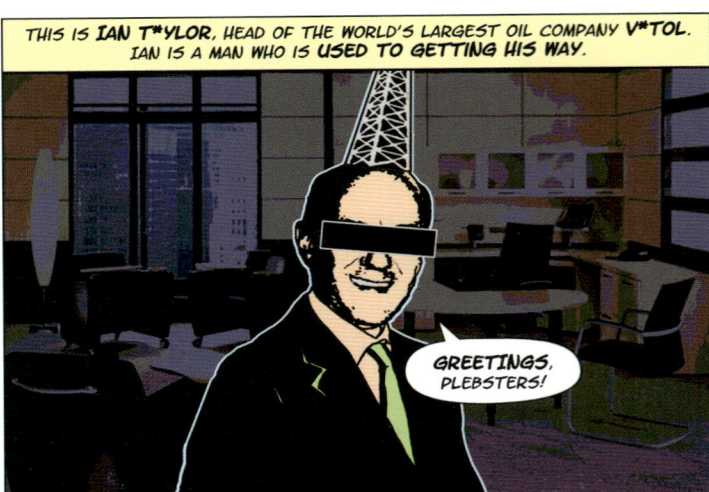

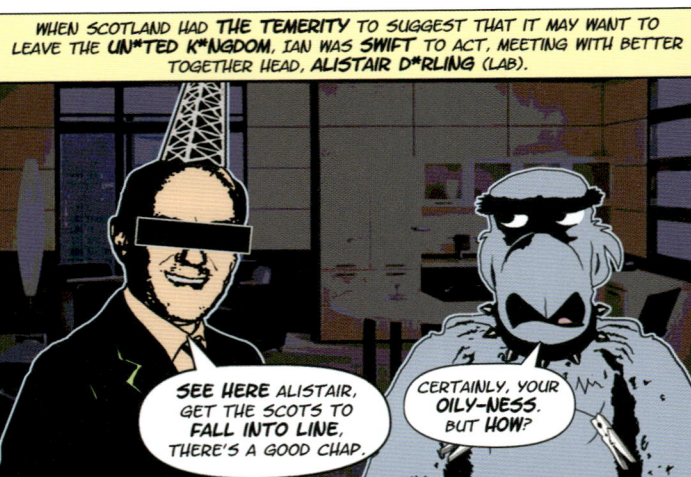

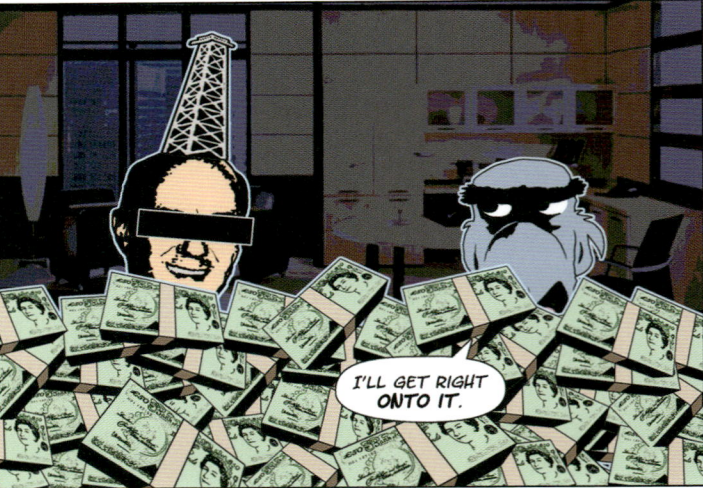

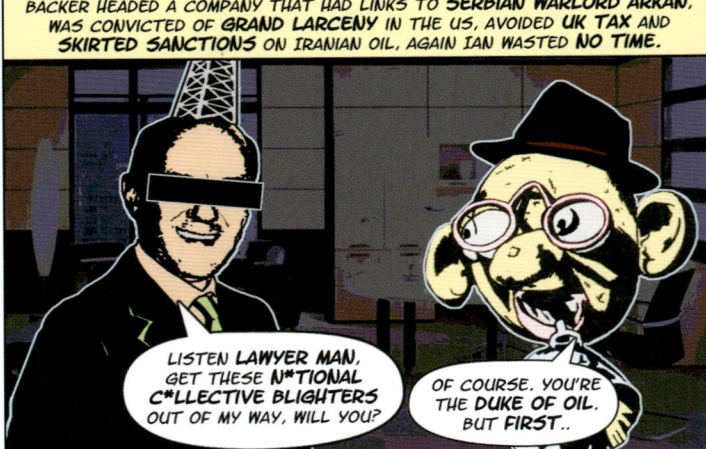

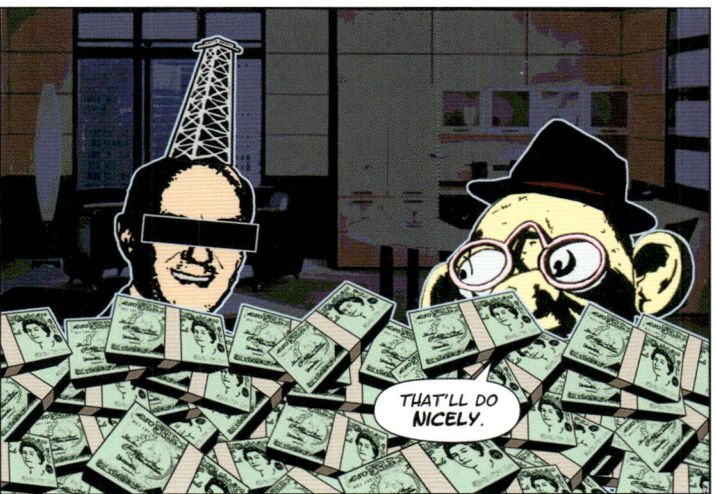

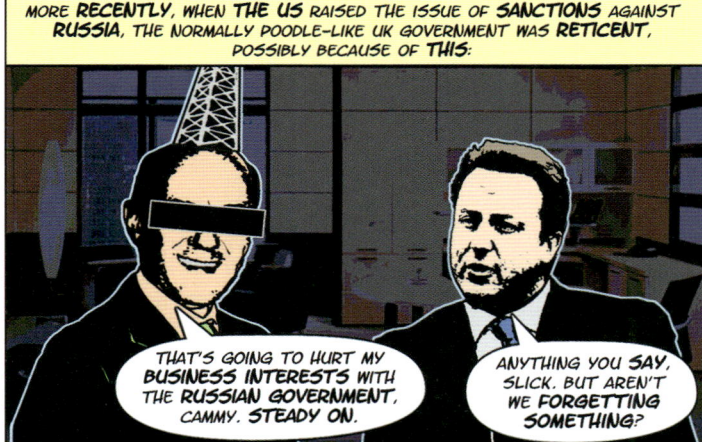

THAT'LL DO NICELY.
MORE RECENTLY, WHEN THE US RAISED THE ISSUE OF SANCTIONS AGAINST RUSSIA, THE NORMALLY POODLE-LIKE UK GOVERNMENT WAS RETICENT, POSSIBLY BECAUSE OF THIS:
THAT'S GOING TO HURT MY BUSINESS INTERESTS WITH THE RUSSIAN GOVERNMENT, CAMMY. STEADY ON.
ANYTHING YOU SAY, SLICK. BUT AREN'T WE FORGETTING SOMETHING?
YOUR WISH IS MY COMMAND.
BUT HERE'S THE THING, IAN. BACK IN SCOTLAND, N*TIONAL C*LLECTIVE DIDN'T BUCKLE. THE 'NO' CAMPAIGN IS FAILING AND HAS JUST BEEN DESCRIBED AS 'MISCONCEIVED, WRETCHEDLY EXECUTED AND POTENTIALLY SELF-DEFEATING'. IT MAY BE THAT, OF THESE EXAMPLES, FUNDING THE TORIES AND ENSURING THE UK WOULDN'T INTERFERE WITH YOUR RUSSIAN WHEEZE WAS THE BEST USE OF YOUR CASH.
WE WISH YOU AND THE REST OF THE SELF-SERVING, MORALLY REPREHENSIBLE BRITISH ESTABLISHMENT ALL THE VERY BEST IN THE NEW RUK. HAPPY ANNIV*RSARY. THE END.
I AM NATIONAL COLLECTIVE

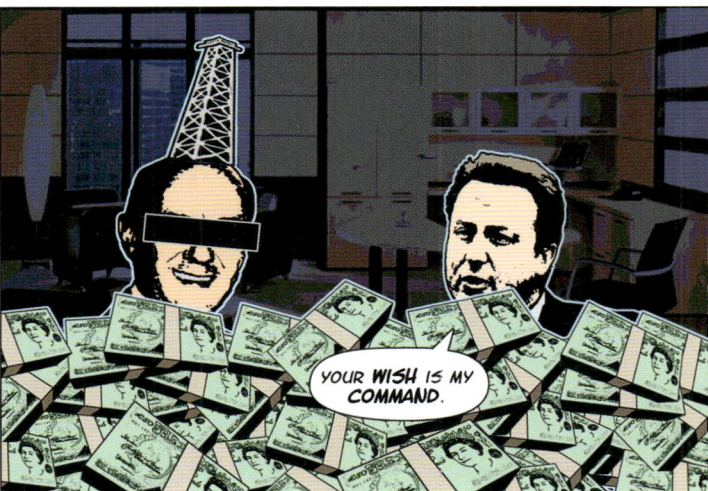

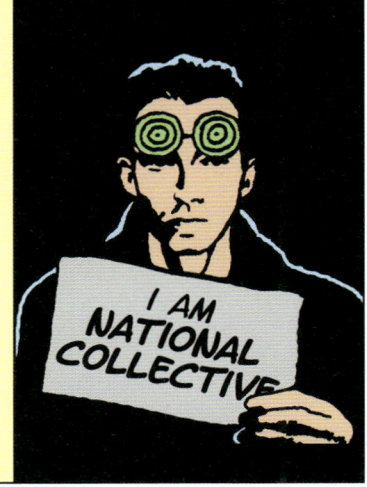

DIGGING A HOLE WITH THE CBI

APRIL 26TH 2014

The CBI like to portray themselves as the impartial voice of business, but when they registered to campaign against independence, they couldn't really maintain the facade. The fun really began, however, once they realised what a bad idea registering was.

THIS IS JOHN CRIDLAND, DIRECTOR-GENERAL OF THE CONFEDERATION OF BRITISH INDUSTRY. WE'VE BEEN FOLLOWING HIM AS HE SET OUT TO DIG THIS IMPRESSIVE HOLE IN THE CBI'S CREDIBILITY.
THE CBI ARE POLITICALLY INDEPENDENT. WE JUST CAMPAIGNED AGAINST DEVOLUTION, THE MINIMUM WAGE AND RESTRICTIONS ON BANKERS' BONUSES.
WE'RE IMPARTIAL ON SCOTTISH INDEPENDENCE, BUT WE REGISTERED WITH THE ELECTORAL COMMISSION TO CAMPAIGN AGAINST IT.
WE BALLOTED OUR MEMBERS ON THE ISSUE, BUT IT APPEARS WE FORGOT TO TELL THEM ABOUT IT.
WE DIDN'T FORESEE THAT THIS PUT MANY OF THEM, WHO ARE BOUND BY IMPARTIALITY RULES, IN AN UNTENABLE POSITION.

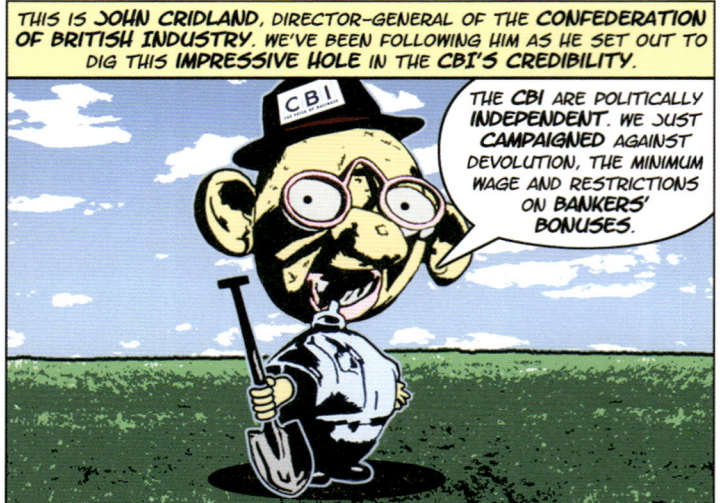

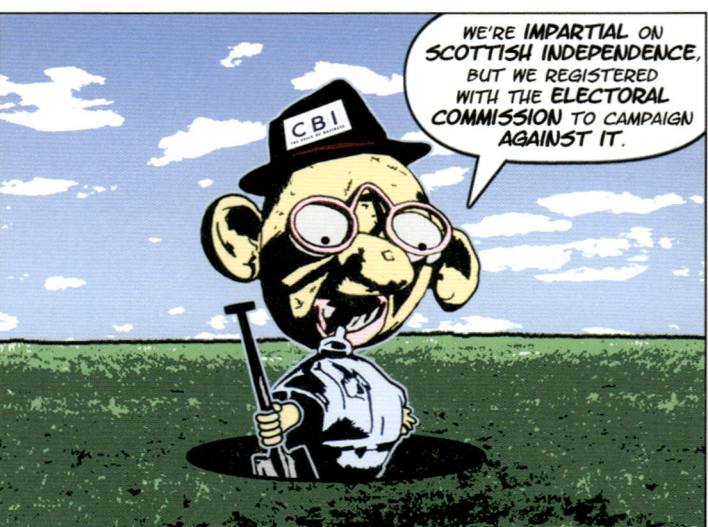

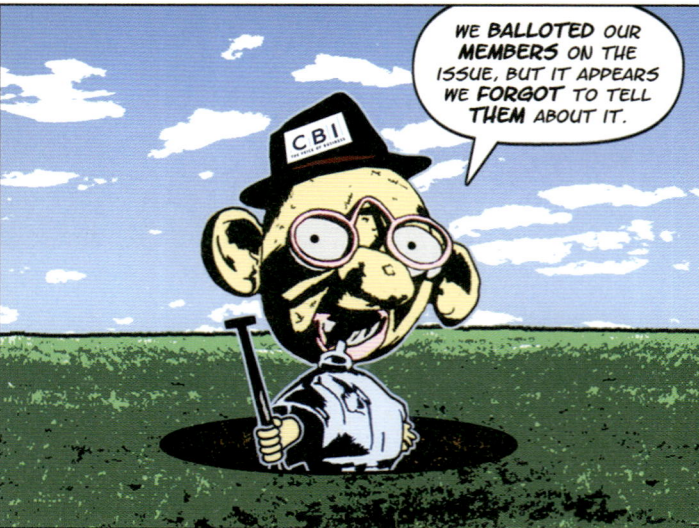

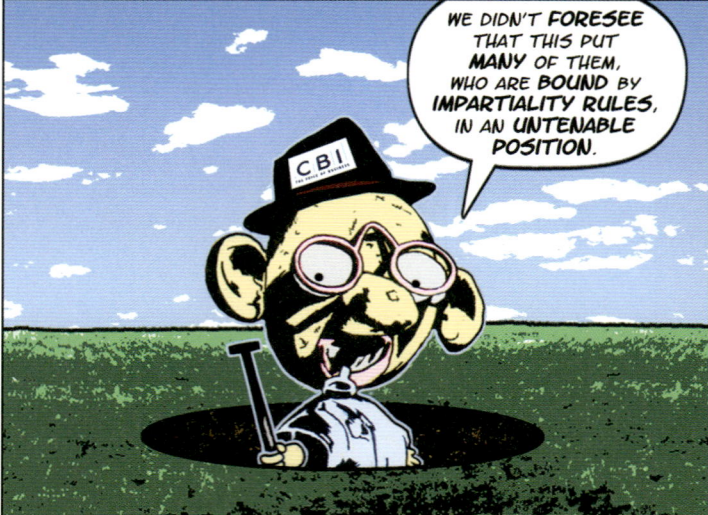

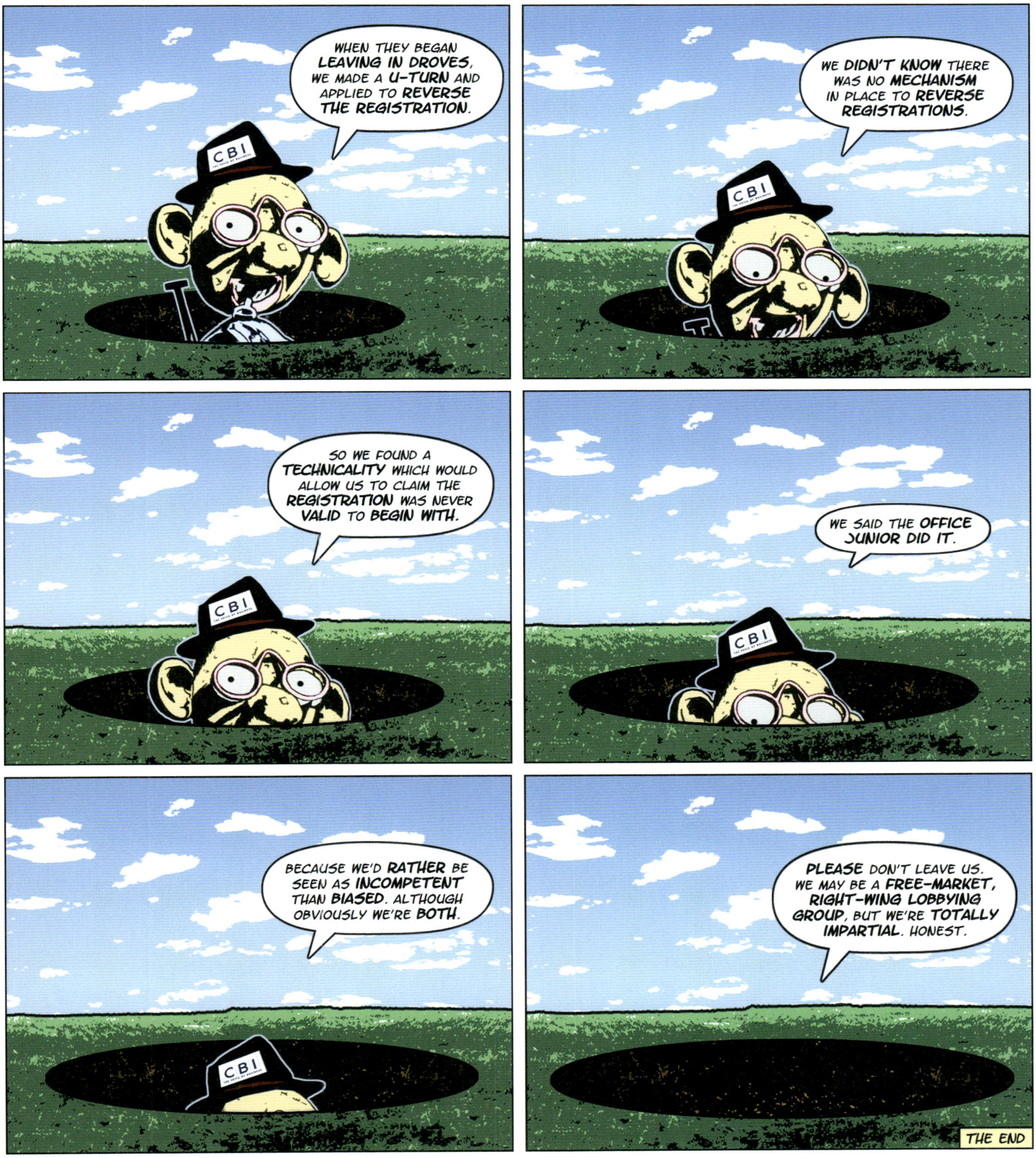
WHEN THEY BEGAN LEAVING IN DROVES, WE MADE A U-TURN AND APPLIED TO REVERSE THE REGISTRATION.
WE DIDN'T KNOW THERE WAS NO MECHANISM IN PLACE TO REVERSE REGISTRATIONS.
SO WE FOUND A TECHNICALITY WHICH WOULD ALLOW US TO CLAIM THE REGISTRATION WAS NEVER VALID TO BEGIN WITH.
WE SAID THE OFFICE JUNIOR DID IT.
BECAUSE WE'D RATHER BE SEEN AS INCOMPETENT THAN BIASED. ALTHOUGH OBVIOUSLY WE'RE BOTH.
PLEASE DON'T LEAVE US. WE MAY BE A FREE-MARKET, RIGHT-WING LOBBYING GROUP, BUT WE'RE TOTALLY IMPARTIAL. HONEST.
THE END

ONE CHRISTMAS AWAY

APRIL 28TH 2014

"We are just one Christmas away from a having a Labour government," said Ed Miliband, "which will take up the cudgel of social justice on behalf of the people of Scotland and the whole of the United Kingdom." Presumably just like it did under Tony Blair.

SCOTLAND, YOU'RE JUST ONE CHRISTMAS AWAY FROM A HAVING A LABOUR GOVERNMENT.
OK, MAYBE NOT A CHRISTMAS, MAYBE A LEAP YEAR OR TWO. A FEW WORLD CUPS.
TWO OR THREE THOUSAND SLEEPS, TOPS.
BUT SOONER OR LATER, I'LL BE COMING DOWN YOUR CHIMNEY AND INTERFERING WITH YOUR MILK AND COOKIES.

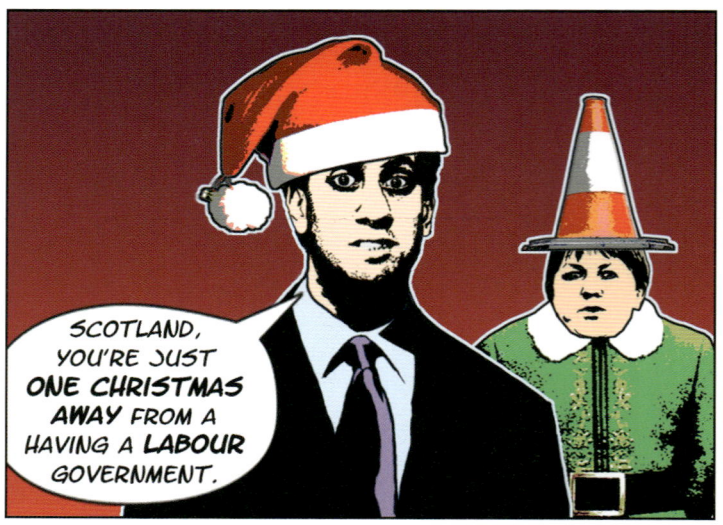

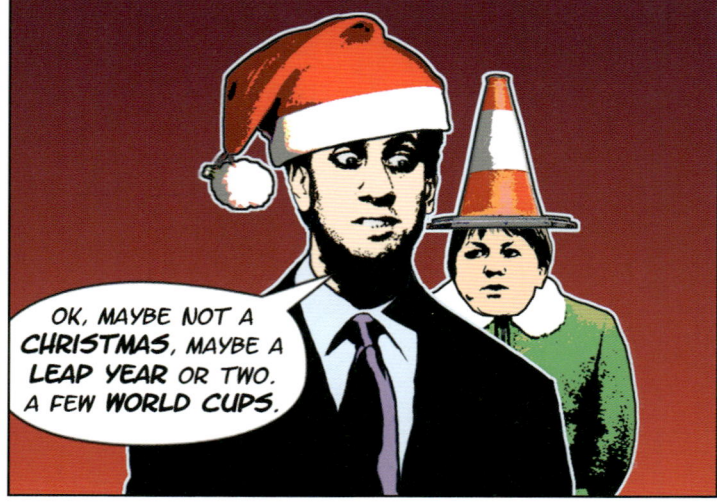

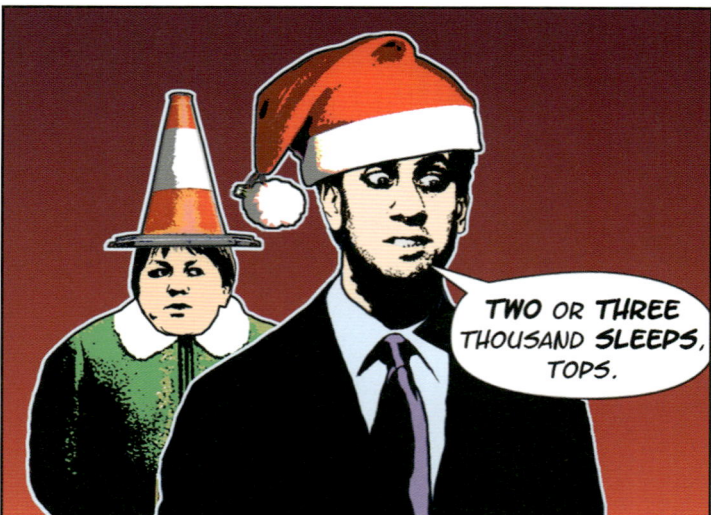

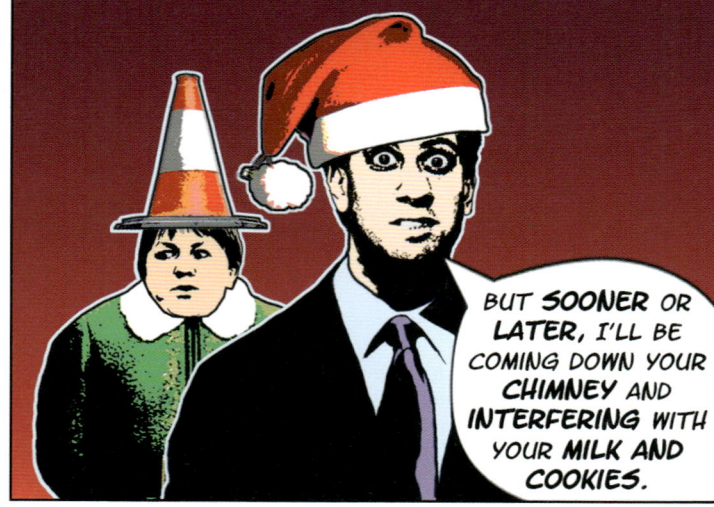

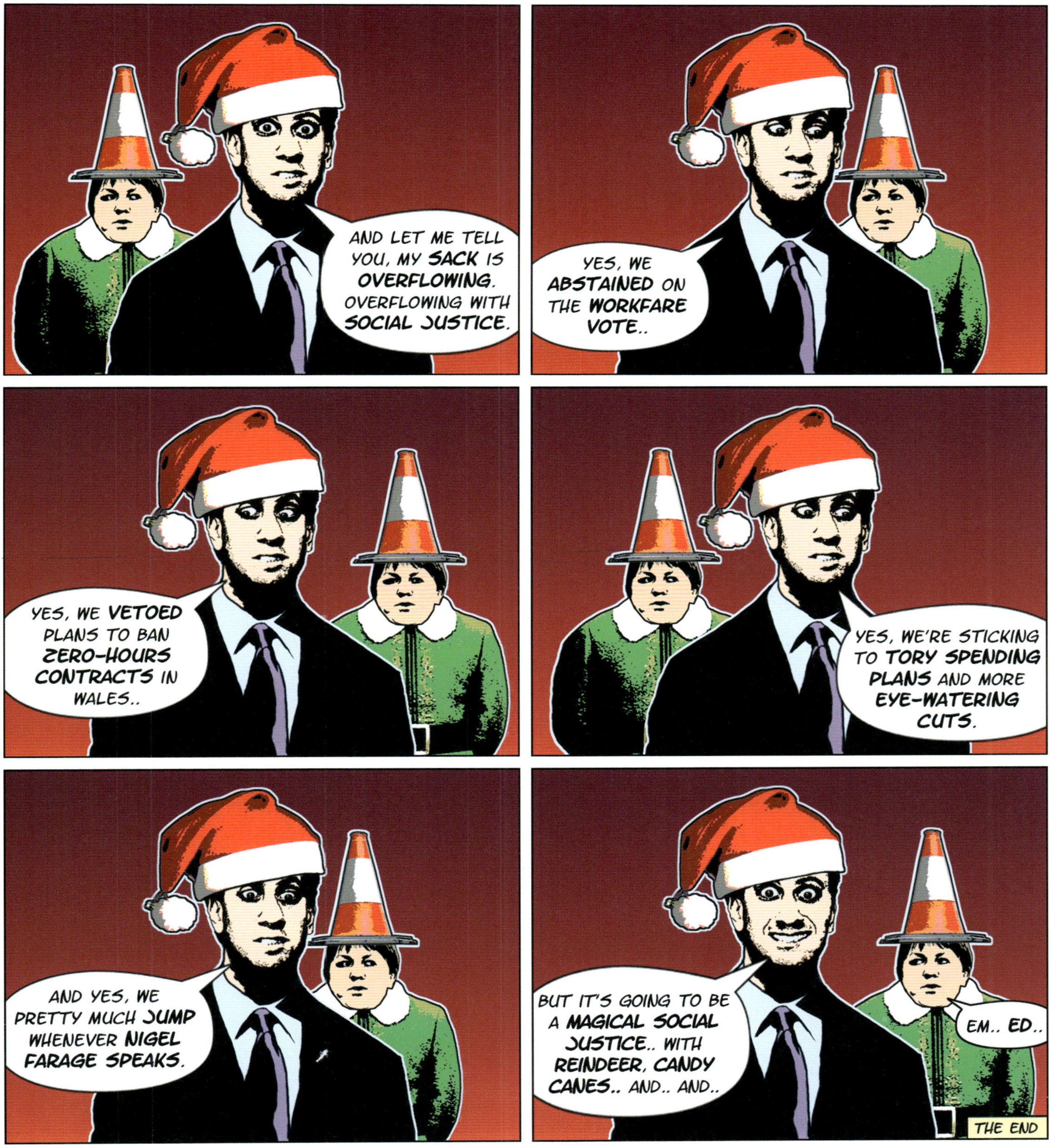
AND LET ME TELL YOU, MY SACK IS OVERFLOWING. OVERFLOWING WITH SOCIAL JUSTICE.
YES, WE ABSTAINED ON THE WORKFARE VOTE..
YES, WE VETOED PLANS TO BAN ZERO-HOURS CONTRACTS IN WALES..
YES, WE'RE STICKING TO TORY SPENDING PLANS AND MORE EYE-WATERING CUTS.
AND YES, WE PRETTY MUCH JUMP WHENEVER NIGEL FARAGE SPEAKS.
BUT IT'S GOING TO BE A MAGICAL SOCIAL JUSTICE.. WITH REINDEER, CANDY CANES.. AND.. AND..
EM.. ED..
THE END

NUCLEAR LOVE: THE PREMIERE

MAY 3RD 2014

When I first saw Zara Gladman she was singing a song about how Alex Salmond was fat so we should all vote No. I insisted she play at the Zine launch and she's been nothing but trouble ever since. We collaborated on a little animated video called Nuclear Love. She has a PHD but she once tried to microwave a tin of soup.

THREE WEEKS AGO, GREG WAS IMPRISONED BY THE WICKED, NAW-VOTING LADY ALBA AND FORCED TO WORK ON THE FOLLOW-UP TO HER INTERNET SENSATION 'BAD ROMANCE', WITH ONLY A THIMBLE OF WINE TO SUSTAIN HIM.
REGARDING THIS AS ATTENTION, GREG BECAME THE FIRST EVER CAPTIVE TO DEVELOP STOCKHOLM SYNDROME WITHIN SECONDS OF INCARCERATION, AND MERELY ASKED FOR A BIGGER THIMBLE.
THE ORDEAL OVER AND THE VIDEO COMPLETED TO LADY ALBA'S HIGH STANDARDS, THEY ARRIVED AT THE RED-CARPET PREMIERE OF 'NUCLEAR LOVE', READY TO WELCOME GUESTS.
YOU KNOW THE VIDEO'S ANTI-NUCLEAR, RIGHT?
DINNAE BE STUPID. IT'S CALLED NUCULAR LOVE, DUMBO.
YEAH, BUT..
I'M THINKING IT MIGHT BE BETTER IF YOU DIDN'T SPEAK.
I AM BLAIR, THE ONE AND ONLY.
SLING YER HOOK, CHOOB-BOY!

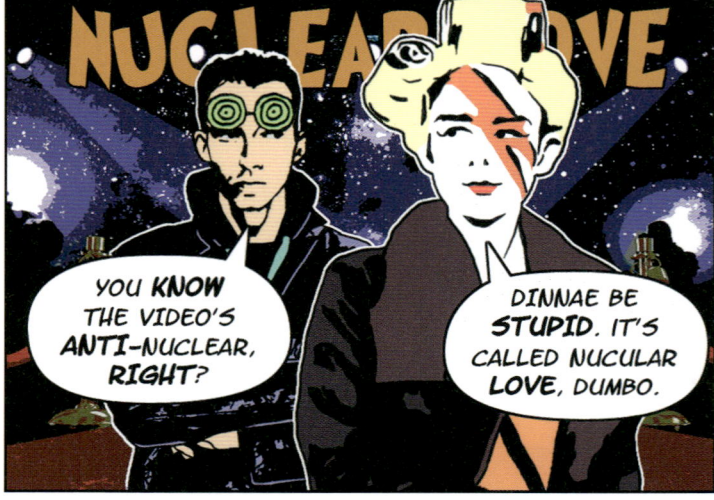

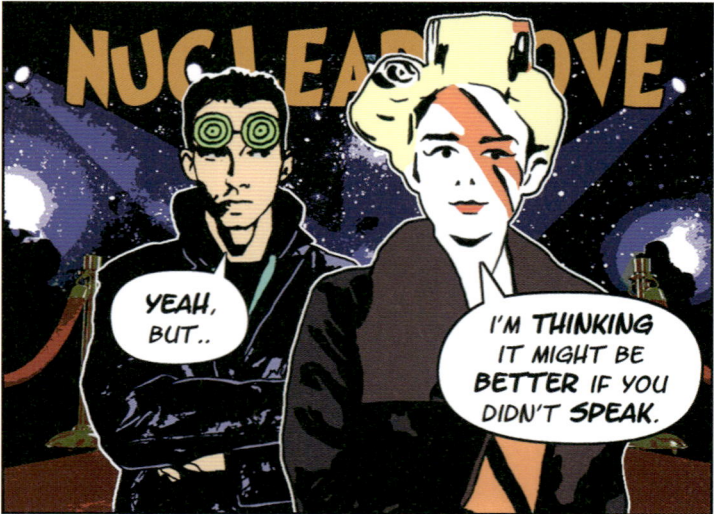

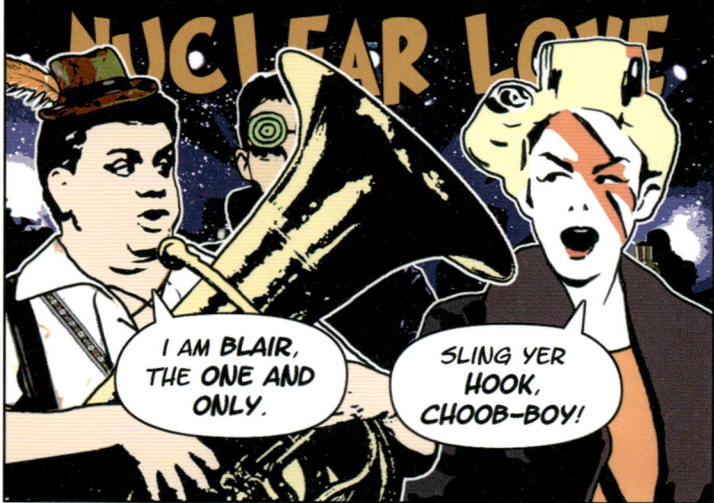

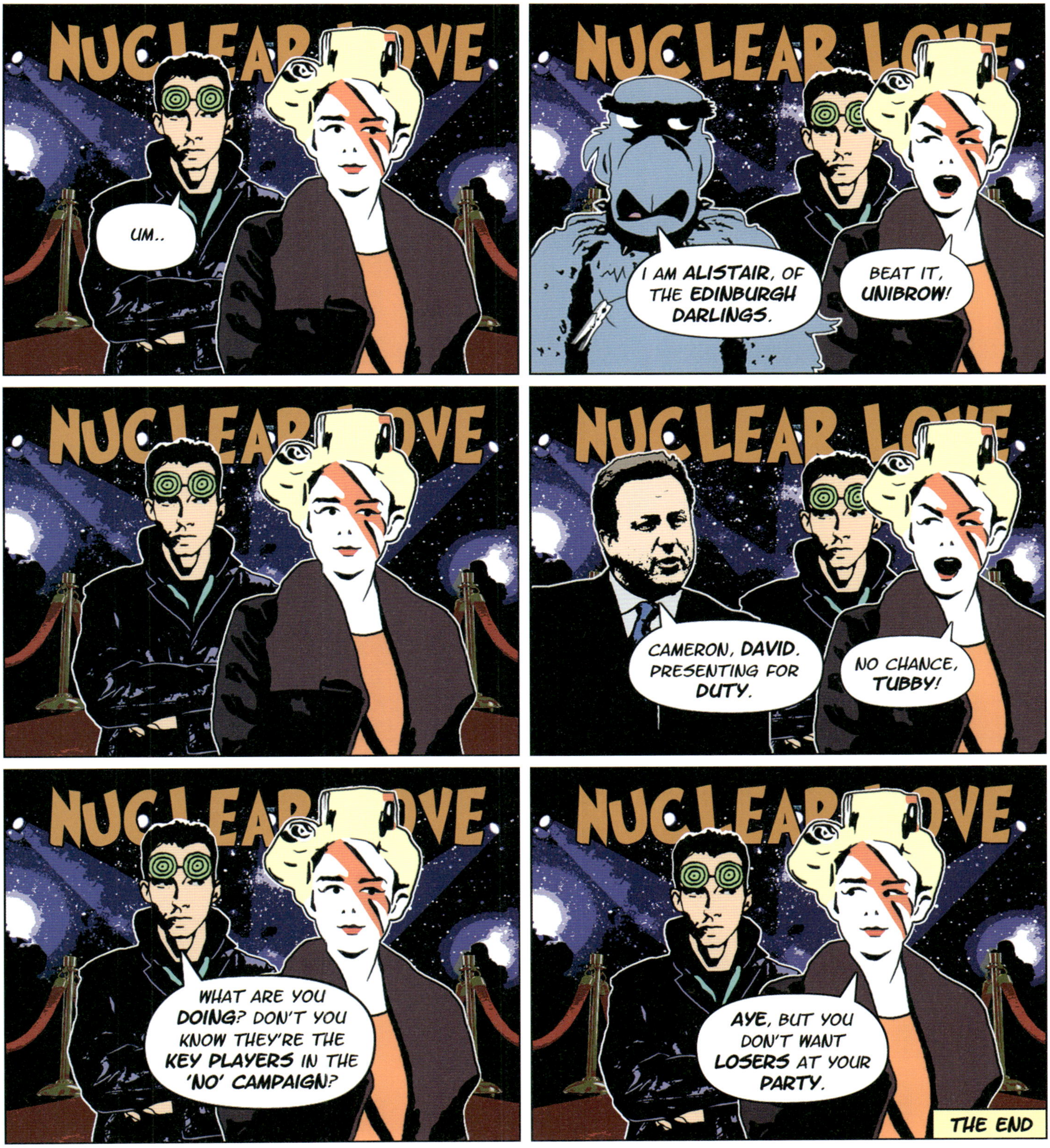
NUCLEAR LOVE
UM..
I AM ALISTAIR, OF THE EDINBURGH DARLINGS.
BEAT IT, UNIBROW!
CAMERON, DAVID. PRESENTING FOR DUTY.
NO CHANCE, TUBBY!
WHAT ARE YOU DOING? DON'T YOU KNOW THEY'RE THE KEY PLAYERS IN THE 'NO' CAMPAIGN?
AYE, BUT YOU DON'T WANT LOSERS AT YOUR PARTY.
THE END

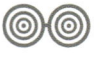

BBC UKIP

MAY 23RD 2014

BBC News became a no-go area before, during and after the European elections as the fawning over Nigel Farage and his merry band of grisly hobgoblins reached alarming new heights. The 'bathcam' was only a slight exaggeration.

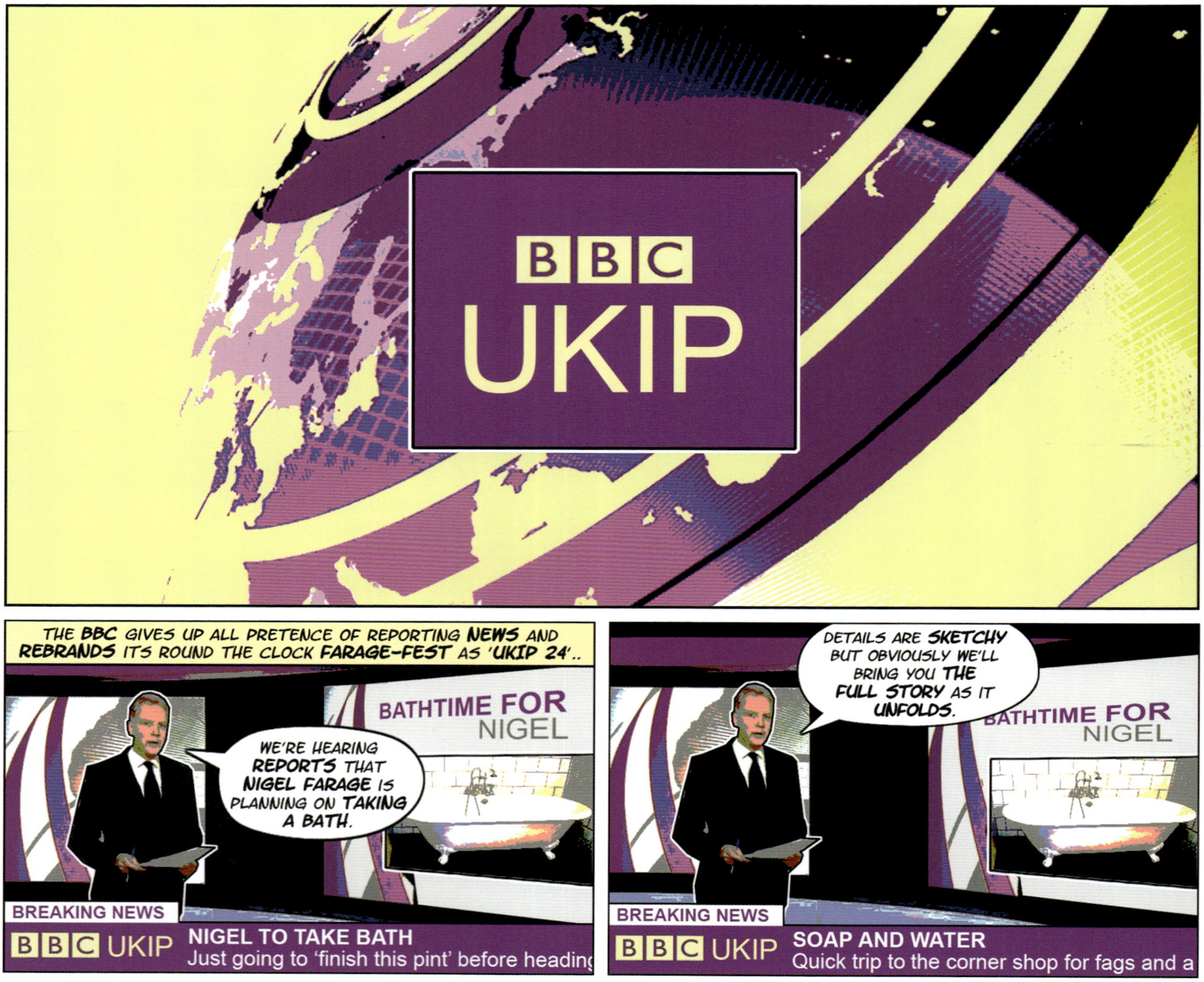

BBC
UKIP
THE BBC GIVES UP ALL PRETENCE OF REPORTING NEWS AND REBRANDS ITS ROUND THE CLOCK FARAGE-FEST AS 'UKIP 24'..
BATHTIME FOR NIGEL
WE'RE HEARING REPORTS THAT NIGEL FARAGE IS PLANNING ON TAKING A BATH.
BREAKING NEWS
BBC UKIP
NIGEL TO TAKE BATH
Just going to 'finish this pint' before heading
DETAILS ARE SKETCHY BUT OBVIOUSLY WE'LL BRING YOU THE FULL STORY AS IT UNFOLDS.
BATHTIME FOR NIGEL
BREAKING NEWS
BBC UKIP
SOAP AND WATER
Quick trip to the corner shop for fags and a

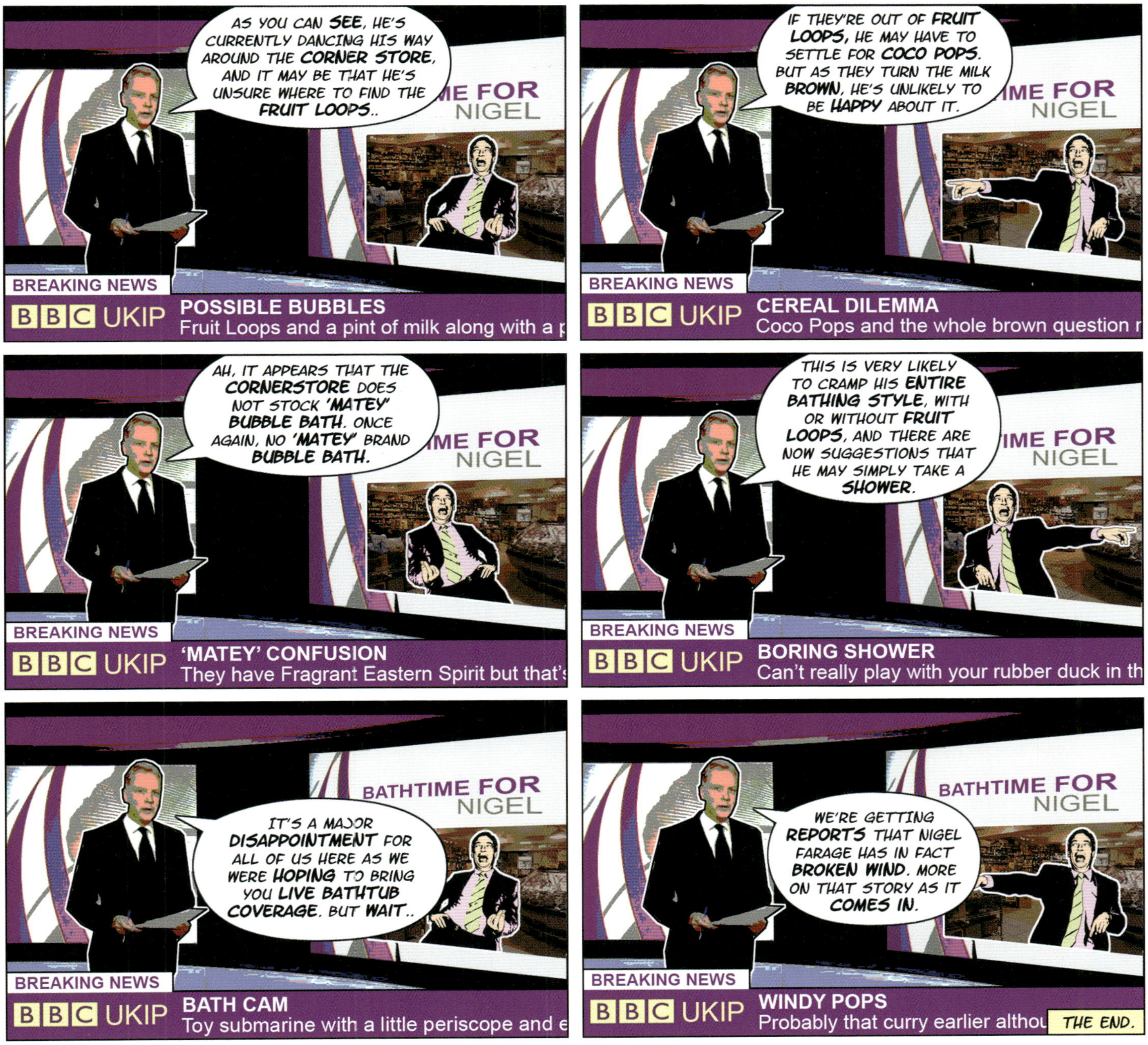
AS YOU CAN SEE, HE'S CURRENTLY DANCING HIS WAY AROUND THE CORNER STORE, AND IT MAY BE THAT HE'S UNSURE WHERE TO FIND THE FRUIT LOOPS..
NIGEL
BREAKING NEWS
BBC UKIP
POSSIBLE BUBBLES
Fruit Loops and a pint of milk along with a
IF THEY'RE OUT OF FRUIT LOOPS, HE MAY HAVE TO SETTLE FOR COCO POPS. BUT AS THEY TURN THE MILK BROWN, HE'S UNLIKELY TO BE HAPPY ABOUT IT.
NIGEL
BREAKING NEWS
BBC UKIP
CEREAL DILEMMA
Coco Pops and the whole brown question
AH, IT APPEARS THAT THE CORNERSTORE DOES NOT STOCK 'MATEY' BUBBLE BATH. ONCE AGAIN, NO 'MATEY' BRAND BUBBLE BATH.
NIGEL
BREAKING NEWS
BBC UKIP
'MATEY' CONFUSION
They have Fragrant Eastern Spirit but that's
THIS IS VERY LIKELY TO CRAMP HIS ENTIRE BATHING STYLE, WITH OR WITHOUT FRUIT LOOPS, AND THERE ARE NOW SUGGESTIONS THAT HE MAY SIMPLY TAKE A SHOWER.
NIGEL
BREAKING NEWS
BBC UKIP
BORING SHOWER
Can't really play with your rubber duck in th
BATHTIME FOR NIGEL
IT'S A MAJOR DISAPPOINTMENT FOR ALL OF US HERE AS WE WERE HOPING TO BRING YOU LIVE BATHTUB COVERAGE. BUT WAIT..
BREAKING NEWS
BBC UKIP
BATH CAM
Toy submarine with a little periscope and
BATHTIME FOR NIGEL
WE'RE GETTING REPORTS THAT NIGEL FARAGE HAS IN FACT BROKEN WIND. MORE ON THAT STORY AS IT COMES IN.
BREAKING NEWS
BBC UKIP
WINDY POPS
Probably that curry earlier althou
THE END.

VOTE NO SHAME

MAY 30TH 2014

in an advert screened in cinemas, mock grassroots organisation (also known as an 'astroturf' organisation) Vote No Borders claimed that, post-independence, Scots would join a "long list of foreigners" waiting for treatment in hospitals such as Great Ormond Street. Unfortunately Great Ormond Street begged to differ and the advert had to be withdrawn.

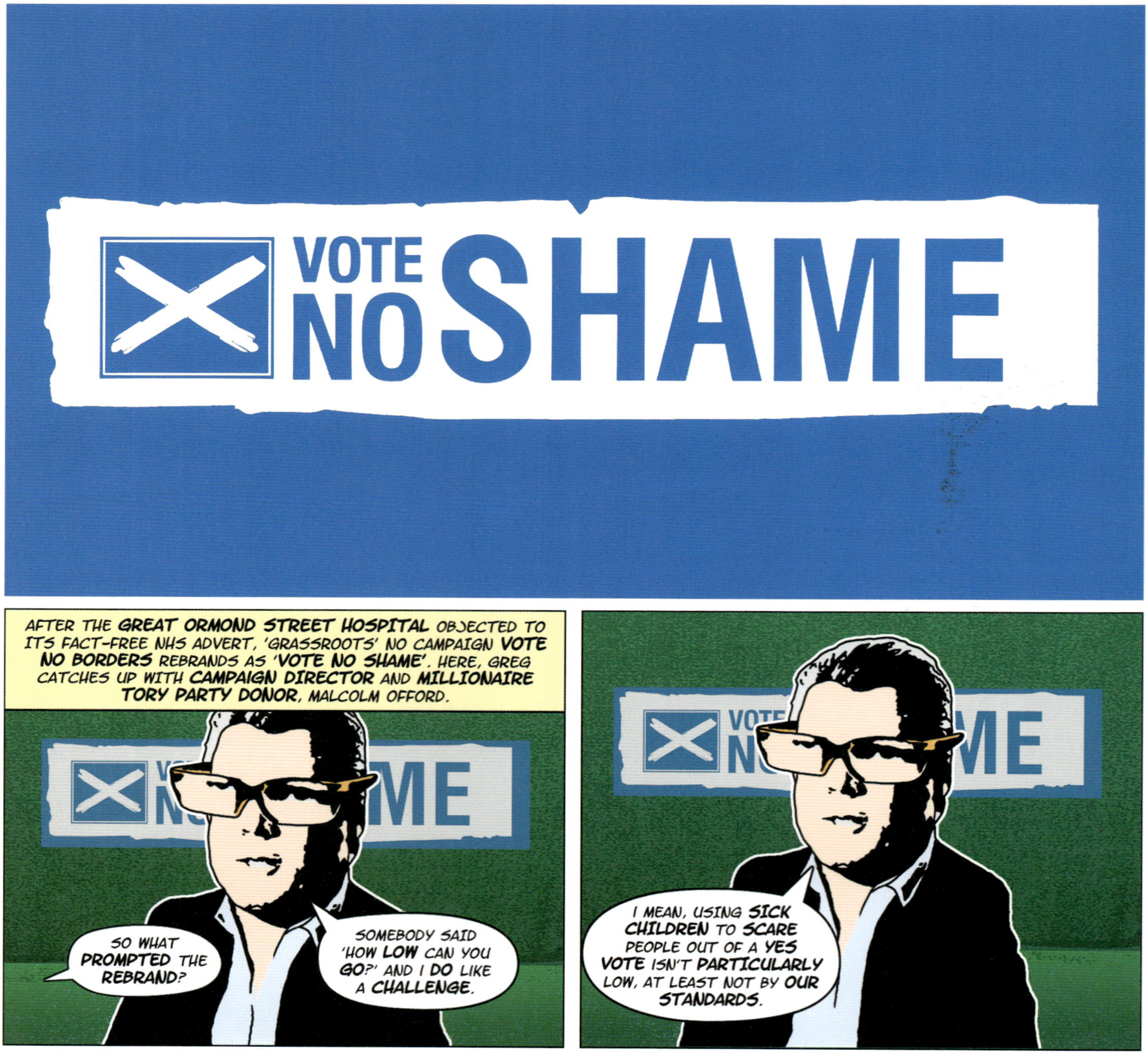

VOTE NO SHAME
AFTER THE GREAT ORMOND STREET HOSPITAL OBJECTED TO ITS FACT-FREE NHS ADVERT, 'GRASSROOTS' NO CAMPAIGN VOTE NO BORDERS REBRANDS AS 'VOTE NO SHAME'. HERE, GREG CATCHES UP WITH CAMPAIGN DIRECTOR AND MILLIONAIRE TORY PARTY DONOR, MALCOLM OFFORD.
SO WHAT PROMPTED THE REBRAND?
SOMEBODY SAID 'HOW LOW CAN YOU GO?' AND I DO LIKE A CHALLENGE.
I MEAN, USING SICK CHILDREN TO SCARE PEOPLE OUT OF A YES VOTE ISN'T PARTICULARLY LOW, AT LEAST NOT BY OUR STANDARDS.

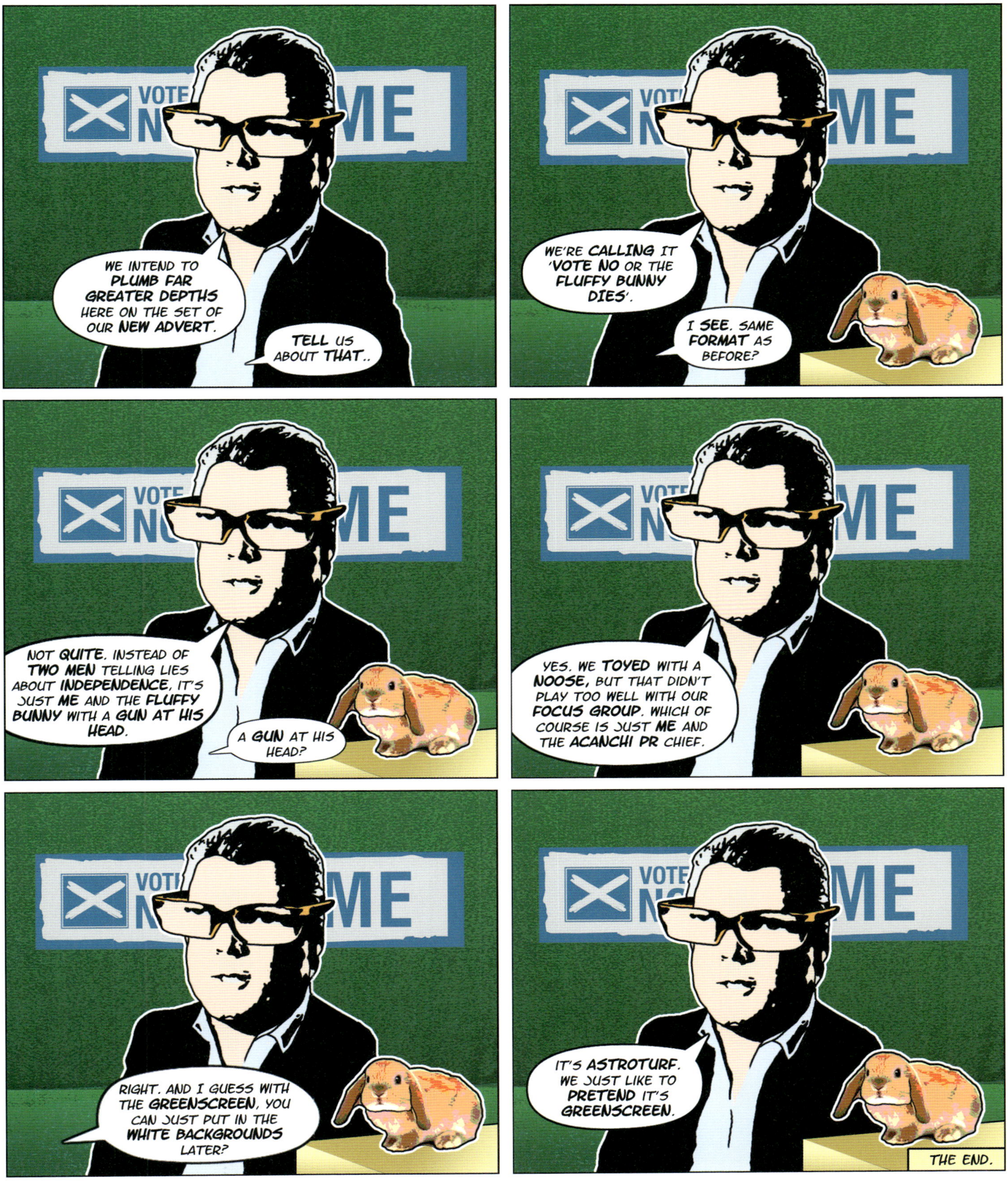
VOTE NO ME
WE INTEND TO PLUMB FAR GREATER DEPTHS HERE ON THE SET OF OUR NEW ADVERT.
TELL US ABOUT THAT..
WE'RE CALLING IT 'VOTE NO OR THE FLUFFY BUNNY DIES'.
I SEE. SAME FORMAT AS BEFORE?
NOT QUITE. INSTEAD OF TWO MEN TELLING LIES ABOUT INDEPENDENCE, IT'S JUST ME AND THE FLUFFY BUNNY WITH A GUN AT HIS HEAD.
A GUN AT HIS HEAD?
YES. WE TOYED WITH A NOOSE, BUT THAT DIDN'T PLAY TOO WELL WITH OUR FOCUS GROUP. WHICH OF COURSE IS JUST ME AND THE ACANCHI PR CHIEF.
RIGHT. AND I GUESS WITH THE GREENSCREEN, YOU CAN JUST PUT IN THE WHITE BACKGROUNDS LATER?
IT'S ASTROTURF. WE JUST LIKE TO PRETEND IT'S GREENSCREEN.
THE END.

THE FREE WORLD. AND SCOTLAND.

JUNE 7TH 2014

Obama on the UK remaining in Europe: "It is hard for me to imagine it would be advantageous for Great Britain to be excluded from political decisions that have an enormous impact on its economic and political life." In the same speech, Obama on Scotland remaining in the UK: "From the outside at least it looks like things have worked pretty well." Guardian headline: "Barack Obama suggests Scotland should stay in UK."

THE LEADER OF THE FREE WORLD GIVES AS CLEAR AN INDICATION AS HE CAN THAT THE UK SHOULD STAY IN EUROPE. BUT NUMBER 10 DOESN'T WANT TO HEAR IT AND THE PRESS DOESN'T WANT TO REPORT IT, ESPECIALLY SINCE HE'D ALSO MADE THIS "STRIKING" AND "UNEXPECTED" SCOTTISH INDEPENDENCE INTERVENTION..
IN THE CASE OF .. AH.. SCATLAND.. I WOULD SAY THAT.. AH.. FROM THE OUTSIDE AT LEAST..
THE UNITED KINGDOM LOOKS LIKE A NICE PLACE.. AH.. IT SEEMS KINDA NEAT..
IT HAS A PRETTY FLAG.. AH.. WITH THE SAME COLOURS AS OURS..
AND AH.. YOU MIGHT WANT TO HANG ONTO THAT.

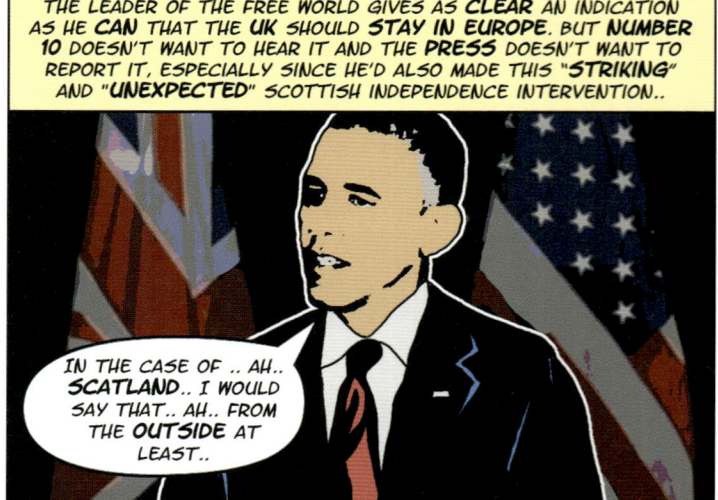

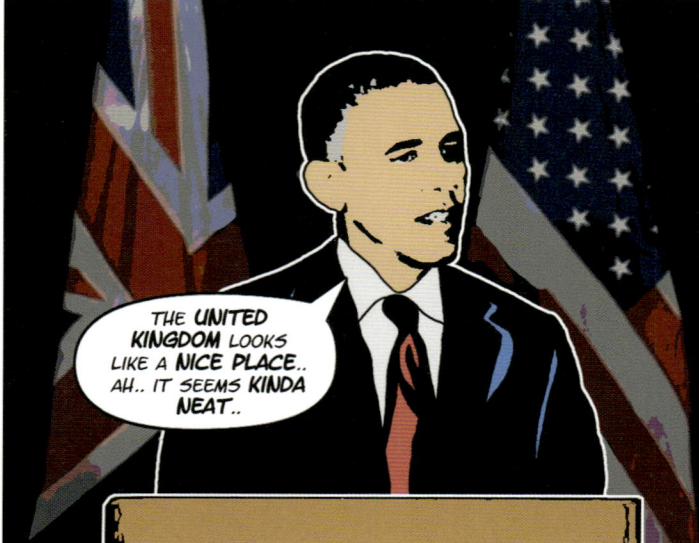

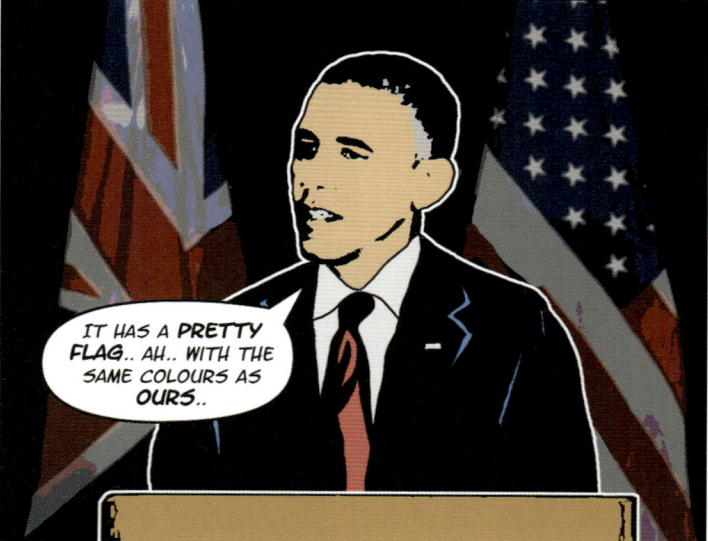

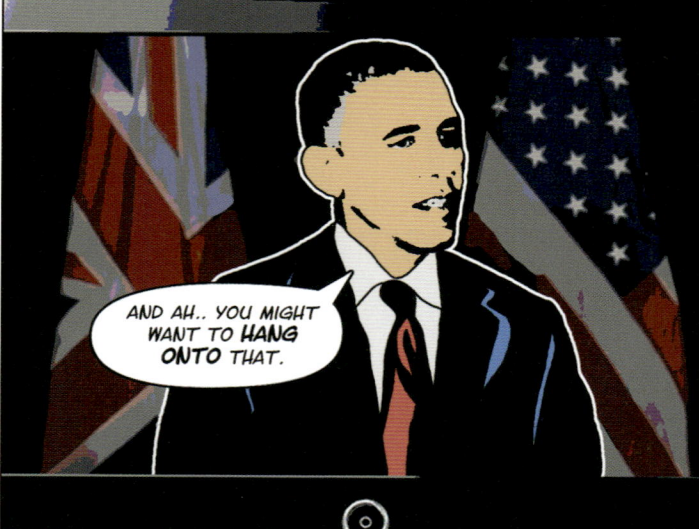

OBVIOUSLY, WE LEFT A LONG TIME AGO.. BUT.. AH..
THAT DOESN'T NECESSARILY MEAN THAT.. AH.. YOU SHOULD.
ULTIMATELY THOUGH.. AH.. IT'S YOUR CHOICE.
IT WAS AN EXTRAORDINARY CONTRIBUTION TO THE DEBATE, AND SCOTTISH VOTERS INDEED MADE A CHOICE..
THE END.

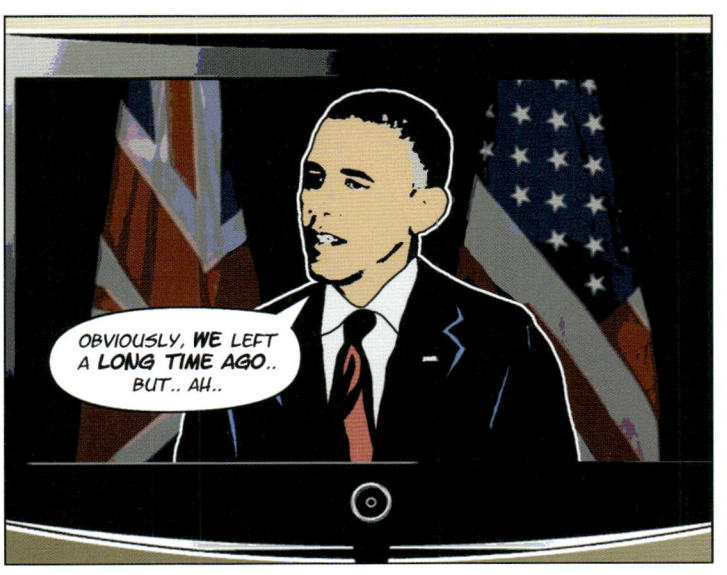

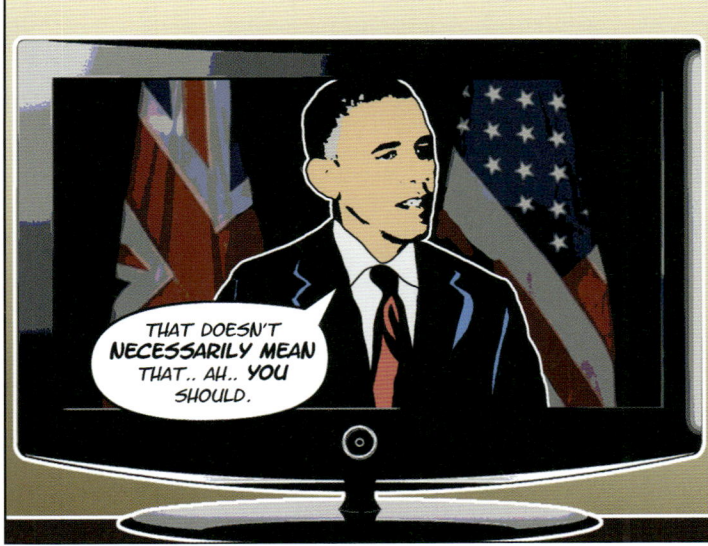

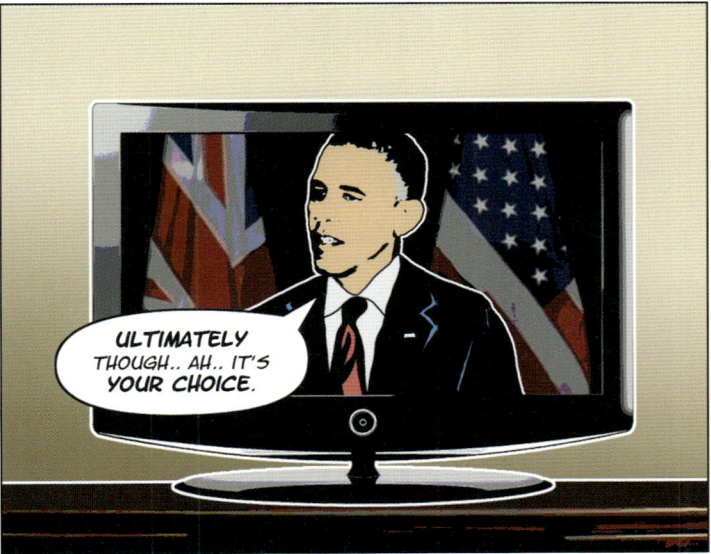

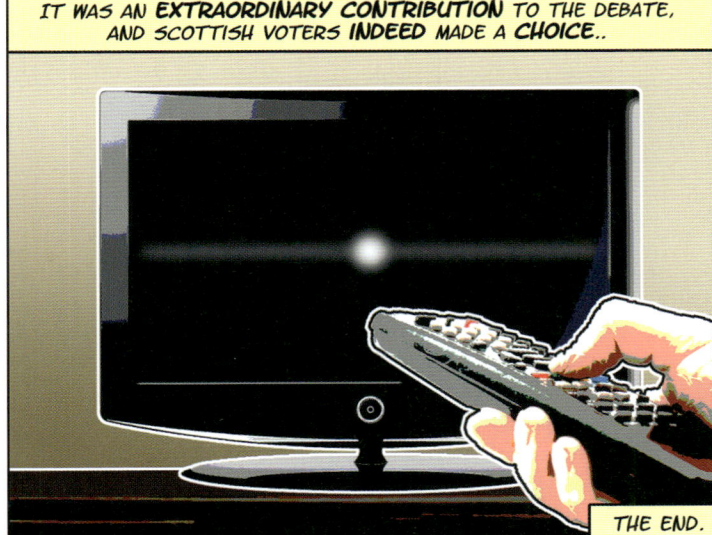

AN ORDINARY MUM

JUNE 14TH 2014

First, Better Together's grassroots 'ordinary mum' Clare Lally turned out to be a member of the shadow cabinet. Then Alistair Darling, when asked if he thought the SNP were 'blood and soil nationalists', replied "at heart." Then we discovered a Better Together advert was made in the BBC's Glasgow studio, flouting the BBC's own guidelines. And here they are, all in one cartoon.

DELIGHTED WITH HAVING PASSED OFF A MEMBER OF THE SHADOW CABINET AS A GRASSROOTS ACTIVIST, THE LABOUR PARTY TRIES TO REVIVE ITS AILING FORTUNES BY INTRODUCING "ORDINARY MUM", ALISTAIR FROM EDINBURGH..
IT'S TOUGH BEING AN ORDINARY MUM. THERE'S THE COOKING, THE CLEANING, AND OF COURSE DEALING WITH THE CONSTITUENTS OF EDINBURGH SOUTH WEST.
I FERRY THE KIDS AROUND, MANAGE THE HOUSEHOLD BUDGET AND THEN TALK UTTER BALLS ABOUT THE CONSEQUENCES OF INDEPENDENCE.
IT'S SO DEMANDING THAT I BARELY HAVE TIME TO FLIP HOMES ANYMORE.
YESTERDAY I WAS OUT DOING THE SHOPPING. A WOMAN APPROACHED AND SAID "HOW DO YOU MANAGE TO BE SUCH AN EXCELLENT ORDINARY MUM?"

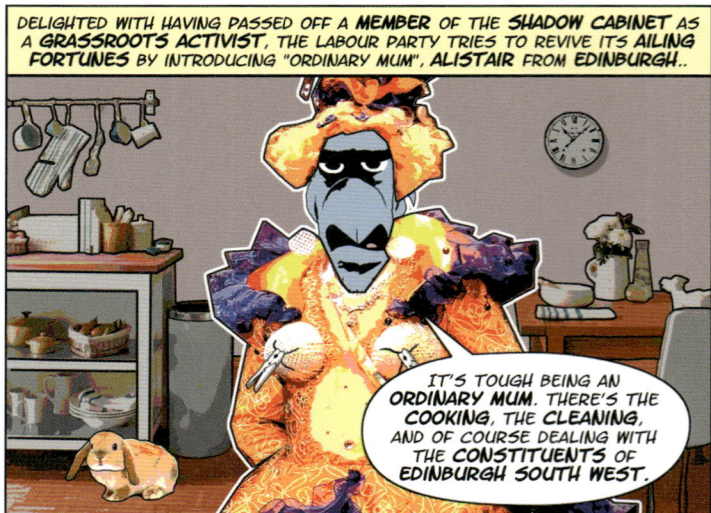

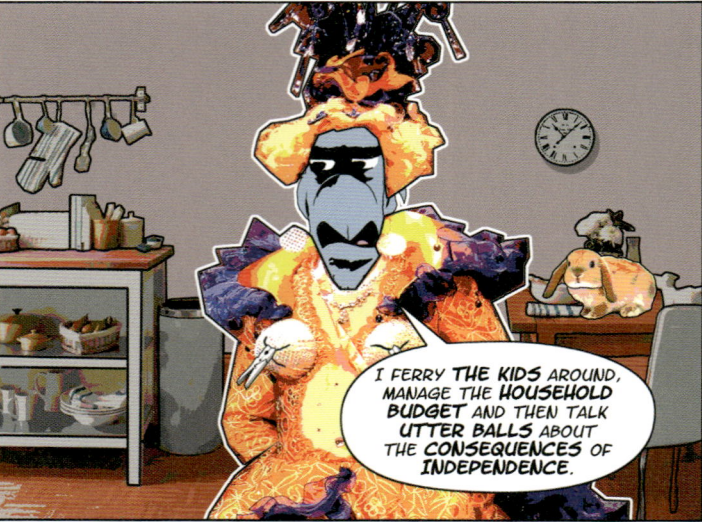

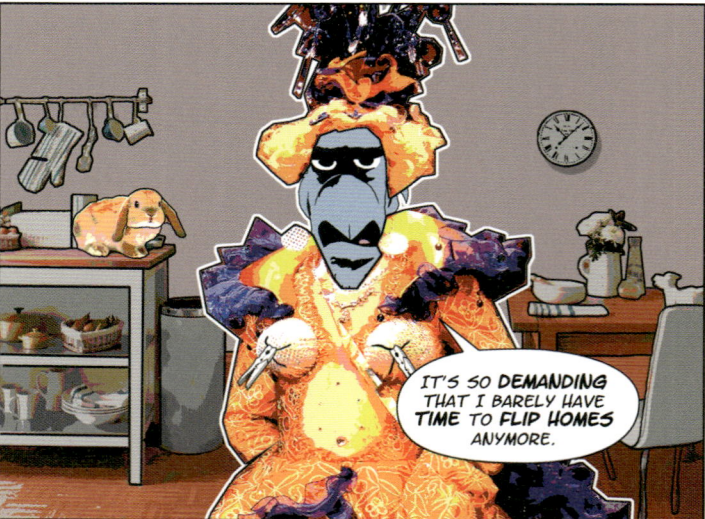

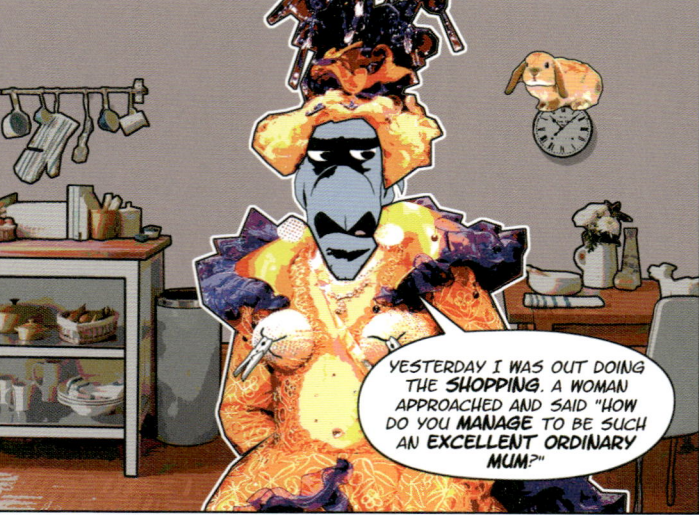

I SAID "LOOK, AT HEART, THE YES CAMPAIGN ARE BLOOD AND SOIL NATIONALISTS WHO WON'T BE HAPPY UNTIL THEY'VE SLAUGHTERED YOUR FIRSTBORN."
SHE LAUGHED AND SAID "THANK YOU, I'LL BE VOTING NO NOW." IT'S MOMENTS LIKE THESE THAT MAKE IT ALL WORTHWHILE.
SUDDENLY, THE BBC STUDIO USED TO FILM THIS CARTOON IS DISRUPTED BY AN OVERSIZED REPTILIAN PREDATOR..
ROAR!!!
WHAT THE..?
MEET MY HUSBAND, GORDON.
HUNGYYY!!!
THE END.

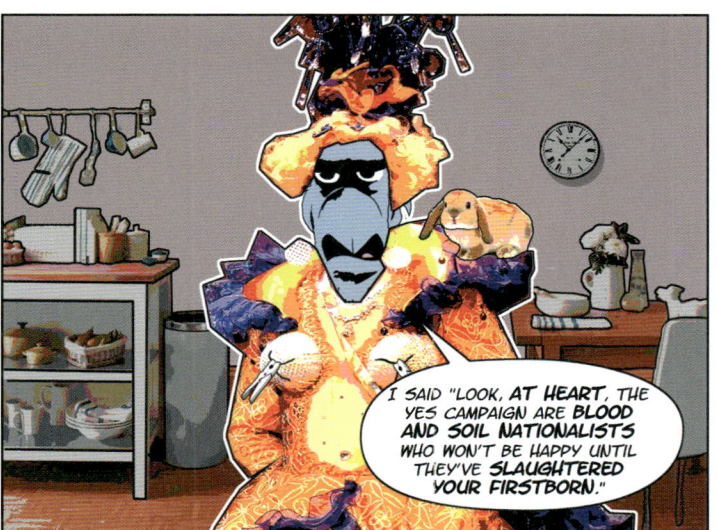

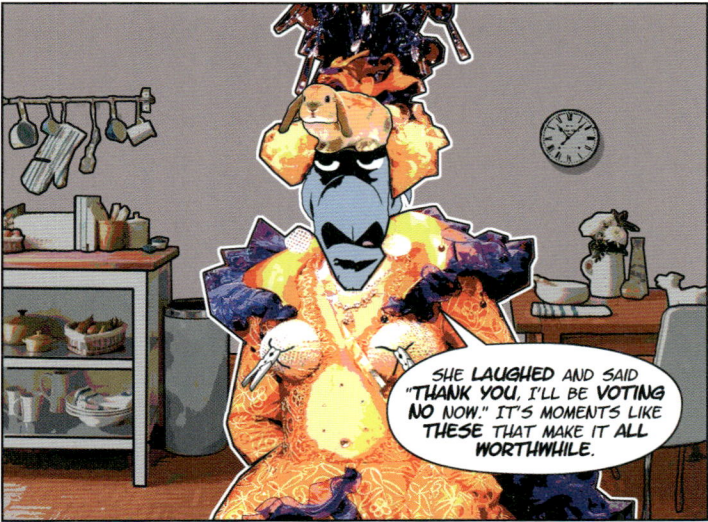

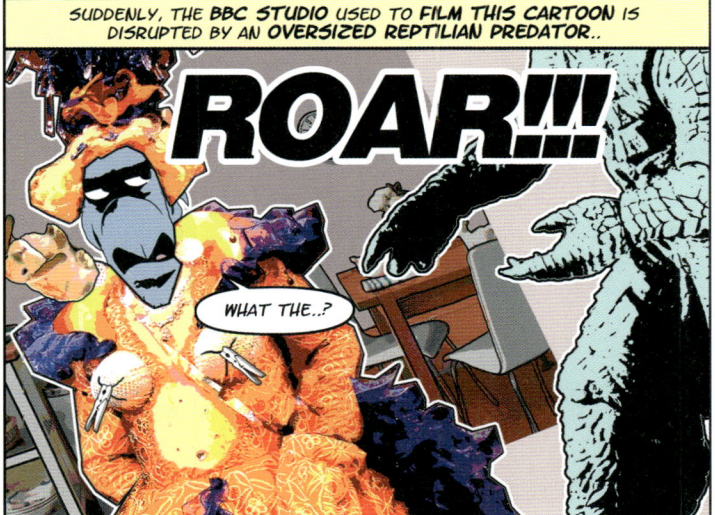

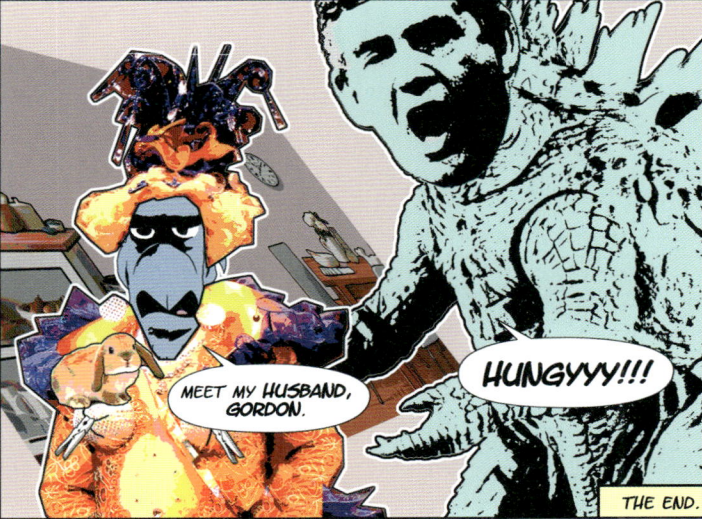

GOD BACKS A NO VOTE

JUNE 20TH 2014

Regardless of who Westminster cajoled into speaking out against independence, it didn't seem to have any effect on the polls. Imagine their frustration. Meanwhile, Labour promised to provide everyone in the country with their own owl after their Twitter account was hacked.

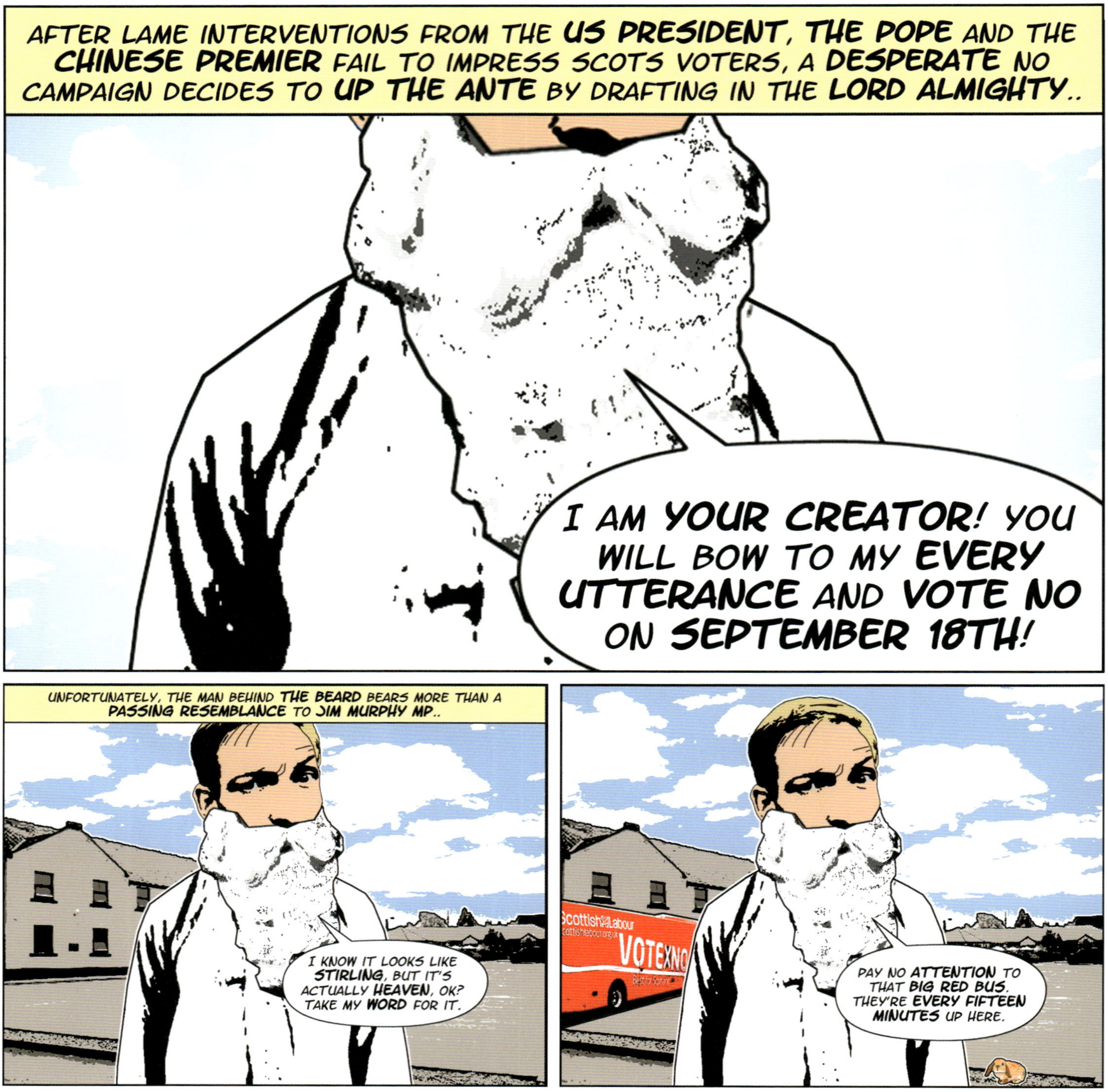

AFTER LAME INTERVENTIONS FROM THE US PRESIDENT, THE POPE AND THE CHINESE PREMIER FAIL TO IMPRESS SCOTS VOTERS, A DESPERATE NO CAMPAIGN DECIDES TO UP THE ANTE BY DRAFTING IN THE LORD ALMIGHTY..
I AM YOUR CREATOR! YOU WILL BOW TO MY EVERY UTTERANCE AND VOTE NO ON SEPTEMBER 18TH!
UNFORTUNATELY, THE MAN BEHIND THE BEARD BEARS MORE THAN A PASSING RESEMBLANCE TO JIM MURPHY MP..
I KNOW IT LOOKS LIKE STIRLING, BUT IT'S ACTUALLY HEAVEN, OK? TAKE MY WORD FOR IT.
PAY NO ATTENTION TO THAT BIG RED BUS. THEY'RE EVERY FIFTEEN MINUTES UP HERE.

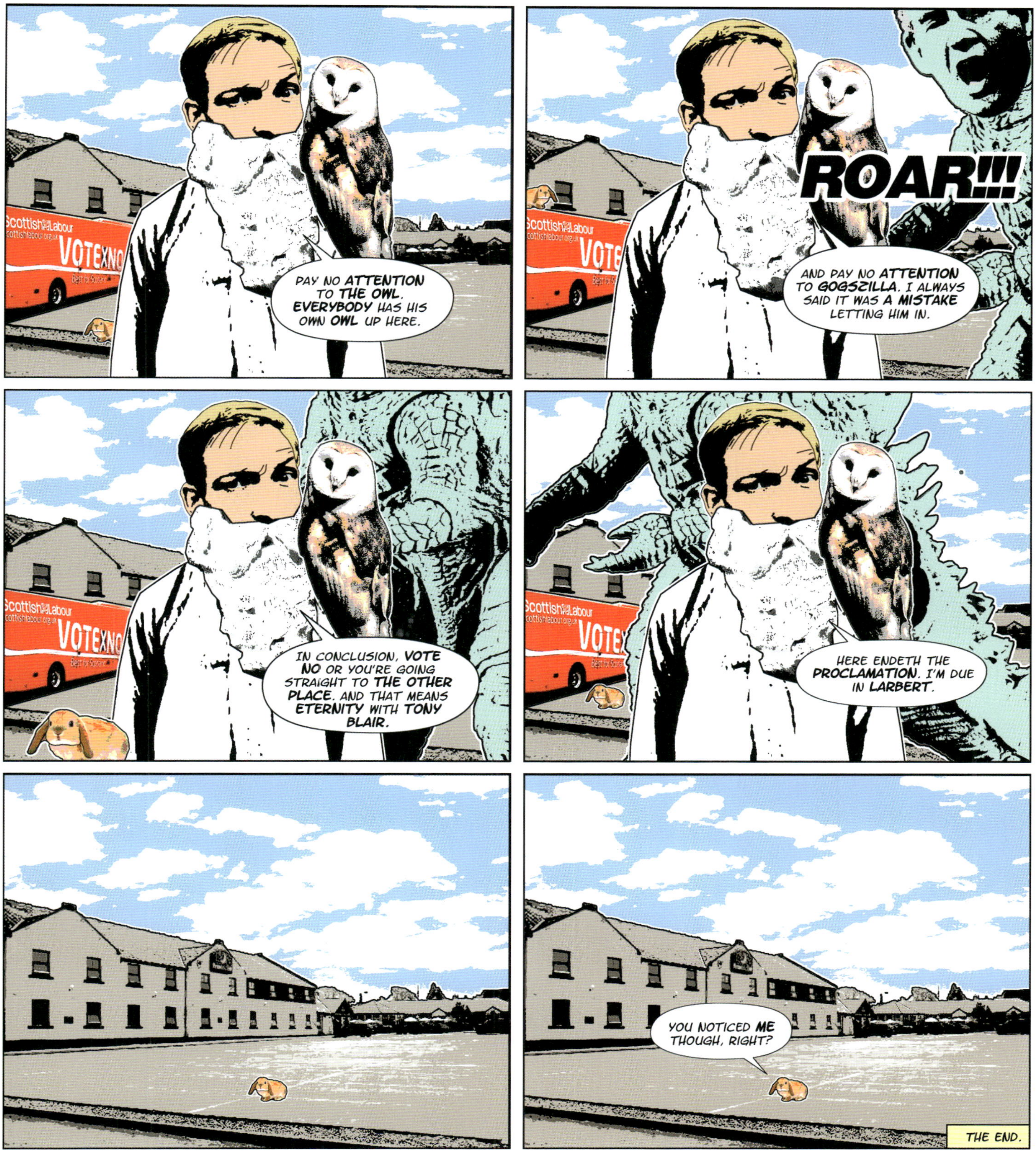
Scottish Labour
VOTE NO
PAY NO ATTENTION TO THE OWL. EVERYBODY HAS HIS OWN OWL UP HERE.
ROAR!!!
AND PAY NO ATTENTION TO GOGSZILLA. I ALWAYS SAID IT WAS A MISTAKE LETTING HIM IN.
IN CONCLUSION, VOTE NO OR YOU'RE GOING STRAIGHT TO THE OTHER PLACE. AND THAT MEANS ETERNITY WITH TONY BLAIR.
HERE ENDETH THE PROCLAMATION. I'M DUE IN LARBERT.
YOU NOTICED ME THOUGH, RIGHT?
THE END.

THE HEEBY JEEBIES

JUNE 28TH 2014

After months of trying to hook up with the debate-shy Prime Minister, Alex Salmond agreed to debate with Alistair Darling instead, and suggested that Darling may have the 'heeby jeebies'. By this point Better Together had rebranded as No Thanks. But it was still Project Fear to me.

HEAD OF 'NO THANKS', ALISTAIR DARLING, CALLS DAVID CAMERON..
NO THANKS
LOOK CAMMY, WHATEVER HAPPENED TO THE WHOLE FIRST MINISTER PRIME MINISTER THING?
I KNOW I SAID I'D DEBATE HIM ANYTIME ANYWHERE, BUT I NEVER THOUGHT IT WOULD ACTUALLY HAPPEN.
ANYHOW, AUGUST 5TH IS SIMPLY OUT OF THE QUESTION.
ct fear
BECAUSE I'M.. HAVING MY NIPPLE CLAMPS TIGHTENED.

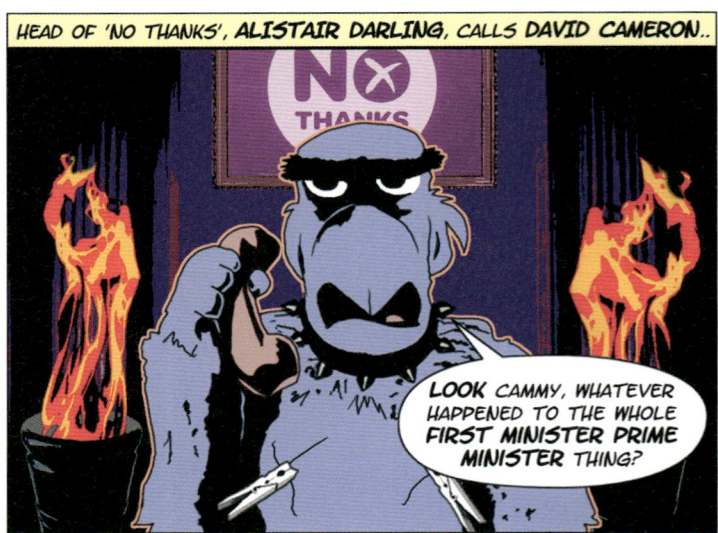

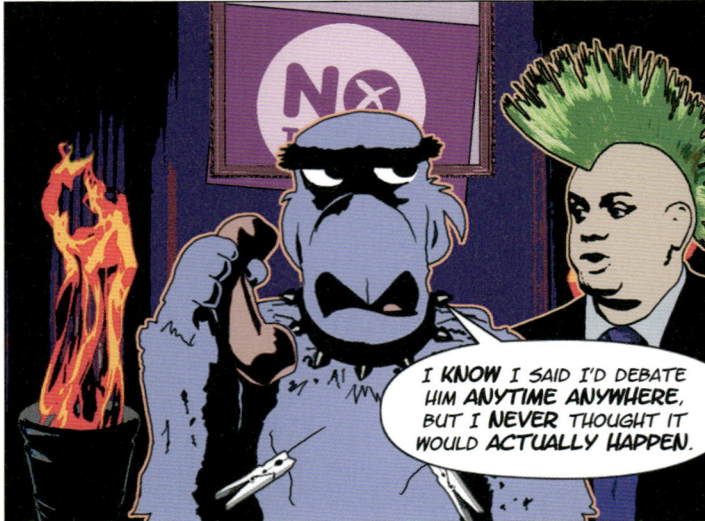

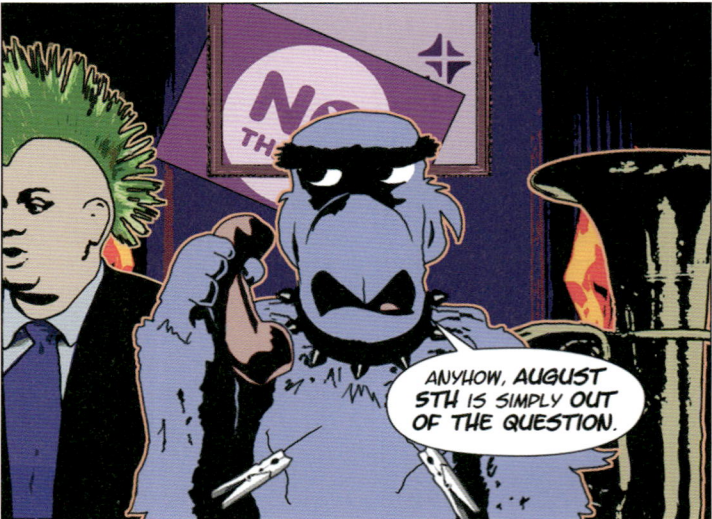

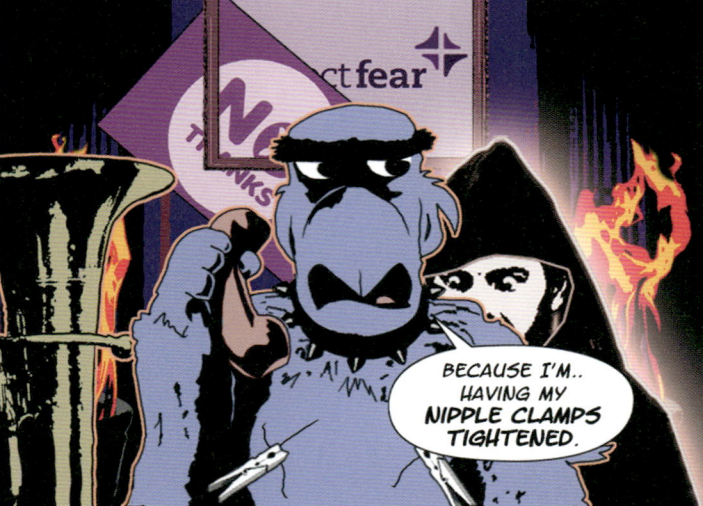

NO, ON THE 6TH, I'M HAVING A BRAZILIAN.
NO, THE 7TH IS MY RHUMBA LESSON.
NO, I DON'T HAVE THE HEEBY JEEBIES! I HAVE FULLBLOWN RUNS IN MY SHORTS!
OF COURSE EVERYTHING ELSE IS FINE!
THE END.

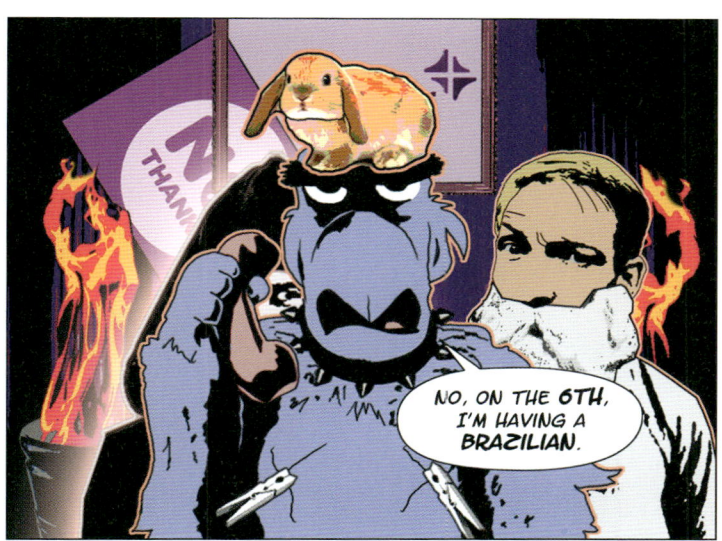

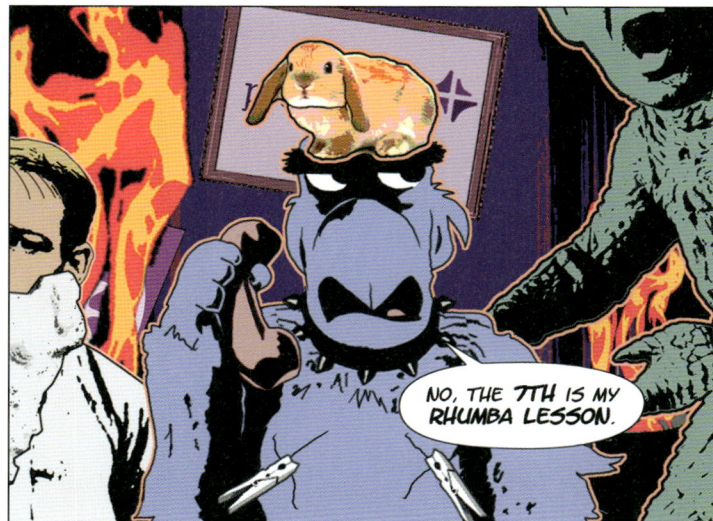

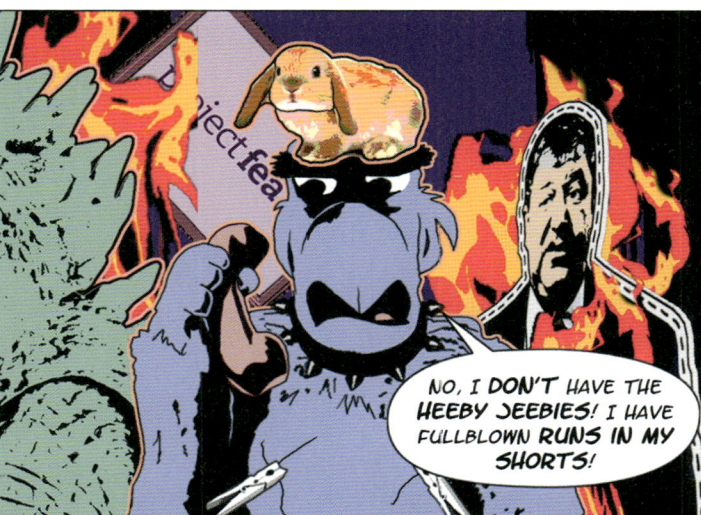

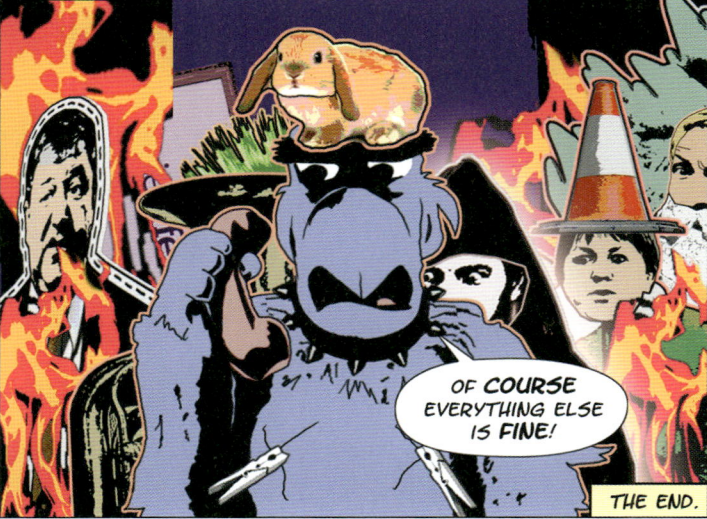

DON'T BREAK MY HEART

JULY 4TH 2014

"It would break my heart to see our United Kingdom break apart," said the Prime Minister at a Conservative Friends of the Union rally in Perth. It had a musical ring to it, but not in a good way. Here he performs outside the aptly-named Deadwood Saloon.

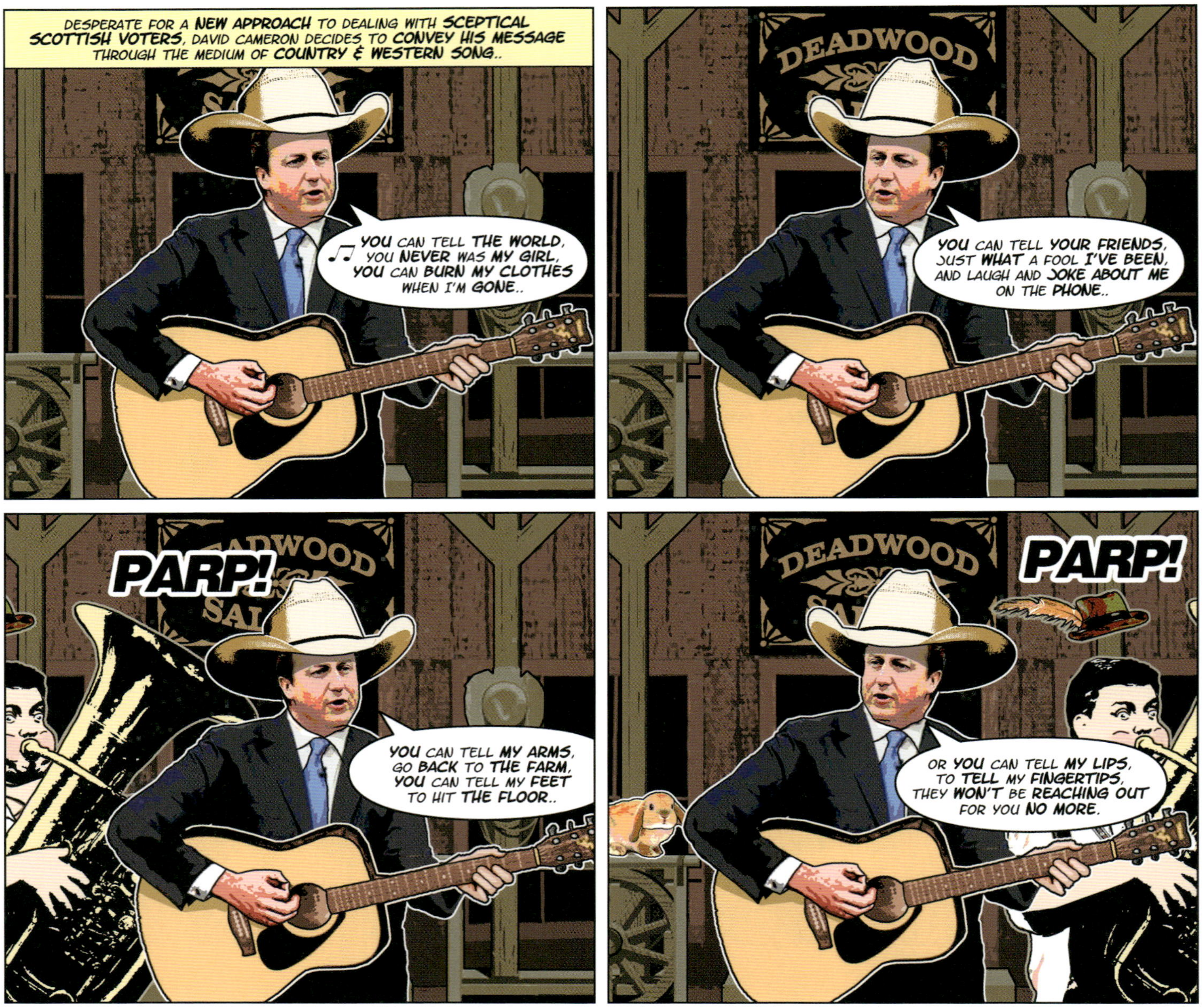

DESPERATE FOR A NEW APPROACH TO DEALING WITH SCEPTICAL SCOTTISH VOTERS, DAVID CAMERON DECIDES TO CONVEY HIS MESSAGE THROUGH THE MEDIUM OF COUNTRY & WESTERN SONG..
♫ YOU CAN TELL THE WORLD, YOU NEVER WAS MY GIRL, YOU CAN BURN MY CLOTHES WHEN I'M GONE..
DEADWOOD
YOU CAN TELL YOUR FRIENDS, JUST WHAT A FOOL I'VE BEEN, AND LAUGH AND JOKE ABOUT ME ON THE PHONE..
PARP!
YOU CAN TELL MY ARMS, GO BACK TO THE FARM, YOU CAN TELL MY FEET TO HIT THE FLOOR..
DEADWOOD
PARP!
OR YOU CAN TELL MY LIPS, TO TELL MY FINGERTIPS, THEY WON'T BE REACHING OUT FOR YOU NO MORE.

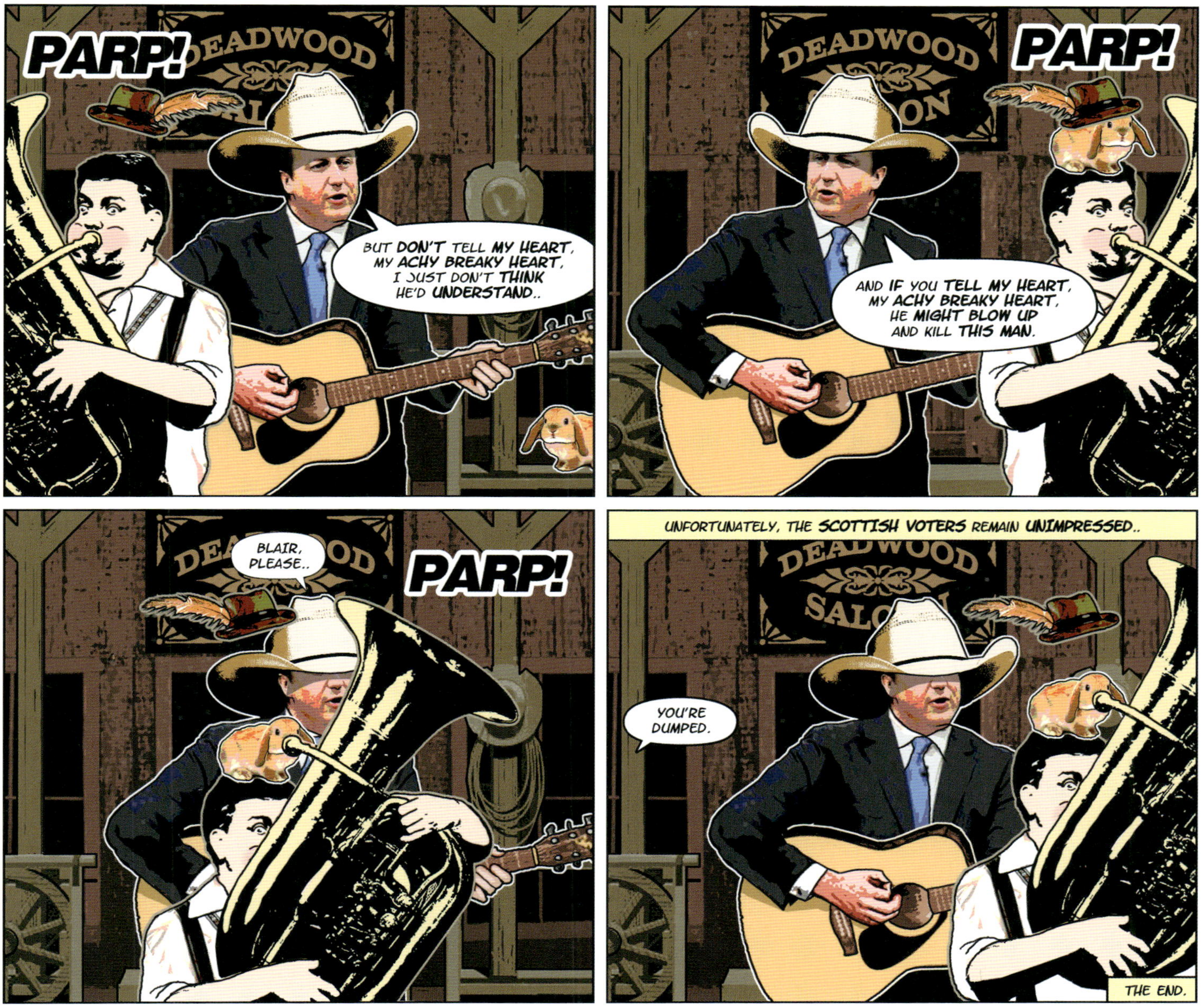
PARP!
BUT DON'T TELL MY HEART, MY ACHY BREAKY HEART, I JUST DON'T THINK HE'D UNDERSTAND..
PARP!
AND IF YOU TELL MY HEART, MY ACHY BREAKY HEART, HE MIGHT BLOW UP AND KILL THIS MAN.
BLAIR, PLEASE..
PARP!
UNFORTUNATELY, THE SCOTTISH VOTERS REMAIN UNIMPRESSED..
YOU'RE DUMPED.
THE END.

GREG MOODIE DANCES WITH THE DEVIL

JULY 11TH 2014

Sometimes the indyref debate feels like an 'us and them' thing. It's easy to think of those with different views as 'other' but it's not particularly helpful. McTernan and The Farq are no more bad guys than Hassan is a good guy. Still, 'Patriots Vote No' was pretty hard to swallow.

THIS WEEK I MET THE SCOTSMAN'S KENNY FARQUHARSON. HE'S THE ONE WHO SAID ARTISTS FOR INDEPENDENCE OUGHT TO HAVE MORE ART, THEREBY LAUNCHING ME INTO THE WORLD OF CARTOONING..
LISTEN FARQ, I WANT YOU TO WRITE THE FOREWORD TO MY BOOK.
CERTAINLY GREG, IN EXCHANGE FOR YOUR..
HERE'S SOME BADGES.
OOOH! BADGES!
I DON'T KNOW WHICH ONE TO WEAR FIRST. MAYBE 'CONES FOR INDEPENDENCE'..
OK, CALM DOWN, SATAN-BOY.
THE DEVIL DIDN'T SEEM SO BAD, ALTHOUGH IT HAS TO BE SAID THIS PARTICULAR INCARNATION WAS FROM DUNDEE.
THE NEXT DAY, I ATTENDED A TALK BY FORMER TONY BLAIR SPINDOCTOR JOHN MCTERNAN. THIS DEVIL'S PATTER WAS A LITTLE MORE CHALLENGING..
PATRIOTS VOTE NO. AFGHANISTAN WAS A GOOD THING. KEEP VOTING LABOUR. I'M A SOCIALIST.
YOU'RE MORE LIKE A JEHOVAH'S WITNESS. BUT NOT AS MUCH FUN.

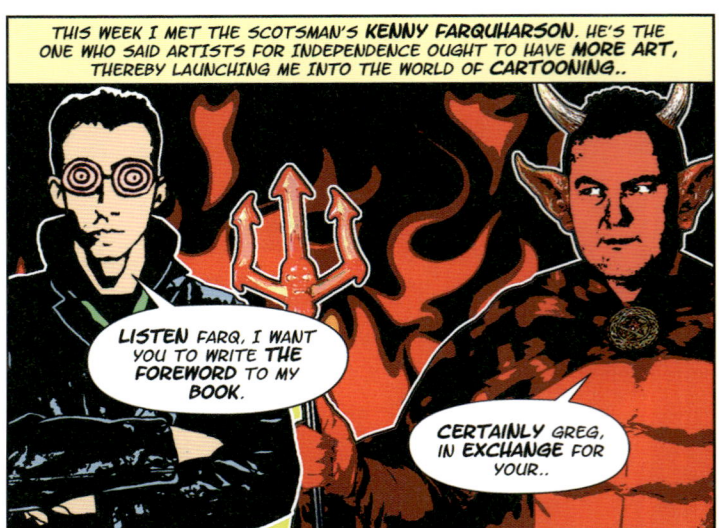

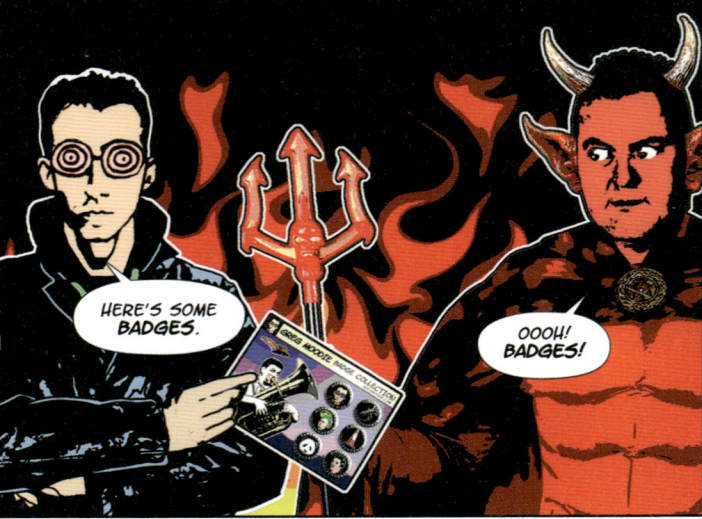

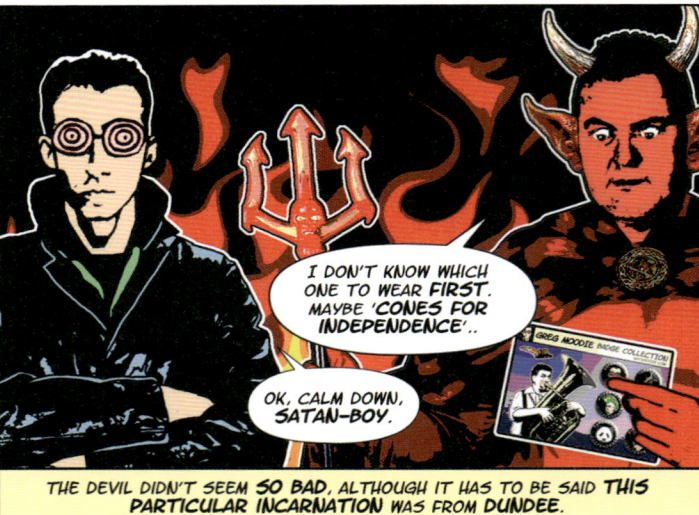

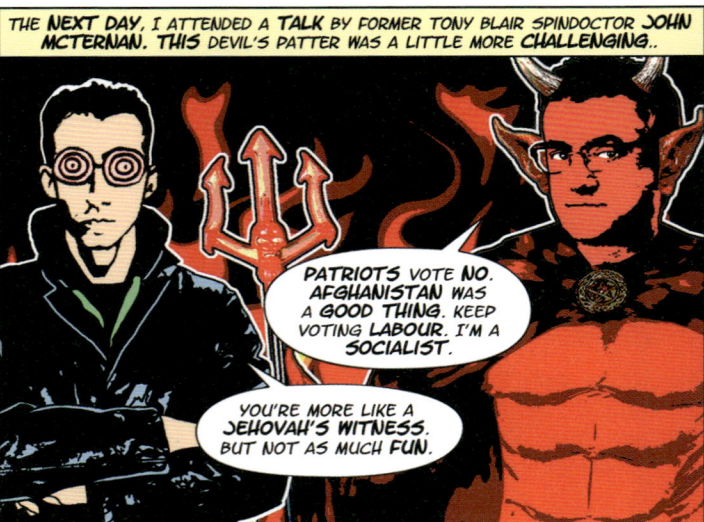

THEN THE DEVIL SAID SOMETHING INTERESTING...
WHAT'S THE POINT OF ATTENDING A TALK BY SOMEONE WHOSE VIEWS ARE IDENTICAL TO YOUR OWN?
YOU'VE GOT ME THERE, CHIEF.
AT THIS POINT I MET THE AUTHOR OF CALEDONIAN DREAMING, GERRY HASSAN..
DID YOU ACTUALLY SAY YOU'RE A SOCIALIST?
THE END

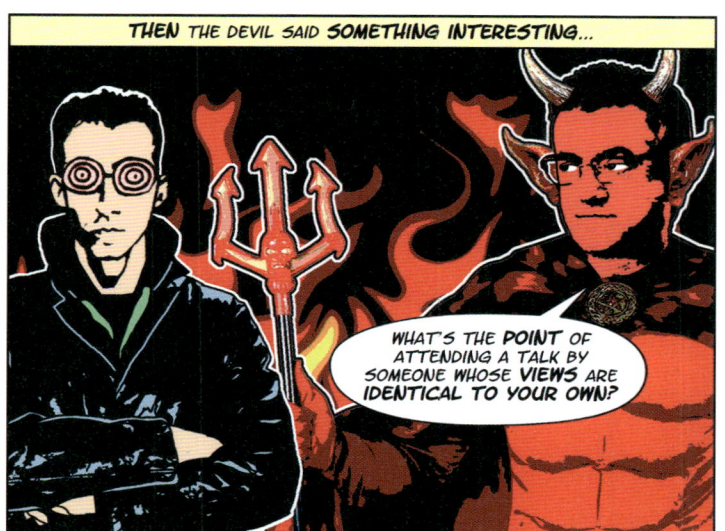

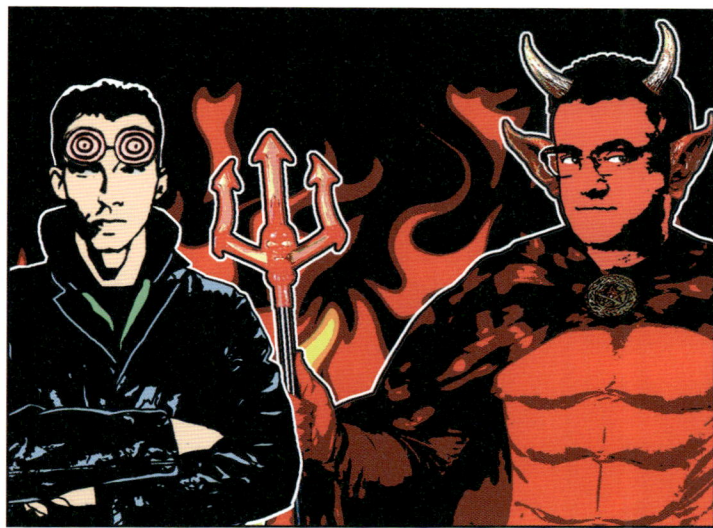

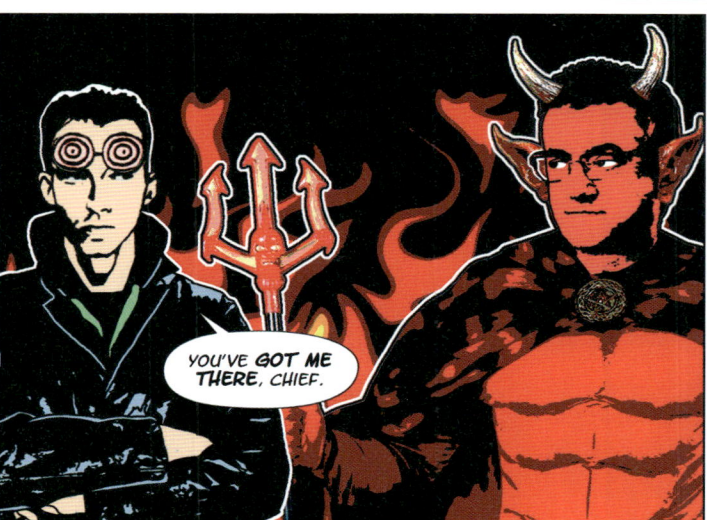

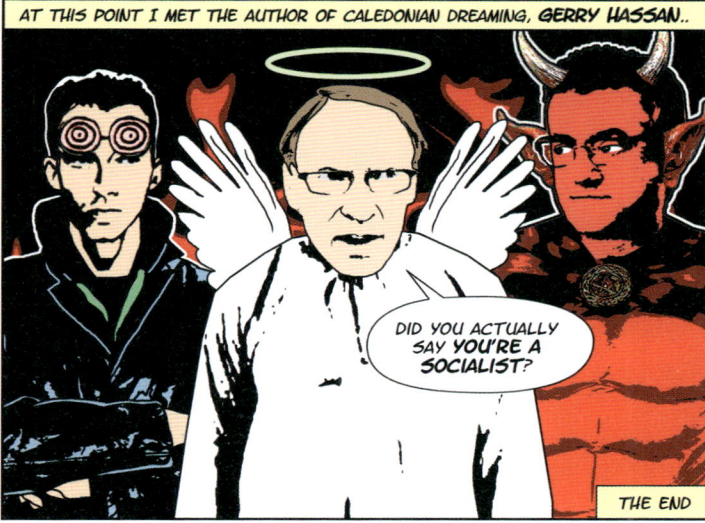

ROSS KEMP PRESENTS THE GREG MOODIE CARTOON

JULY 18TH 2014

I'm not sure why anyone would think it's a good idea to hold up a sign in front of the cameras, but that's what Grant Mitchell, Baldrick and a bunch of other celebs did for a Better Together video that played out to a soundtrack of Queen's 'You're my best friend'.

PARP!
THAT WAS LOVELY, TUBBY. YOU'RE MY BEST FRIEND.
YES, BLAIR.
I'M A BIT UNSURE ABOUT THE WHOLE ROSS KEMP SITUATION, THOUGH.
I KNOW. HE'S TOTALLY BEEN COASTING SINCE 'GANGS'.
NO, I MEAN GETTING A BUNCH OF D-LIST CELEBS TOGETHER JUST SO EDDIE IZZARD CAN BE MAYOR OF LONDON.
OH, THAT. MEH.

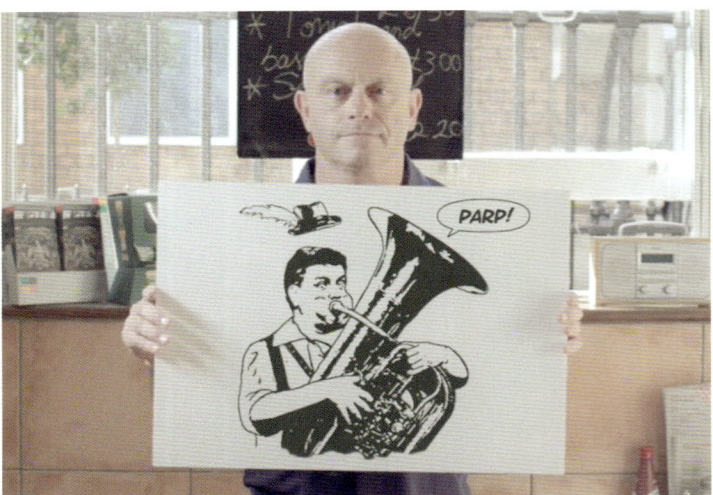

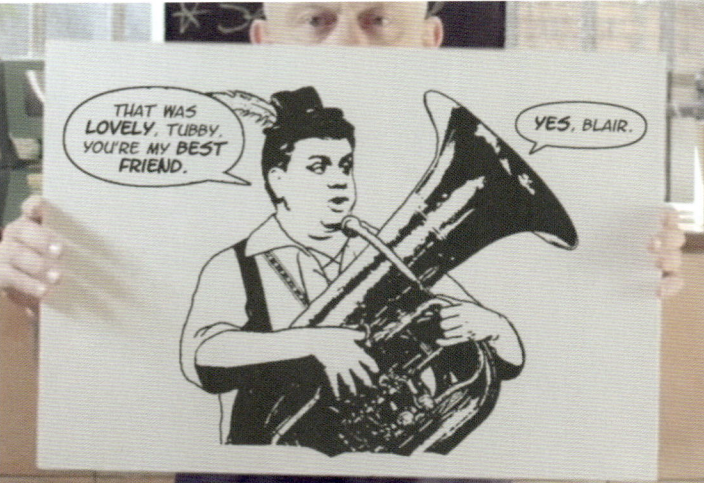

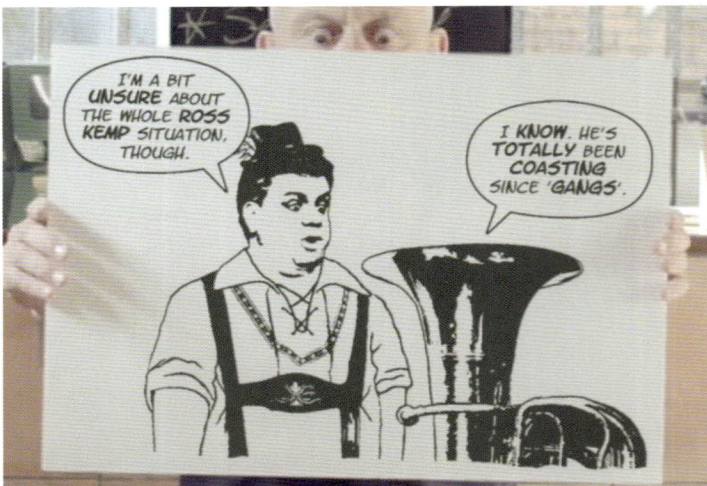

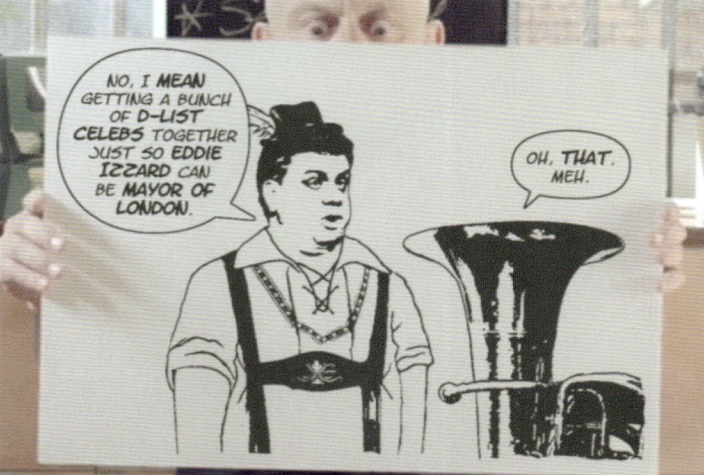

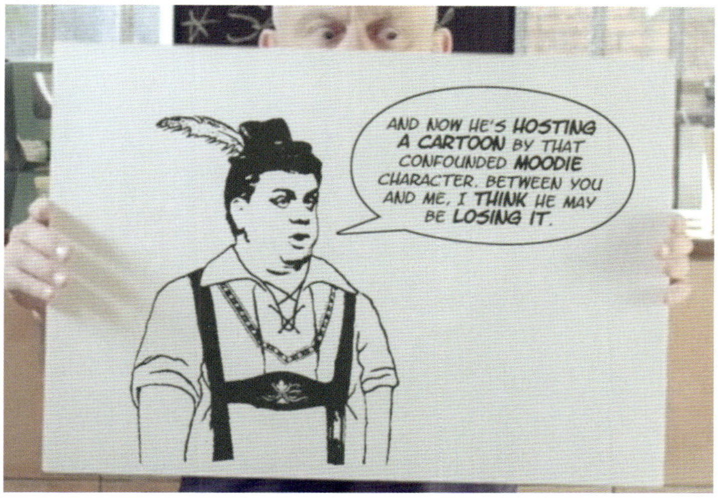
AND NOW HE'S HOSTING A CARTOON BY THAT CONFOUNDED MOODIE CHARACTER. BETWEEN YOU AND ME, I THINK HE MAY BE LOSING IT.

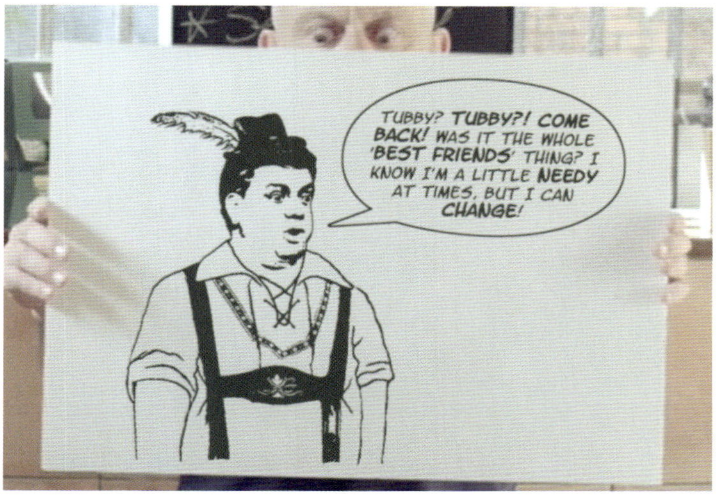
TUBBY? TUBBY?! COME BACK! WAS IT THE WHOLE 'BEST FRIENDS' THING? I KNOW I'M A LITTLE NEEDY AT TIMES, BUT I CAN CHANGE!

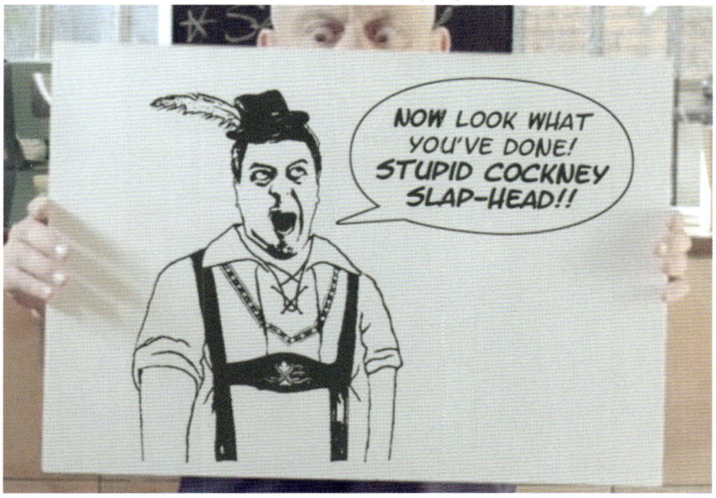
NOW LOOK WHAT YOU'VE DONE! STUPID COCKNEY SLAP-HEAD!!

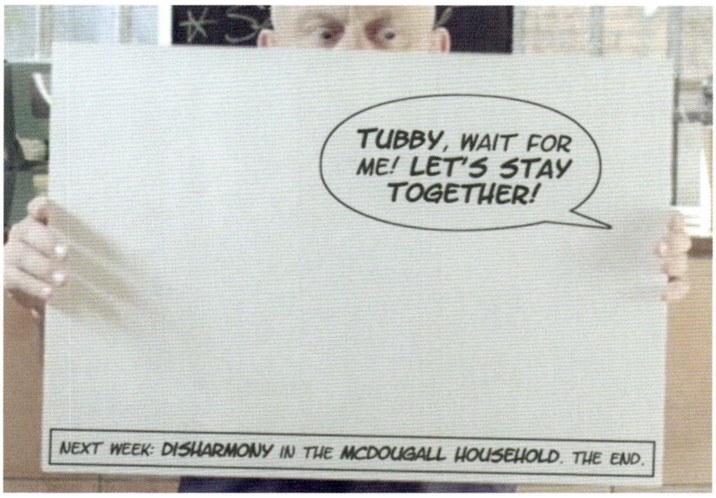
TUBBY, WAIT FOR ME! LET'S STAY TOGETHER!
NEXT WEEK: DISHARMONY IN THE MCDOUGALL HOUSEHOLD. THE END.

JOHN BARROWMAN GOES TO THE PUB

JULY 24TH 2014

I got tired just watching John Barrowman's performance at the Commonwealth Games. But I imagine the effervescent singer and dancer could go on all night in a similar fashion. In keeping with the games, this cartoon is pretty much politics-free.

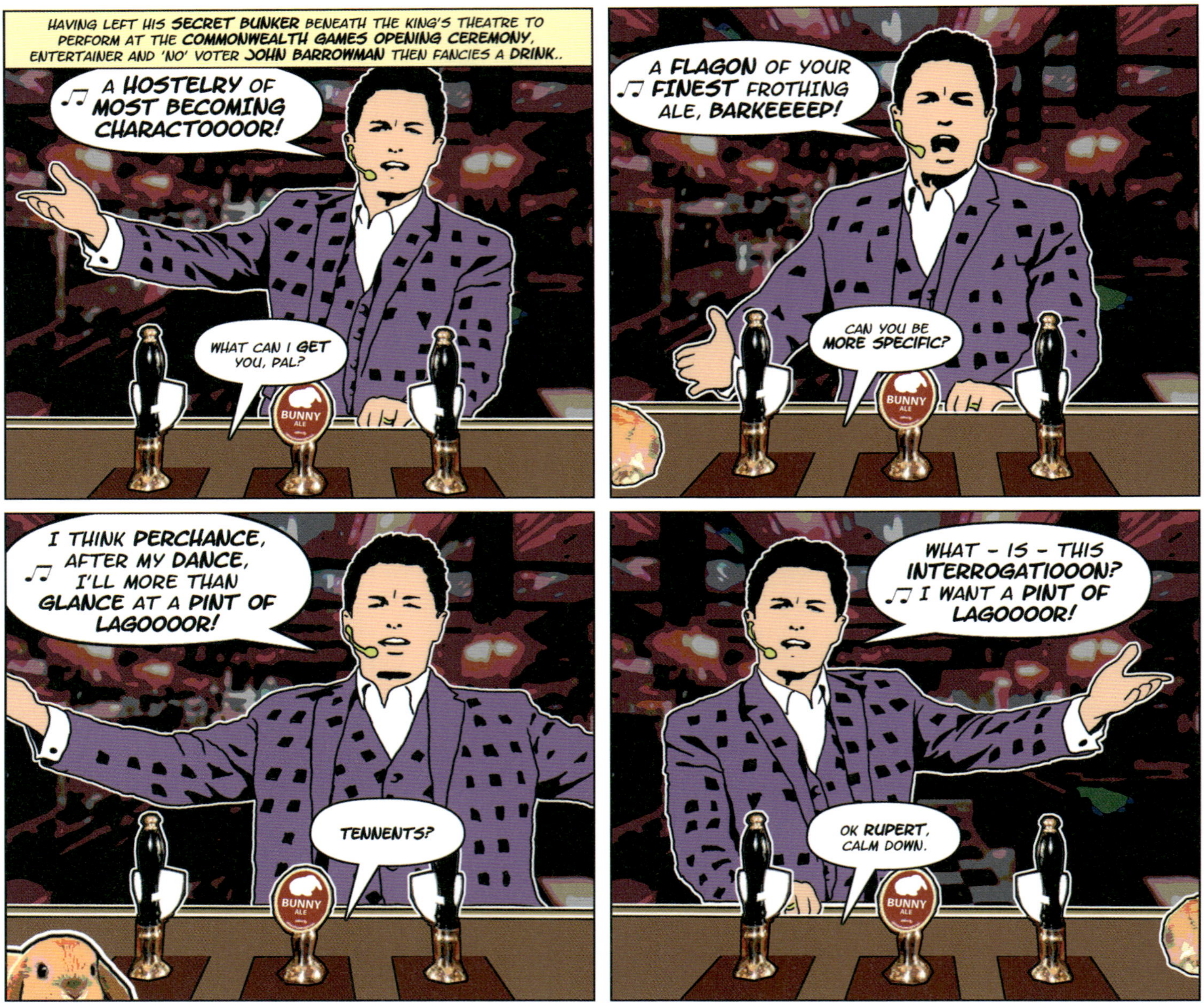

HAVING LEFT HIS SECRET BUNKER BENEATH THE KING'S THEATRE TO PERFORM AT THE COMMONWEALTH GAMES OPENING CEREMONY, ENTERTAINER AND 'NO' VOTER JOHN BARROWMAN THEN FANCIES A DRINK..
♫ A HOSTELRY OF MOST BECOMING CHARACTOOOOR!
WHAT CAN I GET YOU, PAL?
BUNNY ALE
♫ A FLAGON OF YOUR FINEST FROTHING ALE, BARKEEEEP!
CAN YOU BE MORE SPECIFIC?
BUNNY ALE
♫ I THINK PERCHANCE, AFTER MY DANCE, I'LL MORE THAN GLANCE AT A PINT OF LAGOOOOR!
TENNENTS?
BUNNY ALE
WHAT - IS - THIS INTERROGATIOOON? ♫ I WANT A PINT OF LAGOOOOR!
OK RUPERT, CALM DOWN.
BUNNY ALE

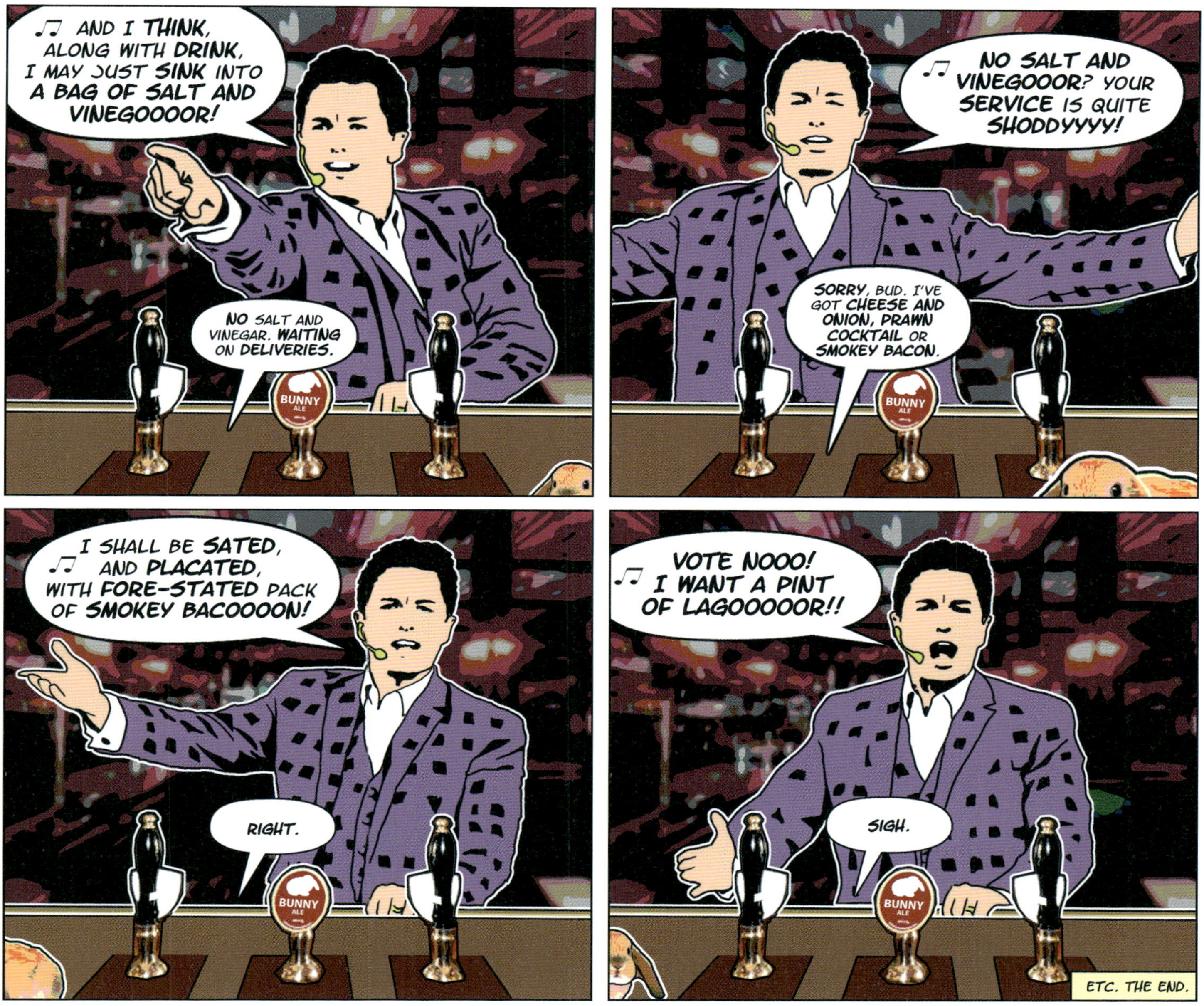
♫ AND I THINK, ALONG WITH DRINK, I MAY JUST SINK INTO A BAG OF SALT AND VINEGOOOOR!
NO SALT AND VINEGAR. WAITING ON DELIVERIES.
BUNNY ALE
♫ NO SALT AND VINEGOOOR? YOUR SERVICE IS QUITE SHODDYYYY!
SORRY, BUD. I'VE GOT CHEESE AND ONION, PRAWN COCKTAIL OR SMOKEY BACON.
BUNNY ALE
♫ I SHALL BE SATED, AND PLACATED, WITH FORE-STATED PACK OF SMOKEY BACOOOON!
RIGHT.
BUNNY ALE
♫ VOTE NOOO! I WANT A PINT OF LAGOOOOOR!!
SIGH.
BUNNY ALE
ETC. THE END.

THE LAST CARTOON IN THE BOOK

AUGUST 2ND 2014

As I write, there are still forty-six days to go until the referendum. I have no intention of hanging up my crayons, but in order to get the book out by September 1st, I have to draw a line under this grand finale and send it on its way. See you on the other side.

IT'S THE LAST CARTOON IN THE BOOK AND BLAIR MCDOUGALL HAS ORGANISED AN 'OOMPAH' PARTY TO CELEBRATE..
FINALLY, THE TORMENT IS COMING TO AN END.
YES, IT REALLY HAS BEEN MOST TRYING.
IF MOODIE'S HANGING UP HIS CRAYONS, I CAN SEE OUT THE REST OF THE PRE-REFERENDUM PERIOD WITH A MODICUM OF DIGNITY.
WELL, I DON'T THINK HE SAID ANYTHING ABOUT QUITTING..
HE DIDN'T?
NO, MORE'S THE PITY. IT WAS JUST SOMETHING ABOUT 'HAVING TO GET TO THE BASTARDING PRINTERS ON TIME.' YOU KNOW HOW PRINTERS ARE..
WELL, YES, BUT..
I'M AFRAID HE COULD BE CARTOONING RIGHT UP TO THE REFERENDUM. MAYBE BEYOND IT.
PRESS

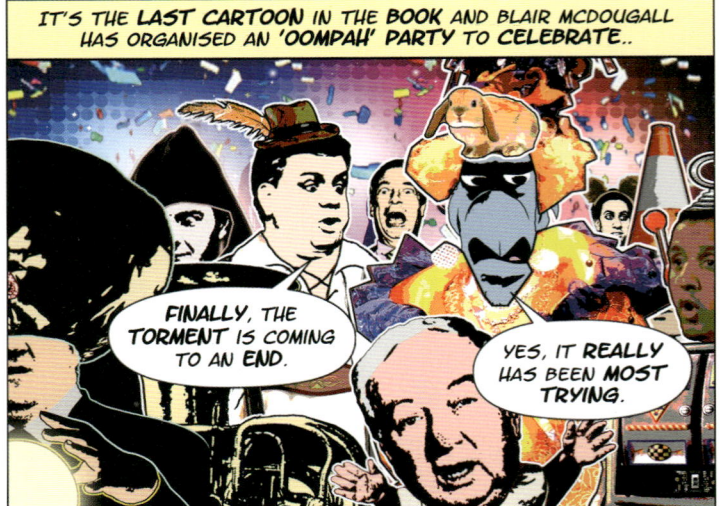

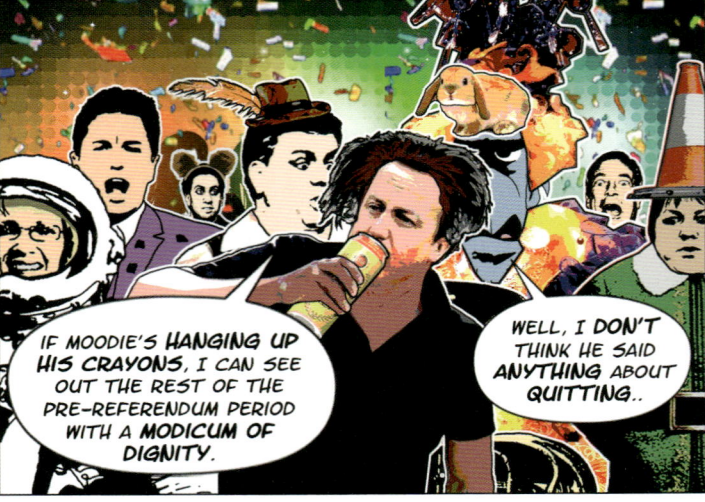

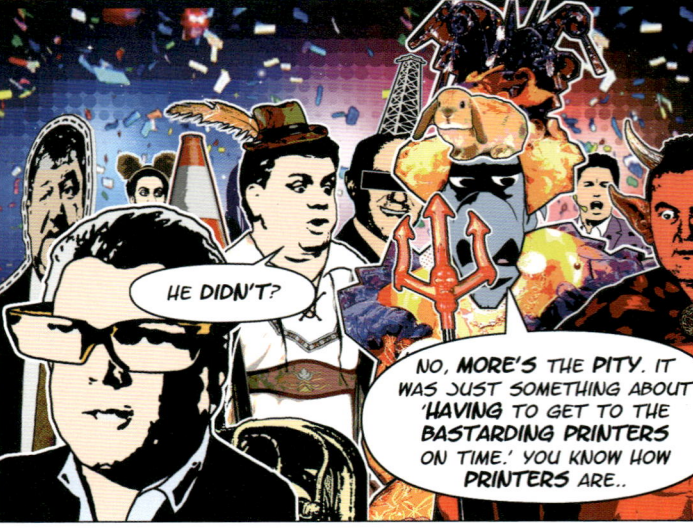

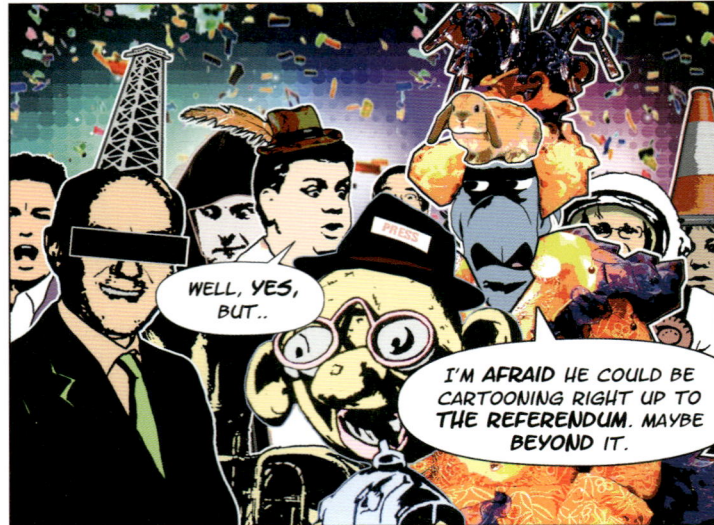

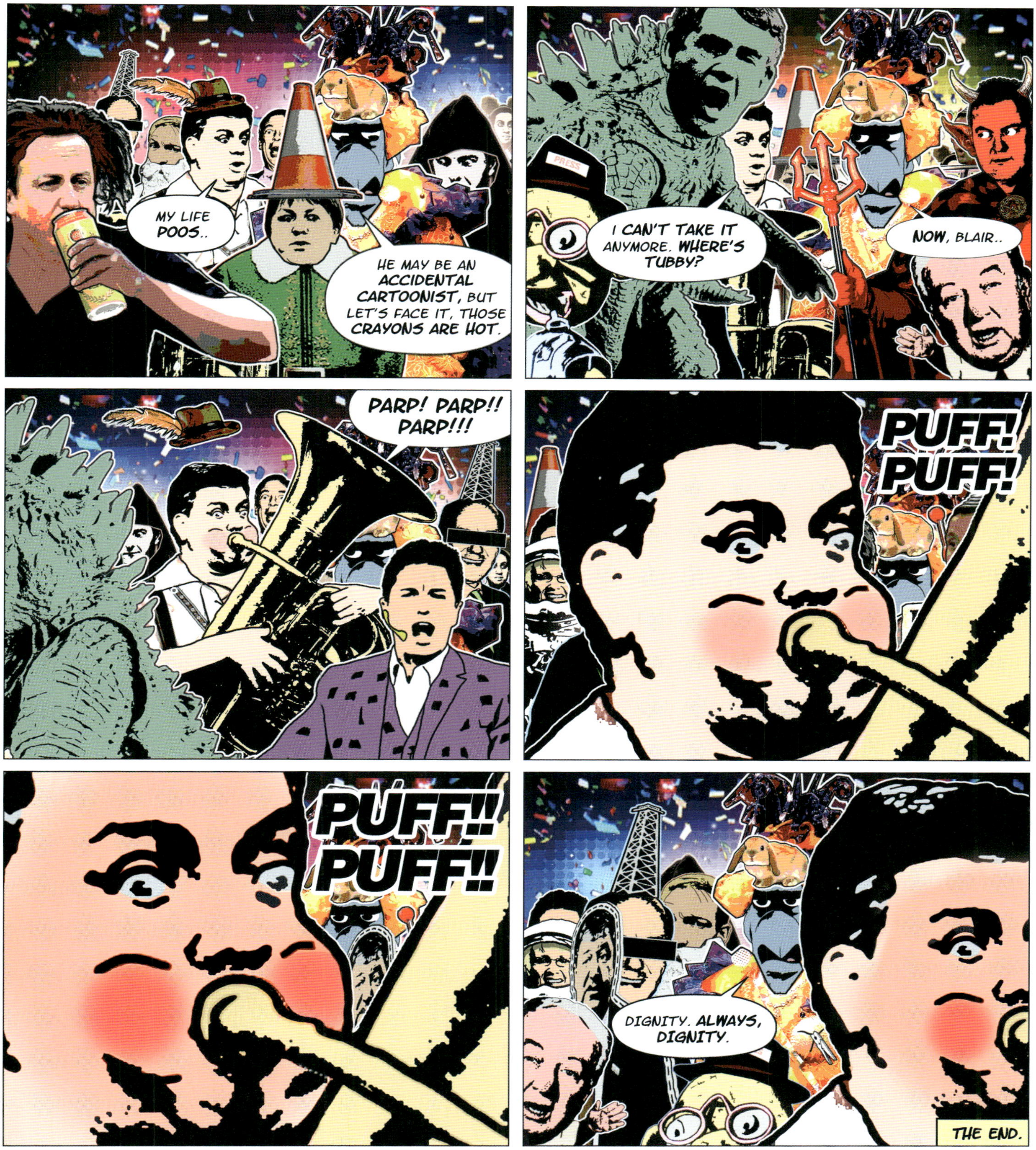
MY LIFE POOS..
HE MAY BE AN ACCIDENTAL CARTOONIST, BUT LET'S FACE IT, THOSE CRAYONS ARE HOT.
I CAN'T TAKE IT ANYMORE. WHERE'S TUBBY?
NOW, BLAIR..
PARP! PARP!! PARP!!!
PUFF! PUFF!
PUFF!! PUFF!!
DIGNITY. ALWAYS, DIGNITY.
THE END.

Under-employed graphic designer Tony Boaks reluctantly accepts a commission from Guy LeSnide QC, an advocate ('like a lawyer, but even more so') with monumental delusions of grandeur. Before settling his bill however, the advocate's delusions turn to madness and he retreats to the fictional English region of Wester - a dense and murky area only accessible by canal - where he commandeers a tribe of indigenous people and junior lawyers.

Unwilling to let madness be an excuse for non-payment, Tony sets out on an epic quest to track him down, narrowboating into Wester's heart of darkness and taking the spikey unrequited love of his life, LaFlamme, along for the ride.

Together they discover that Wester is a wild and dangerous place, alive with magical phenomena and overrun with pedantic boaters and rogue solicitors. After encounters with a psychotic ventriloquist dummy, a deviant gastrophile on his own quest to find a cure for the common hangover, a professional beard-reader, and a man who may or may not have been Victorian stage magician The Great LaFlambé, Tony is no nearer his goal.

But he has more pressing problems. Wanted for a spate of murders he didn't commit and increasingly caught up in his own personal heart of darkness, it is only by finding the elusive advocate that he can clear his name and win over LaFlamme. And get paid of course.

SIX DEGREES OF STUPIDITY A Novel
CHAPTER ONE: THE ADVOCATE FOR SELF-IMPORTANCE

I'm thinking about having my doorbell removed. It makes a pleasant enough sound but all too often heralds the arrival of something disagreeable. For a while I tried ignoring it but I suspected this particular doorbell had some kind of inherent magnetism that drew the disagreeable towards it and made pressing compulsive. I set out to try and understand its subliminal appeal by pretending to be disagreeable myself. It was difficult to get a frame of reference for this until I imagined being one of my clients. Then I began wondering instead how to make it deliver a small electric shock.

I recognised The Advocate For Self-Importance immediately. His finely-chiseled features and rigid jaw had accompanied many a newspaper headline. I wondered if his popularity with the press was due to the squareness of his chin complimenting the lower half of picture frames. But it wasn't so much his appearance that I recognised, as the general aura of self-satisfaction that accompanied it. It had exuded throughout the numerous TV news reports I'd endured and now here it was exuding on my doorstep.

He was completely absorbed in his phone and whatever interest he had in me seemed to end at my doorbell. Despite my presence he continued to press it and I began to regret not having pursued the electric shock idea. Between the doorbell and the phone I felt he had enough to occupy him and made to close the door, but this caught his attention and finally the ringing ceased.

"I'm on the phone," he said to me, as if I had been the one bothering *his* doorbell. I could tell that within minutes I'd want to punch him.

I returned to my knotted ball of string - something I attempted to disentangle periodically as a means of avoiding work - and against my better judgement left the door ajar. The consequence of this was that The Advocate For Self-Importance and his phone conversation followed me in. After several minutes the conversation showed no signs of abating and I wondered if I might be better off outside playing with the doorbell.

Unable to give the ball of string my full attention, I had no choice other than to wait. For The Advocate, the verb 'to wait' didn't conjugate in the first person. It was said that even time, which normally waits for no man, would have to sit around twiddling its thumbs whilst The Advocate completed his current engagement.

"Lovely to talk to you," he said to the caller fortunate enough to command his attention for so long, "but I've had 45 missed calls whilst we've been talking and now I'm with my design interfacer. I have an important matter to attend to." He brought the phone to a position where he could terminate the call, then catching sight of the mobile screen, swiftly returned it to his ear and added: "46."

Considering my hospitality a fundamental right, he slumped in an armchair expectantly. He could be as expectant as he wanted as far as I was concerned; I'd long since given up on hospitality.

"Apologies," he began. "It is an addiction."

"Self-importance?" I said. I wouldn't normally insult potential clients freely like this, at least not on a first meeting, but I felt secure knowing that he wasn't really listening.

"I was in Madrid last week and the network ground to a halt because of my calls. I wanted to tell them their system was quite shoddy as it had only been a moderately busy week. But of course the line was never clear for long enough. Eventually I bought a relief phone to ease the strain." He produced a second phone and both began ringing at once.

"It's tough being popular," I said and, trying to bring the conversation around to what he was doing in my house, added: "Can I help you?"

"Indeed," he replied, setting the phones to one side. "Doubtless you've seen my face in connection with one of the many high profile cases in which I've acted." I knew only that he was an attention-seeker of enormous magnitude and told him so. He thanked me.

"Media visibility may not play a large part in the lives of ordinary legal professionals, but for me it's vital. Being on television and radio and appearing in print means in effect being in several places at once. This helps raise awareness of the many little people my work touches. Were it not for me they would have nobody to represent their interests, nobody to cast a light onto their sad little lives, nobody to hold a mirror up to their hopelessness." Nobody to curse at night, I thought, but I decided to keep this to myself as I didn't want it mistaken for flattery.

"I put everything into my work. It is all-consuming, all-encompassing. It filters through to every moment of my waking life then permeates my non-waking life. My non-waking life informs my waking life. My waking life is already overcrowded, so at times I'm forced to research cases in my non-waking life."

"You're all-singing, all-dancing," I said. "I get it."

"At the moment, the whole world wants me and I owe it to them to deliver. But herein lies the problem. Even if there were an entire channel devoted to my sayings and doings, it would not be enough. I would have to be beamed across all networks at once in order to be fully effective. You see, however magnificent I may be, commanding the utmost respect and god-like awe from all corners of the globe, there is only so much of me to go round. I am limited to being just one man."

I felt sure his phones, which had continued to ring throughout this monologue, were on the cusp of melting. Eventually he succumbed to half of the ringing and, with a sigh, answered phone number one.

"LeSnide," he said. It sounded like a sneeze but was evidently a name. Seconds later he was pontificating at volume in my hallway. I picked up the relief phone from the table. The caller display said 'Mother'. At this point it occurred to me that he may have paid his many callers to ring at regular intervals throughout the day in order to reassure him of his popularity.

This caused me to do some pontificating of my own. Not only did I want the doorbell removed, I wanted it surgically implanted in his back passage. Once implanted, I would instigate the electric shock plan. Whether this would stop him ringing it however, was a moot point.

With LeSnide currently attending to one of his little people, and the relief phone tailing off and resuming repeatedly, I thought I should field the call. There being no fields within throwing distance however, I answered it instead. The caller was 'Dave.'

"Are you there?" said the plummy voice at the other end.

"Yes?"

"I'll be up next week. Are we still on for tennis?"

"Tennis?" I replied, unsure how best to decline. Tennis was my least favourite sport, ranking some way behind cheese-rolling and extreme ironing. Several reasons: Only the over-educated play it. Nobody looks good in white. Cucumber's not really sandwich material. You never know when Cliff Richard might show up. I could go on but that would involve talking about tennis.

"Hello?" said the caller.

"You know me," I said, choosing an alternative approach. "I love tennis."

"Good," he replied. "I took your advice, by the way."

"What advice?"

"The back to work scheme for the over-65's. You know, wheel them out, give them a silver-seeker's allowance instead of a pension."

"Oh, that," I said. "I was really drunk when I said that. I was only kidding."

"You were?" said Dave. "Well it's going down a treat. Not with the over 65s obviously, but the people that matter love it."

"That's nice. Look, I have to go. I'm with this incredibly gifted design interfacer by the name of Boaks."

"Ah."

"He said to tell you you're a knob."

"I see," said Dave. "Well, any more good ideas, let me know. See you next week."

He rang off just before LeSnide returned to the fray. I was concerned that he might have heard me using his phone but I needn't have been. LeSnide's self-absorption was absolute. He practised it like a martial art and would not be distracted by such external stimuli.

"What was I saying?" he asked, as if I was sure to remember his last magnitudinous utterance.

"You were about to tell me what you're doing in my house," I said.

"Ah yes," he replied. "There is only so much of me to go round." This was remarkable. He managed to recall the exact point in his discourse at which he'd broken off, and at which I'd first considered serious verbal abuse. He was a self-absorption black belt.

"If I have been bequeathed a great gift – and I have - the question is how to apportion that gift in order to maximise its efficacy. It's all very well being talented to a ridiculous degree and being in perpetual demand, but if my public are unable to access this talent due to mere physical laws, then I have failed them. Having given this a great deal of thought in recent weeks, it strikes me that there may be a very simple solution to the problem."

He paused, and I wondered if striking him was indeed the solution.

"In short," he said finally, "franchise."

"Franchise?" I said. "You want me to be a franchis-ee?"

"Clearly, franchis-ees would have to be vetted by the franchis-or and, as the franchis-or, it is safe to say you are not franchis-ee material. However, I imagine a design interfacer such as yourself could establish an appropriate design interface for the franchise brand." It seemed a long way round to ask for a logo, but it was actually a relief as I felt sure being a franchis-ee would involve tennis.

I wondered if first I should suggest a couple of weeks in a rest home prior to project initiation, as the man's grandeur had gone beyond delusional into the realms of the supernatural. Two weeks in a rest home might be just what I needed to help me forget.

"Not that I don't appreciate your plight," I said. "But unless your name's Hugo Boss, a man isn't really a brand."

"It's a very sellable brand," he said defiantly. "Try googling LeSnide. I'm so popular you won't get through." I wanted to tell him that wasn't how Google worked, but actually I had no idea how it worked. It may well be the case that people the world over are bringing the internet to a standstill through incessant searching for egomaniacal advocates. I suspected, however, that there would be no problem if he could resist googling himself.

I had only a matter of minutes to weigh up the pros and cons of accepting a commission from someone who could put Narcissus in the shade. On the one hand, a man who was a couple of writs short of a decree could be a difficult client. On the other, a man who needed industrial supplies of red wine in order to ease the pain of being alive had to fund those supplies. But was there really enough red wine in the world? I also had a growing concern for the ratio of sane to insane within my client-base. It was already dangerously favouring the nutters and one more would tip the sanity scale deeper into deficit. I might as well start designing my own brand of straitjacket.

I thought I should let the decision rest on whatever this eccentric goon said next.

"I'm thinking of a coat of arms," he declared finally.

This practically broke the sanity scale altogether and should have clinched it. But the mere thought of red wine had sent me into a misty-eyed reverie and clouded my judgement. Abandoning my misgivings about his mental well-being, I forgave his appalling liberties and crimes against modesty, and welcomed The Advocate For Self-Importance into my increasingly barking client-base.